William Makepeace Thayer

Onward to Fame and Fortune

Climbing Life's Ladder

William Makepeace Thayer

Onward to Fame and Fortune
Climbing Life's Ladder

ISBN/EAN: 9783337350925

Printed in Europe, USA, Canada, Australia, Japan

Cover: Foto ©Thomas Meinert / pixelio.de

More available books at **www.hansebooks.com**

ONWARD

TO

FAME AND FORTUNE

OR

CLIMBING LIFE'S LADDER

BY

WILLIAM M. THAYER

Author of "MARVELS OF THE NEW WEST," "WHITE HOUSE SERIES," "TACT, PUSH AND PRINCIPLE,"
"THE LOG CABIN SERIES," etc., etc.

Containing seventy-five Superb Portraits and numerous
other Illustrations

1897
THE CHRISTIAN HERALD
LOUIS KLOPSCH, PROPRIETOR
BIBLE HOUSE
NEW YORK

Copyright, 1893, WM. M. THAYER
Copyright, 1897, LOUIS KLOPSCH

PREFACE

THE lives of great men are an inspiration to the young. Tact, industry, perseverance, honesty, self-reliance, and the other virtues indispensable to success are incarnated in them. They are *lived*, thereby becoming real things instead of idealities or speculation. Abstractions and mere sentiment impress youth feebly, in comparison with truths which men illustrate by noble deeds. By studying these, the young discover a secret of power, and learn the value of the virtues by seeing the men who practiced them. Human experience invests certain elements of character with a sort of personality; and personality itself is power.

There is no more profitable study for the young than the study of men and women who made things happen. Emerson said, "There is properly no history— only biography." If this be true, acquaintance with the great and good who made history must be doubly profitable to the young.

The incitement of a great cause or principle also stimulates youth to nobler purposes. Great men and women represent great things; as commerce, art science, philanthropy, liberty, education and religion. By studying these representative men and women, the young reader catches the incitement of the principles and enterprises which they represent.

This volume on success has been prepared with these facts in view. It is really the outcome of more than forty years' study of biography, as illustrative of the elements of success. The purpose of the author is to help the young of both sexes to success, by showing how successful men and women achieved. The volume discusses the chief topics that true success embraces, and illustrates them with striking incidents from the lives of those who have won in the race of life. It also introduces the opinions of distinguished persons whose opinions are of real value.

The book is written, not for young men alone, but for young women as well. For the same elements of character that make the young man successful on the farm, in the shop, at the bar, in the forum and pulpit, will make the young woman successful in the kitchen, counting-room, school-room, or learned profession, and as daughter, wife, mother, or public benefactor. The day has gone by when a different curriculum is required for girls. The same preparatory course, the same college, and the same work for both is now the almost universally accepted theory. Womanhood has an equal chance with manhood. With the same opportunities, the same occupations, and equal remuneration, the former will prove a match for the latter.

That older people—parents, guardians, business men—often derive the greatest benefit from books written for the young goes without saying. This is especially true of works that are designed to illustrate the philosophy of character and success. Hence, this volume is commended to the attention of adults for study and information.

The author is conscious of the imperfections of his effort. So grand a subject deserves an abler pen. But his motive is high as the highest—to benefit the young people of our land. With an honest desire to inspire them to live nobly, this book is sent upon its mission.

WILLIAM M. THAYER.

Franklin, Mass.

INTRODUCTION

"*The righteous also shall hold on his way, and he that hath clean hands shall be stronger and stronger.*"—JOB xvii. 9.

A MORE fitting introduction to this volume cannot be written than the following extracts from the experience and counsels of a few of the world's worthies, whose words are as "apples of gold in pictures of silver:"—

"It is not good for human nature to have the road of life made too easy. Better be under the necessity of working hard and faring meanly than to have everything done ready to our hand, and a pillow of down to repose upon. Indeed, to start in life with comparatively small means seems so necessary as a stimulus to work that it may almost be set down as the *secret of success*."   SAMUEL SMILES.

SAMUEL SMILES.

"*My dear Burke:*—You will agree with me that every one must decide and direct his own course in life, and the only service friends can afford is to give us the data from which we must draw our own conclusion and decide our course. Allow me, then, to sit beside you and look over the field of life and see what are its aspects.

"Tell me, Burke, do you not feel a spirit stirring within you that longs to *know*, to *do*, and to *dare*; to hold converse with the great world of thought, and hold before you some high and noble object to which the vigor of your mind and the strength of your arm may be given? Do you not have longings like these, which you breathe to no one, and which you feel must be heeded, or you will pass through life unsatisfied and regretful? I am sure you have them, and they will forever cling round your heart till you obey their mandate. They are the voices of that nature which God has given you, and which, when obeyed, will bless you and your fellow-men.

"Now, all this might be true, and yet it might be your duty not to follow that course. If your duty to your father or your mother demands that you take another, I shall rejoice to see you take that other course. The path of duty is where we all ought to walk, be that where it may. But I sincerely hope that you will not, without an earnest struggle, give up a course of liberal study. Suppose you could not begin your study again till after your majority—it will not be too late then, but you will gain in many respects. You will have more maturity of mind to appreciate whatever you may study. You may say you will be too old to begin the course. But how could you better spend the earlier days of life? We should not measure life by the days and moments we pass on earth.

> "'The life is measured by the soul's advance—
> The enlargement of its powers—the expanded field
> Where it ranges, till it burns and glows
> With heavenly joy, with high and heavenly hope.'

"It need be no discouragement that you will be obliged to hew your own way and pay your own charges. I know this, for I did so when teachers' wages were much lower than they are now. It is a great truth that 'Where there's a will, there's a way.'"

JAMES A. GARFIELD.

The foregoing was written by James A. Garfield when he was a teacher of ancient languages at Hiram College, Ohio, at twenty-six years of age. The letter was addressed to his young friend of nineteen years, Burke Hinsdale, whose environment was repressing his noble aspirations. In twenty-four years after this counsel was given, Garfield was President of the United States, and Hinsdale was president of Hiram College.

* * *

"If our young men miscarry in their first enterprise, they lose all heart. If the young merchant fails, men say he is *ruined*. If the finest genius studies at one of our colleges, and is not installed in an office within one year afterward in the cities or suburbs of Boston or New York, it seems to his friends and to himself that he is right in being disheartened, and in complaining the rest of his life. A sturdy lad from New Hampshire or Vermont, who teams it, farms it, peddles, keeps a school, preaches, edits a newspaper, goes to Congress, buys a township, and so forth, in successive years, and always, like a cat, falls on his feet, is worth a hundred of these city dolls. He walks abreast with his days, and feels no shame in not studying a profession, for he does not postpone his life, but lives already.

He has not one chance, but a hundred chances. Let a stoic open the resources of men, and tell men they are not leaning willows, but can and must detach themselves; that, with the exercise of self-trust, new powers shall appear; that a man is of the word made flesh, born to shed healing to the nations; that he should be ashamed of our compassion, and that the moment he acts from himself, tossing the laws, the books, idolatries and customs out of the window, we pity him no more, but thank and revere him—and that teacher shall restore the life of man to splendor, and make his name dear to all history."

RALPH WALDO EMERSON.

RALPH WALDO EMERSON.

* * *

"My entrance into the telegraph office was a transition from darkness to light—from firing a small engine in a dirty cellar to a clean office where there were books and papers. That was paradise to me, and I bless my stars that sent me to be a messenger in a Pittsburg telegraph office. Young men should begin at the beginning. I was introduced to the broom, and spent the first hours of my business life by sweeping out the office, and several other boys, who afterward attained eminence, were my fellow-sweepers.

"When I was a boy in Pittsburg, Colonel Anderson, Alleghany—a name which I can never speak without feelings of devotional gratitude—opened his little library of four hundred volumes to boys every Saturday afternoon. He was in attendance himself at his house to exchange books. No one but he who has felt it can know the intense longing with which the arrival of Saturday was awaited that a new book might be had. My brother (Thomas) and Mr. Phipps, who have been my principal business partners through life, shared with me Colonel Anderson's precious generosity, and it was when reveling in these precious treasures that I resolved if ever wealth came to me that it should be used to establish free libraries, that other poor boys might receive opportunities similar to those for which we were indebted to that noble man.

"The man who dies rich dies disgraced. That is the gospel I preach, that is the gospel I practice, and that is the gospel I intend to practice during what remains of my life."

The poor boy—Andrew Carnegie—who was running a "small engine" in a dark, dirty cellar at fifteen years of age, became the greatest steel and iron manufacturer in the world at fifty—"The iron king of Pittsburg." He is the head of a company commanding a capital of thirty million dollars—more than half of it his own. He controls twenty thousand operators, whose monthly pay-roll amounts to one million dollars. His munificent gifts to establish public libraries, and to promote other philanthropic and benevolent causes, show that he does not mean to "die rich."

ANDREW CARNEGIE.

"I was talking a few days ago with Mr. George W. Childs, and he gave me an illustration on this very point. Perhaps a little more than a score of years ago there was not a periodical more famous or prosperous than *Graham's Magazine*. It was published in Philadelphia, and every great author of the time wrote for its pages. Washington Irving's best work was published in it. Edgar Allan Poe was one of the regular contributors. Longfellow, Emerson, Bryant, Thackeray, Mrs. Sigourney, Lowell—who did not write for its pages and who did not know its publisher and owner? George W. Childs was then office boy in a store opposite Mr. Graham's publishing house. 'How often,' said Mr. Childs to me, 'have I stood on the sidewalk in front of the store where I was employed, resting my tired hand on my broomstick, and seeing Mr. Graham roll by in his magnificent equipage with some world-renowned author at his side, wondering if ever I would reach such a point of luxury in my struggling existence.' Mr. Graham's Philadelphia home was the Mecca for all famous literary visitors to town, and there he entertained in sumptuous style the greatest literary lights which American literature has ever known. And to-day, lying in a hospital in the interior of New Jersey, is the once successful publisher of

GEORGE W. CHILDS.

Graham's Magazine, sick and nearly blind, almost forgotten by the world, which hears nothing of him; and the boy who stood with his hand on his

INTRODUCTION.

broom on the curb, envying his lot, is now his benefactor. But for the generosity of George W. Childs, sad indeed would be the lot of the forgotten publisher. All his bills are paid by Mr. Childs, every comfort is given him—all met from the purse of him who was a poor boy when Graham was a great publisher and editor!"

EDWARD W. BOK.

This poor boy began his life-work in a book store at two dollars a week, and he worked his way up to great wealth, influence, and distinction by his own persistent efforts. "The most noteworthy feature of his life has been the facility with which he has won the lasting esteem of many great men of America and England—Irving, Bancroft, Prescott, Grant, Garfield, Motley, Gladstone, Farrar, Dickens, and a host of others."

* * *

"Our whole country is a great and speaking illustration of what may be done by native force of mind, uneducated, without advantages, but starting up, under strong excitement, into new and successful action. What man can start in life with so few advantages as those with which our country started in the race of independence! Over whose private prospects can there hang a cloud as dark as that which brooded over the cause of America? Who can have less to encourage, and more to appall and dishearten him, than the sages and the chieftains of the Revolution? Let us, then, endeavor to follow in their footsteps; and each, according to his means and ability, try to imitate their glorious example; despising difficulties, grasping at opportunities, and steadily pursuing some honest and manly aim. We shall soon find that the obstacles which oppose our progress sink into the dust before a firm and resolute step; and that the pleasures and benefits of knowledge are within the reach of all who seek it."

EDWARD EVERETT.

EDWARD EVERETT.

* *

"Lives of great men all remind us
We can make our lives sublime,
And departing, leave behind us
Footprints on the sands of time;

INTRODUCTION.

> Footprints that perhaps another,
> Sailing o'er life's solemn main,
> A forlorn and shipwrecked brother,
> Seeing shall take heart again.
> Let us, then, be up and doing,
> With a heart for any fate;
> Still achieving, still pursuing,
> Learn to labor and to wait."
>
> LONGFELLOW.

*

With the foregoing introductory words of the great, wise, and good, which I have taken the liberty to quote, I send forth this work to do whatever good it may in the broad world of aspiring men and women.

HENRY WADSWORTH LONGFELLOW.

CONTENTS

	PAGE
What is Success?	21
How to Achieve Success,	25
Failure, and How to Avoid It,	31
Application,	35
Minding Little Things,	39
Observation,	43
Discrimination,	47
Thought and Labor,	53
Singleness of Purpose,	57
Perseverance,	63
Self-Reliance,	67
Decision,	71
Courage,	75
On Time; or, Punctuality,	81
Energy,	84
Art of Waiting,	86
Industry,	89
Standing Before Kings,	93
Idleness,	97
Doing Things Well,	99
Work, a Condition of Success,	101
Business a School,	105
Method,	107
Wasting Time,	110
Self-Control,	115
Self-Made or Never Made,	118
Genius,	120

CONTENTS.

	PAGE.
Modesty,	123
Simplicity,	127
Self-Respect,	130
Magnanimity,	133
Courtesy,	136
Accuracy,	141
Practice Makes Perfect,	144
How Delays Begin,	147
Secret of Mental and Moral Growth,	149
An Example That Explodes Excuses,	154
Common Sense,	156
Shortening the Way to Success,	161
Be Yourself,	163
What Spare Moments Will Do,	166
What Difficulties Are For,	168
A Good Start,	173
How to Use Yourself,	175
Choosing an Occupation,	177
Place of Reading in Education,	181
What to Read,	184
How to Read,	188
What One Book May Do for a Youth,	190
Art of Thinking,	193
Reading Newspapers,	196
Honesty,	201
What Honesty Did for Abraham Lincoln,	204
Power of Character,	206
Character as Capital,	208
Greater than One's Business,	211
Making Things Happen,	214
Room at the Top,	216
Tact,	218
Push,	222

Principle, ...
Not Above One's Business,
Self-Possession, ...
Beginning in a Small Way,
Choice of Companions, ...
Money Not a Safe Impulse to Effort,
Make All You Can,
Save All you Can, .
Give All You Can, .
The Wisdom of Self-Help,
Education Not a Foe to Labor, .
Prepared for Possibilities. . . .
Adapting One's Self to Circumstances,
Habit, ...
The Drink Habit, ...
The Tobacco Habit, .
Seizing an Opportunity.
Letting Opportunities Slip, . .
A Sound Body for a Sound Mind,
A Sound Body Made and Kept,
Recreation,
Duty, ...
Keeping Promises . . . . . .
Getting Something for Nothing,
The Filial Tie, .
The Fraternal Tie, ...
The Expense Book,
Keeping a Diary, .
Art of Conversation, ...
The Master Passion . . . . .
Letter-Writing as a Fine Art,
The Discipline of Debate
Worth of an Idea,

Reducing an Idea to Practice.
The Ideal and the Real, . .
Facts, not Theories, to be Followed.
Choice of Permanent Values.
Eye Service. . .
Gratitude, . . .
Patriotism . .
Loyalty, ...
A Reason for Patriotism and Loyalty
Personal Responsibility. .
Perils of Success, ...
Place of Faith in a True Life.
Religion in Business. . .
Infidelity a Foe to Success,
The Bible in Business.

THOROUGHNESS.

Heartiness . . . .
Prosperity and Presumption . . . .
Quiet Meditation . . . .
Chums . . . .
One or Two Fools I Have Met . . . .
Hasting to be Rich . . . .
"As the Man is, so is His Strength " . .
The Divine Plumb-line
A Notable Eleven . . . .
The Compendium of Christian Duty
Keeping the Heart with Diligence
A Complete Life . . . . .
The Bow of Promise . . . .

Companionship with Fools . . .
The Conclusion of the Whole Matter . . .

ILLUSTRATIONS

	PAGE
Samuel Smiles,	5
James A. Garfield,	6
Ralph Waldo Emerson,	7
Andrew Carnegie,	8
George W. Childs,	8
Edward Everett,	9
Henry Wadsworth Longfellow,	10
Death of Archimedes at the Siege of Troy,	24
The Home of the Pioneer,	26
William E. Gladstone,	27
Gladstone Taking Physical Exercise,	28
Girard College,	32
Daniel Webster,	34
Sheridan's Ride,	38
Pizarro, on the Island of Gallo, Spurs His Comrades to the Conquest of Peru,	42
Faneuil Hall, "The Cradle of Liberty,"	44
The Battle of Sadowa,	46
Blaise Pascal,	49
Roman Symposium,	52
Richard Arkwright,	54
James Watt,	55

ILLUSTRATIONS.

Watt Observes the Power of Steam,
Young Wilson at Mrs. Eastman's,
The Night of October 11, 1492,
Jacob Wrestling with the Angel,
George Stephenson,
Christopher Columbus,
W. H. Prescott,
Ulysses S. Grant,
Patrick Henry,
Patrick Henry in the Virginia Convention,
Phil Sheridan,
Abraham Lincoln,
Sir Thomas More being led to Execution,
Milton Dictating "Paradise Lost" to His Daughter,
Old South Church, Boston,
Nathaniel Hawthorne,
Thomas Carlyle,
"Good Tidings of Great Joy,"
Sir Walter Scott,
Franklin at Court,
Admiral Farragut Forces His Way into the Harbor of Mobile,
Samuel Taylor Coleridge,
William Cullen Bryant,
Edmund Burke,
Friedrich von Schiller,
Chariot Race in the Circus Maximus, Rome,
Gladiatorial Combat in the Arena,
William H. Seward,
William the Silent,

ILLUSTRATIONS.

Charles Dickens,
Count von Moltke,
Joseph Addison,
William Shakespeare,
Exterior of St. Peter's, Rome,
Interior of St. Peter's,
William T. Sherman,
Stephen A. Douglas,
The Signing of the Declaration of Independence,
Hoarding Wealth for the Love of Wealth,
Kentucky Home of Abraham Lincoln,
Jonathan Swift,
Alexander von Humboldt,
Arrival of Ben Franklin in Philadelphia,
Michael Angelo,
John Milton,
John Bunyan,
Bernard Palissy,
D. G. Farragut,
Fénelon,
Marie Antoinette,
Marie Antoinette Led to Execution,
Frederick the Great,
Dr. Samuel Johnson,
John Greenleaf Whittier,
Whittier's Birthplace,
Abraham Lincoln,
Martin Luther,
John Ericsson,

ILLUSTRATIONS.

Fight between the Monitor and the Merrimac,
Sir Isaac Newton, ...
Peter the Great,
Stephen Girard, ...
Napoleon, . . .
Sir Walter Raleigh, ...
Henry Ward Beecher, . . .
Lord Francis Bacon, . .
Sir Edward Bulwer-Lytton,
John Wesley, ...
Benjamin Franklin, ...
Michael Faraday, . .
George Washington,
William Lloyd Garrison, .
George Bancroft,
Lord Nelson, ...
Battle of Trafalgar, ...
Christ Tempted in the Wilderness,
The Last Days of Pompeii, . . .
Washington and His Mother, ...
Washington Irving, ...
Christ at the Home of Mary and Martha,
Mrs. Harriet Beecher Stowe, ...
Andreas Hofer Led to Execution at Mantua, . .
David Livingstone,
The First Proof,
Galileo Galilei,
J. L. R. Agassiz, . .
The First Railroad Train,

Robert Fulton,
William Harvey,
Horace Greeley,
Nathan Hale,
Washington Crossing the Delaware,
Aaron Burr,
Thomas A. Edison Trying the Perfected Phonograph the Night before the Public Announcement of His Success,
Columbus before the Doctors of Salamanca,
Arrival of the "Mayflower" at Plymouth Harbor,
Watching the Departure of the "Mayflower,"
S. F. B. Morse,
Three Celebrated Americans,
Moses, by Michael Angelo,

Onward to Fame and Fortune....

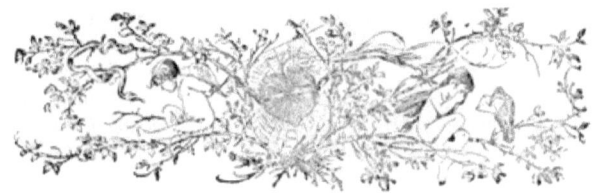

Onward to Fame and Fortune.

I.

WHAT IS SUCCESS?

LONGFELLOW said, "The talent of success is nothing more than doing what you can do well, without a thought of fame." Osborne, writing for the *Merchants' Magazine*, said, "Success in life consists in the proper and harmonious development of those faculties which God has given us." Another writer says, "Success in life is simply a right result from all the factors at work in the days and years as we live them, instead of a wrong result."

All these writers are substantially correct. The youth who makes the most of himself is successful, though he may not become wealthy, learned, or President of the United States. A man with five talents and small opportunities may improve them so as to be of more real service to mankind than one having ten unimproved talents. The former is more successful than the latter. Example more than precept, however, shows what true success is. We have illustrations of it in all the vocations of life.

David Porter was a chimney-sweeper of Yorkshire, England. In early boyhood he was kidnapped, and subjected to an experience of almost abject slavery. But he made the best of what he could not help, devoted himself to the business with great energy, tact and perseverance, and at eighteen years of age set up for himself. From childhood he had a thirst for knowledge, and devoted every spare moment to mental improvement. Business and knowledge increased rapidly, and as dollars accumulated he used them liberally to ameliorate the condition of boy chimney-sweepers. He even wrote and published a treatise on the forlorn condition of the young chimney-sweeps, appealing for help, and distributed it among influential people. By his persistent efforts and frugality he amassed a fortune, at the same time establishing a character for integrity and benevolence that gave him access to the highest circles. He was no less a philanthropist than a man of business. Sir Thomas Bernard asked him the secret of his success, and he answered, "By never having an idle hour or an idle guinea." He is an example of success in one of the lowest occupations of life.

The late George N. Briggs, of Massachusetts, was the son of a blacksmith. Poverty forced his apprenticeship to a hatter at fourteen years of age. Already he had advanced himself very creditably, by giving every leisure moment to culture. During the three years' service in the hatter's shop he never surrendered the idea that somehow he would be educated for the bar, and finally the idea was reduced to fact. Years afterward he wrote, " In August, 1813, with five dollars I had earned at haying, I left home to go to studying law. I had a brother living on the Hudson whom I visited in September, and then, with my trunk on my back, came into Berkshire County penniless, and a stranger to all except a few relatives and friends, most of them as poor as I was, and that was poor enough." Within a few years he became a leading lawyer in Berkshire, then an active and popular member of Congress for twelve years, and then, for seven consecutive years, the beloved, model governor of Massachusetts, as good as he was great. Surely that was success of no doubtful character.

The late Amos Lawrence, merchant and millionaire of Boston, was born on a farm at Groton, Massachusetts. He began mercantile business in Boston when he was twenty years of age. His capital was energy, economy, tact, industry, and Christian character—and not money. He was not seeking for wealth or fame. On his pocketbook was inscribed the text, "What shall it profit a man if he gain the whole world and lose his own soul?" Instead of making everything subservient to money, he made money subservient to character. A fortune was only incidental to the great purpose of his life. Once, confined to his house by illness, he sent a note to his partners for six hundred dollars, in small bills, for charitable objects. A few days afterward he sent for more, quoting, in his letter, the following from some quaint writer: "The good there is in riches lieth altogether in their use, like the woman's box of ointment; if it be not broken and the contents poured out for the refreshment of Jesus Christ, in His distressed members, they lose their worth. He is not rich who *lays up* much, but he who *lays out* much. I will, therefore, be the richer by charitably laying out, while the worldling will be poorer by his covetous hoarding up." Lawrence was eminently successful in business. He became a merchant prince, contributed SEVEN HUNDRED THOUSAND DOLLARS to charitable objects during his life, and left a fortune to relatives at his death.

There are degrees of success. There is the highest round of the ladder, and there is the round next to it. He who cannot reach the former may reach the latter. A young man may become a successful merchant, though he may not be a Lawrence; he may be eminent in the legal profession, though he may not become a Webster; he may make a superior mechanic, though not able to manufacture a piano. Arkwright made the spinning-jenny, but he could not make a watch; Morse invented the telegraph, but we had to wait for Edison to give us the phonograph. The French proverb says, "A man may shine in the second rank who would be eclipsed in the first."

DEATH OF ARCHIMEDES AT THE SIEGE OF SYRACUSE.

II.

HOW TO ACHIEVE SUCCESS.

THERE are four millions of young men in our country who ought to possess a strong desire to win in the battle of life. On these, and as large a number of young women, shortly will rest the burden of a nation's life. The destiny of the republic will be in their hands; for which shall it be—weal or woe?

Never was there such an opportunity to compete for the prizes as there is to-day. There never was so much room for the best as now. The field of exploits stretches beyond the "Father of Waters" to the shores of the Pacific; from Hudson Bay on the north to the Gulf of Mexico on the south; and Providence invites every young man and woman to this vast arena of action extending from sea to sea.

Already the pioneer is found at the utmost verge of this territory, training, mining, farming, surveying; already commerce has appropriated the products of its soil and the minerals of its mountains to swell the nation's wealth; already learning has built her temples where the savage was but recently the only human denizen, and religion reared her altars where the march of enterprise is arrested only by the sea. A fourth of a century hence one hundred millions of people will inhabit this remarkable country, with wealth and commerce, art and science, toil and trade, learning and religion enlarged in like proportion, to make the land an example of work, thrift, and power. The youth of to-day will come into the possession of these immense interests of territory, commerce, manufactures, mechanic arts, political and civil institutions, schools, colleges, churches, and benevolent enterprises.

A golden opportunity surely! Let golden aims and efforts seize the crisis, and the highest prizes will reward the aspirants. The poorest boy may become the richest man; the obscurest girl may preside over the finest home or the noblest Christian institution; the humblest youth may win the brightest fame. Quicker, surer than ever before, aims and efforts that are equal to the grand occasion will surmount obstacles and achieve signal success. How did Wilson, Burritt, Lawrence, Lincoln, Garfield or any other honored American, reach greatness? Each one possessed character, a noble purpose, ability to do, courage to dare, industry, perseverance, and patience, or waiting for results. Whatever other qualities they possessed, these led the van and controlled all. Hon. Stephen Allen, one of the most eminent and useful citizens of New York, perished on the steamer "Henry Clay" which was burned on the Hudson River. In his pocket was found printed

THE HOME OF THE PIONEER.

ONWARD TO FAME AND FORTUNE.

rules by which he had been guided, and among them the following: "Good character is above all things else. Never be idle. If your hands cannot be usefully employed, attend to the cultivation of your mind. Your character cannot be essentially injured except by your own acts. Make no haste to be rich if you would prosper. Never play at any kind of game of chance. Earn money before you spend it. Live within your income. If anyone speaks evil of you, let your life be such that none will believe him."

Here are substantially the qualities which are found in the career of every successful person; and there is success in even the humblest occupation for him who will pay the price. The irresolute, limp young man or woman who expects to find success "marked down" some day, is doomed to disappointment. It is a fair price that God has set upon it, and he is not half a man who attempts to get it for less.

These conditions admit of no such alternative as "luck."

A "lucky hit," a "lucky fellow," are common expressions. There is no such thing as becoming learned or great without forethought, plan, or purpose; it must be the result of well-directed and persevering effort.

When the time comes that idleness reaps rich harvests and industry begs bread; that economy goes to the poor-house and prodigality to the palace; that temperance invites want and drunkenness revels in plenty; that virtue is condemned and imprisoned and vice extolled and crowned—then, and not until then, can a sensible man embrace the popular delusion about luck. It had nothing to do with the triumphs of the great and good in the past, and it can have nothing to do with the triumphs of this class in the future.

WILLIAM E. GLADSTONE.

28   ONWARD TO FAME AND FORTUNE.

Hon. William Ewart Gladstone, the eminent English statesman and orator, is one of the brightest examples of success in modern times. Instead of poor ancestors, his were rich; instead of being born in seclusion, he was born in the royal line. He was not under the necessity of being industrious, economical, self-reliant, persevering, courageous, and irrepressible, for ancestral influence and great wealth

GLADSTONE TAKING PHYSICAL EXERCISE.

were at his command. And yet he possessed all these qualities and more, whereby he rose rapidly in public estimation. Royalty and wealth would have spoiled a youth of less tact, push, and principle than he possessed. As it was, he depended upon himself rather than upon royalty and fortune, and rose all the more rapidly in consequence. He was eminently "the artificer of his own fortune," under circumstances differing widely from those under which Wilson, Burritt, and many others of whom we speak, became renowned.

With the best education his country could afford, and a patriotic interest in the nation's welfare, he entered Parliament at twenty-three years of age, where his ability and honest devotion to public duties soon won a high position for him. Being of a delicate constitution, he very wisely adopted a mode of life suited to improve his health, without which he knew that great success was not possible. By systematic exercise in the open air, walking, riding, chopping wood, and other methods of daily physical exercise, he came into the possession of a vigorous constitution. From his start in public life, he was a great worker, an honest legislator, a true patriot, and a hearty lover of humanity. "The history of Gladstone is the history of England for fifty years." He has made some grave mistakes, for which he has publicly apologized; and yet his career is one of the brightest jewels in England's crown to-day. He is an example of success to which the young men of two hemispheres may be pointed with pride. It may be said truthfully that neither ancestry nor wealth materially assisted him to achieve, but the elements of character that he nurtured.

One friend asked another, "What was it that gave the business bent to John Wanamaker's mind?" "The same thing that has given a bent to many other minds—necessity," was the answer.

"What made him succeed?"

"Capacity coupled with indomitable energy. He has no patent on success. Any other man may use his means if he will. But few men will work as hard as he. I have never known one other man to do so."

"How does he keep his head under it all?"

"By masterful organization, and one bit of philosophy."

"What is the bit?"

"He expressed it once to me in these words, 'Do the very best you can, and leave the rest to Providence.'"

The late Alexander T. Stewart, of New York, said of Wanamaker, at the opening of his business career, "That man Wanamaker, of Philadelphia, will be the greatest merchant in the world." Stewart saw that he possessed not only a capacity for business, but also those business qualities that make capacity available. Capacity without judgment, circumspection, courage, and hope under great difficulties, and the indomitable spirit of a conqueror, may stumble and fall. John Wanamaker started out in life with all these qualities and more, by reason of which his capacity accomplished. His method, industry, economy, energy, and moral principle characterized his career at the very start. Under the control of these attributes, his business increased, and his capacity with it, until he owned the largest store in the world, having fourteen acres of flooring, on which three thousand clerks served. It was a view of this gigantic traffic, so thoroughly organized, so easily handled, that led General Grant to say to George W. Childs,

"Mr. Wanamaker could command an army. He would make a magnificent quartermaster-general." President Harrison made him postmaster-general because of the elements of character that General Grant praised. By his own earnest efforts Wanamaker reached this high distinction.

One has well said: "Every man has a mission to perform in this world, for which his talents precisely fit him, and having found what this mission is, he must throw into it all the energies of his soul, seeking its accomplishment, not his own glory. . . . Having found out what you have to do—whether to lead an army or to sweep a crossing, to keep a hotel or drive a hack, to harangue senates or address juries, or prescribe medicines—do it with all your might, because it is your duty, your enjoyment, or the very necessity of your being."

III.

FAILURE, AND HOW TO AVOID IT.

THE lesson of failure ought to be as instructive as that of success. Wise men learn from their mistakes and unfortunate ventures. It is claimed that more men triumph through failure than otherwise. As the defeat at Bull Run taught the loyal army of the North a lesson whereby Appomattox was assured, so sensible people learn better management, tact, control and use of forces that lead to final success. Dr. Johnson said, "I never knew a man of merit neglected; it was generally by his own fault that he failed of success."

Some years ago, General Dearborn said, in a public address, "After an extensive acquaintance with business men, and having long been an attentive observer of the course of events in the mercantile community, I am satisfied that among one hundred merchants in Boston, not more than *three* ever acquired an independence." A listener doubted the statement, and sought the facts in the case. Subsequently he published the following: "In 1800, a memorandum of all the business men on Long Wharf was taken, and in 1840, as long a time as men usually continue in trade, only *five* remained. All the others had failed or died poor. The Union Bank commenced business in 1798, when there was only one other bank in Boston; and a few years ago they had occasion to look back to its early history, and found that of one thousand persons with whom they opened accounts, only *six* remained. In the forty years nine hundred and ninety-four had failed, or died without property."

To learn the cause of so large a per cent of failures would, indeed, be a useful lesson. The portion lacking tact, economy, judgment, and persistence would not have prospered in any pursuit whatever. Others may have developed manly virtues in their business, become respected and influential, and died honored by all who knew them; that is, they may have been successful *as men*, while unsuccessful as merchants. Some benefactors of the race have been unfortunate as traders, bankers, and financiers, yet have built up noble Christian manhood, which is the greatest triumph of all.

There is a success, so-called, to be avoided, and a failure to be sought. To seek to acquire wealth or fame by sacrificing moral principle is always an unfortunate venture. If money, honor, or pleasure is all that a person can show for his business career, he is an object of pity rather than congratulation. He has paid too much for what he has received. True manhood and womanhood are greater than riches or fame. If these are gotten, life is not a failure though poverty burden its close. Without these, the wealth of Crœsus and the fame of Alexander are worthless possessions.

Astor possessed an inborn passion for money-making. He belonged to a family of conceded business tact. At twenty years of age he came to this country from Germany, and settled in New York City. Within sixteen years he was worth $250,000, and this was but a mere fraction of his wealth when he died. That he possessed many elements of success, such as industry, economy, perseverance, and observation, is quite evident. But his great aim was to make money —nothing higher or nobler. And yet, measured by the true standard, his life was only partially successful. He was successful as a trader, but not *as a man*. The noblest part of him was not brought to the front.

GIRARD COLLEGE.

The same was true of Girard, and others who might be named; and they are not to be held up as examples of eminent success. Horace Mann put the case pointedly and truthfully, as follows: "If a man labors for accumulation all his life long, neglecting the common objects of charity, and repulsing the daily appeals to his benevolence, but with the settled determinate purpose of so multiplying his resources that, at death, he can provide for some magnificent scheme of philanthropy, for which smaller sums or daily contributions would be insufficient, then he becomes a self-constituted servant and almoner of the Lord, putting his master's talent out at usury, but rendering back both talent and usury on the day of account; and who shall say that such a man is not a just and faithful steward, and worthy of his reward? But the day is sure to come which will test the spirit that has governed the life. On that day, it will be revealed whether the man of vast wealth, like Stephen Girard, has welcomed toil, endured privation, borne contumely, while in the secret heart he was nursing the mighty purpose of opening a fountain of blessedness so copious and exhaustless that it would flow on undiminished to the end of time, or whether, like John Jacob Astor, he was hoarding wealth for the base love of wealth, hugging to his breast, in his dying hour, the memory of his gold and not of his Redeemer; gripping his riches till the scythe of death cut off his hands in the twinkling of an eye, from being one of the richest men who ever lived in this world, to being one of the poorest souls that ever went out of it."

DANIEL WEBSTER.

IV.

APPLICATION.

APPLICATION means more than attention. The latter denotes the engagement of the powers in various degrees, and may be divided or concentrated. Application cannot be divided or partial; for then it ceases to be application. The latter is indispensable to the attainment of excellence in any pursuit, and it is the constant exercise of power or use of means to a definite end sought. Application is "sticking to one's business," whatever it is.

A writer in the *Merchants' Magazine* says, "Mark the men in every community who are notorious for ability and equally notorious for never getting ahead, and you will usually find them to be those who never stick to any one business long, but are always forsaking their occupation just when it begins to be profitable. Young man, stick to your business. It may be you have mistaken your calling; if so, find it out as quickly as possible, and change it; but do not let any uneasy desire to get along fast, or a dislike of your honest calling, lead you to abandon it. Have some honest occupation, and then stick to it. If you are sticking type, stick away at them; if you are selling oysters, keep on selling them; pursue the business you have chosen, persistently, industriously, and hopefully, and if there is anything of you it will appear and turn to account in that as well, or better, than in any other calling; only, if you are a loafer, forsake that line of life as soon as possible, for the longer you stick to it the worse it will 'stick' to you."

Sir Isaac Newton repelled the idea of being called a genius, and declared that his success was won wholly by "continuous application." He applied himself so closely that he often forgot his meals, and sometimes he pursued his studies into the night without observing that the sun had set.

Archimedes, the great mathematician of Syracuse, often became oblivious to the passing scenes around him in his enthusiasm to master his subject. When his native city was invaded by a foreign foe, and the inhabitants were driven therefrom at the point of the bayonet, he was in his study endeavoring to solve a geometrical problem. The enemy broke into his study and demanded his surrender, but he only raised his eyes from his work, and politely requested them to wait until he had completed the problem.

Horace Mann, known the world over in his day as an educator and author of the "Common School System of Massachusetts," won his position and influence by the closest application. Born in Franklin, Massachusetts, to an inheritance of poverty and hard work, there was no prospect, seemingly, that he would ever be known beyond the school district in which he received the scanty rudiments of an education. But he carried about in his heart a quenchless thirst for an education. It was the dream of his boyhood. Somehow, he hoped that the advantages of seminary and college would be his in the future, though he could not imagine how. His father was too poor to buy even his few school books, so the boy braided straw to earn money therefor. It was really "all work and no play" with him. In manhood, he wrote, "The poverty of my parents subjected me to continued privations. I believe in the rugged nursing of toil, but she nursed me too much. I do not remember the time when I began to work. Even my play days—not play days, for I never had any, but my play hours—were earned by extra exertion finishing a task early to gain a little leisure for boyish sports. Industry or diligence became my second nature, and I think it would puzzle any psychologist to tell where it joined on to the first. Owing to these ingrained habits, work has always been to me what water is to a fish."

His hard lot was made harder, at thirteen years of age, by the death of his father. Still, he continued to dream of an education, and appropriated every moment he could in the day time, and many hours at night, for mental improvement. When he was eighteen years old a teacher who was qualified to prepare him for college came to town. By the closest application he was prepared to enter in six months, and entered one year in advance. Few such examples of brave resolve and devotion to a given work are on record. His hopefulness got the better of his poverty every time in college, and he wrote to his sister: "If the Children of Israel were pressed for 'gear' half as hard as I have been, I do not wonder that they were willing to worship the golden calf. It is a long, long time since my last ninepence bade good-bye to its brethren: and I suspect that the last two parted on no very friendly terms, for they have never since met together. Poor wretches! Never did two souls stand in greater need of consolation!"

If he did not make fun of poverty, *it* did not make fun of him.

Notwithstanding Horace Mann spent but six months in preparing for college, and then entered a year in advance, he at once rose to the highest rank, and was graduated valedictorian of his class. His heroic purpose and intense application found its reward in early distinction as an educator and statesman. He succeeded John Quincy Adams in Congress, where he served six years with great ability.

ONWARD TO FAME AND FORTUNE.

Then he was nominated for governor of Massachusetts; and, at the same time, was appointed president of the Antioch College. Preferring a literary to a political life, and being deeply interested in the education of young men and women, he declined the former and accepted the latter offer. His career confirms the remark of Disraeli, "Mastery of a subject is attainable only through continuous application."

Often the dull, plodding pupil, faithful in his place, and doing the best he can, in the long run leaves his brilliant, talented companion far in the rear. In the lapse of years, his persistent application, seconded by its invincible purpose, makes for him a place and a name. For the want of these elements of strength, ten talents often fail in the race of life.

The young architect who spent his evenings in hard study was ridiculed by his fellow-associates for his efforts at self-improvement. "The boss will never give you any credit for it," they said; "we won't bother our brains so." But he still bent all his energies to master his calling, and, ere his apprenticeship closed, he won the prize of two thousand dollars for the best plan for a state house, offered by a New England commonwealth. The result confounded his young associate architects, who undervalued his application.

It is this spirit of consecration to a noble purpose that bids defiance to perils, hardships, and difficulties of every sort. It led Locke to live on bread and water in a Dutch garret; Franklin to dine on a small loaf, with book in hand, while his companions in the printing-office were absent a whole hour at dinner; Alexander Murray to learn to write on an old wool-card, with a burnt heather stem for a pen; and Gideon Lee to go barefoot in winter, half clothed and half fed. It was the price they were willing to pay for success.

"A smooth sea never made a skillful navigator," as a smooth road never leads to success.

Says another, "The idle warrior, cut from a shingle, who fights the air on the top of a weather-cock, instead of being made to turn some machine commensurate with his strength, is not more worthless than the man who dissipates his labor on several objects, when he ought to concentrate it on some great end."

SHERIDAN'S RIDE.

V.

MINDING LITTLE THINGS.

GREAT things are the aggregate of littles; great results proceed from little causes. Human life is a succession of unimportant events; only here and there one can be called great in itself. A crushing sorrow, the loss of a fortune, physical and mental suffering, are the exceptions and not the rule of life. Experiences so small as scarcely to leave a trace behind, are the rule, producing, in the consummation, a life that is noble or ignoble, useful or useless, an honor or a disgrace.

Success, in all departments of human effort, is won by attention to little things. The details of all kinds of business demand the closest attention. The pennies must be saved as well as the dollars. Indeed, it is the hundred pennies that make the dollar. So in literary pursuits; careful regard to details, such as correct pronunciation and spelling, good reading, meaning of words, dotting i's and "minding p's and q's" generally, make up what we call an education. Only littles are found in the way to learning, and many of them are a small sort of drudgery; but all of them must be taken up and carried along, if we would "make our lives sublime."

"He who despiseth little things shall perish by little and little." Nevertheless, youth of both sexes are apt to disregard this divine counsel. Like the man in the parable who hid his one talent because it was so small, they want and expect larger things. They may not ask for *ten* talents, but they despise *one*. It is too insignificant to command their interest or admiration. Greater things or nothing.

It is right here that many young people make a fatal mistake, not believing or seeing that with this little they may gain another little, and still another, and so on, up, up, up, to the great. They commit themselves to failure at the outset.

A clerk in New York City was wont to take down the shutters at precisely six o'clock in the morning. While he was taking them down, rain or shine, an old gentleman passed by on his way to his place of business. The latter smiled so benignantly upon the former, that a hearty and familiar "Good morning," became natural to both. Month after month this mutual greeting continued, until one morning the old man was missed, and he never appeared again. He was dead.

Not long thereafter the enterprising and faithful clerk was waited upon by the administrator of the old man's estate, and informed that his store and stock of goods were willed to him. Attracted by the youth's promptness and fidelity, he inquired into his character and circumstances, and was satisfied that he could leave that property to no one so likely to make good use of it as the clerk who took down the shutters at just six o'clock, summer and winter.

Through this legacy the clerk was introduced into a profitable business at once, and became one of the most wealthy, benevolent, and respected merchants of the city.

A banker in the city of Paris, France, said to a boy who entered the bank:—

"What now, my son?"

"Want a boy here?" was the answer.

"Not just now," the banker replied, engaging in further conversation with the lad, whose appearance favorably impressed him.

When the boy went out, the eyes of the banker followed him into the street, where he saw him stoop to pick up a pin and fasten it to the collar of his coat. That act revealed to the banker a quality indispensable to a successful financier; and he called the boy back, gave him a position, and, in process of time, he became the most distinguished banker in Paris—Lafitte.

A young man responded to the advertisement of a New York merchant for a clerk. After politely introducing himself, the merchant engaged him in conversation as a test. Finally, he offered him a cigar, which the young man declined, saying:—

"I never use tobacco in any form whatever."

"Won't you take a glass of wine, then?" the merchant continued.

"I never use intoxicating drinks, under any circumstances," the young man answered.

"Nor I," responded the merchant, "and you are just the young man I want."

He had the key to the applicant's character now, and he wanted no further recommendation.

"Very little things to make so much account of," some one will say. Yes, they are little things; but all the more significant for that. "Straws show which way the wind blows." We say of the man who plans for the half cent, he is avaricious; of the youth who is rude in the company of females, he is ill-bred; and of the letter writer who spells words incorrectly, his education is defective—all little things, but all revelations.

"Little causes produce great results." A gnat choked Pope Adrian, and his death occasioned very important changes in Europe and America. A bloody war between France and England was occasioned by a quarrel between two boy princes. "The Grasshopper War," in the early settlement of our country, was a conflict between two Indian tribes. An Indian squaw, with her little son, visited a friend in another tribe. Her boy caught a grasshopper, and the boy of her friend wanted it. The boys quarreled; then the mothers took sides, and then the fathers, and finally the two tribes waged a war which nearly destroyed one of them. Several centuries ago, some soldiers of Modena carried away a bucket from a public well in Bologna, and it occasioned a protracted war in which the King of Sardinia was taken prisoner, and confined twenty-two years in prison, where he died.

The first hint which Newton received leading to his most important optical discoveries was derived from a child's soap bubbles. The waving of a shirt before the fire suggested to Stephen Montgolfier the idea of a balloon. Galileo observed the oscillations of a lamp in the metropolitan temple of Pisa, and it suggested to him the most correct method of measuring time. The art of printing was suggested by a man cutting letters on the bark of a tree, and impressing them on paper. The telescope was the outcome of a boy's amusement with two glasses in his father's shop where spectacles were made, varying their distance between them, and observing the effect. A spark of fire, falling upon some chemicals, led to the invention of gunpowder. Goodyear neglected his skillet until it was red hot, and the accident guided him to the manufacture of vulcanized rubber. Brunel learned how to tunnel the Thames by observing a tiny ship-worm perforate timber with its armed head.

"Little foxes destroy the vines." Little sins sap the foundation of principle, and lead to greater sins. Cheating to the amount of one cent violates the divine law as much as swindling to the amount of a hundred dollars. The wrong does not lie in the amount involved. The stealing of a pin violates the law "Thou shalt not steal," as really as the taking of a dollar. "He who is unjust in the least, is unjust in much;" that is, he acts upon the same principle that he would in perpetrating far greater sins. Indeed, he who does wrong for a small gain, may incur the highest criminality, since he yields to the smallest temptation, thereby showing a readier disposition to sin.

Smiles says, "As the daylight can be seen through very small holes, so little things will illustrate a person's character. Indeed, character consists in little acts, well and honorably performed."

PIZARRO, ON THE ISLAND OF GALLO, SPURS HIS COMRADES TO THE CONQUEST OF PERU.

VI.

OBSERVATION.

SOLOMON declared, "The wise man's eyes are in his head"—not in his elbows or feet. He meant to extol the faculty of observation, which some distinguished educators place at the front. Dr. Hooker says, "It should be the main business of the school to train the child as an observer. He should not be taken out of the world of beautiful and interesting things, and shut up to the letters and works of the schoolroom. Things, and not mere signs, should constitute the substantial part of his instruction. We should impart to him the spirit of this precept of Hugh Miller, 'Learn to make a right use of your eyes; the commonest things are worth looking at; even stones and weeds, and the most familiar animals.' Then he is prepared in early manhood to 'study men and things' in a way to make success easy and sure." The kindergarten method answers this purpose.

Their eyes "are in their head," the proper place for them, the only place where they can prove of the highest advantage. Not so with a multitude of men, who stumble, blunder, and make mistakes, and dwell "among a wreck of places." Their eyes seem to be anywhere but in their heads. They learn little, or nothing, from the objects and experiences of life.

If the physical eye beholds, the mental and spiritual eyes do not. These are blind. The mind is dull and unobservant. And so the possessor continues to live, listless, unintelligent, and untaught among scenes that ought to lift the soul into a high and grand career.

The late Dr. Charles Jewett, the famous temperance lecturer, was noted for his clear-cut observation. From boyhood, he never allowed a why or wherefore to go unanswered. He waited, searched, and studied until the problem was solved. Patrick Henry never studied "men and things" more thoroughly than he did. Once he went to hear John Quincy Adams speak at Faneuil Hall. While sitting there, he said to Mrs. Jewett, "See that man yonder?" (pointing); "that man does his own thinking." At the close of the meeting, it was found that Rufus Choate was the citizen to whom he pointed.

At another time, the doctor was traveling from New York to Philadelphia in the cars, when two young men, directly in front of him, attracted his attention. One of them made an ungracious remark about a lady who left the car at a certain station, to which the other assented.

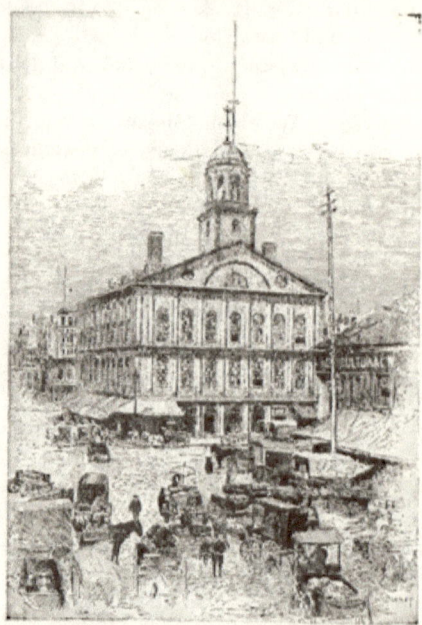

FANEUIL HALL, "THE CRADLE OF LIBERTY."

"Young men," interrupted the doctor, "I think you did not read the character of that woman correctly. Let us have a friendly talk about it. I have made character a study for many years, and it has been a great benefit to me. Students like you—"

"How do you know that we are students?" exclaimed one of them, cutting off the doctor's remark short.

"Ah, that is it," replied the doctor. "I told you that I had made character a study. You are both students."

"It is so," replied one of them, laughing.

"And you are collegians, too," continued the doctor.

Both laughed outright, and one said: "Right again; members of Princeton College; but how can you tell that?" "Simply by observation," replied the doctor; "and what may surprise you more, perhaps, I can tell to what classes you belong. You are a senior," laying his hand on the shoulder of one; "and you are a sophomore," laying his hand on the shoulder of the other. The doctor was right again, and the two students were filled with amazement that observation could do so much.

All the way to Philadelphia their conversation continued, the doctor giving them the best advice concerning the observing faculties, in his inimitable way.

Fifteen years thereafter, a clergyman sat upon the platform from which Dr. Jewett spoke, in the State of New York, and, at the close of the lecture, he introduced himself to the doctor as the senior whom he instructed on the train to

Philadelphia, adding, "I can never be too grateful for that lesson. It has been worth more to me than one whole year in college."

A good pair of eyes, with an active, inquisitive mind behind them, made Newton a philosopher in boyhood, the inventor of the kite and windmill. Keeping his eyes open in his father's workshop when he was a mere boy, observing how tools were handled and things were made, inquiring into the reason of this, that, and the other piece of work, made Watt the renowned mathematician, optician, and inventor that he was. Samuel Budgett was but eight years of age when he heard his mother say to his father, as a new grocer applied for their custom, exhibiting his prices, "I see no advantage in buying of him; the prices are the same that we have been paying." Samuel saw at once where the grocer failed, and thirty years thereafter, he said, "The practical lesson I learned from that scene has been worth to me thousands of pounds in business. Show people that what you propose is for their own interest, and you will generally accomplish your purpose."

The moral use of this noble faculty is pre-eminent. When a youth goes out into the world to seek a livelihood, he will need it at every step. Wily men will seek to entrap him, and he must be able to read them. Temptations will beset his way; he must behold so as to shun them. The lure of wealth and drink will appeal to him in city and country; he must have an eye upon the consequences of following the lure. Misrepresentations, deceptions, and fraud will meet him in social and business life; he must be able to distinguish between right and wrong — the upward tendency of one, and the downward tendency of the other. His safety is found here.

THE BATTLE OF SAHOWA.

VII.

DISCRIMINATION.

A UNIVERSITY professor asked his class, after having discussed the nature and uses of observation, "What is discrimination?" A student answered, perhaps facetiously, "It is observation, and a little more."

He meant to say that discrimination is not a separate power, but a different mode of the same power, sharper in its last analysis.

Observation implies discernment and penetration, which see quickly in spite of artifice and concealment, but it does not necessarily include discrimination; that discovers differences between objects by instituting comparison.

It is generally conceded that the character of Shylock, in Shakespeare, is drawn with sharp discrimination. Observation would embrace the essentials of that character without the sharp analysis.

We say of observation, it is *close;* of discernment, it is *clear;* of penetration, it is *acute;* and of discrimination, it is *nice.*

These descriptive words indicate, not different powers, but different modes of the same power; and it is a valuable mental exercise for young people to study these nice distinctions.

Perhaps there is no better illustration of what discrimination is than the familiar Arabian tale of the *dervis* and the lost camel.

Two merchants met a *dervis* in the desert, who was traveling alone.

"You have lost a camel," he said to the merchants.

"Indeed we have," one of the merchants replied.

"Was he not blind in his right eye, and lame in his left leg?" continued the *dervis.*

"He was," answered the merchants.

"Had he not lost a front tooth?" added the *dervis.*

"He had," replied the merchants, beginning to think that the lost animal was found.

"And was he not loaded with honey on one side and corn on the other?"

"Most certainly he was," the merchants said; "and as you have seen him so lately, and marked him so particularly, you can, in all probability, conduct us to him."

The *dervis* responded, "I have never seen your camel, nor even heard of him but from you."

"A pretty story, truly!" exclaimed the merchants, supposing they were standing face to face with a thief or robber. "But where are the jewels which formed a part of his burden?"

"I have neither seen your camel nor your jewels," insisted the *dervis*.

Satisfied that the *dervis* was a robber, the merchants seized him and carried him before the *cadi* for examination. Nothing was found upon his person to convict him, nor could any evidence of guilt be discovered.

"A sorcerer! a sorcerer!" exclaimed the merchants, and they hastened to get him indicted for sorcery. But the *dervis* put an end to their proceedings by addressing the court thus:—

"I have been much amused with your surprise, and own that there has been some ground for your suspicions; but I have lived long and alone, and I can find ample scope for observation, even in a desert. I knew that I had crossed the track of a camel that had strayed from its owner, because I saw no mark of any human footstep on the same route. I knew that the animal was blind in one eye because it had cropped the herbage only on one side of the path; and I perceived that it was lame in one leg from the faint impression which that particular foot had produced upon the sand. I concluded that the animal had lost one tooth because, wherever it had grazed, a small tuft of herbage was left uninjured in the centre of its bite. As to that which formed the burden of the beast, the busy ants informed me that it was corn on one side, and the clustering flies that it was honey on the other."

The aforesaid merchants were no more unwise in charging the *dervis* with sorcery than thoughtless men are now who ascribe the eminent success of some parties they know, or have read of, to "good luck," for somewhat of that nice discrimination which the *dervis* possessed is found in the career of all successful men. They are discriminating—remarkably so. They see where the ants gather and for what; they discover the evidence of a lame leg in the sand and of a lost tooth in the grass. They are the sorcerers of our day.

When Blaise Pascal, who became one of the most distinguished mathematicians that ever lived, was ten years old, his attention, at the dinner table, was attracted by the sound when he struck his plate with his knife.

"Blaise, what are you doing with that plate? You will break it!" exclaimed his eldest sister.

"See here, sister," answered the boy; "when I strike the plate with my knife, notice how it rings. Hark!" and he struck his plate again. Both listened for a moment, when Blaise continued:—

"Now, see; when I grasp the plate with my hand, the sound ceases;" and he struck the plate again, the ringing of which ceased when he grasped it with his hand.

"Why is this, I wonder?" he asked.

His sister could not enlighten him; but he went on inquiring, examining, and observing the nice distinction of sounds, searching the depths of science, and penetrating its utmost recesses, until he brought forth his elaborate treatise on the subject in manhood.

BLAISE PASCAL.

James Ferguson was a boy who studied machinery for the pleasure of it. He wanted to know how this, that, and the other thing was made. His father's clock interested him beyond measure, but he could not obtain permission to examine it. The temptation, however, was too strong for him one Sabbath day when his parents had gone to meeting. Taking the clock down from the shelf, he took it to pieces, examined every part of it, and then put it together again, so that it was in running order when his parents returned.

One day a gentleman was passing his father's house on horseback, and stopped to inquire the way of young Ferguson, who was playing in the yard. The boy answered the gentleman politely, and then ventured to ask him, "What time is it?" The traveler took out his watch and told him; whereupon the boy, growing bold on account of the kindness and familiarity of the stranger, asked the privilege of looking into the watch. The owner readily granted him permission. His first question on opening it, was:—

"What makes the box go round?"

"A steel spring," answered the man.

"How in the world can a steel spring in a box turn it around so as to wind up all the chain?"

The gentleman explained the operation as well as he could.

"But I don't see it yet," added James.

"Well, my young friend," speaking very tenderly, "I will illustrate. Take a long thin piece of whalebone; hold one end of it fast between your finger and thumb, and wind it round your finger; it will then endeavor to unwind itself; and if you fix the other end of it to the inside of a small hoop, and leave it to itself, it will turn the hoop round and round, and wind up a thread tied to the outside."

The whole operation was clear now to the boy's discriminating mind.

"I see! I see!" he exclaimed with delight; thanked the gentleman for his kindness, and subsequently made a wooden watch, which he put into a case about the size of a teacup.

This quality is invaluable in every-day life, since it can make a youth learn, as Sir William Jones did, "from every person he meets, even the bootblack and hostler." One purchaser notices every defect in cloth or garment that he examines, while another overlooks them; one traveler notes everything on his journey—trees, landscapes, crops, farms, homes, thrift or decay, proofs of enterprise or shiftlessness, and a score of other things, which another traveler fails to see; one reader becomes familiar with the style, purpose, sentiments, and scope of an author, pleased with excellence and pained by defects, while another catches only the general drift of the book, without being able, at the conclusion of his reading, to discuss its subject-matter intelligently, or even to give a passable analysis of the volume; one pupil masters each branch of study to which he gives his attention, never satisfied until he understands each subject so that he is able to give a reason for the belief that is in him, while another is content with a parrot-like recitation or less, neither comprehending the author nor mastering the subject. Discrimination, a power that may be a gift or an acquisition, is the cause of this difference between the two classes. If a gift, it cannot be remarkable without use and improvement; if an acquisition, it may become as serviceable as it could be if a gift.

Morally, this discriminating faculty is even more valuable than it is mentally, for it observes moral distinctions which may save the possessor from ruin. In his youth, Amos Lawrence was a clerk in a store in Groton, Massachusetts. There were several other clerks, five in all. In his last years, Mr. Lawrence wrote of that time: "The five boys were in the habit, every forenoon, of making a drink compounded of rum, raisins, sugar, nutmeg, etc., with biscuit, all palatable, to eat and drink. After being in the store four weeks, I found myself admonished by my appetite of the approach of the hour of indulgence. Thinking the habit might make trouble if allowed to grow stronger, without further apology to my seniors I declined partaking with them."

From that time forward through life he practiced total abstinence. At the same time he put tobacco under the same ban, so that he could say in age, " I have never in my life smoked a cigar;" and he added, " to this simple fact of starting just right am I indebted, with God's blessing on my labors, for my present position, as well as that of the numerous connections around me." His nice discrimination showed him the tendency of certain acts to ruin, and he chose the side of safety.

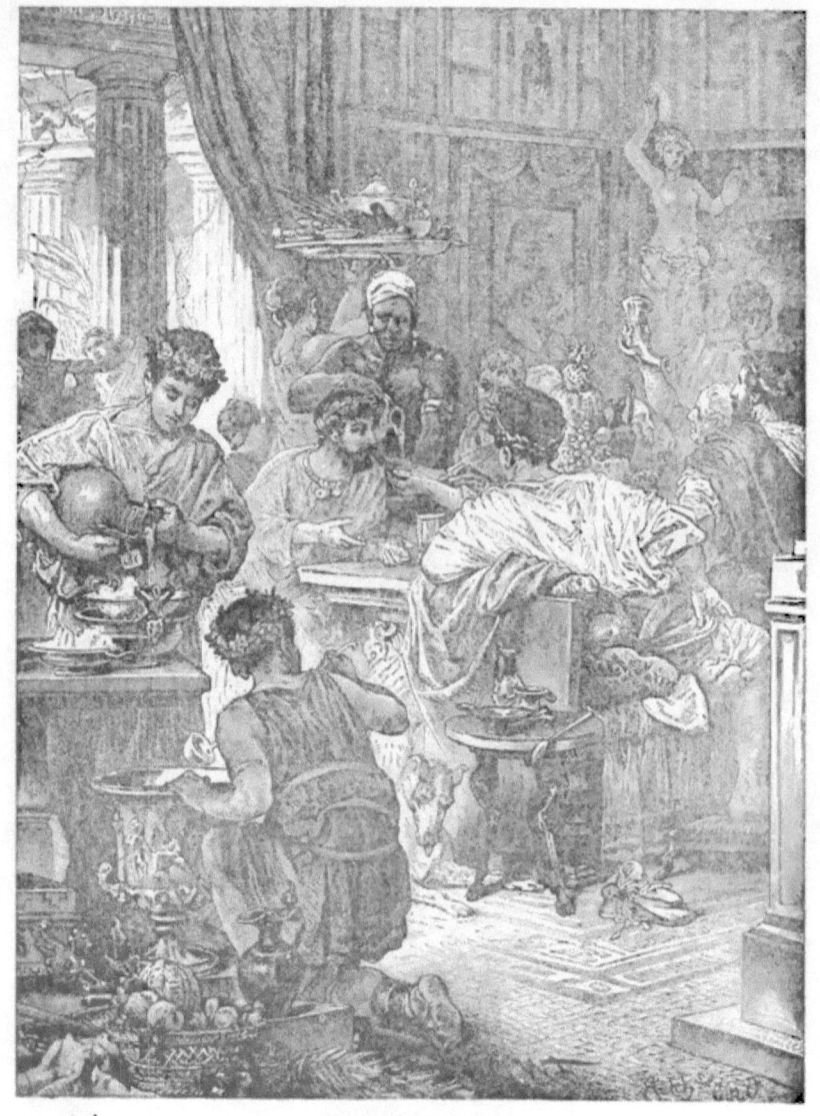

ROMAN SYMPOSIUM.

VIII.

THOUGHT AND LABOR.

CLOSE observers are thinkers as well as workers. Thought is the father of labor. The inventions, discoveries, and enterprises of men call for laborers; work is thus made possible for them. But thinkers are the authors of the inventions, discoveries, and enterprises, without which laborers would find nothing to do.

Not that thinkers are independent of laborers, for, like capital and labor, they are mutually dependent. Unless there were laborers to do the work which thinkers lay out, the occupation of the latter would be well-nigh gone.

On the other hand, unless there were thinkers to create work, laborers would starve.

However, thought ranks higher than labor, for it is greater.

Not so have laborers always regarded their relations to thinkers.

When James Hargraves invented his spinning-jenny, the work-people considered it an assault upon their province of labor. They supposed that their occupation was gone, and they arose *en masse* to vindicate what they claimed to be their imperiled rights. They attacked his house, dragged out his model machine and utterly destroyed it. Learning that he had sold several of them in the country about Blackburn, they scoured the region and destroyed every one.

Before that time, John Kay invented the fly-shuttle, the appearance of which aroused them to violence.

That one of the world's thinkers should dare to invade their domain of work by thrusting upon them a labor-saving machine, aroused a spirit of malignity within them. They pursued him with so bitter persecution that he was forced to flee from his native land to save his life.

When Richard Arkwright perfected his cotton machinery and put up a cotton mill, near Chorley, in 1769, he was denounced as an enemy of the working people

(53)

who wanted to deprive them of labor. Their hostility waxed hotter and hotter, until they attacked his mill and destroyed it in the presence of a strong force of police and military.

Thinkers were in bad odor with the wage people of that day. Nor has this delusive idea of thought being inimical to labor been entirely eradicated from the earth. It crops out occasionally in *our* day.

Several Boston merchants, of sharp observation and marked sagacity, conceived the idea of establishing a manufacturing city on the Merrimac River.

It was a bold and mammoth enterprise for their day.

Without publishing their intentions to the world, they employed a young engineer to explore and secure the most advantageous site. "But keep your own counsels," they said, "and take your dog, gun, and fishing-tackle along with you, so that property owners may not become suspicious."

The young engineer went thither, found board at a farmhouse, went out daily to hunt and fish, and began to investigate. Within a week he became sure that the best site for the contemplated city was on the very farm where he was stopping.

RICHARD ARKWRIGHT.

"Would you like to sell your farm?" he inquired of the proprietor, one day.

"I had not thought of it," replied the farmer.

"Not if you could get twice its real value?"

"Perhaps I would sell it in that case—say if I could get three thousand dollars," answered the owner.

"You will take that amount, will you?" pressed the engineer.

"I think so," replied the farmer.

ONWARD TO FAME AND FORTUNE. 55

The agent took time to report to his employers, who instructed him to purchase the farm. But when he informed the man that he would take his farm at three thousand dollars, the latter replied:—

"You did not take my farm when I offered it to you, and now I am not willing to sell it for less than six thousand dollars."

"You can't be in earnest, sir," the agent replied. "Six thousand dollars for a farm like this!"

"Never was more earnest in my life than I am now," replied the farmer; "and my present offer must be accepted within twenty-four hours."

The agent hastened to close the bargain at once. When the papers were signed and passed, the agent asked the farmer the cause of doubling his price. The farmer answered:—

"The day after I offered you my farm, I saw two men on the opposite side of the river, sitting on a rock and talking very earnestly. Then they parted; one went up the stream, and the other down. After a while they returned and talked together again. I did not know what it meant, but I thought it had some connection with your purchase, and so I decided to double my price."

JAMES WATT.

In this incident there appears prominently the close observation of the Boston merchants in locating the city of Lowell on the Merrimac. Equally sharp is the observation of the farmer, who learned from the conduct of the engineer and the two men on the opposite side of the river, that some great enterprise was on foot which would make his acres cheap at six thousand dollars.

The fact proves, also, that thought is the parent of labor. The thinkers planned and located before laborers were wanted. Marvelous, indeed, are the labors made possible by the Boston thinkers! Vast armies of laborers have been required to do the work laid out by three or four thinkers. "The City of Spindles" will always stand as a monument of thought and labor in their harmonious action, while thought is the author of all that we behold of the magical metropolis.

In consequence of this relation of thought to labor, every object, enterprise, and event becomes a teacher to the observing boy or girl. There are more teachers for this class outside of the schoolroom than there are inside. They read and study more things and experiences in the world about them than they do books, and learn vastly more from them. Unless this had been true of the boyhood of some distinguished men, they would have lived and died in oblivion.

The inventor of the suspension bridge, Samuel Brown, was a boy who carefully observed everything. When he became a man, he was a quick-witted, sharp observer, and learned from the web of a spider, which he found one morning stretched across his path in the garden, how to construct a suspension bridge.

So James Watt, another boy who kept his eyes wide open as he went along, made a very thoughtful, practical man; and, from the examination of a lobster shell, with its singular head and dangling claws, he learned how to carry water in tubes under the Clyde. From watching the power of the steam which lifted the lid of the tea-kettle, he discovered that secret which brought forth the modern steam-engine.

No book or professor could have taught him; a lobster and a tea-kettle became his teachers. No thanks to the lobster or the tea-kettle, however, but to the man who saw with his mind.

The captain of the canal boat on which young Garfield served as mule driver, said of him, "His observation served him a good purpose in the absence of books; it set him to thinking."

IX.

SINGLENESS OF PURPOSE.

ARCHBISHOP LEIGHTON said, "To him that knoweth not the port to which he is bound, no wind can be favorable." One wind is about as good for him as another.

He may be well equipped, a good craft, sails set, ballast right, cargo well packed; but he wants somewhere to go, a port to enter.

All his activity and preparation are useless without a purpose. A ship without a rudder, chart, or compass, on a trackless sea, tossed about like a cockle-shell by wind and wave, is an apt symbol of thousands of youths who undertake to cross the ocean of life without a definite aim. They are more likely to make shipwreck than a safe harbor.

By singleness of purpose we mean an early decision to follow a certain occupation or profession as a life-work, keeping that object constantly in view, true as the needle to the North Pole, and pushing for it through sunshine and storm to the goal. That is what the great apostle meant when he said, "This one thing I do." That single purpose took possession of his soul, and all the powers of his nature combined and bent to its accomplishment. In his triumphant declaration, "I press toward the mark for the prize," is not only a dauntless spirit, but also the lofty aim that never knows defeat.

Perhaps the wise man put it best of all, when he said to the young, "Let thine eyes look right on, and let thine eyelids look straight before thee. Ponder the path of thy feet, and let all thy ways be established. Turn not to the right hand nor to the left." That is singleness of purpose.

Seventy years ago there lived a boy in Farmington, New Hampshire, who thought more of a book and school than he did of anything else. He was then only six years of age. When he was eight years old, a neighbor, wife of Hon. Nehemiah Eastman, and sister of Hon. Levy Woodbury, seeing him passing her house, called him in and gave him some clothes, of which he was in great need. At the same time she inquired if he knew how to read.

"Yes; pretty well," he answered.

"Come, then, to-morrow, and see me at my house," she continued.

She knew of the lad's fondness for books, and her object was to encourage him.

Early the next morning, little Henry Wilson (for that was his name) presented himself before the good lady, when she said to him:—

"I had intended to give a Testament to some good boy who would be likely to make a proper use of it. You tell me you can read; now, take this book and let me hear you."

WATT OBSERVES THE POWER OF STEAM.

He read a whole chapter.

"Now, carry the book home," she added; "read it entirely through, and you shall have it."

Seven days from that time, he called again at Mrs. Eastman's house, and announced that he had read the book through.

"Why, so soon? It cannot be!" Mrs. Eastman exclaimed; "but let me try you."

So she examined him until fully convinced that he had read the Testament through.

ONWARD TO FAME AND FORTUNE.

"The book is yours now," she kindly said; and this was the first book he ever owned.

When he was ten years old, his father, who was a poor day-laborer and worked in a sawmill, bound him by indenture to a hard-working farmer, to serve

YOUNG WILSON AT MRS. EASTMAN'S.

him on his farm until the age of twenty-one. The bargain was that he should have one month schooling each year in winter, but none in summer, with board and clothes, and, at the close of his service, should receive six sheep and a yoke of oxen.

He proved a faithful worker, and endeared himself to his guardian and family.

At twenty-one, he received his six sheep and a yoke of oxen, and sold them at once for eighty-four dollars. This was a large amount for one who had never possessed so much as two dollars, and who had never spent so much as a single dollar.

But, during the eleven years of hard service on the farm, he had become rich in manly thought and aims. Every moment of leisure, and many hours at night, when he ought to have been in bed, he devoted to reading and study. Mrs. Eastman and Judge Whitehouse loaned him books from their ample libraries.

At twenty-one, he had read nearly a thousand volumes, including all the numbers of the *North American Review* published at that time. These books embraced the leading works of British and American statesmen and historians, together with the works of such writers as Irving, Cooper, and Scott. His strong desire for learning, as well as his love of country, were strengthened by this course of reading; so he resolved to remove to Natick, Massachusetts, where he could earn much more in making brogans, and, at the same time, enjoy greater facilities for mental improvement.

In twenty years from the time he began to make brogans in Natick, he became United States senator, taking the seat vacated by Hon. Edward Everett. In less than forty years from the time he became the "Natick cobbler," he was vice-president of the United States.

His single aim made it possible for him to surmount the difficulties and endure the privations that crowded between those two extremes.

When a Southern member of the United States Senate called Northern workingmen "mud-sills," Mr. Wilson rose in his seat, with the fire of indignation flashing in his eyes, and repelled the charge, saying:—

"Poverty cast her dark and chilling shadow over the home of my childhood, and want was there sometimes an unbidden guest. At the age of ten years, to aid him who gave me being in keeping the gaunt spectre from the hearth of the mother who bore me, I left the home of my boyhood, and went to earn my bread by daily labor."

It was such a fearless, withering rebuke of Southern aristocracy, that despised honest toil, as to fairly make it stagger.

Such men as Wilson, under the control of a lofty aim from boyhood, have made our country what it is—its commerce, manufactures, mechanic arts, liberty, learning, government, and Christian institutions.

As the burning-glass focalizes the rays of the sun upon a single point, increasing the heat a hundred-fold, so singleness of purpose concentrates the

ONWARD TO FAME AND FORTUNE.

mighty native powers of these men upon the nation to push it forward in the path to glory.

It is the absence of this magical quality that leaves thousands of youth to waste their lives in changing from one occupation to another, bringing nothing to pass, and accomplishing nothing for their country or race.

There is no grander spectacle than that of a youth girding his loins for the battle of life, his sharp eye upon the flaming goal in the distance, his soul on fire with enthusiasm for victory, and all barriers crumbling beneath his feet.

These are the few who were not born to die. They live for one noble object, and so they live for all.

THE NIGHT OF OCTOBER 11, 1492.

X.

PERSEVERANCE.

PERSEVERANCE is singleness of purpose and application on the "home stretch." It is the going to the end of the "long pull, strong pull, and pull altogether."

The negro expressed it well, though in a homely way:—

"It means," said he, "take right hold, hold fast, hang on, and no let go." It is this process of holding on to a purpose formed with unfaltering determination.

President Lincoln was asked, "How does Grant impress you as a leading general?"

"The greatest thing about him is cool persistency of purpose," he replied. "He is not easily excited, and he has the grip of a bull dog. When he once gets his teeth in, nothing can shake him off."

That is perseverance—putting the teeth of invincible purpose into the object sought, and holding on until it is yours! Even in religion this is the condition; the angel will go if you will let him; Jacob wrestled with him, and compelled him to stay or bless. He cried aloud, "I will not let thee go, except thou bless me."

Success yields to such persistency, as the angel did.

It is only when a person is sure of being in the right way, that perseverance becomes a great blessing to him. The Bible calls it "patient continuance in well-doing." This is perseverance of the saints.

But "patient continuance" in evil-doing is the perseverance of sinners, which every wise and thoughtful youth will shun.

Stephenson, the inventor of the locomotive, addressed an audience of mechanics in the city of Leeds, his purpose being to encourage them in persistent efforts to reach a higher standard in their pursuits.

"I stand before you," he said, "as an humble mechanic. I commenced my career on a lower level than any man here. I make this remark to encourage young mechanics to do as I have done—to persevere. The humblest of you occupy a much more favorable position than I did on commencing my life of labor. The civil engineer has many difficulties to contend with; but if the man wishes to

JACOB WRESTLING WITH THE ANGEL.

rise to the higher grades of the profession, he must never see any difficulties before him. Obstacles may appear to be difficulties, but the engineer must be prepared to throw them overboard or to conquer them."

It is characteristic of perseverance not to see difficulties, or expect defeat. It anticipates success.

When Columbus was searching for the New World, his ship's crew became discouraged, and rose in rebellion. They insisted upon turning back, instead of persevering on a fool's errand. There was no New World to be found, in their view. But this commander expected to find it; he had not the least doubt of it. Still, under the circumstances he was obliged to compromise with them; and he promised that, if they would be patient and faithful three days longer, he would abandon the enterprise, unless land should be discovered.

Before the three days expired, however, the New World burst upon their view.

ONWARD TO FAME AND FORTUNE.

That last three days was the gift of perseverance, and it saved the expedition from disaster and disgrace. The three days were only a fractional part of the time consumed by the voyage, but they were worth to Columbus all that his life and the New World were worth. Months and years of labor, study, and care had been spent, requiring decision, energy, industry, and courage clear up to the last three days, all of which would have been worse than wasted had Columbus yielded to the mutiny and abandoned the enterprise.

Such is frequently the value of even one day or hour in accomplishing a purpose. That brief time, wrested from ignoble failure, is not only worth more than all the rest, but it gives value to all the rest.

Robert Bruce took this hint from a spider. He had made several unsuccessful attempts to possess his kingdom and crown, and his heart began to fail him. He was exhausted, and was seeking concealment from his foes in a shattered barn, where, lying upon his back, he discovered a spider casting its silken line from one beam to another. Six times in succession the attempt was made and failed,

GEORGE STEPHENSON.

but the seventh time the persistent little creature succeeded. Bruce took the hint and sprang to his feet, his soul on fire with hope revived, and his heart expectant of victory; and he soon sat upon the throne of Scotland.

He learned that the value of the seventh effort was greatest of all; indeed, that all previous efforts were valueless without it.

Many years ago, a student lost his eyesight by a missile thrown by a classmate. His father was an eminent jurist, and was educating the son for the bar, but this calamity prevented the prosecution of the original plan.

5

66   ONWARD TO FAME AND FORTUNE.

Strange as it may seem, however, the son resolved to become an author. He spent ten years of close systematic study, using the eyes of an assistant, of course, before he selected his theme. Then he spent another ten years in careful research, exploring archives, libraries, correspondence, and consulting official documents and old chronicles. Then followed his great history, "Ferdinand and Isabella," when he was forty years old; "Mexico," "Peru," and "Philip the Second" appeared in due time, establishing his reputation as a profound historian on both sides of the Atlantic.

The perseverance of Prescott is almost unparalleled in human effort.

XI.

SELF-RELIANCE.

A YOUTH may rely upon himself or another person. The one is self-reliance; the other is dependence. He may depend on persons or things; but he can rely only on a person, and that person may be himself, in which case he is self-reliant. Dependence may have reference to the present or the future, while reliance serves for the future only; dependence has more reference to external circumstances, reliance to the feelings.

It is clear, then, that true self-reliance is in no way related to self-conceit, but is that manly confidence in one's ability to make his way in the world that awakens admiration.

When Samuel J. Mills, who was really the author of the great foreign missionary enterprise, was a member of Williams College, he said to a fellow-student, "You and I are little men, but before we die our influence must be felt on the other side of the globe."

There was no conceit in the remark. He was a noble, Christian young man, on whose soul had dawned the light and glory of missionary work for the heathen world, and his language was that of a trusting, self-reliant soul, as confident of success in missionary labors as he was conscious of being in the line of duty. He simply had faith in himself to carry the Gospel to the perishing, and the result proved that his confidence was not misplaced.

He explored every nook and corner of moral destitution in the West, carried the Word of Life to India, and died when he was performing herculean labors for the redemption of Africa.

His was a noble, unselfish self-reliance, which put all his faculties upon the *qui vive* for a definite work. He trusted in God and himself, instead of depending upon influential ancestors, rich fathers or uncles, and favorable circumstances, to assure success, as the unreliant youth does.

It is said of a former United States judge that he was a carpenter in his youth, employing all his leisure moments in mental improvement with reference to the legal profession some time in the future. One day he was planing a board that was to become a part of a "judge's bench" building in the shop, when a friend, observing his careful labor, inquired:—

"Why do you take so great pains to make it smooth?"

Instantly the self-reliant young carpenter replied:—

"Because I want a smooth seat when I come to sit upon it." He continued to make the most of himself by application and persistent effort, until he was able to remove from the carpenter's shop to college; and thence on to the bar and rostrum. A remarkable career of a few years brought him to that "judge's bench," on which he sat. The distance between the carpenter's and the judge's bench was paved, not with broken resolutions, but with granite purposes and heroic struggles.

CHRISTOPHER COLUMBUS.

True self-reliance leads to such results. "God helps those who help themselves."

The celebrated Richter said, "I have made as much out of myself as could be made of the stuff, and no man could require more."

The human race, as a whole, is not inclined to be self-reliant. Men depend on others. The Chinaman plows with a stick because his ancestors did; the American is a protestant, and the Irishman a Roman Catholic, because his father, grandfather, and great-grandfather were. In a thousand things men show how disposed they are to depend upon others, rather than themselves. Others do their thinking, planning, and overcoming for them.

But here and there men appear who accept Carlyle's advice, "Pin thy faith to no man's sleeve. Hast thou not two eyes of thy own?" *They* strike out for themselves; they leave the beaten track; they penetrate the unknown and unexplored; they dare to think and act for themselves; they despise laziness and cowardice; they court hardships and difficulties; they expect hard fare and hard work; and they also expect to succeed. These are the self-reliant.

General Grant was an eminent illustration of self-reliance from his boyhood. His wonderful tact aided him in this direction, and, at the same time, his self-reliance gave expression to his tact.

He was only eight years old when he took his father's unbroken colt, put the harness on him for the first time, and drew brush with him all day long, without any fracas with the untrained animal.

He was but nine years old when he used twenty dollars which he had laid by, for the purchase of a colt. He did it with his father's consent and the latter thought that the bargain was a good one.

Less than two years afterward, his father sent him to another town to purchase a horse for him. He was but eleven years old when he drove a pair of horses, carrying passengers to Cincinnati, forty miles distant, going one day and returning the next.

W. H. PRESCOTT.

In the late war this trait made General Grant conqueror. If he had been a book soldier instead of one who relied on his common sense, he would have been as great a failure as some other generals were. To prosecute his own plans he was obliged to ignore both books and orders. Knowing that General Halleck would not approve of his plan to invest Vicksburg, because it was contrary to the instruction of all military books, he stopped communication on the Mississippi River with St. Louis, Halleck's headquarters, for seven days, so no order could reach him from his superior officer. Badeau says, in his Life of Grant, "He was never averse to availing himself of the ideas of others; but the suggestion of others were simply presented, and either accepted or rejected, as his judgment dictated: he was never persuaded. And if he took up an idea that he found, it was so developed by his own mind that it became as original in reality as if he had conceived the germ. Every one who might be called an associate felt this. Sherman resented the ascription to himself of the origin of the Vicksburg campaign, and has often told the story of his objection to the movement with loyal and splendid magnanimity."

ULYSSES S. GRANT.

The Duke of Wellington was visiting the celebrated school of Eton, where he spent many happy days of his boyhood, and as he stood watching the boys at their sports on the playground, he remarked, "It was there the battle of Waterloo was won."

The self-reliant person is more likely to have a correct view of the business of life—what it is really for. Thousands have no higher conception of it than that it is only to assure a livelihood. This is a very low idea of one's occupation or business. If it is only to get a living—an expedient for earning bread and butter—there is little manhood or womanhood in it. But it is altogether more than that: it is to discipline the physical, mental, and moral faculties, that true manliness and womanliness may be the outcome of pursuing an occupation faithfully. The farmer, mechanic, and merchant, no less than the lawyer, physician, clergyman, and statesman, should become abler and nobler by the work they are obliged to put into their chosen pursuits. This view of one's business is necessary to the highest achievement; and the truly self-reliant person is most likely to possess it.

XII.

DECISION.

THE elements of success lock and interlock; it is difficult to separate them—to tell where one ends and another begins, so it is with decision; it is involved in the operation of other qualities. Yet it has a character of its own. It was the spirit of our fathers when they arose to cast off the British yoke, and adopted the Declaration of Independence.

Patrick Henry voiced it in the convention of Virginia in that impassioned speech in which he said:—

"If we mean not basely to abandon the noble struggle in which we have been so long engaged, and which we have pledged ourselves never to abandon until the glorious object of our contest shall be obtained, we must fight! I repeat, sir, we must fight! An appeal to arms and to the God of hosts is all that is left us. It is vain, sir, to extenuate the matter. Gentlemen may cry 'Peace, peace!' but there is no peace. The war is actually begun! The next gale that sweeps from the North will bring to our ears the clash of resounding arms! Our brethren are already in the field. Why stand we here idle? What is it that gentlemen would have? Is life so dear, or peace so sweet, as to be purchased at the price of chains and slavery? Forbid it, Almighty God! I know not what course others may take; but as for me, give me liberty, or give me death."

John Foster cites an example of decision of character worthy of our study:—

A young Englishman inherited a vast estate just when his wild nature was yielding to dissipation. The great legacy served only to hasten his progress to ruin. Within a few years the last dollar of his patrimony was spent, and poverty and degradation stared him in the face.

One day, in his deep despair, he rushed out of the house resolved to take his own life in the field yonder. Reaching an eminence that overlooked the estates which had passed out of his hands, he stopped, entranced by the splendid panorama that spread out before him, and finally sat down to reflect.

Then and there, with mighty difficulties and apparent impossibilities before him, he resolved to regain the estates which his immorality had wasted.

At once he decided to carry out his decision by performing the first work that offered.

A load of coal was dumped at a fine residence; he sought, and obtained the job of carrying it into the cellar. Other menial work was offered, and he did it.

PATRICK HENRY.

Step by step, onward and upward, he advanced, until he became a prosperous and wealthy merchant, and purchased the estates which his folly once squandered.

These facts are a signal illustration of the maxim, "Where there's a will, there's a way."

Pompey was entreated by his friends not to risk his life on a tempestuous sea that he might be in Rome at a certain time, when his soul bounded to the climax of dignity, investing all his powers with greatness, and he replied, "It is necessary for me to go, but it is not necessary for me to live."

The great English orator, Richard Brinsley Sheridan, made a ridiculous failure of his first attempt to speak in Parliament. The sneering laugh of the members mortified him exceedingly, and, at the same time, aroused the noblest elements of humanity within him, so that he exclaimed, as he sat down in humiliating confusion, "It is in me, and it shall come out." And it did come out. Under the power of heroic decision, he, of whom the schoolmaster said when he was a boy, "He is a dunce," became the eloquent statesman of whom it is said, "Had his character been reliable, he might have ruled the world."

ONWARD TO FAME AND FORTUNE.   73

In like manner, our American Sheridan (Phil), the great general, turned defeat into victory by his remarkable decision. He was miles away from his army when the booming of cannon assured him that his men were engaged in a hot battle. Putting spurs to his horse, he struck into his famous ride down the

PATRICK HENRY IN THE VIRGINIA CONVENTION.

"Winchester Road" toward the seat of conflict. Within a few miles he met his beaten and retreating forces ingloriously running from the foe; whereupon, rising to his full height in his saddle, he cried, "Halt! Halt!" and commanded them "to right about face" and follow him. On, on, he dashed, his valiant men rallying at the sound of his voice, and inspired with fresh hope of triumph by his decisive act; nearer and nearer to the foe they came, more and more invincible under their leader's contagious heroism, until commander and men fell upon the foe like an avalanche, surprising them when flushed with victory, and completely routing them, horse, foot, and dragoon.

It was when General Grant was fighting the bloody battles of the Wilderness, and the whole loyal North was watching every movement of his army to learn what hope there was of his ever capturing Richmond, that he rose to the sublime decision which sent a thrill of joy through the country, "I shall fight it out on this line, if it takes all summer." That settled the fate of the Rebellion; the people accepted it as the harbinger of victory and the return of peace.

PHIL SHERIDAN.

Decision answers the questions: Can you do it? Will you do it? and answers them in the affirmative. We know better than we do; decision helps us to do even better than we know.

In his "personal memoirs," General Grant speaks of the sense of "trepidation" with which he took command of his first regiment, yet we know that his decision of character quickly fitted him to lead a thousand regiments. Persons who are weakened by indecision are always subservient to circumstances; while circumstances are subservient to manly decision.

It is decision of character which makes a youth proof against the lures to excessive play and pleasure, to gaming and drink, and to all other forms of temptation that are inimical to study, uprightness, and virtue. Decision thunders "No!" and the devil of temptation flees.

It is indecision that hesitates, delays, fears, and finally says "Yes," and becomes the slave of immorality or vice.

Many people, young and old, know what duty is, but fail to do it for the want of decision. They know very well what labors and self-denials are necessary to obtain an education, master a trade, or attain to excellence in any pursuit; but their ignoble indecision, which is a sort of mental and moral debility, disqualifies them for the undertaking.

"The will, which is the central force of character, must be trained to habits of decision; otherwise, it will never be able to resist evil, nor to follow good."

It is not an exhibition of manly or womanly character for youth to waste their breath in laments over their present situation; to think if their circumstances, or friends, or talents were different, they might achieve something worth recording. This is indecision, which often leads a person to think that embarrassments are especially numerous in his own experience, and that he does not have his full share of advantages falling to the common lot of humanity.

Nothing can be more unmanly and belittling. Rise above this unmanly view of life! Decide for the best in everything!—and then win it.

COURAGE.

PERSEVERANCE and self-reliance are proof of courage; their continuance depends upon it. By courage, we mean that power of the mind which bears up under all dangers and difficulties.

Fortitude may express one element of this noble virtue, since fortitude is the power that enables one to endure pain. The man of fortitude will endure the amputation of a limb; the man of courage will do that, and also face the cannon's mouth. "Courage comprehends the absence of all fear, the disregard of all personal convenience, the spirit to begin, and the determination to pursue what has been begun."

Such a quality is needed every hour. The most humble life will find abundant use for it; the cares, labors, and embarrassments that are the common lot of humanity, make it indispensable.

The burdens which boyhood and girlhood must bear in acquiring an education, learning a trade, resisting temptations, and building spotless characters, demand better physical and moral courage.

A faint-hearted man would never undertake to prepare a dictionary, or a history of the United States.

ONWARD TO FAME AND FORTUNE.

Only the most resolute and determined spirit would take up such a burden. Here is ample scope for courage that can forego pleasure and personal comfort, endure privation and wearisome labor and conquer opposition of every kind.

At sixteen years of age Samuel Drew was a wild, reckless youth, given to idleness, orchard-robbing, and even worse practices. A serious accident that nearly cost him his life, together with the sudden death of his brother, checked him in his mad career. He had lost his reputation by evil conduct, and education by avoiding schools, and yet he resolved to regain one and acquire the other. A youth of less courage would have yielded to despair, declaring that it would be impossible to surmount the difficulties in his way. But, rising in the strength of regenerated manhood, he resolved to become a true man and scholar. He appeared to realize that the gist of the matter was in him, and to resolve that it should come out.

Yet he must gain a livelihood on the shoemaker's bench, where he went to work with a will. Every leisure moment was devoted to reading and study, and often night contributed materially to this end. Referring to this period, twenty years thereafter, he said, "The more I read the more I felt my ignorance, and the more I felt my ignorance the more invincible became my energy to surmount it.

"Every leisure moment was now employed in reading one thing or another. Having to support myself by manual labor, my time for reading was but little; and to overcome this disadvantage my usual method was to place a book before me while at meat, and at every repast I read five or six pages. Locke's 'Essay on the Understanding' awakened me from my stupor, and induced me to form a resolution to abandon the groveling views I had been accustomed to maintain."

Without prolonging his story, Drew became an active parishioner of Dr. Adam Clarke and a local preacher before he left the shoe-bench. Subsequently he became a distinguished author, known to every generation since his day as the author of an "Essay on the Immateriality and Immortality of the Soul." His fame was spread world-wide. Courage did it.

When President Lincoln was renominated for a second term of office the army was in great need of recruits. He resolved to issue a call for five hundred thousand men, but leading members of Congress said, "It will endanger your re-election;" and they advised him to withhold the order. But he persisted, and finally went personally before the congressional military committee, where a similar attempt was made to induce him to withhold the order. But the attempt only evoked a higher and grander expression of courage. Stretching his tall form to its full height he replied, with the fire of indignation flashing in his eyes, as if he had been asked to do an act of meanness: "It is not necessary for me to be re-elected, but it is necessary for the soldiers at the front to be

ONWARD TO FAME AND FORTUNE.   77

reinforced by five hundred thousand men, and I shall call for them; and if I go down under the act I will go down like the Cumberland, with my colors flying." That was courage culminating in the highest principle.

It was in the terrible battle of Atlanta that the brave and idolized McPherson fell. The news of his death spread with the speed of lightning along the lines, sending a pang of sorrow through every soldier's heart. For a moment it seemed as if despair would demoralize the whole army, until General John A. Logan, on whom the command now rested, took in the situation and, on his furious black stallion, dashed down the lines, crying at the top of his voice, as he waved his sword in the air, "McPherson and revenge! McPherson and revenge!" An eye-witness wrote: "Never shall I forget —never will one of us who survived that desperate fight forget to our dying day—the grand spectacle presented by Logan as he rode up and down in front of the line, his black eyes flashing fire, his long black hair streaming in the wind, bareheaded, and his service-worn slouch hat swinging in his bridle-hand and his sword flashing in the other, crying out in stentorian tones, 'Boys! McPherson and revenge!'

ABRAHAM LINCOLN.

Why, it made my blood run both hot and cold, and moved every man of us to follow to the death the brave and magnificent hero-ideal of a soldier who made this resistless appeal to all that is noble in a soldier's heart, and this, too, when the very air was alive with whistling bullets and howling shell! And if he could only have been painted as he swept up and down the line on a steed as full of fire as his glorious rider, it would to-day be one of the finest battle pictures of the war." This impromptu act of courage was even more inspiring than a

ONWARD TO FAME AND FORTUNE.

reinforcement of ten thousand men, and converted his almost despairing command into mighty conquerors; and the day was won. Such a deed of heroism adds lustre to human glory.

Courage is so noble a trait that men respect it, even in a pirate. Pizarro was a pirate, bent upon plundering Peru no matter what perils and h a r d s h i p s blocked his way. At Gallo, disease and hunger drove his men to madness, and they demanded that the enterprise should be abandoned. Just then a vessel arrived that offered to take them back to Panama. But Pizarro spurned the offer, and with his sword drew a line on the sand from east to west. Then turning his face to the south, he said to his brother pirates:—

"Friends and comrades! On that side are toil, hunger, nakedness, the drenching s t o r m, d e s e r t i o n, and death; on this side, ease and pleasure. There lies Peru with its riches; here, Panama with its poverty. Choose each man what best becomes a brave Castilian. For my part, I go to the south."

SIR THOMAS MORE BEING LED TO EXECUTION.

ONWARD TO FAME AND FORTUNE.

Put that courage into a saint and he will become a missionary like Judson, a reformer like Howard, a preacher like Paul, or a martyr like Sir Thomas More. It is this spirit that has withstood the opposition of wicked men in the progress of the race, and achieved victory in the face of trials and death. The courage of one's conscience is the highest kind of courage, inspiring the whole being to do and dare. Even gentle woman, full of tenderness and love, has endured contumely and persecution beyond measure under the power of Christian courage, which has its source in God.

Time would fail to tell of the deathless names of men and women whose courageous adherence to principle was a forcible illustration of the triumph of David, with his sling and stone, over Goliath, because he stood for the "armies of Israel" in the name of Jehovah. Higher courage is this than that of the battlefield, where the watchword is that of Napoleon, "Glory," or even that of Wellington and Nelson, "Duty."

True courage is both tender and magnanimous. A braver man than Charles Napier never carried a sword or fought a battle. Yet he declined sporting with a gun, because he could not bear to hurt an animal.

General Grant had no fear of "iron hail and leaden rain;" but when Lee surrendered, and the Union men began to salute him by firing cannon, Grant directed the firing to cease, saying, "It will wound the feelings of our prisoners, who have become our countrymen again."

MILTON DICTATING PARADISE LOST TO HIS DAUGHTER.

XIV.

ON TIME, PUNCTUALITY.

A RIPE scholar was the neighbor of Dr. Adam Clarke, the commentator, when the latter had become quite renowned. On the same evening both saw a copy of the Greek Testament of Erasmus advertised. As soon as the ripe scholar had swallowed his breakfast, on the next morning, he hastened to the book-store to purchase the volume. "You are too late; the book is sold," replied the book-seller, to the inquiry of the gentleman. "Too late!" exclaimed the scholar, in surprise; "why, I came as soon as I had eaten my breakfast!" "Yes, but Adam Clarke came *before breakfast*," responded the merchant. The incident shows that the man who is on time has the inside track, and the inside track is nearest the goal.

In 1788, Washington, the father of his country, visited Boston, and he decided to leave for Salem at eight o'clock on the morning of a certain day. A company of cavalry volunteered to escort him to Salem. While the clock of the Old South Church was striking eight, Washington mounted his horse and started, though his escort had not put in an appearance. A few minutes later, however, they arrived, and were greatly mortified to find that Washington was gone. Putting spurs to their horses, they galloped forward, and overtook him at Charles River bridge. When they came up, Washington said, "Major, I thought you had been in my family too long not to know when it was eight o'clock." The major made a poor apology, and learned a lesson he never forgot.

Another incident from the life of Washington confirms the foregoing. He wanted to purchase a pair of horses, and arranged with the owner of a span to be at his office at five o'clock in the morning. Washington was prompt, but the owner of the horses was fifteen minutes late. He found Washington engaged with other parties when he reached his office, and he was obliged to wait a whole week before he could have another interview. Being behindhand fifteen minutes upset his plans for a week. He never recovered that quarter of an hour. It was lost forever.

Hawthorne makes one of his prominent characters say, "I have spent all my life in pursuit of to-morrow, being assured that to-morrow has some vast benefit or other in store for me. But I am now getting a little in years, and must make haste, for unless I overtake to-morrow soon, I begin to be afraid it will finally escape me." He died, probably on the day before he expected to overtake it. Had he started in life with the inspiration of that maxim, "One to-day is worth two to-morrows," he would never have pursued to-morrow at all —all days would have been to-days; but a good many years ago he lost a day by indolence or tardiness, and was never able to make up the loss. He could not tell just what had become of it, but it dropped out sometime and somewhere, and his whole life was incomplete in consequence. That advertisement was not a mere figment of the imagination. "Lost—two golden moments! No reward is offered, as they are gone forever."

OLD SOUTH CHURCH, BOSTON.

Samuel Budgett, the great English merchant, was distinguished for being on time. His employes said that he was as good as a chronometer about the warehouse, where six hundred of them were engaged. He trained them all to promptness by his example and methods. Even those of them who lived four miles away managed to reach the store at six o'clock in the morning, from January to January again. "By the gate hung a blackboard, divided into squares; each square was numbered, and contained a nail; on the nail hung a little copper plate. Each man had his number, and as he went out he took a plate with him, leaving his number exposed on the board. As he entered he placed the plate on the nail, so covering his number. The moment the bell ceased ringing the board was removed, and all whose numbers were not covered were at once set down as defaulters. He who did not appear once on that list during a year received at its end a sovereign as his reward." In this way, Budgett trained to signal efficiency a large number of employes, who served him many years. His warehouse was known throughout Great Britain for the systematic and successful conduct of an immense business. Promptness was the secret of its success, for in the train of that followed industry, economy of time, dispatch, and a whole cluster of other virtues.

The late Amos Lawrence, of Boston, wrote to a friend, " I practiced upon the maxim, ' Business before friends,' from the commencement of my course. During the first seven years of my business in this city, I never allowed a bill against me to stand unsettled over the Sabbath. If the purchase of goods was made at auction on Saturday, and delivered to me, I always examined and settled the bill by note or by crediting it, and having it clear, so that in case I was not on duty on Monday, there would be no trouble for my boys, thus keeping the business *before* me, instead of allowing it to drive me."

The youth who is always punctual at school, store, or shop, becomes the man who shares the confidence of the public, because he is on time in meeting his engagements, paying his debts, fulfilling his promises, discharging official duties, and doing the multitudinous other things which are expected of a reliable citizen. He is a chronometer on legs. Each twenty-four hours can be measured by his daily duties. He keeps the whole time, even to the seconds. His deeds strike the time of day. The sun itself is not more exact in its rising and setting than is he. Nature is always on time, and so is he. Were a planet to get behindhand in the movement of the great system of worlds, there would be such a smash up as would remind us of " chaos and old night." But planets never lag. A minute of time never drops from their orbits. The seasons come and go on the mark. Night and morning always observe the nick of time. Even the comet, that pays

NATHANIEL HAWTHORNE.

us a visit only once in a thousand years, arrives on the very second it is due. And this "sublime precision leads the earth, after a circuit of five hundred million miles, back to the solstice at the appointed moment, without the loss of one second—no, not the millionth part of a second—for the ages on ages during which it has traveled that empyreal road." To be on time as nature is, should be the rule of every young aspirant for success.

ENERGY.

DECISION is more of the head; energy more of the heart. The latter is "the power to produce positive effects."

It is recorded of Hezekiah: "And in every work that he began in the service of the house of God and in the law, and in the commandments to seek his God, he did it with all his heart, and prospered."

Doing "with all the heart" is energy. Without it, no one prospers in anything.

It is necessary to maintain decision; it is the force that reduces decision to practice, or supplements it.

Success comes to the class who pursue their life-work "with all the heart."

The motto on the pickaxe well expressed it: "I will find a way, or make it."

The Spartan father understood it when he said to his son, who complained that his sword was too short, "Then add a step to it."

Another says, "Hence it is that, inspired by energy of purpose, men of comparatively mediocre powers have often been enabled to accomplish such extraordinary results. For the men who have most powerfully influenced the world have not been so much men of genius as men of strong convictions and enduring capacity for work, impelled by irresistible energy and invincible determination; such men, for example, as were Mohammed, Luther, Knox, Calvin, Loyola, and Wesley."

The hearts of all these reformers were in their work; and "he who has heart has everything." Hence, in the most important of all concerns, this sort of energy is required. "Whatsoever thy hand findeth to do, do it with thy might." God does not accept half-hearted work. His servants must throw their whole souls into service they render to Him, if they would count. "Thou shalt love the Lord thy God with all thy heart, and with all thy soul, and with all thy mind." It would be difficult to state the case more strongly.

God knows exactly the measure of human power that we can put into any work, and He demands the full measure.

ONWARD TO FAME AND FORTUNE.

Eighty years ago a youth of eighteen years, residing on Cape Cod, resolved to seek his fortune in Boston, and started for that city with only four dollars in his pocket—all the money he could raise. On reaching the city he set himself to work at once to find a situation; and he traveled and traveled, applying in vain here and there for a place, but finding none.

A single day satisfied him that there was no opening for him, and he was strongly tempted to return home, but his stout heart rose in rebellion against the thought. He would not return to his native town discomfited. He had too much force of character for that. He was a live boy, and his energy said, "If I can't find a situation, I'll make one."

And he did. He found a board about the right size, which he converted into an oyster stand on the corner of a street. He borrowed a wheelbarrow and went three miles to an oyster smack, where he purchased three bushels of the bivalves, and wheeled them to his place of business.

He was a Boston merchant now. He had made a situation that he could not find.

He sold all his oysters on the first day, and was well satisfied with his profits.

He continued this method of doing business until he had laid by one hundred and thirty dollars, with which he purchased a horse and cart. He removed his place of business, also, from out of doors into a convenient room.

On the first day in his new place of traffic, he made seventeen dollars; and from that time he continued to enlarge his business rapidly, taking on other departments, adding daily to his property, until he became a Boston millionaire, blessing others with his money, and leaving hundreds of thousands at his death to found the Boston University, where young men and women are educated for usefulness.

Such was the career of the late Isaac Rich, an example of energy and perseverance worthy of the highest praise. The life of Rich confirms the view of Whipple, the late famous essayist, who said, "What common quality distinguishes men of genius from other men, in practical life, in science, in letters, in every department of human thought and action? This common quality is vital energy of mind, inherent, original force of thought and vitality of conception. Men in whom this energy glows seem to spurn the limitations of matter, to leap the gulf which separates positive knowledge from discovery, the actual from the possible; and, in their grasp at spiritual realities, in their intense life, they seem to demonstrate the immortality of the soul that burns within them. They give palpable evidence of infinite capacity, of indefinite power of growth. It seems a mockery to limit their life by years; to suppose that fiery essence can ever burn out or be extinguished. This life, this energy, this uprising, aspiring flame of thought,

"'This mind, this spirit, this Promethean spark,
This lightning of their being.'

has been variously called power of combination, invention, creation, insight; but in the last analysis it is resolved into vital energy of soul to think and to do."

When Sir Rowell Buxton was a boy, neighbors thought that his great energy, in connection with much waywardness, would be his ruin. But his good mother said, "Never mind; he is self-willed now, but you will see that it will turn out well in the end."

Subsequently he became very intimate with the Gurney family, who were highly respected for their social qualities, mental culture, and philanthropy. He married one of the daughters, and entered upon his business career with a will. His mother's prophecy, that his will power and mighty energy would be a blessing in the end, proved true. Some said that he could do more work in a given time than any two men in England. He became wealthy, was a member of Parliament at thirty-two, and a leading spirit of Great Britain thereafter.

One of the Gurney family, Priscilla Gurney, entreated him on her deathbed, in 1821, "to make the cause of the slave the great object of his life." He was already engaged in the cause of British emancipation, but her dying words fired his heart anew, and he resolved to give himself no rest until the shackles were broken from the last slave in the British realm. With unsurpassed energy he gave himself to the work year after year, and, on the day of his daughter's marriage, August 1, 1834, he wrote to a friend: "The bride is just gone; everything has passed off to admiration; and there is not a slave in the British colonies."

Such men "never strike sails to a fear;" they "come into port grandly, or sail with God the seas;" they never join "communities," so called, where everything is held in common. Their self-reliance, independence, and force of character, lift them high above such dependent relations.

"We love our upright, energetic men. Pull them this way and that way and the other, and they only bend, but never break. Trip them down, and in a trice they are on their feet."

ART OF WAITING

DR. MAISTRE said, "To know how to wait is the great secret of success." Thousands of youth and older persons have made a failure of life-work because they did not know how to wait. Their impatience to achieve caused them to overlook some of the conditions, especially that historic one that time is an element of success. Enduring progress is of slow growth: this is true of all great enterprises. Slow and sure is the rule of Providence, and in this way the present standard of Christian civilization has been attained. Successful workers have waited patiently for results.

Patience is the art of waiting; really a fine art, it is so rare. It is a homely virtue, but strong and healthy, always timely, and always indispensable. Sydney Smith said, "No man can end with being superior who will not begin with being inferior;" and just here is where patience may have its "perfect work." It is a long road to great excellence in any pursuit, and few there be that find it. Many waste life in looking for a shorter route, which they never find. Only "time and patience can change the mulberry leaf to satin," is the truthful proverb.

The great world is in pressing need of this quality. Men can't wait to be rich, or great, or good. To wait forty years for a fortune has a discouraging outlook to many. Half that time is longer than they want to wait. Ten or fifteen years' labor for an education is too much for a multitude of youth. They would be educated in half that time. Not a few youth become disheartened at the very beginning of their efforts for an education, and turn back depressed. They cannot see the end of the road from its beginning, and so it seems endless to them. Many part with their resolution in nearly every branch of study, because too much time and labor are necessary to master it, content to bury themselves for life in ignorance or mediocrity. With more disposition to labor and wait, a great amount of poor scholarship would be avoided.

It is evidence of mental weakness, and, perhaps, of moral weakness too, when a young man or woman becomes disheartened over the continuous efforts necessary to success. Any one can give up the contest, but only the bravest and best can follow it up to victory. It requires no particular talent or wisdom to lose courage and decline to go forward, a very ignorant and inefficient person can do that; but the nobler attributes must push to the front to overcome difficulties and triumph; and patience is by no means the least important of these.

On the other hand, human nature is ennobled by strong endeavors long continued. Manhood and womanhood take on dignity, power, and honor by bending all their energies to a task as long as it is necessary to win. Gibbon, working twenty years upon his "Decline and Fall of the Roman Empire," Bancroft devoting twenty-six years to his "History of the United States," and Noah Webster thirty-six on his dictionary, appear greater and grander for the service. Perhaps there is no more remarkable record of laboring and waiting in the annals of the past than the last mentioned. Thirty-six years of close study in the dry field of philology! Collecting and defining words more than one-third of a century without interruption! Ordinary exhibitions of patience dwindle into insignificance in comparison with this enthusiastic devotion to one purpose.

Newton spent several years upon his "Chronology of Ancient Nations," and then was so dissatisfied with it that he rewrote it. Perceiving wherein he might improve it, he rewrote it again; and he continued this method of improvement until he had rewritten it sixteen times. He knew how to wait for results, and how to work for them, too. The amount of patience involved in such an enterprise is beyond computation; and it is grand in the highest degree. The real greatness of the man appears in such stupendous work.

The life of the late Hon. Simon Cameron at ninety years of age, was a forcible illustration of our theme. Left an orphan at nine years of age, in utter destitution, his prospects were dubious indeed. But he sought the position of errand boy in a printing office, where his tact, industry, and intelligence soon won a high place for him. In a few years he became a journeyman with good wages. At twenty-one he became an editor, and from that time his career in business and political circles was remarkable. He became wealthy, occupied many positions of trust in the State, and was elected United States Senator in 1845. In 1861 he was a member of President Lincoln's cabinet.

THOMAS CARLYLE.

This is a marvelous record to be made by a poor orphan boy, who never went to school one day in his life. While his tact, perseverance, application, and industrious habits were conspicuous elements of his success, they would not have won such victories without his great patience. He knew how to wait. He was never in a great hurry to achieve and to possess, but took up the duty nearest to him and discharged it without expecting quick returns; then the next one, and the next one, and thus on to the end. He proved that "a patient waiter is no loser."

Carlyle wrote, "How much grows everywhere if we do but wait! Not a difficulty but can transfigure itself into a triumph; not even a deformity, but if our own soul have imprinted worth upon it, will grow dear to us."

> "Let us then be up and doing,
>   With a heart for any fate;
>   Still achieving, still pursuing,
>   Learn to labor and to wait."

INDUSTRY.

THE shepherds of Bethlehem were busy watching their flocks by night, when the angels appeared to them with "good tidings of great joy."

God sends angels to the industrious only, to gladden them; there is no such vision for the idle and lazy.

When generals and statesmen tilled the soil of Italy, and labor was considered

"GOOD TIDINGS OF GREAT JOY."

honorable by the magistrates of the land, the Roman empire flourished. But the introduction of slaves wrought a great change in public opinion. Labor became discreditable to those who could live without it, and indolence and ease usurped the place of industry. The ruling classes gave themselves up to pleasure and luxury; and soon corruption, in high places and low, sapped the foundation of the empire, and it fell.

Industry is a virtue; and it is the duty of all to practice it.

Believing this, Sir Walter Scott wrote to his son Charles, "I cannot too much impress on your mind that labor is the condition which God has imposed on us in every station in life; there's nothing worth having that can be had without it, from the bread which the peasant wins with the sweat of his brow, to the sports by which the rich man must get rid of his *ennui*. As for knowledge, it can no more be planted in the human mind without labor, than a field of wheat can be produced without the previous use of the plough. Labor, therefore, my dear boy, and improve the time. In youth, our steps are light, and our minds are ductile, and knowledge is easily laid up; but if we neglect our spring, our summer will be useless and contemptible, our harvest will be chaff, and our winter of old age unrespected and desolate."

Scott himself was a remarkable example of industry. Sometimes his health was impaired by his great labors. At one time the physician besought him to abridge his literary work, to which the inveterate worker replied:—

"As for bidding me not to work, Molly might just as well put the kettle on the fire and say, 'Now, kettle, don't boil.'"

At fifty-five years of age he became heavily involved through the failure of his publishers, with whom he was connected as silent partner. His indebtedness amounted to the enormous sum of six hundred thousand dollars. Men of ordinary courage and industry would have sunk down in utter despair under such a pecuniary burden; but Scott had boundless faith in the achievements of persistent industry, and he resolved that the last dollar should be paid by the product of his pen.

Summoning all the faculties of soul and body to the task, he set himself to work with more earnestness and determination than ever. Volume after volume rolled from his pen, as if it were as easy for him to write books as it was for sugar to be sweet, each one illustrating more and more the greatness of the man, and each one greeted with increasing delight by the reading public.

Year after year he performed these prodigious labors, inspired by the thought of being able to liquidate the mammoth debt, and thereby vindicate his honor.

His purpose was accomplished. The last dollar of his indebtedness was paid, and he was satisfied, though his physical constitution was seriously impaired by the excessive toil. He died, in consequence, a martyr to his uprightness and sense of honor. The patriot who dies for his country, or the Christian who dies for the truth, is not more of a martyr to his convictions than he. The most industrious habits in secular pursuits do not interfere with intellectual culture, as a multitude of facts prove. Spenser was secretary to the lord deputy of Ireland;

ONWARD TO FAME AND FORTUNE.

Bacon was a hard-working lawyer; Milton was secretary to the commonwealth; Locke was secretary to the board of trade under Charles II., and afterward under William III., was commissioner of appeals and of trade, and of plantations; Addison was secretary of state; Steele was commissioner of stamps, and Cowley "held various offices of trust and confidence" in the reign of Charles. I. The labor and drudgery of business did not unfit them for the best literary work. Rather, it stimulated them to nobler efforts in literary life.

In Italy, nearly every distinguished man of letters in the time of Dante was a hard-working merchant, physician, statesman, diplomatist, judge, or soldier. Villani was a merchant; Dante was in the public service, after he was chemist and druggist; Galileo was a physician; Petrarch was an ambassador, and Goldoni a lawyer.

In Great Britain, Isaak Walton was a linen-draper; De Foe a shopkeeper; Isaac Taylor an engraver of patterns for Manchester calico printers; John Stuart Mill was "principal examiner in the East India House," where Charles Lamb and Edwin Morris were clerks; Macaulay was secretary of war when he wrote his "Lays of Ancient Rome;" Sir Henry Taylor, Anthony Trollope, and Matthew Arnold were all holding important public offices when their most popular literary works appeared.

SIR WALTER SCOTT.

In our own land, it is equally true that hard toil in secular life has contributed largely to literary and public distinction. If we cannot say, with Louis XIV., "It is by toil that kings govern," we can say, truthfully, that our country has been governed and moulded by self-made men, who have risen from the ranks of the industrious in humble pursuits by their own brave and self-denying efforts.

The names of Washington, Jackson, Clay, Roger Sherman, Lawrence, Jay, Lincoln, Garfield, Grant, and a host of others, are familiar as belonging to this class, whose memory posterity will not willingly let die. Their industry in early life seemed to command every faculty, sharpening them for greater and better service, until they were as well qualified to rule the nation as to run a shop or farm.

The biographer of Samuel Budgett says, " He seemed born under a decree to do. Doing, doing, ever doing; his nature seemed to abhor idleness more than the natures of the old philosophers a vacuum. An idle moment was an irksome moment, an idle hour would have been a sort of purgatory. No sooner was one engagement out of his hand, than his instinct within him seemed to cry out, ' Now, what is the next thing?' Among such memoranda as escaped destruction by his hand, one note tells of a 'joyless and uncomfortable Sabbath; and no wonder, for I did not rise until half-past five o'clock.'" When this man died it was said, "No death in England, but that of the Queen herself, would have touched hearts so tenderly." A stranger, at his funeral, remarked to a man by his side, "This is a remarkable funeral."

"Yes," the man addressed answered, "such a one as we never had in Kingwood before. Ah, sir, a great man has fallen."

"No doubt he was an important man in this neighborhood," responded the stranger.

"In this neighborhood!" exclaimed the man; "there was not his equal in all England. No tongue can tell all that man did."

The connection between his industry and success was clear as day.

"If any man will not work, neither shall he eat." God's decree is, Work or starve. "The hand of the diligent maketh rich." Industry is the source of all the wealth of our nation, and of all nations. Idleness never maketh rich, physically or morally, but industry creates both material and moral wealth, the latter being best of all.

Horace Mann said, "Let the young man remember there is nothing derogatory in any employment which ministers to the well-being of the race. It is the spirit that is carried into an employment that elevates or degrades it. The ploughman that turns the clod may be a Cincinnatus or a Washington, or he may be brother to the clod he turns. It is every way creditable to handle the yardstick and to measure tape: the only discredit consists in having a soul whose range of thought is as short as the stick and as narrow as the tape."

STANDING BEFORE KINGS.

WHO shall stand before kings? "Seest thou a man diligent in his business? *he* shall stand before kings; he shall not stand before mean men." The kind of diligence spoken of in these words embraces much more than the superficial reader supposes. To be diligent in one's business as above, enlists all the powers. All that is good in a man is brought to the front. He must be sincere, earnest, honest, persevering, self-reliant, industrious, enterprising, and courageous, if he would be "diligent in business." Even more than this will appear; for the whole triumphal train of virtues that assure honorable success will file into the grand march to the king's throne. They are all necessary to pursue a noble purpose, and make it great and successful enough for kings to honor. For the man does not "stand before kings," cringing like a slave or crawling like a beggar; he stands there every inch a man, dignified in his consciousness of having won, with a life record he is willing that royalty itself should scan; not the royalty that flourishes in robe and crown, but the royalty of goodness and truth. "He shall not stand before mean men." A king may be mean; there have been such. He will not stand before a monarch who is "mean." No! The "kings" that he will stand before are the great, good ones of the earth, who have been true to themselves and God. He may be their equal, and the bearing of his royal life will command their respect.

Prove the foregoing by a fact. The late Hon. William E. Dodge had poor but Christian parents. He was obliged to work when he was a mere boy. He had no idle moments, and scarcely any leisure moments even in boyhood. Poor schools offered their small advantages only a few weeks in a year, and out of school he was expected to be "diligent in business." Industry being a law of the family, he was early trained to industrious habits, so that when he took up his residence in New York City, an inexperienced youth, he was well equipped for work. It was immaterial to him how early his day's work began, or how late it closed, if so be that his employer's interests were faithfully served. The work he had in hand engaged his attention as if it were his own. There was not the slightest disposition in him to avoid labor or responsibility. He had no fear or dread of these; he rather sought them. As a consequence, he won the confidence of his employer at once, and that of all other men around him. His industry marshaled a fine array of attributes: uprightness, courtesy, perseverance, singleness of purpose, loftiness of aim, thoroughness, tact, energy, decision of character, self-reliance, courage, and purity of life—a combination of traits well suited to find or make a way to success.

Two temptations of a great city he especially tried to escape: the intoxicating cup and Sabbath-breaking. Treating was common, but no one had an opportunity to treat him; Sabbath-breaking was contagious, but he did not take the evil. Always in the public place of worship on Sunday, "diligent in his business" six days in the week, his evenings devoted to reading, study, literary and religious lectures—this was the routine which he followed month after month, and year after year. His employer would have entrusted his whole property to his care had it been necessary; and so would any other merchant who knew him. The lures of the metropolis that had carried thousands of youth down to ruin made no impression upon him. He paid no attention to them, and pursued the even tenor

FRANKLIN AT COURT.

of his way, as if temptations were not. "Every man is tempted, when he is drawn away of his own lust and enticed."

His advance upward was rapid. Within a few years he was doing business for himself. His character was his capital—better capital than money. "When poverty is your inheritance, virtue must be your capital." There was no limit to his credit, for his capital was moral. Money is not a guarantee against duplicity, cheating, or overreaching; but character is. "A good name is rather to be chosen than great riches." It is as true in a warehouse as it is in the chapel or church.

ONWARD TO FAME AND FORTUNE.

Young Dodge prospered. He was getting ready to meet kings.

Wealth began to accumulate; his business grew; friends multiplied. Though his time was now his own, he had none to waste. Even his recreation was found in philanthropic and benevolent deeds. Down into the slums of the city he went and rescued many a boy. He was a pillar in his church. He became an animating spirit in home, foreign, and other missionary societies. "City Missions," "Freedmen's Aid Societies," "Jerry McAuley's Mission," the "Female College at Beirut," and a score of other organizations to bless the world shared his counsels, labors, and munificent benefactions. Some years he gave away one thousand dollars a day. That was getting pretty near a throne. He "never lost the prayers of the poor."

He became a wise counselor, sought after by leading men in great enterprises —banks, insurance companies, temperance and anti-slavery societies, railroad corporations, colleges, theological seminaries, and other institutions watched over by the wise and learned of the age. His counsel was sought at Washington in the dark hour of his country's peril. There he stood "before kings," the greatest and best statesman of the land. His name and fame crossed the Atlantic, and the high and low in the mother country desired to see him and hear him speak. He went thither. He was invited to address many public bodies where learned professors and renowned statesmen gave him the warmest welcome. He dined with Gladstone, Lord Shaftesbury, and other representatives of England's noble queen. There he stood literally "before kings." The divine promise was fulfilled, "Seest thou a man diligent in his business? he shall stand before kings; he shall not stand before mean men."

Dr. Franklin said in his autobiography, that his father gave him line upon line in regard to the virtue of industry in his boyhood, enforcing his lessons by repeating the text, "Seest thou a man diligent in his business? he shall stand before kings; he shall not stand before mean men." In his last days, Dr. Franklin honored the wisdom and sagacity of his father by saying, "*I have stood before five kings, and dined with two.*"

ADMIRAL FARRAGUT FORCES HIS WAY INTO THE HARBOR OF MOBILE.

XIV.

IDLENESS.

THE great preacher of London, Spurgeon, said, "Idle men are common enough, and grow without planting; but the quantity of wit among seven acres of them would never pay for raking. Nothing is needed to prove this but their name and their character: if they were not fools, they would not be idlers; and, though Solomon says, 'The sluggard is wiser in his own conceit than seven men that can render a reason,' yet in the eyes of every one else his folly is as plain as the sun in the sky."

A good reason, this, for the contempt that respectable people feel for the idle, and for the humiliating description of them in the Bible. "An idle soul shall suffer hunger," and we are all willing that it should. "If he will not work, neither should he eat;" that is fair. Feeding tramps keeps them vagrants. The lockup, instead of the loaf, has forced some of them into better business.

"By much slothfulness, the building decayeth; and, through idleness of hands, the house droppeth through." A most truthful description of the idle man's estate—when he has one. And here is another: "I went by the field of the slothful, and by the vineyard of the man void of understanding, and, lo! it was all grown over with thorns, and nettles had covered the face thereof, and the stone wall thereof was broken down. Then I saw and considered it well: I looked upon it and received instruction. Yet a little sleep, a little slumber, a little folding of the hands to sleep. So shall thy poverty come as one that travaileth, and thy want as an armed man." A very vivid picture of a common curse! The slothful man pleads for sleep, but it is not restful.

"The sleep of the laboring man is sweet." Labor contributes to his health, and the sleep of health is refreshing. But idleness enervates by interrupting the functions of man's threefold nature. In his nervous restlessness one cried out, "Why is there not sleep to be sold?" He would have bought some, if he could, with his laziness; but there was none in the market. Stocks of every kind were quoted; but sleep was not in the quotation.

The terms idle, lazy, slothful, indolent, and sluggish have a common idea, differing in the cause and degree of the quality. It is not necessary to trace their distinctive qualities here, since they belong to the same family, and are all opposed to industry. An idle man may rank a little higher than the lazy or slothful one, but he cannot disown his own relations with any degree of propriety. He is a brother to the useless drone of the proverb, "Who hideth his hand in his bosom, it grieveth him to bring it again to his mouth." Hence the choice between them is not worth discussing. For what Spurgeon said of the best of the three is true, "If the devil catch a man idle, he will set him to work, find him tools, and, before long, pay him wages." If he can do any worse with the lazy and slothful, God pity them.

SAMUEL TAYLOR COLERIDGE.

Idleness is the sepulchre of the living man. To be dead, and yet alive! What can be worse? A dead man out of his coffin, walking among men, is no more out of place than the idle man mingling with the industrious.

There is no use to which idleness can be put to advantage. A chimney-sweep and scavenger are useful men, and we respect them if they are best in their business; but idleness never made a dollar, nor cultivated an acre of ground, nor founded a school, nor built a canal or railroad, nor invented even a clothes pin. It is powerless to accomplish anything good. It can pull down, however, about as fast as industry can build up; and it can rear almshouses and prisons and then fill them to overflowing. It is the mother of poverty, vice, and crime, having a family too numerous to be counted.

Idleness is more prevalent among girls than boys. The manners and customs of society have made it so. Society has not demanded that girls be educated for a definite pursuit. It is expected that a boy will be educated with reference to his life-calling, so that when he becomes a man, he will be master of some trade or profession, and be able to support a family. One is educated for a clergyman, another for a lawyer, another for a physician, another for a merchant, another for a farmer, and thus on.

Not so with a multitude of girls. There is so much indefiniteness in their plans, and in the system of education under which they are taught, that it cannot be said they are instructed to be teachers, housekeepers, seamstresses, or even wives and mothers.

Of course, society must share the blame for such a state of things. If its rule is shops, warehouses, and reading-rooms for males, and nothing in particular for females, it must reap accordingly. It is true that a change has been wrought for the better, along this line, within the last two decades, the doors of many useful employments having been flung wide open to girls, inviting them to choose a life-work, and be disciplined accordingly. They will have fewer idle moments in the future than they have had in the past.

Coleridge was a man of brilliant intellect, but his indolence circumscribed his influence. Near friends called him lazy, and claimed that but for his laziness his great talents would have called public attention to him as the most remarkable scholar of his time. Robert Nicoll wrote of him, "What a mighty intellect was lost in that man for the want of a little energy, a little determination." At one time Southey, who was a tremendous worker, supported Coleridge's wife and children. Even great talents cannot carry the burden of laziness.

As we began this paper with words of Spurgeon, so we will close it with his words: "I would as soon drop my half-pence down a well, as to pay some people for pretending to work, who only fidget you and make your flesh crawl to see them all day creeping over a cabbage leaf. Live, and let live, say I; but I don't include sluggards in that license; for they who will not work, neither let them eat."

DOING THINGS WELL.

MANY youth are more anxious about what they do than about how they do it, and, as a consequence, they are unsuccessful. Dr. Johnson said, "Whatever is worth doing at all is worth doing well." Experience and observation declare that this is the only rule that promotes progress in art, science, or industrial and literary pursuits. To observe it, requires the enlistment of all the powers of application, singleness of purpose, observation, perseverance, and whatever else enters into the composition of a competent man or woman.

David Maydole was the inventor of the modern hammer. He was known as the hammer-maker. He made the first one for his own use, being dissatisfied with any he could buy. He made it so well that a neighbor ordered one for himself, and then another neighbor, and then the town merchant, until, finally, a hardware dealer from New York City seeing one of them, ordered as many as Maydole could manufacture. In this way his business grew to large proportions, and his fortune was assured.

James Parton said to him, when his business had become very large, "By this time you ought to be able to make a pretty good hammer." Maydole replied, "No, I can't. I can't make a pretty good hammer; I make the best that's made." Once a party applied for several hammers, to whom Maydole was indebted for some favor, and the party said to him, "You ought to make my hammers a little better than the others." Maydole responded, "I can't make any better ones. When I make a thing, I make it as well as I can, no matter who it is for." Doing his best every time led him on to fortune. He never pushed his business; he never advertised. Making the best hammer in the market created all the business he wanted.

Something of this quality is found in every successful man, whatever his occupation may be,—farmer, mechanic, merchant, painter, lawyer, doctor, or clergyman. Thoroughness appears to be the key to success. Sir Joshua Reynolds, the painter, replied to a gentleman who asked him, "How do you attain to such excellence in your profession?" "By observing one simple rule, namely, *to make each picture the best.*" That rule produced the painting as well as the hammer. The same rule produced the finest piano, sewing-machine, and locomotive. We make the best merchants out of the best clerks, the best generals out of the best soldiers, the best railroad president out of the best employe, and so on to the end.

Samuel Budgett said, "In whatever calling a man is found, he ought to strive to be the best in his calling: if only a shoeblack, he should try to be the best shoeblack in the neighborhood." Budgett conducted his immense business, in which he employed six hundred men and boys, on this principle. When a boy was introduced into his store, he set him to straightening old nails. If he straightened nails well, he was promoted to bag mending; if he did not do it well he was dismissed. The thorough nail-straightener and bag-mender moved upward into larger and higher fields of work; and so the great English merchant could boast of having the most efficient and faithful class of employes in the British realm. Training them to do their best did it.

The well-known publishing house of New York—the Harper Brothers—established in 1817, built up its mammoth business on the basis of doing everything well. When apprentices in a printing-office, they were the best. When their sign was put out in 1817, "J. & J. Harper, Printers," a book-seller told them that there were more printers in New York than could get a living. Nevertheless, he gave them a book to print. The work was done so thoroughly and promptly that this publisher gave them all the work he had thereafter. Soon other publishers did the same. It was their rule of doing things well that made them thrifty enough to start a noted publishing house of their own. They have always issued the best things in the best style.

We are wont to apply the "blessed" of Rev. xiv. 13, "and their works do follow them," to spiritual things only; but it is just as true of the secular. Why not? In the material world, God provides the best of everything. The leaf, flower, and blade of grass are perfect; even the moss of the African desert, which no one but Mungo Park ever saw, made to live and perish in the wilderness, was as perfect and beautiful as the flower in a window-garden.

Thoroughness is a principle of the Divine government, and we may say truthfully of all men who imitate it, in their secular pursuits, "Their works do follow them."

WORK, A CONDITION OF SUCCESS.

IN these papers we are setting forth the elements of true success, and one of them is work. By this we mean something more than the occupation of one's time; we mean a resolute, invincible determination to accomplish one's purpose, even though absolute hardship of labor be required. To many youth this is not congenial. They prefer to live without hard work. To possess a fortune without hard work, to have a profession without hard study, and to occupy a post of honor without earning it, is their ideal of life. They want ease instead of work to be a condition of success. Somehow they expect to succeed without that intense application which circumstances require; and so they fail, becoming mere ciphers among men.

Gideon Lee, who was so poor in his boyhood that he went to work barefooted even in winter, believed that he must make a bargain with himself for so much hard work or he could not succeed. After he became a wealthy merchant and mayor of New York City he said, "I had made a bargain with myself to labor each day a certain number of hours, and nothing but sickness and inability should make me break the contract. It was known to my young friends in the neighborhood, and on some convivial occasion, a quilting frolic, I believe, they came to my shop where I worked and compelled me to leave my work and go with them. There being girls also in the deputation my gallantry could not resist. I lost my night's rest in consequence, for the morning soon found me at work, redeeming my lost time." It was the bargain with himself that made him invincible. He could not violate that contract without sacrificing his sense of propriety and his conscientious scruples. The bargain held him to hard work.

Dr. Franklin's proverbs set this virtue in fine gold: "Dost thou love life? Then do not squander time, for that is the stuff life is made of." "He that riseth late must trot all day, and shall scarce overtake his business at night; while laziness travels so slowly that poverty soon overtakes him." He once wrote to a young tradesman: "The sound of your hammer at five in the morning or nine at night, heard by a creditor, makes him easy six months longer; but if he sees you at a billiard table, or hears your voice at a tavern when you should be at work, he sends for his money the next day, demands it before he can receive it in a lump." By this advice Dr. Franklin meant the young man should understand that work was his capital. Ten thousand dollars capital alone would not win public confidence as quickly as large capacity to work. A rich lazy man has a slimmer hold upon the public than a poor, persistently industrious one. President Wayland, of Brown University, used to say to his students, "Young gentlemen, remember that nothing can withstand days' works."

Many young people believe in geniuses; and, hence, that a successful man is some sort of a genius. They mistake work for genius. The most gifted men are usually the greatest workers. The celebrated Turner was once asked the secret of his success, to which he replied, "I have no secret but hard work." This is a secret that many never learn, and they don't succeed because they don't learn it. Labor is the genius that changes the world from ugliness to beauty, and the great curse to a great blessing. Even Daniel Webster said, "I know of no superior quality that I possess, unless it be power of application. To work, and not to genius, I owe my success." His famous reply to Hayne has generally been regarded as a remarkable contemporaneous effort—proof of genius in a high degree. But Webster himself denied it, and said, "I was thoroughly conversant with the subject of debate from having made preparation for a totally different purpose than that speech;" and after showing how he prepared himself to discuss Foote's resolution to sell the public lands, and to reply to Calhoun's denial of the right of petition on the subject of slavery, neither of which debates took place, he added: "I had my notes tucked away in a pigeon-hole, and when Hayne made that attack upon me and upon New England I was already posted, and only had to take down my notes and refresh my memory. In other words, if Hayne had tried to make a speech to fit my notes he could not have hit it better. No man is inspired with the occasion. I never was."

Webster might have said, also, that in addition to having his notes prepared, he possessed the mental discipline which the hard study of years affords, without which that grand reply to Hayne could not have been made. A sculptor prepared a bust for a Venetian nobleman, for which he charged "fifty *sequins.*" On receiving it, the nobleman, considering the price extravagant, said, "You charge me fifty *sequins* for a bust that cost you only ten days' labor!" The artist replied, "You forget that I have been thirty years learning to make that bust in ten days." The nobleman forgot just what many young men do when they see the rich, honored, learned public men challenging universal respect—the twenty, thirty, and perhaps forty years' hard labor which make it possible for them to occupy the positions they do. They have fulfilled that condition of success—work—and have their reward. Bryant rewrote his "Thanatopsis" a hundred times, and then considered it imperfect. What patience, perseverance, and hard study were involved in a hundred rewritings! But that was the price. George Eliot said of the years of close work upon her "Romola," "I began it a young woman, I finished it an old woman." One of Emerson's biographers says, referring to that author's method of rewriting, revising, correcting, and eliminating, "His apples were sorted over and over again, until only the very rarest, and most perfect, were left. It did not matter that those thrown away were very good and helped to make clear the possibilities of the orchard, they were unmercifully cast aside. His essays were, consequently, very slowly elaborated, wrought out through days and months and even years of patient thought." Gibbon rewrote his "Memoirs" nine times, and Butler his "Analogy" twenty times. Even Edmund Burke did not produce his famous works without persistent, long-continued labor. He wrote the conclusion of his speech at the trial of Hastings sixteen times. Hume wrote thirteen hours a day, for successive years, to produce his "History of England." He believed, with the old German who

WILLIAM CULLEN BRYANT.

engraved upon his key, "If I rest, I rust." These facts show that real work will win. Nor should the reader forget that the highest discipline comes from this relentless labor. Horace Greeley called it "the genius of persistence," which caused the faculties to shine like a used key. Sir Walter Raleigh was a sharp, bright thinker; and Cecil remarked as an explanation of the fact, "He could labor terribly."

It is hard work that adds the chief value to many possessions. Labor will raise the value of five dollars' worth of crude iron to ten dollars by converting it into horseshoes; to one hundred and eighty dollars by converting it into table knives; to six thousand eight hundred dollars by converting it into needles; two hundred thousand by making it into watch-springs; and four hundred thousand by making it into hair-springs— all the value of labor except five dollars to start with! While a criminal was exchanging his own for a prison suit in the penitentiary of Connecticut, he remarked. "*I never did a day's work in my life.*" No wonder that he brought up at the state-prison! "The idle brain is the devil's work-shop." "The devil tempts all other men, but idle men tempt the devil." Higher authority still has declared, "An idle soul shall suffer hunger." The idle man may become a tramp, but the industrious, never! The former may occupy the cell of a prison; the latter, a king's palace. One will become the "companion of fools," while the other "stands before kings." One life is a failure, the other a success.

EDMUND BURKE.

BUSINESS A SCHOOL.

MANY persons, young and old, think of education as belonging only to the schools. This is a grave mistake. If the school alone can give culture, such men as Henry Clay and Abraham Lincoln never would have been known, for their best teachers were outside the schoolroom. Scores and hundreds of our successful men—statesmen, merchants, manufacturers, and even scholars— owe their distinction to the culture of business, supplemented by the discipline of leisure moments devoted to reading or study.

The late William B. Spooner, one of the most accomplished and honored merchants Boston ever had, never went to school after he was twelve years of age, except a short season at an academy after he was sixteen. Yet he became one of the most intelligent, and even gifted, men of New England. Business was a school to which he went every day, never absent, never tardy. He early determined to make it more than a college curriculum to himself; and he did achieve through it the highest elements of manhood, which were of more value to him and the world than his large fortune that followed as a matter of course. The writer once called at Mr. Spooner's office, when the latter showed him three elaborate reports which he had prepared for that week. One of them was to be presented to the Board of Trade, of which he was president; another to the directors of a bank, of which he was also president; and the third to a benevolent society, whose president he was, also. He prepared all such papers with as much ability as a college graduate; and business did it. True, he improved his leisure moments, which were few, in reading and attending lectures; and this, without doubt, had its decided influence in his rise and progress. But, after all, his business was his school, and here his powers were developed and trained. A business run by industry, tact, honesty, perseverance, and philanthropy, will make a noble man of the proprietor in any age and anywhere.

Webster defines education to be "that series of instruction and discipline which is intended to enlighten the understanding, correct the temper and the manners and habits of youth, and fit them for usefulness in their future stations." Hence, there may be education without the schoolroom. It is possible for a youth to be more truly educated out of college than in it. Abraham Lincoln was better educated than half the graduates of Harvard and Yale. Proof of this is found in the fact that he was fitted for "usefulness in his station." The farm, shop, and warehouse teach eminently practical lessons. They teach much even about science and art. The successful man of business knows more about philosophy, mathematics, and psychology, after he has amassed a fortune, than he did before. Experience is a good schoolmaster.

When Edison had wrought his first invention, he had acquired ability to bring out a half dozen others. The discipline of one year's business enables a man to do better work the next year. He is more of a man at the close of a year's work if he has been true to himself. His mind is constantly on the alert to discover the reason of things, and so he is constantly improving and acquiring power.

When Schiller was a boy, the inquisitive characteristic of his mind in manhood was foreshadowed as follows: During a terrific thunder shower his father missed him, and ran out of doors to learn his whereabouts, when he discovered him perched in the top of a tree which the storm was rocking like a cradle. Much frightened at the peril of the boy, the father called out, "What are you there for?" Promptly the answer came back, "I want to see where the lightning comes from." The lad had a reason for being there, and a good one, too. The inquiring mind which led him to ascertain where lightning comes from was the secret of his manhood success; and the same would have been true of him had he been a merchant instead of a scholar.

FRIEDRICH VON SCHILLER.

The late Hon. William E. Dodge, who was known throughout our land as a wealthy merchant and Christian philanthropist, derived all the advantage he ever had from schools before he was fifteen years of age. At that age his distinctively business life began in New York City—a school that was in session as long as he lived. Like Mr. Spooner, he determined that manhood should stand for more than wealth with him—that everything about his time and business should contribute strength to his personal character. Consequently, his business was his university. In it he had his daily drill. Both his head and his heart were disciplined by the duties of his warehouse. The standard he set up made industry, tact, honesty, and economy absolutely indispensable. He grew mentally and morally here. It was public school and Sunday school together, exerting a powerful influence upon his life. Mr. Dodge's career illustrates what an English journal recently said: "There can be no question nowadays that application to work, absorption in affairs, contact with men, and all the stress which business imposes on us, give a noble training to the intellect, and splendid opportunity for discipline and character. . . . The perpetual call on a man's readiness, self-control, and vigor which business makes, the constant appeal to the intellect, the stress upon the will, the necessity for rapid and responsible exercise of judgment —all these things constitute a high culture. Hence the most successful men have been those who began the world in their shirt-sleeves."

James Harper, founder of the publishing house known as Harper Brothers, of New York, began his business life in that city at fifteen years of age. He began in a printing-office in Franklin Square. He commenced with the resolution to make the most out of the business possible, and, by doing that, to make the most of himself. He applied himself so closely to his work, declining to engage in pleasures which others sought, as to draw down upon himself the ridicule of his companions. They laughed at his clothes, his awkward gait, and his large and homely shoes. Finally, one day a fellow-workman said to him, "Give us your card." Forgetting himself for the moment, Harper kicked the young scamp downstairs, exclaiming, "That is my card; take it!" In five minutes he was very sorry for the act and made an apology, adding, "When I get to doing business for myself, I will let you have work." In thirty years Harper was a wealthy publisher and mayor of the city, and among his employes was the scapegrace whom he kicked downstairs. The latter came to him in a miserable plight, and he gave him a job to keep him from starving. It is one thing to make business a school, but quite another thing to make it the road to ruin.

METHOD.

"ORDER is heaven's first law," it is said; also, "Method consists in the right choice of means to an end." Here is a distinction, though the two words cover the line of thought we wish to express.

We select "method" because it is the term used in speaking of all kinds of business. "Without method, little can be done to any good purpose."

We say of one person, referring to business, he is methodical or systematic; of another, he is orderly, meaning what the proverb does, "A place for everything, and everything in its place." This is the ground our subject covers, including, perhaps, the thought embraced in another maxim, "A time for everything, and everything in its time."

The benefits of method are dispatch, larger achievements, better quality, and greater ease and comfort in work. There is attraction, even beauty, also, in a business that moves, like the works of a clock, without friction. The systematic division of time and labor in our day, in all large manufactories, is to secure larger and quicker results, as well as better goods. In an armory, thirty men, each producing his particular part of the musket, will make more and better muskets in a given time. In a store where each employe knows his time, place, and work, and is true thereto, more is done, and better done and done at less cost, than would be possible otherwise. In the home where time and labor are adjusted with reference to the best results, the orderly housewife, rising at an appointed time, regular as the sun, doing her work as methodically as the state department is run, more is accomplished, all is better done, and that home is more attractive. In the schoolroom, the pupil who yields cheerfully to the method of the teacher, observing the precise time for studying this, that, and the other lesson, with books, papers, slate, pencil, and other helps arranged in order on his or her desk, will do far better work, and contribute more to the success of the school, than the pupil who is restive under rigid method, and whose desk is suggestive of chaos.

Method has industry, punctuality, observation, perseverance, self-control, and other indispensable virtues in its train. It cannot exist without them, and carries them along up into manhood and womanhood to bless the whole life. Method in early life assures method in later life.

John Kitto, a poor boy who lost his hearing by an accident, had so great a thirst for knowledge that a benevolent gentleman took him out of the poorhouse and sent him to school. His strong desire to make the most of his time and opportunities, led him into very methodical ways. After a little, he wrote to his benefactor that "he had reduced his labors to a system," so that he "might be able to tell where he was and what he was doing at any time of the day or week," at the same time sending to his benefactor a copy of the following diagram. The spaces in the original diagram were distinguished by the colors of which here only the names are given.

	MORN.	A. M.	P. M.	EVENING.	NIGHT.
Sunday	Red, 1	Brown, 2	Brown	Brown	Pink
Monday	Yellow, 4	Yellow	Pink, 3	Pink	Pink
Tuesday	Red	Yellow	Pink	Pink	Pink
Wednesday	Green, 5	Yellow	Green	Green	Pink
Thursday	Yellow	Yellow	Pink	Pink	Pink
Friday	Red	Yellow	Blue, 6	Blue	Pink
Saturday	Red	Scarlet, 7	Red	Red	Pink

1—Optional. 2—Writing to Mr Woolcombe. 3—Reading. 4—Grammar. 5—Writing to Mr. Harvey. 6—Extracting. 7—Church.

He added: "Those portions of time which I have used optionally will be occupied in reading, writing, or walking, as circumstances may dictate or permit. I shall spend all the time I possibly can in the library rather than at my lodgings; but when not at the library, I shall be at Mr. Barnard's, unless I take a walk during one of the optional periods."

With this diagram and explanation, Mr. Harvey could tell where his protégé was at any given time, and what he was doing. Indeed, he might have regulated his watch by this rigid method.

Kitto carried this method into the exhausting labors of manhood, when he prepared his "Bible Illustrations," and other great works. He claimed that it would have been impossible for him to have produced these works without systematic labor. He was such a thorough believer in method to assure dispatch that, in manhood, he required his daughter to clean his study by the following rules: —

1. Make one pile of religious books.
2. Another of books not religious.
3. Another of letters.
4. Another of written papers other than that of letters.
5. Another of printed papers.
6. Put these piles upon the floor.
7. The table being now clear, dust and scour it.

The celebrated Nathaniel Emmons claimed that he could not work at all, unless order reigned about him. For more than fifty years the same chairs stood in the same places in his study, his hat hung on the same hook, the shovel stood on the north side of the open fireplace, and the tongs on the south side. During all these years he sat in the same chair to write his sermons, and the chair occupied the same place; he wore a hole through the floor where he sat, so that a new floor for that spot was necessary. One of his students of theology, who resided in his family, says of his orderly habits:—

"One day I was sitting by the fire with him, when a brand fell upon the hearth. I arose and put the brand in its place, but put the tongs on the north side of the fireplace. The doctor immediately removed the tongs to the south side, but said nothing. In a few minutes another brand fell, which I replaced with the tongs, then setting the tongs again on the north side with the shovel. The doctor arose again and changed the tongs from the north to the south side. Soon the brand fell a third time, and, as the doctor's movements appeared to me very singular, I determined to find out what they meant. Having adjusted the brands, therefore, I placed the tongs designedly along with the shovel on the north. The doctor arose, put the tongs in their place on the south side, and said:—

"'My young friend, as you are going to stay with me, I wish to tell you now that I keep the shovel on the north side of my fire, and the tongs on the south.'"

Students, like business men, can accomplish much more by this methodical way of doing than would be possible otherwise.

Cecil, who was a prodigious worker, said:—

"Method is like packing things in a box; a good packer will get in half as much again as a bad one."

That quaint old divine, Fuller, was wont to advise: "Marshal thy notions into a handsome method. One will carry twice more weight trussed and packed up in bundles than when it lies untowardly flapping and hanging about his shoulders."

Noah Webster never could have prepared his dictionary in thirty-six years, unless the most exacting method had come to the rescue. That saved him ten or twenty years and a vast amount of anxiety and trouble.

The biographer of Gideon Lee says of him, "He was so systematic that he kept all accounts posted up to each night, and all correspondence answered, so that up to the evening preceding his last illness everything was in its place. Without this system and regularity he could not have accomplished a tithe of his projects." It is equally true of Amos Lawrence in keeping his business accounts; and he gave as a reason for his method, "I may not be here to-morrow."

The Bible says, "To everything there is a season, and a time for every purpose under heaven." That certainly includes human plans; and there is no way of adjusting one's life to this fact of Providence except by method.

WASTING TIME.

SUCCESSFUL men and women never waste time. They have not enough of it for present, urgent use. The days are too short for them; dinner comes too soon; they could use more time than they have to good advantage. They believe, with Franklin, "If time be of all things the most precious, wasting time must be the greatest prodigality."

Yet much time is wasted by both old and young. Hundreds who complain that they have no time to devote to reading and study, waste enough of it in worthless musing, building air castles, games, and pleasures to class them with literary people, if such time were improved in that direction.

Mary Lyon, founder of Mount Holyoke Female Seminary, observed this tendency among young ladies in this institution to waste much valuable time. Long before that she had observed the tendency in herself, and guarded against it by constant watchfulness.

She was a poor girl and kept house for an unmarried brother, at sixteen years of age, for one dollar per week. This was extra large pay for those times, but the loving brother wanted to assist her to acquire an education for which she thirsted. Every moment was precious to her, both night and day. She improved them in reading and studying. She would have wasted dollars as soon as she would have wasted moments. It was this care-taking against wasting time that she carried with her into the Mount Holyoke Seminary. The students were blessed thereby, for they learned that wasting time was the worst wastefulness known to men.

After her death a paper was found among her effects, containing seven ways of wasting time, against which she guarded, as follows:—

1. Indefinite musings.
2. Anticipating needlessly.
3. Needless speculations.
4. Indulgence in reluctance to begin a duty.
5. In doubtful cases, not deciding at once.
6. Musing needlessly on what has been said or done, or what may be.
7. Spending time in reveries which should be spent in prayer.

Samuel Budgett said to a clerk one day, "If you waste five minutes, that is not much; but probably if you waste five minutes yourself you lead someone else to waste five minutes, and that makes ten; if a third follow your example, that makes a quarter of an hour. Now, there are about one hundred and eighty of us here, and if everyone wasted five minutes in a day, what would it come to? Let me see; why it would be fifteen hours! and fifteen hours a day would be ninety hours, about eight days' working time, in a week, and in a year would be four hundred days. Do you think we could ever stand waste like that?"

This way of putting the matter was new to the clerk, and he never forgot it. From that moment he imitated his employer in never wasting time. Mr. Budgett became quite a literary man, even with an immense mercantile business on his hands, and he became so by keeping a book on his desk that he could catch up for a few moments at a time during each day.

When Benjamin Franklin worked in his brother's printing-office in Boston, he thought that much time was wasted in going to dinner. A whole hour was spent in getting this meal, half of which, at least, he thought was wasted. He could not act for others, but he could act for himself. He says in his autobiography:—

"I proposed to my brother that if he would give me weekly half the money he paid for my board, I would board myself. He instantly agreed to it, and I presently found I could save half of what he paid me. This was an additional fund for buying books; but I had another advantage in it. My brother and the rest going from the printing-house to their meals, I remained there alone, and dispatching, presently, my light repast, which was often no more than a biscuit or a slice of bread, a handful of raisins or a tart from the pastry cook's, and a glass of water, had the rest of the time until their return for study, in which I made the greater progress from that greater clearness of head, and quicker apprehension which generally attends temperance in eating and drinking.''

That was reducing the time question pretty fine, but it was done by the youth who said, forty years thereafter, that wasting time was the greatest prodigality.

Much time is wasted by attending entertainments and games. After allowing a wide margin for necessary recreation, it is still true that many young

CHARIOT RACE IN THE CIRCUS MAXIMUS, ROME.

people, and older people as well, spend much time in this way, that ought to be given to mental culture. This was always true. Cicero said, "What others give to public shows and entertainments, to festivity, to amusements, nay, even to mental and bodily rest, I give to study and philosophy.'' In other words, the improvement of time that others wasted in amusements, won for him renown as a scholar, orator, and statesman.

Many youth of both sexes waste more time by reading worthless books, journals and magazines, than by any other way. There is no dearth of good and useful literature. In this age of public libraries, there is no excuse for reading dime novels. Indeed, if there were no town libraries, the price of good books is within the ability of a multitude of families who do not buy them. A short time ago, a gentleman paid five thousand dollars for an autograph of Shakespeare; but a boy or girl can buy and own all Shakespeare's works for one dollar; and all the boys and girls of any given community can take them out of the library and read them for nothing.

All time spent in profitless reading, when useful reading is abundant, is wasted time.

Good reading has made scholars, philosophers, and statesmen; but worthless reading never made a decent man. With history, biography, and first-class literature, including the world's great poets, within the reach of all, it is worse

GLADIATORIAL COMBAT IN THE ARENA.

than waste of time to read the average novel, which never did, and never can, make the reader better.

When Drexillius was asked by a friend how he managed to accomplish so much, he replied, "The year has three hundred and sixty-five days, or eight thousand four hundred and sixty hours; in so many hours great things can be done; the slow tortoise made a long journey by losing no time."

Rev. Daniel Wise beautifully exposes the waste of time thus:—

"Imagine the spectacle of a light boat floating gaily over the sea. Its sole passenger is a lady. Suddenly awakening from sleep, she clutches for a pearl necklace that has become unfastened during her sleep. One end is still hanging about her neck, the other is loosely dangling over the water. Pearl after pearl has slipped off into the deep abyss. The lady's brow is sad and self-reproachful. Each lost pearl reproves her; each remaining one reminds her of those which are gone. . . . Do you perceive the idea embodied in this spectacle? It is that if the opportunities of early life for self-improvement are wasted in idle day dreams, the loss can never be repaid. Lost opportunities are sunken pearls.

Lost moments, like lost opportunities, are sunken pearls.

XV.

SELF-CONTROL.

THERE is a distinction between self-possession and self-control. The former refers to a certain grip which the will has upon the powers under great and sudden temptation to evil or fear, producing calmness when excitement would be almost excusable. The latter refers to a deeper, stronger grip upon the faculties, holding them to that which is true under all circumstances, that the highest manhood and womanhood may be the result. Hence, the highest authority declares, "He that ruleth his own spirit is greater than he who taketh a city." "Self-control is only courage under another form." One writes: "We think it is far more than that—it is master of all the virtues, including courage. If not so, how can it control them so as to develop into the noblest, purest character?"

Herbert Spencer says: "In the supremacy of self-control consists one of the perfections of the ideal man; not to be impulsive, not to be spurred hither and thither by each desire that in turn comes uppermost; but to be restrained, self-balanced, governed by the joint decision of the feelings in council assembled, before whom every action shall have been fully debated and calmly determined."

The late William H. Seward was in college where many students paid for a four years' course with less than a thousand dollars. But his father gave him one thousand dollars when he entered college, saying, "That will pay your bills through the whole course." The first collegiate year closed, and young Seward spent his vacation at home. As the time drew near for the second year of his course to begin, his father could not see that he was preparing to return.

"William," said his father one day, "are you not going back to college?"

"My money is all gone, father, and I can't return," was William's answer.

"Well, then, you must take the consequences; I have no more to give you," rejoined his father, very much disappointed, as well as provoked.

William had self-possession under certain circumstances, but he was destitute of self-control. There was not a student in college who was cooler and more self-possessed than he when danger threatened. At a fire, or on an imperiled steamer, he was as calm as an "old salt." He could assist a surgeon in the amputation of a limb without the tremor of a nerve, but had so little self-control that he yielded to the influence of reckless college mates, neglected his studies, indulged his appetites and passions, and lived "fast" through his first college year, costing him more than it did many students for four years.

WILLIAM H. SEWARD.

The interview with his father set him to thinking. "I have fooled away my time and money for a whole year," he said to himself, "and I will do it no longer." He resolved then and there to work his own way through college, and he returned to a mighty struggle with science and the classics. He brought every appetite and passion into complete subjection, and denied himself pleasure, sport, and luxuries of every kind. He led his class along from term to term until he was graduated with its highest honors—valedictorian. Self-control managed his faculties from the second year of his collegiate course, and managed them thereafter until he died. He became governor of the State of New York in his early public career, then member of the National House of Representatives, then United States Senator, and then Secretary of State under President Lincoln.

Seward's life proves that self-control is as necessary for a man of great talents as it is for one of small talents. Though possessing marked abilities, it was absolutely necessary for him to say "No," with emphasis, when tempted to dissipate or idle away his time. The law of fidelity to God and one's self has no exceptions.

Ten talents must come under self-control as really as one talent, or five. Clarendon said of the great Hampden, "He was supreme governor over all his passions and affections, and he had, thereby, great power over other men's." Smiles very truthfully says that Motley, the historian, "compares William the Silent to Washington, whom he in many respects resembled. The American, like the Dutch patriot, stands out in history as the very impersonation of dignity, bravery, purity, and personal excellence. His command over his feelings, even in moments of great difficulty and danger, was such as to convey the impression, to those who did not know him intimately, that he was a man of inborn calmness. Yet, Washington was, by nature, ardent and impetuous; his mildness, gentleness, and politeness and consideration for others, were the result of rigid self-control and unwearied self-discipline, which he diligently practiced even from his boyhood." The man of self-control is reliable; so is the boy. People know where to find him. He who does not possess it is like "a wave

WILLIAM THE SILENT.

of the sea, driven with the wind, and tossed;" and he is the one who goes down under the surging billows. But self-control weathers all storms, and goes into port with streamers flying.

The self-control which we commend has its root in true self-respect. The wayward, drifting youth or man cannot respect himself. He knows that there is no decision of character in drifting with the current, no enterprise, spirit, or determination. He must look the world squarely in the face, and say, " I am a man," or he cannot respect himself; and he must stem the current and row up stream to command his destiny.

It has been said, " No society is as large as one man." It is claimed, also, that " a man can govern a state more easily than he can govern himself." If true, self-control becomes doubly important to old and young. It is because man is so great and important among the " powers that be " that self-control becomes an indispensable attribute.

Self-control is an every-day necessity. We need it "every hour," as we sing of the Saviour Himself. The young of both sexes, now qualifying themselves in the schoolroom for the higher and more responsible duties of life, need its constant ministrations. They will not need arithmetic or algebra at all times and in all places, but they will need this cardinal virtue. It may be well for them to learn the names of all the bones of the human body, but it will be of vastly greater service for them to have their powers under complete control. They will need the latter morning, noon, and night, from this time until the close of life, while the former will be of use only at certain times and in certain places. " The courage of self-control exhibits itself in many ways, but in none more clearly than in honest living."

SELF-MADE OR NEVER MADE.

THE term "self-made" is usually applied to persons who succeed without the aid of seminary or college. But it is really as true of college graduates that they are "self-made or never made."

Neither the best teachers nor institutions can make a scholar out of a dunce. There is no curriculum that can make a young man or woman successful without his or her persistent effort. The seminary and college can assist industry, application, and perseverance, but their opportunities are wasted on the indolent and lazy.

The largest and most renowned mercantile house will do no better for the inefficient clerk than the smallest and most obscure one. The active, aspiring, and quick-witted clerk will gain more advantages from the small, unknown warehouse, than the shiftless and negligent clerk will from the large, famous one.

It is because the young person must make himself what he desires to become, whether mechanic, merchant, accountant, teacher, scholar, orator, lawyer, physician, clergyman, or statesman. No institution can do it for him; no man can do it for him. The best opportunities are nothing to laziness. Ordinary opportunities are everything to application and tact.

Robert Bloomfield was a poor boy at twelve, and aided his father what he could in caring for sheep, hogs, and other animals, without going to school. A writer says, "I have him in my mind's eye; a little boy, not bigger than boys generally are at twelve years of age. When I met him and his mother at the inn in London, he was dressed just as he came from keeping sheep and hogs."

After that he learned shoemaking, and laid the foundation of his future greatness by devoting every moment he could snatch from business to self-culture. His biographer says:—

"His literary acquirements appear to have been all made during the time he was learning the business of a shoemaker, and afterwards, while he worked at the same business as journeyman." By his own personal exertions he made himself one of the best and most noted men of his age.

The life of Bloomfield illustrates the remark of Dr. Kitto, "I think that all the fine stories about natural ability, etc., are mere rigmarole, and that every man may, according to his opportunities and industry, render himself almost anything he wishes to become."

Dr. Kitto himself was an example of a "self-made man." He had a drunken father, whose cruelty made extreme poverty more grievous to bear. An accident made him deaf for life; and then, as the family was reduced to a condition of beggary, John was sent to the poorhouse. But his thirst for knowledge triumphed over all.

He astonished every observer by his progress. His improvement of time and his dauntless spirit won the admiration of all who knew him. He became one of the most renowned Biblical scholars and authors in the world.

Perhaps there is no more remarkable illustration of a self-made man than Frederick Douglass, the colored orator and statesman. He was born a slave, in 1817, on the eastern shore of Maryland. The more he read the more he knew, and the more he hated slavery. His master was kind, but kindness only showed him what real freedom would be. He was "hired out" to a ship-master, in Baltimore, because he was difficult to manage, at eighteen years of age.

He liked Baltimore because it was nearer freedom, and freedom he meant to have. He learned rapidly from experience and observation, as well as from books. He kept his own secret and laid his own plans. He early learned that the more intelligent he became, the better it would be for him; so he was bound to be intelligent. At twenty-one he took to his heels and ran straight into freedom. He settled in New Bedford, Massachusetts, where he set about self-education with a will. He worked in the daytime, and studied at night. He soon became a noted exhorter in the Methodist Church. He became acquainted with Garrison, who encouraged him to speak in public for the emancipation of his race. In 1841, he made a speech at an anti-slavery convention in Nantucket, which attracted general attention, and established his reputation as an orator and a *man*. For a slave to make himself into a scholar, orator, editor, and statesman by his own efforts, is wonderful indeed. He said to his fellow-negroes, "We must not talk about equality until we can do what white people can do." Frederick Douglass soon became the peer of the best white man.

Many of the most influential Americans of our time, engaged in shaping the destiny of the nation—merchants, inventors, scientists, clergymen, teachers, lawyers, physicians, and statesmen—have made themselves what they are by the best improvement of their time and abilities. The success of this class illustrates the remark of a distinguished writer, "It is not that which is done for a young man that is most valuable to him and others, but that which he is led to do for himself." Their youth and early manhood, also, answered the view of Lord John Russell, who said, "Instead of assisting a young man with money, we should say to him, 'You have your own way to make, and it depends on your own exertions whether you starve or not.'"

GENIUS.

MANY people believe that genius is a born possession, and that only those to whom it is a gift of nature ever have it. Some, in consequence, think that a genius does not have to work or study much to do great things in his line—that it is easier for him to achieve great things *without* labor than it is for another person to do small things *with* labor. That such a view is foolish in the extreme appears from the statement of geniuses themselves. Giardini, the musical genius of his time, was asked how long it would take to learn to play the violin well. He replied, "Twelve hours a day for twenty years together," meaning to convey the idea that he himself had achieved success by the most laborious practice. Sir Joshua Reynolds said, "If you have great talents—and great talents are what some people call genius—industry will improve them: if you have but moderate abilities, industry will supply the deficiency. Nothing is denied to well-directed labor; nothing is to be obtained without it." Doctor Johnson defined genius to be a "mind of large general powers accidentally determined in some particular direction." John Foster said, "Genius is the power of lighting one's own fires,"—meaning that true genius condescends to do anything that must be done in order to succeed. Buffon said, "Genius is patience,"—meaning, no doubt, that it accomplishes its brilliant deeds by accepting toil, obstacles, and delays, continuous and great, as a part of the price.

The man who can do many things is called a genius as well as the man of many talents. Indeed, the man who can do one thing better than any one else is called a genius, especially if his aptitude in that direction was born with him. Shakespeare, Scott, Newton, Franklin, Burritt, and Edison are illustrations. No doubt they were born with those gifts which won success in their special lines of thought and work; and if that is what constitutes a genius, then they are rightfully called geniuses. But their born qualities never superseded the necessity of hard work, and the wise use of their powers. No persons ever lived whose industry, perseverance, and use of spare moments were more conspicuous than theirs.

CHARLES DICKENS.

Carnot was chairman of the Committee of Public Safety during the French Revolution, and directed the operations of fourteen armies, which turned back the invaders who rushed down from the Alps and Pyrenees. As a proof and explanation of his great military genius, it is told of his boyhood that he was taken to the theatre when six or eight years of age, to witness the representation of a battle scene.

At one stage of the play he saw that the attacking party was exposed to the sweep of a battery, and he startled the audience by crying out to the commanding officer to change his position or his men would be shot. The connection between that episode of his boyhood, and the successful manipulation of fourteen armies in his manhood, may establish his claim to being a military genius; but it must not be forgotten that he was a busy student of military science, and one of the sharpest observers and hardest workers known all along through the years between boyhood and manhood. Without these incessant labors, his gifts of nature never would have made him famous in the French Revolution. Such a fact exposes the absurdity of a common opinion, that genius is a quality of indolent, lazy persons. This opinion had its origin in the fact that a class of men, having a knack of seizing some things by intuition, and consequently promising much, have turned out shiftless and unsuccessful, bringing little or nothing to pass, and going out of the world devoid of fame or a name.

Charles Dickens was a genius in the literary world. But he said to a public assembly in London, when at the zenith of his fame, "I have tried with all my heart to do well; and whatever I have devoted myself to, I have devoted myself to completely: that in great aims and in small I have always been thoroughly in earnest. I have never believed it possible that any natural or improved ability can claim immunity from the companionship of the steady, plain, hard-working qualities, and hope to gain its end. There is no such thing as such fulfillment on this earth."

Whipple says, "Genius is not a single power, but a combination of great powers. It reasons, but it is not reasoning; it judges, but it is not judgment; it imagines, but it is not imagination; it feels deeply and fiercely, but it is not passion. It is neither, because it is all. It is another name for the perfection of human nature; for genius is not a fact, but an ideal."

Matthews says, "And geniuses, no doubt, there are in the world; but, depend upon it, there are no geniuses in this nineteenth century that reap without sowing; none that are idlers till the moment a demand is made upon their mind, and then answer it by intuition. All such have disappeared from the world with ghosts. The geniuses of our day are distinguished by their power of intense application, application not always spread over a great lapse of time, but which hits the nail on the head, which has a fine aim for the heart of a subject or the hinge of a difficulty." Discard, then, the idea of a genius that was born to succeed anyway, whether the possessor be shiftless or enterprising. The world has no place for such; if it had, God has no such monstrosities for the world. The youth who thinks that his natural endowments, whether called genius or something else, will assure him future success without effort, is a failure already. With equal wisdom he might conclude that his fine physical powers assure health and longevity without eating or drinking. Physical starvation is as inevitable in one case, as mental starvation is in the other. "The secret of success is constancy of purpose."

MODESTY.

IT is generally conceded that modesty is a crown jewel in female character. It is no less indispensable to the symmetry and beauty of character in men. The world's verdict is in favor of modesty every time, in man or woman. In its striking contrast with conceit, which is always disgusting, it becomes a royal virtue for both sexes.

Great talents and real worth are modest: the ripest scholars are modest; the best class of wealthy men are modest; the most popular rulers are modest; philanthropists and public benefactors of former generations were modest, as well as those of the present generation. Superficial scholars, useless millionaires, aristocratic rulers, and petty philanthropists are conceited, and they always have been and always will be.

The mother of the late General U. S. Grant was never known to praise her children. She abhorred self-praise, and next to that was praise of her children. Even when her son commanded the Union army, and victory had finally perched upon his banner, she would blush whenever he was highly praised in her presence. The journals which she read teemed with praises of the conqueror, and nearly every man and woman with whom she conversed was equally emphatic in their expressions of admiration, but she could not get used to the praise of her son. No doubt that in her heart of hearts there was real joy over his success. But her modesty exerted such controlling power over her life as to prevent all external demonstration of such internal pleasure.

Her son inherited her modesty. Who ever knew of his indicating by word or deed that he had accomplished great things? When a grateful country laid its proudest honors at his feet, and when other nations vied with each other to swell his fame, the least gleam of pride was never seen in his eye. When the government fêted him at the close of the war, in Washington, he suppressed his personal distaste, and submitted from a sense of duty; but when the ovation ceased, he could not withhold the exclamation:—

"I am tired of this show business."

When General Grant went to Washington to receive the commission of "Lieutenant-General of the Armies of the United States," he stopped at Cincinnati to spend the Sabbath with his father. The latter sent his carriage to the station for his son, but the driver could find no dashing army officer, with epaulettes and gold braid, and so concluded that the great general was not on the train. But while he was looking for the head of the American army in gay military costume, the famous general, with carpet bag in hand, had slipped away unobserved to the home of his parents. His modesty was equal to his mother's; and his, too, was just as useful and ornamental to him as his mother's was to her.

Modesty should be cultivated, not only for its beauty, but also for its use. It is difficult to tell whether it is more ornamental or useful, and *vice versa*. It is certainly essential to the attainment of the highest controlling influence over society. No person can fulfill the mission of life without it. Crabbe says, "Modesty shields a man from mortification and disappointments, which assail the self-conceited man in every direction. A modest man conciliates the esteem even of an enemy and a rival; he disarms the resentments of those who feel themselves most injured by his superiority; he makes all pleased with him by making them at ease with themselves. The self-conceited man on the contrary, sets the whole world against himself, because he sets himself against everybody; every one is out of humor with him, because he makes them ill at ease with themselves while in his company."

COUNT VON MOLTKE.

Count von Moltke, late Field-Marshal of the German Army, was the General Grant of the German Empire. He died at ninety years of age, and was one of the most remarkable men the world has ever known. No other great general ever received more public honors heartily bestowed and royally generous. The seventieth anniversary of his entrance into the army was celebrated on March 8, 1889. Emperors and empresses, princes and princesses, sovereigns and generals, governments and institutions, showered congratulations upon him; and the Grand Duke of Baden conferred the Order of Fidelity in diamonds. After his great military triumphs at Sadowa there seemed to be no limit to the honors a grateful people bestowed upon him, from the king down to the humblest peasant. In reply he said, "*I have only done my duty.*" As he returned to Berlin, ovations awaiting him at every step, he said, "I dislike this, it unsettles me. I have only done my duty, just as my comrades have done theirs. After all, it was God who gave us the victory." When he captured Napoleon III., and Paris surrendered, in "that inevitable war with France," the emperor embraced his "Silent General," as he called Moltke, saying, "Germany owes this to you." He was made Count von Moltke, field-marshal, honorary citizen of every city, and statues were erected everywhere. But all this rather shocked his modesty. "Let me go home to Kreisau," he said, "and attend to my rose garden." Modest, noble, Christian man! How much like our own victorious Grant.

"Mary, the mother of Washington," appeared scarcely to think of the distinguished honors conferred upon her son in her intercourse with him and others. After an absence of seven years, in the great conflict for independence, he returned to pay a visit to his mother. Towns and cities were prepared to greet him with more enthusiastic devotion than was awarded to Grecian and Roman conquerors in ancient days; but no demonstration of respect and love caused the good woman to speak or act in any other than the most unassuming, modest way. She met him at the door of her dwelling and embraced him by the endearing name of his childhood—George. She inquired after his health, and remarked upon the traces of time and care upon his once youthful brow. She had much to say about former days and former friends, but made not the slightest allusion to his achievements and honors.

JOSEPH ADDISON.

Subsequently there was a grand gathering of French and American officers in Fredericksburg, and it was arranged that Washington should conduct his mother thither, to introduce her to foreign officers who were anxious to see her. Judging from European examples, they expected to behold a woman of proud and haughty bearing, exulting in the triumphs of her son, and proud to be his mother. What was their surprise to behold a woman of the most simple manners, arrayed in the plainest garb of old Virginia style!

They showered attentions upon her during the evening, none of which elevated her in the least. To all her modesty appeared as her most conspicuous virtue. Her son, in this regard, was a worthy descendant of his mother.

Addison said, " A just and reasonable modesty does not only recommend eloquence, but sets off every great talent which a man can be possessed of. It heightens all the virtues which it accompanies; like the shades in paintings, it raises and rounds every figure, and makes the colors more beautiful, though not so glaring as they would be without it."

XVI.

SIMPLICITY.

A LECTURER upon art, to whom we listened recently, said, "Simplicity is the crowning excellence in art." He proved his statement on the blackboard by rapid, yet superior, drawing: a straight line here, a curved line there, an oblique stroke, a bar, a quirk, a flourish, and the picture was complete, symmetrical, life-like, beautiful. The process was so simple that we said mentally, "Why am I not an artist? Anybody can become a good artist, even a child." The lecturer said, "A knowledge of a few fundamental rules is all that is necessary," and there was the fact on the blackboard. He did not ask his auditors to believe his statement, but to believe the blackboard. The picture we beheld was produced by a few strokes made according to rule: nothing could be more simple.

Here is one secret, if not *the* secret, of success in all pursuits and positions. Humanity puts on airs; it does so to make a profound impression. It must be elaborate and imposing in order to be influential, it seems to think. So the artificial comes to the front, and simplicity is crowded out of social and public life. In dress, manners, customs, education, and even in religion, the elaborate is sought rather than the simple; a grave and sad mistake, for "the crowning excellence" of nature is simplicity. The closer men can get to nature, the more simple will they be in their manners, aims, and habits. To be natural is to be simple, and not artificial. And this applies to man in his threefold nature and in all relations of life.

The following incident, recently rehearsed by several American journals, confirms the opinion of the art lecturer spoken of in the opening of this paper:—

"The Russian sculptor Kamensky, one of the most noted of Russia's artistic guild, has come to America, and intends to settle in New York and to become an American citizen. The story of his first rise in the world is very pretty. He went to Rome to complete his studies, and on his return to St. Petersburg, did not undertake any remarkable and gigantic work which was certain to prove a failure, as so many other sculptors had done; he contented himself with modeling from a lump of clay a little bird trying its wings for the first time. Whether it was the simplicity and beauty of the model, or the prettiness of the allegory, the attention of the court was at once called to the work by the Grand Duchess Marie, the sister of the Czar. Then came an order to copy the little bird in marble, and when finished it was placed in the Winter Palace."

A father called upon a music-dealer to purchase a certain piece for his daughter, who was taking lessons on the piano.

WILLIAM SHAKESPEARE.

"That is an elaborate piece of music for a learner," said the dealer, "and not half so sweet as something more simple."

The father, who had often listened to elaborate German music, and wondered why it could be so famous, accepted the music-dealer's suggestion, and bought a piece so simple that a child could readily learn it. Subsequently his daughter became an expert pianist, and could execute the most difficult music ever written; but for years, whenever she particularly wished to delight visitors, she would play the piece her father loved so well for its charming simplicity.

John Kitto became one of the most renowned biblical scholars who ever lived; and it might have been said of him, "simplicity was the crowning excellence" of his character. He wrote in the journal of his manhood: "I must remember my humble origin, and never forget that some unexpected circumstance may again consign me to that poverty and wretchedness from which I have emerged."

He thought, as he wrote in his journal, that the recollection of his early poverty and obscurity was necessary to success; and this preserved his simplicity. A noble contrast with the dude-like conceit of Scaliger, who was so mortified that he was the son of a miniature painter that he claimed, in his autobiography, to be "the last surviving descendant of a princely house of Verona."

It is this spirit, reaching out for some "princely house of Verona" rather than accept the facts of humble life, which makes dudes, ambitious imitators in all pursuits, and unnatural, would-be leaders in society.

Wendell Phillips, the silver-tongued orator, was not more distinguished for elegance than he was for simplicity of diction and manners on the platform. His earnestness was not more conspicuous than his artlessness. There was no apparent effort to be eloquent. He never appeared to impress his audience by his oratory. The ease, grace, and wealth of speech that captivated his hearers, were made possible by his simplicity. The secret of his great power lay here.

Mr. Phillips' simplicity appeared in every other relation of life. It characterized his domestic and social life. Everything about his home was suggestive of this quality. His manners, intercourse with his fellows, methods of philanthropic work, personal appearance, and public labors—all were more or less marked by this attribute.

The same quality distinguished the famous preachers of the past—Griffin, Channing, Stow, Finney, Beecher, not to mention others. They were unassuming and natural, and, therefore, without affectation. There was no studied effort to impress or please, but to convey the truth clearly, pungently, and effectively, and herein is the highest kind of simplicity. Many preachers of our day sacrifice their pulpit power to their ambition to shine as scholars and orators.

The wife of a New York millionaire attracted much attention on a state occasion at Washington by the simplicity of her dress. The reception was signalized by the costliest display of apparel and ceremonies. Diamonds, pearls, and other precious gems glittered in bewildering profusion. But this woman, whose wealth could command the most elaborate *trousseau*, appeared in apparel so simple and becoming as to challenge universal admiration. It was said that two trunks would answer her purpose for a season at Saratoga or Newport, when some showy wife of a merchant with half her wealth would require twenty-eight. Vanity too often selects the wardrobe, turning simplicity out of doors, thus becoming cruel as well as foolish.

This quality always characterizes true greatness, whether in citizenship, scholarship, or statesmanship. The pretentious man or woman is never great. Such ambition proceeds from a narrow mind. Shakespeare rebuked it when he said:—

"Man, proud man,
Dressed in a little brief authority,
Plays such fantastic tricks before high heaven
As make the angels weep."

SELF-RESPECT.

TRUE self-respect challenges the respect of others. No man has reason to claim the respect of his fellows unless he first respects himself, for this latter act is the outcome of the only elements of character that can command the sincere regard of men. A mean man, a dishonest man, a niggardly man, a lazy man, or a conceited man does not respect himself. He knows that he is not worthy of his own respect even, unless he is living under the power of some strong delusion. The boy who was importuned by another to perform a wrong act by the plea, "Nobody will see you," replied, "I shall see myself." He possessed genuine self-respect, and would not see himself do an ignoble thing with any complacency. The eye of self-respect is always turned inside. Its knowledge

EXTERIOR OF ST. PETER'S, ROME.

alone lays the foundation for confidence. Cicero says of self-knowledge, "A mind by knowing itself, and its own proper powers and virtues, becomes free and independent. It sees its hindrances and obstructions, and finds they are wholly from itself, and from opinions wrongly conceived. The more it conquers in this respect (be it in the least particular), the more it is its own master, feels its own natural liberty, and congratulates with itself on its own advancement and prosperity."

Raphael, the great Italian painter, belonged to a family of artists, of whom it was said, "Their self-respect was inborn." His ancestral line was distinguished by probity, talent, and honor. His ancestors were held in grateful remembrance.

ONWARD TO FAME AND FORTUNE.   131

Raphael's boyhood was manhood in miniature. Some said that he was never a boy, because of his true manliness. His self-respect and self-reliance, coupled with his desire to succeed as an artist, caused his thoughts, plans, and purposes to savor of manhood instead of boyhood. He was described as a "discreet and amiable youth." From a mere child painting engrossed his attention; first, under

INTERIOR OF ST. PETER'S.

the tuition of his father; afterward, at twelve years of age, under the instruction of Perugino. Raphael had no time to be a boy, because his high aims and persevering efforts consumed it all in preparation for actual manhood.

At twenty years of age he visited Florence to see the famous works of Leonardo da Vinci and Michael Angelo, then on exhibition, and the study of them inspired him with a new zeal. From that time his progress was remarkable. Although he died at thirty-seven years of age, his famous paintings were counted by the score, to which must be added eighty portraits of great men like Julius II. and Leo X. One of his biographers says, "If, in addition to his paintings and portraits, we mention that he directed the construction of St. Peter's from his own plans, subsequent to the death of Bramante in 1514, besides executing several other architectural works; that, in the latter part of his life, he had commenced important researches into the architectural remains of Roman antiquity; and that he executed at least one statue in marble, besides designing others, we have the record of a life, which, considering its brevity, is without a parallel in the history of art."

Mrs. Jameson said of him, "We may now reflect with pleasure that nothing rests on surer evidence than the admirable qualities of Raphael; that no earthly renown was ever so unsullied by reproach, so justified by merit, so confirmed by concurrent opinion, so established by time."

Self-respect had much to do with Raphael's successful career as an artist and a man. One story is told of him that deserves to be repeated in this connection. While he was engaged in painting his celebrated frescoes, he was visited by two cardinals who were disposed to play the critic without a correct knowledge of the subject. Their self-assurance and hypercritical attitude disgusted Raphael, so that when one of them remarked, "The Apostle Paul has too red a face," Raphael retorted, "He blushes even in heaven to see what hands the church has fallen into."

His self-respect always prompted true courtesy, but in this instance, it prompted a just rebuke. He could not have said less and preserved his self-respect.

Frederick Tudor, the original ice exporter of Boston, was a man whose word counted for as much as his bond. His personal character and methods of doing business won for him universal respect. In his business career it was a frequent remark with him, "I could not do that and respect myself." First of all, he desired to live and do business so that he could respect himself. If he could do that, the respect of others would follow. His ice business proved a success, and for twenty-five years he pursued it without engaging in any other enterprise. At the close of twenty-five years, however, friends persuaded him to engage in other business also, the result of which was bankruptcy. Calling together his creditors, whom he owed two hundred thousand dollars, he assured them that his honor was pledged to pay that debt; and that if they would give him time, every dollar, with interest, should be paid from the ice business, which continued to be profitable. His proposition was accepted, and in fourteen years his entire indebtedness with interest, amounting to nearly three hundred thousand dollars, was met, his self-respect attaining its maximum power when he paid the last dollar. The praises of his fellow-men were lavished upon him deservedly, but it was his own honest self-respect that won for him an enviable reputation. Up to the time of his misfortune, he had respected himself because his life had been guided by principle, and the only way to continue to maintain self-respect was to pay the debt.

Tudor's career shows that self-respect embraces self-knowledge, self-control, self-denial, self-discipline, self-reliance, and most of the other heroic virtues that combine to make a true man. It confirms the following words of another: "Self-respect is the noblest garment with which a man may clothe himself, the most elevating feeling with which the mind can be inspired. One of Pythagoras' wisest maxims in his 'Golden Verses,' is that in which he enjoins the pupil to 'reverence himself.' Borne up by this high idea, he will not defile his body by sensuality, nor his mind by servile thoughts. This sentiment, carried into daily life, will be found at the root of all the virtues—cleanliness, sobriety, chastity, morality, and religion. To think meanly of one's self is to sink in one's own estimation, as well as in the estimation of others. And as the thoughts are, so will the acts be. A man cannot live a high life who grovels in a moral sewer of his own thoughts. He cannot aspire if he looks down; if he would rise he must look up. The very humblest may be sustained by the proper indulgence of this feeling, and poverty itself may be lifted and lighted up by self-respect."

Self-respect maintains a close alliance with virtue. So long as a youth of either sex has true self-respect, vice has little allurement for him or her. It is when this sterling virtue is sacrificed, and the thoughtless or reckless one ceases to care what is thought of him or her, that vice claims its victim. He who cares not whether men think well or ill of him does not possess self-respect; and so he is easily lured into sin, becoming more and more indifferent to the good-will of others, and more abandoned and criminal in his daily life. With the loss of self-respect, he is likely to lose all that makes manhood true and ennobling.

MAGNANIMITY.

WEBSTER'S definition of magnanimity is, "Greatness of mind; that elevation or dignity of soul which encounters danger and trouble with tranquillity and firmness; which raises the possessor above revenge, and makes him delight in acts of benevolence; which makes him disdain injustice and meanness, and prompts him to sacrifice personal ease, interest, and safety for the accomplishment of useful and noble objects."

The youth of either sex who fills this bill in mature life, is an ornament to his or her kind. The aims and efforts leading up to such a standard must be sincere and lofty, for such a goal cannot be attained without calling into exercise the highest faculties of the soul. To be magnanimous is to be great in the best sense. It is the opposite of human littleness, selfishness, and commonplace. It is not artificial, but spontaneous and devoid of conceit. Magnanimity is derived from *magnus* (great) and *animus* (mind), and hence it always commands respect and admiration.

WILLIAM T. SHERMAN.

Historic illustrations of magnanimity, still fresh in the memories of many citizens, are to the point here. General Grant had been for several months in front of Petersburg, apparently accomplishing nothing, while General Sherman had captured Atlanta, and completed his grand "march to the sea." Then arose a strong cry to promote Sherman to Grant's position as lieutenant-general. Hearing of it, Sherman wrote to Grant:—

"I have written to John Sherman [his brother] to stop it. I would rather have you in command than any one else. I should emphatically decline any commission calculated to bring us into rivalry." General Grant replied: "No one would be more pleased with your advancement than I; and if you should be placed in my position, and I put subordinate, it would not change our relations in the least. I would make the same exertions to support you that you have done to support me, and I would do all in my power to make our cause win." Two great souls striving to be equally magnanimous! Could anything be more beautiful or noble in public life, where jealousy, selfishness, and double-dealing appear to rule the hour, than such self-abnegation, where "each esteems the other better than himself?" General Grant's magnanimity at Lee's surrender is known all over the world. "I will instruct my paroling officers that all the enlisted men in your cavalry and artillery who own horses are to retain them just as the officers do theirs. They will need them for their spring plowing and other farm work. I will furnish your soldiers with a parole to protect them from Confederate conscription officers." And he issued twenty thousand rations for the conquered enemy, hungry and exhausted.

A Southern brigadier said to him, "You astonish us by your generosity;" and General Badeau recently wrote, "The men whom he conquered never forgot his magnanimity. A few months after he made a tour of the Southern States, and then entered Richmond for the first time. Had he been the savior instead of the captor of the town, he could hardly have been more cordially received. The most important Southerners, civilians and soldiers, made it their duty to welcome him, and show him their gratitude."

When Abraham Lincoln was candidate for United States Senator in Illinois, Lyman Trumbull, a political opponent, was put forward as a candidate by Democrats opposed to forcing slavery upon Kansas and Nebraska, a scheme to which Lincoln was also opposed. Governor Matheson was the candidate of the Douglas party in favor of abandoning the above States to slavery, and, on the third or fourth ballot, lacked but four votes of an election. "Withdraw my name at once," said Lincoln, "and support Trumbull."

"Never; we can never do it," replied one of his friends.

"But we cannot afford to risk another ballot; four more votes for Matheson, and our cause is lost," answered Lincoln, with much feeling.

"Nevertheless, we shall not withdraw your name," returned his friend.

Rising to his full height, and with an emphasis that could not be misinterpreted, Lincoln said, "It must be done; my name is withdrawn."

Some of his political friends wept as they abandoned his candidacy, and voted for Trumbull, who was elected; but none of them were ever more in love with his magnanimity than they were then. He sacrificed all political ambition to the cause of freedom.

When he was President, and friends were trying to persuade him to reply to some of the attacks made upon him by certain journals of the day, he replied: "Oh, no; if I were to try to read, much less answer, all the attacks made on me, this office might as well be closed to any other business. I do the very best I know how, the very best I can; and I mean to keep doing so to the end. If the end brings me out all right, what is said against me will not amount to anything; if the end brings me out wrong, ten angels swearing I was right would make no difference."

When tidings of the heavy losses in the battle of the Wilderness reached him, he exclaimed with deep emotion, "My God! My God! Twenty thousand poor souls sent to their account in one day! I cannot bear it! I cannot bear it!"

At another time he said to Secretary Seward, "This dreadful news from the boys has banished sleep and appetite. Not a moment's sleep last night, nor a crumb of food this morning. I shall never more be glad."

In another line, there is now an eminent illustration of our subject before the public. John Wanamaker has a store in Philadelphia larger than the famous *Bon Marche* of Paris, in which are four thousand employes. Believing that he is personally under obligations to make these people thrifty, reliable, and happy, if possible, Mr. Wanamaker has established a civil service system, and a plan of working by which he knows the yearly, monthly, and weekly record of each one employed. In connection with this is a profit-sharing arrangement, by which about one hundred and fifty thousand dollars annually are apportioned among them, according to their standing, in addition to their salaries. Two spacious restaurants, where those who bring dinners from home, and those who wish to buy at the bare cost, are provided. Here plenty of tables are spread, many easy chairs, and a large library are furnished, so that the full hour allowed for dinner may be restfully and profitably spent. By this arrangement, Mr. Wanamaker has accomplished his purpose—secured the most reliable and best working force in any store in the United States. Magnanimity is the word to apply to the author of a scheme so unselfish and philanthropic.

These illustrations of magnanimity from the public walks of life are cited because they are historic. In private and social life, however, are found equally striking examples of the virtue. The humblest persons can be magnanimous. The farmer and mechanic can vie with the general and president on this line. The quality is not confined to age, occupation, sex, or nationality. All can possess it.

COURTESY.

ACCORDING to Webster, courtesy is "elegance or politeness of manners, or especially politeness connected with kindness; civility."

The same lexicographer defines civility to be " good breeding, politeness, complaisance, courtesy," and politeness, by the same, is "elegance of manners, good breeding, ease, and gracefulness; obliging attentions."

We employ the term "courtesy" as embracing the best meaning of the other two. A courteous person must be both polite and civil in the best sense, as neither civility nor politeness can exist without courtesy. Each courts the presence and co-operation of the other. " Civility is to a man what beauty is to a woman; it creates an instantaneous impression in his behalf." As much may be said of genuine courtesy and true politeness.

The phrases " good manners," " a real gentleman," " an obliging man," " a pleasing appearance," so frequently heard, denote the popular idea of courtesy. It is more readily recognized than described, and is always the outcome of heart qualities. Of course, its creation and nurture are not dependent upon books of etiquette, dancing masters, or the rules of fashionable life, but it is an indispensable passport to success.

The model merchant wants his clerks to be " gentlemen;" not foppish, not clownish, not boorish. He does not object to a high polish on their boots, but he does not want it all there. Officiousness, pride, and gruffness he will not tolerate. He requires and expects of them just about what the Bible does when it teaches: " Be courteous;" " Be gentle unto all men;" " In honor, preferring one another;" " Honor all men." Slang, vulgar, and profane language does not harmonize with such behavior.

Not only in warehouses, but everywhere else, such character is current. A lady met the late President Humphrey, of Amherst College, and she was very much impressed by his manners. Although belonging to another denomination, she subsequently gave a liberal subscription to the college, offering as a reason for the act, " President Humphrey is a man of genuine politeness; a college with such a president deserves to be supported."

Daniel Webster was noted for his polite bearing. A Washington official went to see him at Marshfield one summer. On leaving the stage, the driver directed him to the Webster homestead. Thinking to shorten the distance, the visitor struck across lots, but soon found himself on the banks of a stream. Observing an " old farmer " near by, he called out:—

" Look here, old fellow, I am going to see Webster; how am I to get across the stream?"

"Jump or wade it," replied the farmer.

He could not jump it, nor was he willing to wet his feet.

" I will give you a quarter to take me across, old fellow," continued the stranger.

Without making himself known, Webster carried him across, declined to accept his quarter, and politely directed him to the homestead. Soon after Webster joined the visitor in his own house, to the evident and great mortification of the guest. Not a word, however, passed between them respecting the affair. Webster was too courteous to allude to it, and the visitor was too much ashamed to speak of it.

A prominent merchant of New York City went to the Shoe and Leather Bank to open an account.

"You may like to know why I open an account here," he remarked to the president, who was distinguished for true politeness.

"Perhaps you think your money will be safer here," answered the president.

"No; I come here because you are civil. I went into my old bank, and accidentally laid my hat on the cashier's desk. He looked at me with the air of five millions, and said:—

"'Take your hat off my desk, sir!' I took it away, when he said, 'Now, I will hear you.'

"'No, you won't; I will have nothing to do with you,' I replied."

A writer said, some years ago, and his words are equally true now, "Universal politeness has become a primary law in all mercantile houses. It characterizes the entire course of the Barings, the Rothschilds, Laboucheres, and all the most respected American houses. Every Boston merchant remembers with pleasure the genial urbanity which graced the energy, success, grand beneficence, and important public services of Abbott Lawrence, the distinguished merchant and statesman. The feeling and courtesy of the true gentleman marked his eminent character." Women, more than men, possess courtesy and its kindred qualities in a high degree. It is to their character what beauty is to the rose, form to the lily, and odor to a blossom.

An auctioneer in a western city engaged a youth for his clerk at two dollars a day. The clerk's genial, polite bearing carried the crowd on the first day, and he was invited to teach one of the public schools. He accepted the position, studied law while teaching, and was admitted to the bar at twenty-one. A year later, the legislature elected him attorney-general of the State. The next year

STEPHEN A. DOUGLAS.

he became a member of the legislature; then secretary of state, then judge of the supreme court, then member of Congress, where he served until he died. That was Stephen A. Douglas, whose courtesy was his leading quality. A writer says of him, " Though he had high talent, his pleasant manners from the beginning to the end of his career were what gained him the larger part of his popularity."

So essential to success is courtesy that dishonest men counterfeit it in order to accomplish their base purposes. "A wolf in sheep's clothing" is a compliment to the sheep. A man may "smile and smile, and be a villain still."

"The Christian gentleman and lady are such because they love their neighbor as themselves; and to be a thorough Christian without being a gentleman or a lady is impossible. He who is pure in heart can never be vulgar in speech, and he who is meek and loving in spirit can never be rude in manners."

THE SIGNING OF THE DECLARATION OF INDEPENDENCE.

XVII.

ACCURACY.

WE use the word accuracy in the popular sense; a more positive term than correct, though perhaps no more significant. We say of a man, "he is exact"—meaning the same quality as another does when he says of the same person, "he is accurate." The quality is indispensable to a successful career. Without it, confidence cannot be inspired.

To be inaccurate is to be untrustworthy. "A little knowledge, of an exact and perfect character, is always found more valuable for practical purposes than any extent of superficial learning." The superficial scholar, mechanic, or merchant, is not accurate. Accuracy lies deeper down. One must dig down to it in order to possess it.

"Only two cents!" exclaimed a clerk to his employer, who rebuked him for a mistake in a customer's account. He thought that a mistake of two cents was hardly worth mentioning, but had it been two dollars it would have been quite another affair. He did not see that the clerk who would make a mistake of two cents was likely to make one of two dollars. He did not set a high value upon accuracy. To approximate it, in his estimation, was enough for all practical purposes.

But even he would think otherwise, and become enamored of accuracy by a little wise reflection. Let him consider the satisfaction of having his computations just right—the honorable distinction of being known in the warehouse as an accurate accountant who detests mistakes, even the smallest, and he can scarcely fail of falling in love with accuracy.

Besides, the discipline of being exact is very uplifting. Progress is never more rapid than it is when we are studying to be accurate. The effort taxes all the powers. There is positive education in it. Arthur Helps says, "I do not know that there is anything, except it be humility, which is so valuable, as an incident of education, as accuracy; and accuracy can be taught. Direct lies told to the world are as dust in the balance when weighed against the falsehoods of inaccuracy. They are fatal things; and they are all-pervading. I scarcely care what is taught to the young, if it will but implant in them the habit of accuracy."

It is not enough to be "chiefly correct," "exact in the main," "nearly accurate," as thousands of the old and young believe; for that is not accuracy. To be nearly honest, or honest in the main, is not to be honest. A person must be unequivocally and absolutely honest, if he would be above suspicion. There is no half-way work about it. And it is the same with accuracy. A man is accurate or inaccurate, one or the other, for there is no middle ground between them on which we can stand. If he is not accurate, he must be inaccurate.

A young man was highly recommended to a mercantile house in New York City, and he expected to secure a position in the well-known warehouse. But he had occasion to address a letter to the firm, in which he wrote *Toosday* for Tuesday; and this inaccuracy defeated his purpose. The gentleman of the firm concluded that if he knew no more about Tuesday than that, he might not know any more about the other days of the week; and they had no place for him. They must have an exact man or none.

An educator, who insisted upon cultivating the observing faculties of pupils, tried an experiment upon the members of a large school for the benefit of their teacher. He asked the pupils to tell him the difference between a cat and a dog. Probably the first thought of each pupil was "that is easy enough;" but it did not prove so easy after all. Not one scholar could answer the question. They had never observed the difference between the two animals critically enough to tell exactly what it was. So they sat in silence, apparently surprised that they could not answer so simple a question. After a little, the educator called their attention to the feet of the two creatures, appealing to their observation. Then one and another could tell the difference between their feet. In this way they compared different parts of the two animals, until their entire bodies were taken into view. But the original question proved that they had not observed the cat or dog, with all their familiarity with them, critically enough to describe the difference. Sharp observation is indispensable to accuracy.

Our attention has recently been called to certain inaccuracies of speech among well-educated, and even literary men, and the facts show that this subject demands more careful attention.

"He learned him good manners," remarked a gentleman, concerning a successful teacher, in our hearing. He meant that the teacher taught him good manners. This is a very common error, as well as that other remark which even a minister dropped yesterday: "I done this," for "I did this."

Not long since, on a visit of two hours to a school, we heard a very successful teacher use two ungrammatical expressions. They were these:—

"Now, scholars (he spoke to a class called to the recitation seat), be on the alert; either of you are at liberty to ask questions." He should have said "either of you is at liberty to ask questions." The other inaccuracy was: "John, turn to page thirty-one, first paragraph, and render the two first words." John did render two words, but only one of them was first. The teacher did not mean "two first words;" he meant the first two words.

An interesting debater, a young man of real intelligence and much culture, said, "I differ with my colleague." He meant, "I differ from my colleague."

The same young man said, in the same speech, "Neither one or the other." He should have said, "Neither one nor the other."

A lady of refinement, usually careful in the choice of language, said of another, "I see her most every day." Almost every day would have been more in keeping with her taste and culture.

A clerk in a store, gentlemanly in his bearing, called the second month of the year "Febiwerry," and his employer called it "Febuary," when, correctly, it is Febru-a-ry.

The late Alexander T. Stewart, of New York, was noted for accuracy in statement and business, and he demanded the same of others. He had no confidence in a clerk who was incorrect in his figures, or who exaggerated or misrepresented the quality of goods. He believed that success in business depended more upon accuracy than any other quality. He used to say, "A salesman is valuable to me, not when he disposes of goods through a misrepresentation, but when he states fairly what my goods are, and what are the prices. Exaggeration, misrepresentation, and having two prices for articles, are as damaging to merchants as they are wrong in principle." He adopted rules and regulations, imposing heavy penalties in fines for breaches thereof, in order to secure accuracy as a habit. It was a severe discipline to which employes were subjected; and yet scores of young men and women were constantly applying for situations, for it was a good certificate of character to have served honorably in Stewart's store, and opened the way to positions of trust elsewhere. Stewart's clerks were exact in their computations, their representation of goods, their promptitude, their fulfillment of promises—everything. This merchant prince maintained that a high standard of success could not be attained by any business house without such accuracy.

Accuracy challenges confidence in all pursuits, and confidence yields satisfaction. To be accurate is to be trusted, to be trusted is to be self-respecting, and to be self-respecting is to be happy, other things being equal.

Another says, "The accurate man is more likely to be the honest man, for his disposition will be to be accurate in morals as well as in knowledge." Doubtless this is a correct opinion, especially when accuracy becomes a habit, as it should be. It requires more watch and care to be accurate than it does to be inaccurate, but the former may become a habit as really as the latter. As we positively know that the habit of being inaccurate is readily formed, so we should know with equal certainty that the habit of accuracy may become fixed and irrepressible. There is no doubt that, in that case, it has an influence upon honesty and all the other virtues that are found in its company.

Accuracy is uplifting. Effort to attain and maintain it elevates the best part of human nature. Inferior qualities are necessarily brought into subjection. If they are not suppressed they are forced into the background, and are powerless. The mastery over them is achieved by striving for a definite and high excellence.

PRACTICE MAKES PERFECT.

WE had the privilege, recently, of examining a work of art by one of our best landscape painters.

The first scene this artist ever put upon canvas added nothing to the value of the canvas. It was a mere daub by an inexperienced artist, and such a picture is worth no more in the market than the canvas is worth; possibly not as much. But twenty-five years of close practice has made him an expert, and his last painting is worth ten thousand dollars. The difference between ten dollars, the original price of the canvas, and ten thousand dollars, the value of his painting, is found in the quality of his work. "Practice makes perfect." What he has put upon the canvas constitutes its value now, and practice only has enabled him to do that. What is true of the fine arts is true of all the arts of work and living.

The manner of Ole Bull bringing music out of the violin was wonderful. He was the only violinist who ever aroused Edison sufficiently to note and appreciate the charm of sweet sounds, for the click of the electric battery had become the "music of the spheres" to him.

But Ole Bull, without practice, would have been a failure. He said, "If I practice one day, I can see the result; if I practice two days, my friends can see it; if three days, the great public can see it." No doubt, genius figured in his successful career, but it was through persistent practice.

The modern plan of dividing labor so as to secure skill is the outcome of the idea that "practice makes perfect." Formerly one man made the gun, but now it takes about forty. Each man makes a particular part of the weapon, and does not know how to make any other part. He becomes an expert in his line, because his practice is expended upon it, and upon no other.

Edison employs three hundred and fifty hands in his works—all experts; that is, each one has become eminently skilled in his department by devoting himself to it persistently for years. He can be relied upon under all circumstances. His practice has been so thorough and has continued so long, that he stands at the head—the best there is.

A few years ago a teacher in New Haven, Connecticut, drilled two pupils in mental arithmetic until they could readily multiply twenty-one figures by twenty-one figures without recording a figure, the multiplication being entirely mental. It required forty-two figures to express the product, and yet these two students performed the elaborate mental process, and gave the result without an error, one of them being forty, and the other forty-five minutes in going through the operation. Mr. Lovell, the teacher, claimed that several of his scholars could perform the mental feat of Voltaire—multiply the nine digits by nine digits, without putting down a figure, and do it in five minutes. It was not genius, but practice that did it. Only those who aspired to superior attainments accomplished this remarkable multiplication. The youth whose ambition is content with the mental process of multiplying two or three figures by two or three figures, will never compete with the New Haven students. He lacks those qualities that enable him to surmount obstacles in the way to excellence.

Our attention was called to a boot-bottomer, who was an expert in that business.

"How many boots can you bottom in a day?" we inquired.

"Forty," he answered; "I have done more."

"How many pegs are there in a boot?"

"One hundred and five," he replied.

We computed the number of pegs he drove in a day—about eight thousand—one at a time; almost fifty thousand pegs driven in a week! Let the uninitiated ponder the work on a Monday morning—drive fifty thousand pegs, singly, by Saturday night! The task seems quite impossible! The amateur cannot accomplish the feat; it requires practice, close and long continued. This boot-bottomer had been at it from his boyhood, and the celerity and skill with which he performed his task seemed to make both hammer and pegs instinct with life. One could almost believe, on seeing him work, that a sort of intelligence characterized both hammer and pegs, fitting them exactly for their respective places. Practice did it. In the outset, his fingers were clumsy, his hammer heavy, and his motions slow and awkward. At last, his nimble fingers were suggestive of ease, his hammer was light and quick, and his movements apt and graceful. Repetition had eliminated everything like awkwardness and hesitation from his work.

At this point many persons make a mistake in their judgment of labor. That a surgeon should receive a thousand dollars for amputating a limb; a public lecturer one or two hundred dollars for a single address; an elocutionist be remunerated at the rate of fifty dollars an hour; a lawyer be paid twenty thousand dollars for conducting a suit; a preacher have a salary of ten thousand dollars; the president of a bank, railroad corporation, or insurance company, be paid twenty or thirty thousand dollars annually, and a salesman find constant employment at five or ten thousand dollars a year, many persons cannot understand. It appears to themselves enormous pay for little work. But they overlook the "practice" that "makes perfect."

Ten, twenty, and even thirty years of incessant toil preceded these positions of trust and honor. The way up to them was paved with self-denial, work, and sacrifice—the same thing over and over, year after year. Others fell out by the way. They might have enjoyed equally well-earned remuneration and distinction, but they lacked the resolution and vim to continue the "practice." Ten, twenty, or thirty years of unremitting endeavor was a monstrous lion in their way. They cowered before such an obstacle. So much practice was too large a price, and so they do not occupy these lucrative and honorable positions; and they do not deserve them. Society, on the whole, was just and fair. It rewards practice as it does virtue, but it does not reward inaction and cowardice. The man who does his "level best" will never go begging for bread or friends. Society will do as well by him as it can, and he will have no just reason to complain.

It is practice that makes execution easy. When a man has attained to his best, his work is the most easily done. Difficulties were encountered before he reached his high standard of excellence. When he has become an expert, doing is by no means difficult. It is easy for a wise man to be wise, just as it is for a fool to be foolish.

It is easy for a really honest man to be honest, the industrious man to work, the expert to be best. Practice has run into a habit, and habit is easy.

Will Carleton, the "poet of the farm," was reared in the wilderness of Michigan, his father being one of the pioneers on what was then our frontier. He was more in love with books than he was with the farm, and his father was willing that he should be. He was allowed the best schooling that part of the country could furnish. That he was a born poet his parents never dreamed. But a public lecturer chanced to speak in that vicinity and young Carleton went to hear him. The speaker was eloquent and instructive. His young hearer was thoroughly enthused; he must become a public speaker. From that moment both poetry and prose oozed from him as readily as perspiration. The farm was nothing, but public speaking was everything. He spoke in the cornfield and woods, in the barn and stable. He addressed audiences of cattle and cornstalks, trees and fence-posts. He did it, not only daily, but several times in a day, until his father became alarmed; he feared that his son would come out at the little end of the horn, and suggested as much to him. But Will believed that practice makes perfect, and he continued the practice. Writing poetry and orating in the barn and cornfield, occupied his time more than ever. His improvement was in proportion to his practice. He practiced much and his improvement was much. At twenty-six he wrote the poem "Betsy and I Are Out," and it made him famous. Recently Mr. Carleton said, "It is a pleasant memory that my father lived to see me earning a hundred dollars a night, and admitted, with a twinkle in his eye, 'that there was more money in me than he had supposed.'" Practice did it.

HOW DELAYS BEGIN.

EVERY delay has a beginning; stop the beginning, and there will be no delay. It is the same with this as with all other evils: the first step therein is the dangerous one. Refuse to take that and the last one in that line is impossible.

"It is the first step that ruins," it has been well said; steps that follow are easy. The contest comes on crossing the line between right and wrong, good and evil. Once across the line, and the rest is not difficult; it is a down grade then, with constantly accelerating speed. "Delays have dangerous ends," says Shakespeare, but their beginning is more dangerous, for the reason named.

La Fontaine said, "It is no use running; to set out betimes is the main point." Here the truth is found in a nutshell. Only begin in season, and delay becomes impossible. Decision must emphasize starting, since it is easier to continue than to start.

Running to overtake lost time or opportunity only exhausts the breath: one can never catch up. Failing to begin one task or duty promptly shoves it upon the heels of the next; and soon they all crowd and jostle each other, and confusion and inefficiency ensue. Each duty has a place, and that place has beginning and end; give it the beginning, and it is sure of the end.

When the late William H. Seward was in college, he had a room-mate who was more distinguished for delays than anything else. He was a talented young man, but his passion for reading interfered seriously with his hours for hard study. Absorbed in an interesting volume, when the time of preparing for a recitation arrived he would say to himself, "Not quite yet," and read on. "I can make up the time I take here by closer application." This delusion lured him on until he had not more than half time enough to get his lesson, to which he would rush with desperate intent; and thence to the recitation-room, to fail or make an indifferent effort.

This kind of service continued for some time, when Seward said to him :—

"You might rank with the best students of your class instead of with the poorest, if you chose."

"How so?" responded his room-mate, not a little surprised.

"Begin to study your lessons in season, and read after you are well prepared for recitation; and never compromise the rule."

His chum sat in silent reflection for a moment, and then replied:—

"You are right, Seward, I see it; I will heed your advice."

From that time he became one of the most prompt and reliable students in college. He had not thought that delay has a beginning, and his trouble was right there. Seward caused him to see it, and he had wisdom enough left to stop delay at the beginning.

Daniel Webster claimed that this was the only way to gain time for other things instead of losing it for everything. The time he spent on his farm at Marshfield was when public duties pressed less heavily upon him. Hence, improvements upon his farm, hunting and fishing, provided him with needed recreation. But, in order to enjoy this, his rule was to rise very early and attend to his correspondence before breakfast. He would often write twenty or thirty letters before breakfast, and then would come to the table, saying:—

"Well, my day's work is done. Now I am ready for hunting, fishing, or farming, or anything that may come to hand."

Had he continued in bed until the breakfast call dragged him out, and allowed his correspondence to await "a more convenient season," and hunting, fishing, and farming set up their clamor together for attention, things would have been badly mixed on his farm, and in his office; and the "danger of delay" been sadly illustrated. But he adopted the only possible way of circumventing delay, by tabooing it in the outset.

Hamilton set forth the beginning of delay in so terse and pleasant a way, that we quote his entire paragraph:—

"A singular mischance has occurred to some of our friends. At the instant when He ushered them into existence, God gave them a work to do, and He also gave them a competency of time; so much time that, if they began at the right moment and wrought with sufficient vigor, their time and their work would end together. But a good many years ago a strange misfortune befell them. A fragment of their allotted time was lost. They cannot tell what became of it, but, sure enough, it has dropped out of existence; for just like two measuring lines laid alongside, the one an inch shorter than the other, their work and their time run parallel, but the work is always ten minutes in advance of the time. They are not irregular; they are never too soon; their letters are posted the very minute after the mail is closed. They arrive at the wharf just in time to see the steamboat off; they come in sight of the terminus precisely as the station gates are closing. They do not break any engagement nor neglect any duty; but they systematically go about it too late, and usually too late by about the same fatal interval."

Many persons are so long considering when and how to begin a task, enterprise, or duty, that it becomes too late to act at all. They lack decision, and procrastination, that "thief of time," takes advantage of their hesitation to make them linger until it is too late to begin.

Some one has said that "it is easier to delay than to begin." No doubt this is true of a class, but not necessarily so. It is easier to delay, just as it is easier to do anything that is wrong, than to do right. To do the latter requires that all the noblest qualities of humanity shall spring to the front, and stay there, but to do the former requires nothing of the kind; only yield to indecision, and hesitation will follow, and then delay and failure.

There is no doubt, however, that the highest enjoyment is always found by avoiding the beginning of delays. A person can respect himself when he enters upon a duty promptly, at the time required, so that he is on time at the end of it. He has begun, executed, and completed his work within the allotted time, and is, consequently, ready and fresh for the next task; without hurry, flurry, or disappointment. In this is found unalloyed satisfaction.

SECRET OF MENTAL AND MORAL GROWTH.

THE secret of growth is to do to-day what we could not have done yesterday. It requires no striving, or extra effort, to do to-morrow what we can do to-day as well as not. The effort of doing something greater and better is necessary; for this keeps the faculties at their highest tension, in which there is growth. It is in this way that a youth acquires culture, and eventually becomes learned; in this way the artisan becomes an expert, and contributes to the skilled labor of the world; in this way, too, the artist becomes able to execute the most difficult music or transfers his beau ideal to the canvas. It is the effort to improve or excel, taxing the powers more and more, that develops manhood and womanhood, mentally and morally.

When Edison was thirteen years of age, he sold papers on the trains of the Grand Trunk Railway, his home and headquarters being at Port Huron, Michigan.

A boy by the name of James A. Clancy was his partner in the business. Their homes were a mile apart, and it became quite indispensable for them to have some speedy way of corresponding with each other. Edison proposed a telegraph, so they purchased a quantity of stove-pipe wire and put up the line, trees serving them for poles. An operator in the place taught them the telegraphic alphabet, and how to use it. Here was Edison's initiation into the mysteries of electrical science. If he had been content with that short line telegraph, and the good he derived from it, the world would never have heard of his phonograph. But he was not content. That smattering of knowledge stimulated his inventive genius, so that he has been acting upon the principle ever since of doing to-morrow what was not possible to-day. His growth has been phenomenal because his method of reducing the principle in question to practice has been phenomenal. He is still advancing on this line, and is doing to-day what he could not have done yesterday. Hence, one invention follows another naturally, as he expects it will so long as his inventive powers are stretched to their utmost tension for greater acquisitions. Between his one-mile telegraph in 1861, and his present position as "The Wizard of Menlo Park," there are personal struggles, studies, and masterly efforts beyond computation.

The mere money-maker may grow in shrewdness and worldly wisdom, but his manhood does not enlarge and become ennobling. His mind must grasp higher themes, that will tax something more than his avaricious nature, to secure real growth. He may become rich as Crœsus, but a miser has no real manhood; he is a small specimen of humanity. If, while acquiring a fortune, he allows himself to acquire knowledge by dint of perseverance, and become personally and deeply interested in philanthropic enterprises, his whole man feels the force of his efforts. The higher and nobler themes of thought and study make his mental and moral growth inevitable.

Many farmers do not grow in manly character as they advance in years. They till the soil as their fathers did before them, content to plant, sow, and reap as the seasons come and go, without improvement of themselves or their farms. But it is not so with all. Agricultural science taxes their mental powers. They study the nature of the soils, the methods of improving crops and stock, and the many other scientific subjects that are involved in successful agriculture. They grow constantly in intelligence and manly qualities. Higher thoughts lift them out of the old humdrum life of their grandfathers, and they dwell in a new sphere of labor, in which social and intellectual growth is certain. Taxing the mind is the secret of making farming a real discipline.

Of two young men or women, of equal ability and like circumstances, one may attend divine worship on the Sabbath constantly, and the other may not attend at all. The former becomes far more intelligent than the latter. His

ONWARD TO FAME AND FORTUNE. 151

intellect is more active and sharper, so that the difference is apparent to every observer. The explanation is that the mind of the first has been taxed in the house of God by the discussion of higher and grander themes. He has been

HOARDING WEALTH FOR THE LOVE OF WEALTH.

prompted to think and reflect on a higher plane, while the other has groveled in that lower life that characterizes those who neglect public worship. Not one subject of thought was high enough, or noble enough, to lift him above his surroundings. David said, "I know more than the ancients, because I have kept

Thy precepts"—and David was right. Every person who is obedient to God, not only knows more than he who is not, other things being equal, but he has acquired a mental power by grasping greater themes, to which the disobedient is a stranger. Of two children, alike in natural endowments and in opportunities, the obedient one knows more than the disobedient. He practices all the higher qualities that obedience involves, and, therefore, he knows all about them, while the other knows absolutely nothing of them. To know honesty a man must be honest, just as to know astronomy he must master it. So with the good life: the effort for it stimulates both intellect and soul by the necessity of studying and comprehending the highest themes.

These facts show why the dude never grows except in vanity—his passion for dress furnishes food for little else. His thoughts do not rise above his personal appearance, his mind grasps only belittling themes. So with the girl who lives only in a world of pleasure and apparel—she grows vain, but she does not grow brighter and better. She never can grow mentally and morally on this low plane of life. We learn, also, why the constant reader of dime novels, and other trashy literature, knows no more at forty or fifty years of age than at fifteen. He has had nothing uplifting to think about, so that mental and moral growth was impossible. The mind was made to think with; and, in order to grow, it must have something worth thinking about.

The most eminent example of our theme, in our day, is that of Dwight L. Moody, the evangelist. A wide-awake boy, poor and naughty, causing his good Christian mother great anxiety, he possessed, nevertheless, decision, firmness, self-reliance, and indomitable force of character. Just the boy to go to ruin under certain circumstances! Just the boy to make a John Knox or Whitfield under other circumstances! "Uncle Samuel Holton," boot and shoe dealer of Boston, knowing how headstrong and unmanageable he was, advised his mother "to keep him at home in Northfield; such a boy will be ruined in three months in Boston."

But young Moody's ardor was not dampened by his uncle's opinion. At sixteen, he packed up his clothes and left Northfield for Boston. "Uncle Holton" was somewhat dumfounded by his presence, but, speedily taking in the situation, he said, "Dwight, I will give you a place in my store on these conditions: you shall board where I wish to have you; you shall go to meeting with me every Sabbath; and you shall join the Sabbath school."

Dwight accepted the conditions, and went to work with a will. His tact, energy, intelligence, and remarkable efficiency, soon made him an indispensable helper in the store; and his brightness, punctuality, and constancy at church and Sabbath school, drew the attention of both pastor and teacher. He was converted to Christ, and united with the church; and now he must work for his new Master in the church, as he did for the old one in the store, *with all his might*. He was on fire for Christ, and therefore irrepressible. He spoke and prayed in meeting, mutilating the King's English shockingly, and grammar suffered martyrdom at his hands with every effort. Pastor and people hung their heads—the young Christian hero was too rough on the refinement of Boston. But he must work for the Lord or be unhappy, and seeing a field in Chicago for his powers, thither he went. He became salesman in a large boot and shoe house of that city, and stepped to the front at once in the business. Other salesmen complained that he got most of the customers. "Gets them fairly," replied his employer. He joined Plymouth Church, and at once rented four pews and filled them the next Sabbath with young men from the street, showing as much tact in drumming up recruits for the Lord as he did in bringing customers to the warehouse. He offered to teach a class in the Sabbath school. "Gather a class from the streets, and you may teach them," replied the superintendent. The next Sabbath he had a class of "street Arabs," numbering eighteen, some of them hatless and shoeless. Within a few weeks he had a mission school of his own, where two hundred drinking and gambling hells flourished around it. He quit business and devoted his whole time to Christian work. Soon he had a church, and became a preacher of the Gospel. Onward and upward he continued, until he addressed more people at any one time, and at all times, than any other preacher on earth, brought more sinners to Christ than any pastor or evangelist who ever lived, and became known as the model expository preacher of the nineteenth century, at whose feet the graduates of theological seminaries gladly sit to learn how to preach.

What is the secret of such a life? In business he worked with all his might, and prospered. He kept his physical and mental powers on the stretch all the time, so that he grew and stood at the head of salesmen. In like manner he kept his moral and spiritual powers on the stretch constantly, growing surprisingly in mental and moral power. This taxing all his powers to the utmost, year after year, has produced a life almost without a parallel.

Many youth and adults make a fatal mistake by thinking that the way to grow morally, and become strong in principle, is to have a personal acquaintance with the vicious side of life. They must know from personal observation what its sins and pitfalls are. They must peer into that land of darkness. This has often proved a fatal delusion. It is necessary to know only the way to honor and usefulness in order to get there. To know the opposite is no help at all. It is not necessary to learn the way to perdition in order to reach Heaven. A passenger said to the pilot on a Mississippi steamer, "How long have you been a pilot on these waters?" The old man answered, "Twenty-five years, and I came up and down many times before I was pilot." "Then," said the passenger, "I should think you must know every rock and sandbank on the river." The pilot smiled at the man's simplicity, and replied, "Oh, no, I don't! But I know where the deep water is; that is what we want—to know the safe path and keep to it."

AN EXAMPLE THAT EXPLODES EXCUSES.

MANY youth of both sexes might know much more if they would. There is no valid excuse for the commonplace manhood and womanhood which they make. These might be of higher type, more commanding and influential, as well as not. Neither lack of time nor opportunities is the real cause of their indifferent standing in society. If Elihu Burritt could attain to high distinction in knowledge in spite of poverty and obstacles, surely most of the class in question might accomplish much more than they do. In 1838 Governor Everett read a letter from Elihu Burritt to a convention of educators in the city of Taunton, Massachusetts. The letter was written to a friend in Worcester, in response to his inquiry as to the reasons of his success; and no young person can read it without feeling rebuked, unless he has made the most possible of his opportunities. The letter is as follows:—

"I was the youngest of many brethren, and my parents were poor. My means of education were limited to the advantages of a district school; and those, again, were circumscribed by my father's death, which deprived me, at the age of fifteen, of those scanty opportunities which I had previously enjoyed.

"A few months after his decease I apprenticed myself to a blacksmith in my native village. Thither I carried an indomitable taste for reading, which I had previously acquired through the medium of the social library, all the historical works in which I had, at that time, perused.

"At the expiration of a little more than half my apprenticeship, I conceived the idea of studying Latin. Through the assistance of an elder brother, who had himself obtained a collegiate education by his own exertions, I completed my 'Virgil' during the evenings of one winter.

"After some time devoted to Cicero and a few other Latin authors, I commenced the Greek. At this time it was necessary that I should devote every hour of daylight, and a part of the evening, to the duties of my apprenticeship. Still I carried my Greek grammar in my hat, and often found a moment, when I was heating some large iron, when I could place my book open before me against the chimney of my forge, and go through with *tupto, tupteis, tuptei*, unperceived by my fellow-apprentices, and, to my confusion of face, with a detrimental effect to the charge in my fire. In the evening I sat down, unassisted and alone, to the 'Iliad' of Homer, twenty books of which measured my progress in that language during the evenings of another winter.

"I next turned to the modern languages, and was much gratified to learn that my knowledge of the Latin furnished me with the key to the literature of most of the languages of Europe. This circumstance gave a new impulse to the desire of acquainting myself with the philosophy, derivation, and affinity of the different European tongues. I could not be reconciled to limit myself, in these investigations, to a few hours after the arduous labors of the day. I therefore laid down my hammer and went to New Haven, where I recited to native teachers in French, Spanish, German, and Italian. I returned at the expiration of two years to the forge, bringing with me such books in those languages as I could procure. When I had read these books through I commenced the Hebrew, with an awakened desire of examining another field; and by assiduous application I was enabled, in a few weeks, to read the language with such facility that I allotted it to myself, as a task, to read two chapters in the Hebrew Bible before breakfast each morning; this, and an hour at noon, being all the time that I could devote to myself during the day.

"After becoming somewhat familiar with this language I looked around me for the means of initiating myself into the fields of Oriental literature, and, to my deep regret and concern, I found my progress in this direction hedged up by the want of requisite books. I immediately began to devise means of obviating this obstacle; and, after many plans, I concluded to seek a place as a sailor on board some ship bound to Europe, thinking in this way to have opportunities of collecting, at different ports, such works in the modern and Oriental languages as I found necessary to this object. I left the forge and my native place to carry this plan into execution. I traveled on foot to Boston, a distance of more than a hundred miles, to find some vessel bound to Europe. In this I was disappointed and, while revolving in my mind what step next to take, I accidentally heard of the American Antiquarian Society, in Worcester.

"I immediately bent my steps toward that place. I visited the hall of the Antiquarian Society and found there, to my infinite gratification, such a collection of ancient, modern, and Oriental languages as I never before conceived to be collected in one place; and, sir, you may imagine with what sentiments of gratitude I was affected when, upon evincing a desire to examine some of these works, I was kindly invited to an unlimited participation in all the benefits of this noble institution. Availing myself of the kindness of the directors, I spent about three hours daily at the hall, which, with an hour at noon, and about three in the evening, make up the portion of the day which I appropriated to my studies, the rest being occupied in arduous manual labor. Through the facilities afforded by this institution I have been able to add so much to my previous acquaintance with the ancient, modern, and Oriental languages as to be able to read upward of fifty of them with more or less facility."

This letter bore the date of September 6, 1838, and Governor Everett said, as he closed the reading of it, "It discloses a resolute purpose of improvement, under obstacles and difficulties of no ordinary kind, which excites my admiration—I may say, my veneration. It is enough to make one who has had good opportunities for education hang his head in shame."

The mass of youth enjoy vastly better opportunities than the author of the foregoing letter ever did. Let them study that epistle carefully, until they catch the spirit that animated the soul of its author. The average student of to-day needs the application and indomitable perseverance that made such achievements possible. If the small opportunities of Burritt yielded so great results, what have we a right to expect from the greater opportunities which the average student of to-day enjoys! Such an example leaves the youth of even fewer talents absolutely without excuse.

COMMON SENSE.

"COMMON sense is the most uncommon kind of sense," said Dr. Emmons; and a truer remark never was made. It is the kind of sense for which we have the most use; and, therefore, it ought to be more common than it is. But the schools cannot furnish it. Teachers cannot teach it. Pupils must possess it in the natural way, by birthright, or cultivate it by sharp observation. It is what some writers call "tact," or is closely related to it.

It is told of four men who met in Australia, that three of them were college graduates who worked on a sheep farm for the fourth, who was too ignorant to read and write, or to keep accounts. One of the three employes had taken a degree at Oxford, another at Cambridge, and the third at a German university, and here they were, at last, on a sheep farm! College educated to take care of brutes! Evidently they had missed the mark. Educated to be leaders of thought, they became drivers of sheep. They had failed in every undertaking for want of common sense, and finally became the servants of a man who knew as little about school as they did about the common affairs of life. But the ranchman had a practical turn of mind, and had become wealthy by his business. Without an education he had accomplished more by his common sense than his employes had, though drilled in the curriculum of famous universities. The fact shows that education does not create common sense. It was a born quality in the ranchman, but left out of the students' make-up, and the best university could not supply the deficiency. Culture against ignorance, the college against the ranch; and the ranch beat every time; not because the ranchman knew more, nor because he knew less, but because of the practical use he made of what he did know. It is no argument against the highest education, but it is an argument for the cultivation of common sense. All the knowledge in the world is of little use to him who does not know how to use it.

A professor of mathematics in a New England college was called a "bookworm." Books were all he knew. His knowledge of common things was very limited indeed. One day, as he was going out, his wife asked him to call at the store and get some coffee. Before returning he called for the coffee. "How much will you have?" inquired the merchant. The inquiry was unexpected by the professor, and related to a practical matter, about which he knew nothing, so he answered, after a little, "Well, I declare; my wife did not say, but I think a bushel will be enough." The fact does not discount mathematics, but it does plead eloquently for acquaintance with common things.

Dr. Emmons, who made the wise remark quoted at the beginning of this paper, had very little knowledge of the common affairs of life.

KENTUCKY HOME OF ABRAHAM LINCOLN.

He did not know how to harness or unharness a horse. He was never known to attempt to harness one; but, on one occasion, in peculiar circumstances, he did unharness the faithful old family horse, but in doing so took the harness entirely to pieces, unbuckling every strap, so that it took his hired man some time to put it together again. The hired man said, "That horse was too much unharnessed."

How can we account for such lack of common sense? The author could scarcely credit a fact like the foregoing had he not seen it with his own eyes. How can it be explained? In this case, another incident will answer. We were getting the doctor's best hay into the barn. There were three loads of it. On reaching the barn with the second load, the hired man observed a shower coming up very rapidly, and he said to the doctor who was near by, "The other load will get wet unless the boy has some one to help him take it away." The doctor took the hint, but answered promptly, "Making hay is your business, and making sermons mine." He went to his study, and the hay got wet. Here was singleness of purpose with a vengeance. Dr. Emmons did not believe in knowing how to do but one thing, so he gave common sense no show at all. Such examples illustrate the importance of becoming familiar with common things, and the process of doing so cultivates common sense. In this way men become practical. They learn, thereby, not only what to do, but how to do it; and the former is of little value without the latter.

The schools give learning, but experience in the daily business of life gives wisdom, and wisdom is better than learning. Abraham Lincoln's hard experience in the backwoods, and his struggles to enter the legal profession, were of more value to him than a college diploma. These qualified him to conquer secession, and steer the ship of state through the roughest political waters ever sailed over. A well-trained mind, rather than learning, makes a great statesman, and his was well trained by the stern necessities and experiences of early life.

JONATHAN SWIFT.

Gibbon says, "Every person has two educations—one he receives from others, and the other he gives to himself." Doctor Emmons had only one, that he received "from others"—the college. Lincoln had only one, that which he gave to himself in the practical things of life. Both might have accomplished more by the two educations combined. General Grant was a "matter-of-fact man"—that

ONWARD TO FAME AND FORTUNE.

is, a man of sound common sense. General Sherman recognized this dominating quality in him when he wrote that famous letter that contained these words: " My only point of doubt was in your knowledge of grand strategy, and in books of science and history; but I confess your common sense seems to have supplied all these." Common sense did more for Grant and the country than whole libraries of military science and tactics. It studied "details." In like manner, the wisdom of Napoleon and Wellington compassed the smallest matters—"shoes, camp-kettles, biscuit, horse-fodder, and the exact speed at which bullocks were to be driven."

Common sense adapts men to circumstances, and makes them equal to the occasion. Without it, they "may say even their prayers out of time," and may aspire to take the second step before the first has been taken. For this need, Dean Swift nearly starved in an obscure country parish, while Stafford, his blockhead classmate, with practical sense, reveled in wealth and popularity. Beethoven, the great musical composer, exposed himself to ridicule when he sent three hundred florins to the store to pay for a pair of shirts and six handkerchiefs. He lacked common sense in common

ALEXANDER VON HUMBOLDT.

affairs. When a merchant acts like a statesman, it is proof that he has common sense, but when a statesman acts like an inferior merchant, it is proof that he has none. Wellington "never lost a battle, because he was a good business man," his biographer said. That is, he had common sense. Common sense that successfully manipulates the smaller things of life, is competent to utilize the greater; therefore, have it at any cost. Some one has said that "more men of ordinary than of extraordinary ability possess common sense." Whether true or not, one of the most famous men of science that ever lived, Baron Humboldt, possessed this attribute in a high degree. His judgment was equally good in great and little things. He was familiar with the common affairs of life, as well as with the most difficult problems of science. He was always sensible and wise. His opinions, in consequence, were of great value. He was the author of "Kosmos," and other great works in which are manifest both "his common and his uncommon sense." To the personal influence of Humboldt is due nearly all that the Prussian government did for science in the latter part of his life. Agassiz said of him, "The influence he exerted upon science is incalculable. With him ends a great period in the history of science, a period to which Cuvier, Laplace, Arago, Gay-Lussac, De Candolle, and Robert Brown belonged."

XVIII.

SHORTENING THE WAY TO SUCCESS.

THE shortest and quickest route to one's destination is a factor in the problem of life. Busy people desire and seek it, for it saves time and energy. The "longest way round" is not popular, though it may sometimes prove the best; for it requires more patience, and seems to absorb more time and force than is necessary. The shortest and quickest route is the demand of men who mean business.

So it is with the way to success; men desire to shorten it, and it can be shortened, though it may not always be best. Youth are apt to think the way is too long, and become impatient and disheartened. They want to diminish the distance, and they might do it if they only knew how. Whether it is done or not, depends upon themselves—their tact, force, enterprise, and determination.

Benjamin Franklin's route to success was long and crooked. He was born in Boston, and, at ten years of age, left school to assist his father in making candles. Poverty allowed him but two years at school before it forced him into the candle-shop. But in two years he became so disgusted with the work that his father allowed him to leave it to learn the trade of a cutler. Circumstances, however, terminated his career in the cutlery establishment, and he was apprenticed to his brother, who was a printer.

Here he made rapid progress, for he liked the business and pursued it with all his heart. He improved every leisure moment by reading and study, even boarding himself that he might save money to spend on self-culture. His brother published the *New England Courant*, a weekly paper, and Benjamin edited it when he was sixteen years of age, the youngest editor, perhaps, who ever lived. Then he was, by far, the most talented and enterprising boy of his age in Boston. Friends prophesied that he would be renowned at thirty. But the abuse of his

ONWARD TO FAME AND FORTUNE.

brother caused him to run away at seventeen, and several years of straightened circumstances and unusual hardships followed.

He appeared to be on the way to ruin instead of success, when he walked up Market Street, Philadelphia, on the morning of his arrival, eating a baker's roll from one hand and carrying two others, one under each arm. He was between forty and fifty years of age when he began his studies in electricity, and between fifty and sixty when he really entered upon the public life which made him a great statesman at seventy. He was almost old enough to die when he reached the zenith of his renown and usefulness, so long and circuitous was his way thither. It is plain now where it might have been shortened. Could he have lived his life over again, he could have shortened it materially.

ARRIVAL OF BEN FRANKLIN IN PHILADELPHIA.

On the other hand, the great English statesman, William Pitt, went straight and quick to his goal. His celebrated father, the Earl of Chatham, decided to educate him for the public service. He was but eight years of age when his education for the forum began, and from that time he was made to realize that he must accomplish a public career worthy of his illustrious father. To this one object he devoted his powers, even in boyhood developing remarkable abilities for one of his years. Whatever studies he pursued in school or college, whatever labor he performed, and whatever position he enjoyed, all appeared to be conceived and used to fit him for the intended sphere. There was no change of occupation, no turning aside to other objects, no dreaming away time or building air castles; but one look and purpose forward, onward, and upward, straight to success.

At twenty-two years of age he became a member of Parliament, at twenty-three chancellor of the exchequer, and prime minister of England at twenty-five. His way to success was not half as long as Franklin's. It was so straight that he could see from the opening to the end of it. He resolved what he would be in the outset, and stuck to it, nothing diverting him from his purpose. Likes and dislikes yielded to his lofty aim. Whatever he studied and did fitted him for Parliament. All roads conducted him to that body. He was there at an earlier age than Franklin set up the printing business for himself. He fulfilled his mission and was ready to die at the age Franklin began his public career. We cannot see how he could have made his way to success any shorter. It was short enough.

The author is familiar with a wealthy man who left the farm at eighteen years of age for work in a straw-hat factory. His father was not quite in favor of his choice, but yielded thereto because the son was determined upon a business career. Each employe had his particular work, but this young man used leisure moments in studying other branches of the business. He examined the bleachery, spent many evenings in making pattern hat-blocks, had an eye upon the styles, and was ready, at any time, to perform extra work for his employer.

"You are a fool to spend your time and strength in work you get nothing for," said one of his companions.

"It will shorten my way to the head of the manufactory," he replied.

His fellow-laborer only pitied him for his folly.

In three years the young man from the farm was superintendent of the establishment, and a good one, too. That was what he started out for, and he obtained the object he had in view sooner than he expected. He shortened the distance by serving his employer to the very best of his ability, watching for opportunities to learn what he did not know, doing often more than his employer required of him and proving, by actual service, that he meant to master the business.

It is quite evident, then, that the way to success may be shortened by the early choice of an occupation or profession, and then bending all the energies of the soul to realize the beau ideal. Certainty of achievement appears to be as essential as the desire to achieve. Dalliance or diversion lengthens the distance, and lack of enthusiasm prolongs the journey; while a single, strong purpose, supplemented by resolve, work, invincible courage, and practical wisdom, makes the route short and quick.

BE YOURSELF.

THAT person, old or young, who tries to be other than himself, makes a failure of life, and yet many do this very thing. One preacher tries to be like another whom he regards as a model; one lawyer to be like another lawyer who is famous; one orator like another whose eloquence is a charm; one woman like another whose manners are easy and graceful; and so on, to the end of the alphabet. Few only are satisfied to be themselves. The Methodist bishop rebuked this spirit when he told the student, after listening to his trial sermon, "I do not forbid you to preach, but nature does." To undertake to fill a coveted place in the face of nature is a sure failure. It is necessary to be "called" to a pursuit or enterprise, in order to succeed.

Another says, "One of the most disgusting sights in this world is that of a young man with healthy blood, broad shoulders, presentable calves, and a hundred and fifty pounds, more or less, of good bone and muscle, standing with his hands in his pockets, longing for help." He would have him, instead, start out for what he is worth, asserting his individuality by positive endeavors, even though he never prove a great winner. Better to be himself and fail to reach the top of the ladder, than ape another and thereby become the laughing-stock of observers. To be yourself is a virtue, even though yourself is of small consequence in the body politic. Better be that than to be weak in trying to be another.

What is called "society" is cumbered with fashions and customs, including "rules of politeness," whose direct tendency is to destroy individuality. These things cause many men and women to appear what they are not. They are artificial, formal, and assuming. The evil is met and overcome only by sound common sense, culture, and humility.

It is not unusual for persons to claim rank and wealth for their ancestors, who were really commonplace and poor. Frequently men and women will praise a popular book which they never have read, in order to leave the impression of literary taste. A class furnish houses and support turn-outs to give the appearance of riches where they do not exist. All that is done in society simply for appearance tends to make people vain and showy, instead of real and sensible. It is only decision and determination that can resist this pressure of social life to be what one is not. The highest kind of courage alone is required to *be* and not *seem* in these circumstances. When the English government resolved not to recognize Napoleon as Emperor, but only as general, he replied grandly, "They may call me what they please; but they cannot prevent me from being myself." Napoleon's career and fame were the outcome of this individuality. He was unlike any other general, because he was only Napoleon.

Sincere, frank, honest, true, candid, and ingenuous, are adjectives we must apply to the man who means to be himself. He cannot assume to be what he is not, because these qualities forbid. *Seeming* is out of the question; *being* is imperative. Steele says, "He who does not wish to obtain false applause will *ingenuously* disclaim his share in the performance which has obtained the applause." Crabbe says, "The *frank* man is under no restraint; his thoughts and feelings are both set at ease, and his lips are ever ready to give utterance to the dictates of his heart. He has no reserve." It is the man who is trying to be somebody else who is under restraint. He must do much for appearance only. He is anxious, nervous, and apprehensive lest he should fail to seem. In this is the most irritating restraint. It is slavery, and not freedom.

ONWARD TO FAME AND FORTUNE.

If General Grant had followed the best treatises on military tactics and science, or sought to be Cæsar, Napoleon, or any other general of ancient or modern times, in the late Civil War, he would have been a failure. But he was General Grant, and no one else. Sherman wrote to him: "You are now Washington's legitimate successor, and occupy a position of almost dangerous elevation; but if you continue, as heretofore, *to be yourself*—simple, honest, and unpretending—you will enjoy through life the respect and love of friends, and the homage of millions of human beings." His power lay in being himself; his individuality doomed the Rebellion. A person can be himself and study all the models he pleases. There is nothing in the foregoing to forbid his careful analysis of character and methods; they may intensify his resolution to be himself. Webster studied the orations of Cicero so thoroughly that he could repeat most of them verbatim; but they did not destroy or compromise his individuality, because he did not try to be Cicero. It has been said that Michael Angelo, who was the most original of ancient or modern artists, was more familiar with the model statues and paintings of the world than any other man. He studied the excellences of all the great works of art, not to copy or imitate them, but to develop his own powers. As the food he consumed became bone and muscle by assimilation, so, by mental assimilation, the knowledge he acquired by art models entered into the very composition of his mind.

MICHAEL ANGELO.

Research, investigation, and study of models may help and not hinder individuality. Says Matthews, "No doubt the most original writer, like the bee, will have drawn his capital stock of ideas, his funded store, from a variety of sources; but, as the bee, though it rifles all the flowers of the field of their sweets, lets not the honey betray the prevailing flavor of any single nectary, so it will be with him who makes the honey of Hymettus. He will lay all literature under contribution to supply his stores, but every foreign thought will be passed through the alembic of his own brain, and its elements recombined before it is again given to the public. Like old coin, it will be melted and reminted before it is again put into circulation."

Sydney Smith insisted upon this quality of manhood and womanhood as indispensable. He said, "There is one circumstance I would preach up morning, noon, and night, to young persons for the management of their understanding: Whatever you are from nature, keep to it; never desert your own line of talent. If Providence only intended you should write posies for rings, or mottoes for twelfth-cakes, keep to posies and mottoes; a good motto for a twelfth-cake is more respectable than a villainous epic poem in twelve books. Be what nature intended you for, and you will succeed; be anything else, and you will be ten thousand times worse than nothing."

WHAT SPARE MOMENTS WILL DO.

THE old adage is, "Time is money;" but the time of which we speak is worth more than money; it is culture, usefulness, and character to every person who improves it.

Spare moments made Elihu Burritt the "learned blacksmith," Hugh Miller a renowned geologist, Isaac Taylor a famous author, Abraham Lincoln a statesman and president, Benjamin Franklin a great philosopher, and a long line of other worthies what they became in literature, science, and statesmanship.

Dr. Franklin said, "Leisure is time for doing something useful;" not the time for lounging and idleness. Leisure moments should not be idle moments, as is too often the case. They may become the most profitable moments of the whole life, leading up to higher and grander aims.

Amos Lawrence says in his diary: "When I first came to this city, I took lodgings in the family of a widow who had commenced keeping boarders for a living. I was one of her first, and, perhaps, had been in the city two months when I went to this place; and she, of course, while I remained, was inclined to adopt any rules for the boarders that I presented. The only one I ever made was that, after supper, all the boarders who remained in the public room should be quiet, at least for one hour, to give those who chose to study or read an opportunity of doing so without disturbance. The consequence was that we had the most quiet and improving set of young men in the town. The few who did not wish to comply with the regulation went abroad after tea, sometimes to the theatre, sometimes to other places; but all, to a man, became bankrupt in after life, not only in fortune but in reputation, while a majority of the other class sustained good characters, and some are now living who are ornaments to society and fill important stations. The influence of this small measure will, perhaps, be felt throughout generations. It was not less favorable on myself than it was on others."

Young people of both sexes have many spare moments. Perhaps girls have more such moments than boys. One writer claims that the average girl could read a hundred pages in the spare moments of each day. Seven hundred pages a week! Thirty-six thousand four hundred pages in a year! Three hundred and sixty-four thousand pages in ten years! About one hundred volumes a year, of four hundred pages each! Nearly one thousand volumes of this size in ten years! There is no excuse for ignorance here.

If a girl or boy can command but one hour a day for reading, twenty pages could be read thoughtfully in that time, or one hundred and forty pages in a week. In a single year, more than seven thousand pages, which is equal to eighteen large duodecimo volumes! In twenty years, one hundred and fifty thousand pages, or three hundred and sixty-five volumes of the size named above! Divide this amount of reading between history, philosophy, chemistry, biography and general literature, and the reader will be well versed in these several departments of knowledge.

We have an eminent illustration of the result of one hour's reading per day for forty years, in the life of the late Charles G. Frost, of Vermont. At fourteen years of age he was apprenticed to a shoemaker; and he resolved, on going to his trade, to read and study one hour daily on the average. In thirty-one years from that time, at the age of forty-five, it was said of him: " In mathematical science he has made so great attainments, that it is doubtful whether there can be found ten mathematicians in the United States who are capable, in case of his own embarrassment, of lending him any relief." At forty-five, Mr. Frost said of himself, " The first book which fell into my hands was ' Hutton's Mathematics,' an English work of great celebrity, a complete mathematical course, which I then commenced—namely, at fourteen. I finished it at nineteen without an instructor. I then took up those studies to which I could apply my knowledge of mathematics, as mechanics and mathematical astronomy. I think that I can say that I possess, and have successfully studied, all the most approved English and American works on these subjects. Next, natural philosophy engaged my attention, which I followed up with close observation, gleaning my information from a great many sources. The works that treat of them at large are rare and expensive, but I have a considerable knowledge of geology, entomology, and conchology."

Botany was a favorite study of his. He made extensive surveys, in his own State, of the trees, shrubs, herbs, ferns, mosses, lichens, and fungi, and possessed the third best collection of ferns in the United States. He turned his attention to meteorology, and devoted some time to the study of storms and the movement of erratic and extraordinary bodies in the air and heavens. He found that a knowledge of Latin was indispensable to the prosecution of some of his studies, and he acquired it and could read it with great freedom. He made himself familiar with the standard poets of England and America, as well as the history of his own and other countries. Books that he read and studied were added to his library, of which he said, " I have a library which I divide into three departments—scientific, religious, literary—comprising the standard works published in this country, containing five or six hundred volumes. I have purchased these books, from time to time, with money saved for the purpose by some small self-denials."

As an author, Mr. Frost ranked among the most useful, having prepared and published several popular historical and other works. These remarkable achievements were what spare moments did for him, although in his later literary life he devoted more time to mental and less to manual labor.

Julius Cæsar wrote his famous " Commentaries " in moments that he snatched from the cares and toils of military campaigns. Robert Bloomfield's literary acquirements were made when he was learning the trade of a shoemaker, and afterward while he worked at the same business as a journeyman. When Albert Barnes first thought of preparing his commentary on the Bible, his hands were full; but finally he decided to accomplish the great work by rising and spending an hour before breakfast upon it. He made spare moments for the emergency, and in this way achieved what is marvelous in our eyes.

WHAT DIFFICULTIES ARE FOR.

DIFFICULTIES have their use. Their mission is not to dishearten applicants for success; they are not sent to turn a youth back from a noble career.
They are discipline. Rightly used, they develop manhood and womanhood, and assist in making true men and women. All difficulties come to us, as Bunyan says of temptation, " like the lion which met Samson; the first time we encounter them they roar and gnash their teeth, but once subdued, we find a nest of honey in them."

When Benjamin Franklin set up the printing business in Philadelphia he found a formidable rival in a well-to-do printer who commenced business about the same time. Franklin was poor, and comparatively a stranger in the city; but the superior advantages of his rival did not discourage him. On the other hand,

ONWARD TO FAME AND FORTUNE.

he was disciplined thereby to increased economy, industry, and perseverance. He moved into a back room of his shop, where he boarded himself upon the smallest possible allowance. One day his rival called at the shop, and Franklin took him into his living-room, where, pointing to part of a roll of bread on which he had just made a meal, he said:—

"Now, unless you can live cheaper than I can, you must perceive that it is utterly vain to think of starving me out."

Sir Charles Napier said, "Difficulties only make my feet go deeper into the ground. The more trouble, the more labor must be given." When Milton was struck with blindness, "he bore up and steered right onward." Others might have interpreted the calamity as a plain hint of Providence to stop short, but he regarded it rather as a command to move forward, and produced his greatest works when he was under the darkest cloud.

The world received the great legacy of "Pilgrim's Progress" from Bedford jail. But for Bunyan's incarceration in that prison, the remarkable allegory would never have been written. His "Grace Abounding," and the "Holy War," were written there also. The bitter experience seemed to set his mind aglow and start him forth upon a career that neither his friends nor himself had dreamed of. A man called upon him one day with "a message from the Lord," as he claimed, and remarked:—

"I have been to half the jails in England, and now am glad to find you at last."

JOHN MILTON.

Bunyan replied:—

"If the Lord sent you, you would not have needed to take so much trouble to find me out, for He knew that I have been in Bedford jail these seven years past." He continued in prison five years longer. A quaint writer says, "A certain amount of opposition is a great help to a man. Kites rise against, not with, the wind. Even a head wind is better than none. No man ever worked his way anywhere in a dead calm. The best wind for anything, in the long run, is a wide wind. If it blows aft, how is he to get back?"

JOHN BUNYAN.

To a soul bent on a grand achievement, difficulties become the occasion of greater efforts. Everything yields to its controlling passion. No sacrifice is too great for the prize sought. Palissy, the potter, absorbed in discovering for himself the process of white enameling, when he saw that the heat of the furnace in which he fired his models was about to fail him, at once cast in his furniture, even to the bed of his children, ready to consume everything rather than that which he considered to be his greatest work should prove a failure.

Of the examples of success in spite of towering difficulties, all are tame in comparison with those we might adduce from the blind, deaf, and dumb, who have become renowned in science, art, and letters. Perhaps the most wonderful case of all is that of Laura Bridgman, who possessed only the sense of *touch*, yet learned to study, work, and converse through that sense alone. Dr. Howe said, "When Laura is walking through a passageway, with her hands spread before her, she knows, instantly, every one she meets, and passes them with a sign of recognition."

ONWARD TO FAME AND FORTUNE.

Laura had charge of her own wardrobe, and displayed much taste about her toilet. She became expert and ingenious with her needle, making ornamental and useful articles with even more skill than many other girls endowed with eyes and ears. Her progress in the various branches of knowledge was rapid, and her scholarship high. In social life she was animated, bright, joyous, and genial, the sense of touch putting her into intimate and pleasant communication with the company about her. She was educated to be all this and more.

Pupils who falter and complain before difficult tasks, when the five senses wait to do their bidding, should blush for shame with such an illustration of the "pursuit of knowledge under difficulties" as Laura Bridgman affords. For well-endowed people to be content to be second-rate scholars and artisans with this example to inspire them, is as discreditable as it is lamentable. If Laura could overcome and acquire an education, is there any excuse for the shortcomings of students who are a thousand times better situated to master science and learning? Education was available to her only by *touch!* Yet she got the education!

BERNARD PALISSY.

The hill Difficulty should not be tunneled for the student or artisan: he should tunnel it himself. Neither should the rich and enterprising build a railroad over it for him: he should build it himself. Then, and only then, does he get the most good out of tunnel or railroad. To go round it is as belittling and foolish as to sit down in front of it in despair. *Over it or through it*, should be the motto. In this there is manly and womanly enterprise and character. Once on the summit of the hill, and the reward is great! A panorama of indescribable beauty and grandeur spreads out before the toiler. There is nothing like it in the valley below. No sacrifice was too great for such an opportunity. The price was not too dear; the work was not too hard; the way was none too rough; the summit was not too high. On the Mount of Triumph all are satisfied.

One writer says, "The beginning of all things is difficult." Another, "Difficult things are the only things worth doing." And Garfield said, "Poverty is uncomfortable, as I can testify; but nine times out of ten the best thing that can happen to a young man is to be tossed overboard and compelled to sink or swim for himself. In all my acquaintance I never knew a man to be drowned who was worth saving."

XIX.

A GOOD START.

WHAT many people consider a good start in the world may prove the poorest start of all. A capital of ten thousand dollars, inherited, or loaned by some rich friend, may prove less fortunate for a young man than poverty and a good character.

There can be no doubt that money capital that is earned before it is used, serves the business man a higher purpose than the same amount of capital inherited or borrowed. Earning the capital is a good start of itself. It booms the noblest qualities of manhood.

Principle alone is a good start, and will earn a good name more surely and quickly than money. "Good principles and good habits were all the capital I had to start with," said Amos Lawrence, and it was all the capital he needed, as his successful career proved. At one time he wrote to his son who was in France:—

"Good principles, good temper, and good manners, will carry a man through the world much better than he can get along with the absence of either. The most important is good principles. Without them, the best manners, although for a time very acceptable, cannot sustain a person in trying situations."

Admiral Farragut said to a gentleman at Long Branch, after the close of the late war:—

"Would you like to know how I was enabled to serve my country?"

"Of course I should," responded the person addressed. "I should enjoy it hugely."

"It was all owing to a resolution that I formed when I was ten years old," continued the admiral. "My father was sent to New Orleans with the little navy we had, to look after the treason of Burr. I accompanied him as a cabin boy. I had some qualities that I thought made a man of me. I could swear like an old salt, could drink as stiff a glass of grog as if I had doubled Cape Horn, and could smoke like a locomotive. I was great at cards, and was fond of gambling in every shape. At the close of dinner one day, my father turned everybody out of the cabin, locked the door, and said to me:—

"'David, what do you mean to be?'

"'I mean to follow the sea,' I said.

"'Follow the sea!' exclaimed father: 'yes, be a poor, miserable, drunken sailor before the mast, kicked and cuffed about the world, and die in some fever hospital in a foreign clime.'

"'No, father,' I replied, 'I will tread the quarter-deck, and command, as you do.'

"'No, David; no boy ever trod the quarter-deck with such principles as you have, and such habits as you exhibit. You will have to change your whole course of life if you ever become a man.'

"My father left me and went on deck. I was stunned by the rebuke, and overwhelmed with mortification. 'A poor, miserable, drunken sailor before the mast, kicked and cuffed about the world, and die in some fever hospital!' That's my fate, is it? I'll change my life and change it at once. I will never utter another oath, never drink a drop of intoxicating liquor, never gamble; and, as God is my witness, I have kept these three vows to this hour. Shortly after I became a Christian, and that act settled my temporal, as it settled my moral, destiny." It was a good start for Farragut, when his father started him off in the direction of total abstinence and purity. But for his good resolve on that memorable day, he would have been a ruined sailor before the mast, instead of the famous admiral that he was.

D. G. FARRAGUT.

The late William B. Spooner, of Boston, was but seven years old when poverty forced him out of his home into a tanyard, where he drove the horse in the bark-mill. A very poor outlook it was for the homesick boy! But it proved a good start, because it introduced him, after fifteen years, to the leather business in Boston. His early training in the tannery familiarized him with the details of the business, and his excellent principles won the confidence of all who knew him. At twenty-two he was serving a large and successful leather dealer, when a gentleman who had observed his tact, industry, and transparent honesty, invited him to become his partner in the same kind of business.

"I have no capital to put into business," said Spooner.

"Yes, you have," responded the gentleman; "you have character and experience, and I have money. I will put my money into the firm, and that is all the money we want; and you put in your experience and principles."

The bargain was concluded on this basis, as Spooner knew the young man who had the money capital to be entirely reliable. The end of that new departure was that in forty-five years he was worth half a million dollars, and he had lost and given in charity another half million.

At the same time, he had become one of the most influential and honored citizens of Boston. Poverty gave him a good start at seven years of age; and tact, integrity, and hard work, supplemented it at twenty-two. Neither a favored ancestry, nor money, rendered him essential aid.

The renowned Dr. Channing once wrote to a young man:—

"At your age I was poor, dependent, hardly able to buy my clothes; but the great idea of improvement had seized upon me— I wanted to make the most of myself. I was not satisfied with knowing things superficially, and by halves, but tried to get some comprehensive views of what I studied; I had an end, and, for a boy, a high end, in view. . . . The idea of carrying myself forward did a great deal for me. . . . I never had an anxious thought about my lot in life; when I was poor, ill, and compelled to work with little strength, I left the future to itself."

The good start which Dr. Channing had was when he resolved "to make the most of himself."

HOW TO USE YOURSELF.

"KNOW thyself" was the wise counsel of an ancient philosopher. It is absolutely necessary to know yourself in order to know how to use yourself. You cannot use what you do not have. You cannot use five talents if you do not have but one or two; you cannot be wise if you are otherwise; you cannot exercise sound judgment if you do not possess it; you cannot make a successful merchant or minister if you have no qualifications for those positions. Make the most of such material as you have, and the best results will follow. Hence, self-acquaintance is indispensable to the proper use of yourself.

Some young people may lack certain qualities which they can cultivate, but they must know what they are. Observation may be deficient; love of work languish; patience and perseverance may be wanting; and other qualities may be weak and inefficient; but they can be improved, when a person knows what it is that he must improve. He must know himself in order to undertake intelligently self-improvement. Whether to use check or spur, and when or where, is indispensable knowledge.

When Hugh Miller was seventeen years of age, his two uncles, who had been his guardians since his father died, suggested to him that he was old enough to choose a life-pursuit. They wanted him to be educated for one of the learned professions; they were not particular which. But he protested against their plan, claiming that he had no fitness for any of them: that he would make a failure as physician, lawyer, or clergyman. His views on the subject were so emphatic that his uncles acquiesced in his choosing an occupation, but they were somewhat confounded when he consented to become the apprentice of a stonemason. But the boy knew himself better than did his uncles. They had regarded his fondness of nature, and his frequent excursions over the country in search of minerals, rather as boyish freaks instead of indications of a "natural bent." They had, indeed, thought that he possessed more than ordinary talents; and, for this reason, no doubt, desired that he might choose one of the learned professions.

Young Miller knew that he loved nature with a passionate love; that he enjoyed himself more when traversing the hills and valleys to increase his knowledge of her treasures than he did anywhere else. He delighted in caves and quarries. With hammer in hand, he found more real enjoyment among crags and rocks than the average bright boy finds in astronomy or Latin grammar. He knew that a quarry would be more than a college to him, and that he could sit at the feet of nature to learn with more faith than he could sit at the feet of a professor, so that it was not blind reasoning that made him a stonemason; it was the call of a soul for knowledge in that line. He might never have been known beyond his own immediate circle had he become a lawyer, doctor, or rector. He certainly would not have been favorably situated to develop into a great geologist. He devoted himself to that pursuit which appealed to the strongest and best elements of his being. He was fitted for it. He could make the most of it possible, and it could make the most of him possible. He became the world-renowned geologist because he selected a pursuit for which nature had fitted him.

One of the best artists of New England was educated for the medical profession against his own taste and judgment. From a child he manifested a strong love for art, and was drawing and painting every chance he could get. His father witnessed his precocity in this direction, and was annoyed rather than pleased by it. He was determined to make a doctor of him, so that tact and talent in another line was not acceptable.

"Artists can hardly keep soul and body together," he said; "and my son must pursue a more lucrative and substantial business." So he was educated for a physician.

"I have no taste for the profession, and no talent for it" said the son; "but I yield to my father's strong desire. I know that I possess both taste and talent for art, and could distinguish myself therein, but my father orders otherwise."

He entered the medical profession; but his heart was not in it. He felt continually that he was out of his place—that he was engaged in a pursuit for which nature did not intend him. He was dissatisfied and unhappy, of course. His profession was a burden to carry; and the time came when he resolved to lay it down and take up art, which was so congenial to his nature. He knew himself better than his father did, as the sequel proved. He was not a born physician, but he was a born artist, and, knowing that fact, he knew how to use himself to the best advantage.

John Bright was a remarkable illustration of our theme. He was a good scholar, fond of books, and yet he had an eye to business. Having completed his education, he entered upon a business career with his father. At the same time, he gratified his love of learning by improving leisure time in reading. He was passionately fond of poetry, and it commanded a good share of his spare moments. In school he belonged to a debating society, in which he developed finely as a speaker. He did not undervalue these sources of intellectual and popular strength after he became a business man. He became an expert in the study of poetry and English literature; he spoke in public, also, and became a famous orator. In this way he advanced constantly, and became a leader in the British Parliament. A correct knowledge of himself led him to self-improvement on lines that assured his renown as a statesman.

CHOOSING AN OCCUPATION.

THE choice of an occupation is a very important factor in the success of life. The earlier it can be done the better. The more nearly the aptitudes of the man or woman fit the occupation, the more congenial and successful is the career. To follow the "natural bent," whenever it is possible, appears to be eminently wise, for "square men should be put into square holes, and round men into round holes." Failing to regard the drift of one's being in the choice of an occupation, is almost sure to put square men into round holes, and round men into square holes.

A good mechanic has often been spoiled to make a poor clergyman or merchant, and a good minister has been spoiled to make a commonplace artisan. Overlooking the "natural bent," the youth has selected an occupation for which he has no special aptitude, and he brings little to pass.

Strong minds readily indicate the pursuit for which they are naturally fit; others do not. When Dr. Watts was a boy his propensity for rhyming was irresistible. His father became disgusted with his habit in this direction, and finally proceeded to expel it from his soul by a flogging. In the midst of the punishment, with the tears running down his cheeks, young Watts cried out:—

> "Dear father, do some pity take,
> And I will no more verses make."

His father saw that what was bred in the bone could not be expelled with the rod, and he very wisely concluded to let the boy develop into a poet.

The celebrated English engineer, Smeaton, displayed a marvelous ability for mechanical pursuits even in his childhood. Before he had donned jacket and trousers in the place of short dresses, his father discovered him on the top of his barn putting up a windmill that he had made. But his father paid no regard to his aptitude for this or that position. He was determined to make a lawyer of him, and sent him to school with that end in view. But the boy thought more of windmills and engines than he did of Euclid or Homer, and the result was unfavorable. His father was trying to crowd a square boy into a round hole, and it was too repugnant to the born engineer. Nature fitted him for a particular place, and he got it.

The mother of Benjamin West, too, showed her good sense by recognizing the natural bent of her boy toward art. One day he drew a picture of his chubby little sister as she lay in the cradle asleep, and the likeness was so striking that his mother observed it with admiration, and then imprinted a kiss on Benjamin's cheek. "That kiss," said West, forty years thereafter, "made me a painter." Instead of seeing nothing but a freak of childhood in the act, Mrs. West beheld the foreshadowing of a distinguished artist, and acted accordingly.

Sir John Franklin was an illustration of our theme. His father designed that he should be a preacher, but in his heart of hearts the boy meant to be a sailor. This was somewhat singular, as he lived twelve miles from the sea and never saw it until he was twelve years of age. On that day, accompanied by an intimate companion, he walked that distance for the purpose of gazing upon the ocean. It was the grandest spectacle he had ever seen, and for hours he sat and gazed in silence upon its restless bosom. His desire for a life "on the ocean wave" grew stronger than ever. He talked about it by day and dreamed about it by night. He must go to sea, a denial would break his heart. As he was deaf to all entreaties and counsels of his parents, who were thoroughly opposed to a seafaring life for their son, there seemed to be no alternative. His father yielded to the boy's wish for a seafaring life, and procured a situation for him as cabin-boy in a merchant vessel bound for Lisbon. This voyage was selected for its roughness, his father thinking that enough hardship would sicken him of the sea. But from the time the vessel set sail it was one continuous festival for the adventurous and fearless cabin-boy. He returned more enthusiastic than ever for the life of a sailor, and his father secured for him a midshipman's place on board of a seventy-four gun ship of the royal navy.

He was then fourteen years of age, and from that time he began to make his mark. At fifteen his ship was in the battle of Copenhagen, under Nelson; and his valor, tact, and efficiency in that conflict proved that he was a gifted naval commander in embryo. Obedience to orders, loyalty to his country, and the habit of doing the best he could, were his traits. He was in the battle of Trafalgar, where he performed the perilous duty of signal officer when his comrades were falling fast about him—a youth of nineteen displaying the courage and military skill of a veteran. By devotion to his profession and fidelity to his superiors he worked his way up to knighthood. Great Britain delighted to honor him. He was the naval commander above all others selected in 1845 to undertake a voyage of discovery in the Arctic Ocean. From that voyage he never returned.

Had his father's plan to make him a minister, in spite of his taste for the sea, been carried into effect the world would have lost the services of one of the greatest and noblest explorers whose memory it delights to honor.

But such examples as the foregoing are exceptional. The aptitudes of most boys and girls are not so manifest. There is little or nothing to show whether nature designed them for this, or that, or the other occupation. The choice of a profession is more difficult with them. Time, thoughtfulness, and sound judgment are indispensable in making the choice. Since almost every one will do better in a certain occupation than he can in any other, the choice becomes doubly important because so difficult. But forethought, circumspection, and a sincere desire to make the most of one's life, will overcome the difficulty and guide to the best employment. Emerson said, "The crowning fortune of a man is to be born with a bias to some pursuit which finds him in employment and happiness." But youth who have not that "crowning fortune" must fall back upon their own good sense.

When the occupation is selected, adherence to it is a condition of success. "A rolling stone gathers no moss," is the maxim, and it fairly describes the man who often changes one occupation for another. Matthews says, "The great weakness of our young men is fickleness, and where one of them perseveres in a calling which he ought to abandon, a dozen abandon their calling when they ought to stick to it. The better the profession, the more likely they are to do this; for all those kinds of business which are surest in the end, which pay best in the long run, are slowest in beginning to yield a return." Therefore his advice is, choose an occupation and stick to it.

XX.

PLACE OF READING IN EDUCATION.

THERE is no substitute for reading. There are no means of culture so available to the masses as this. It can be taken up at odd moments, and can be continued a longer or shorter time, as circumstances demand. It is indispensable to all classes, but especially to the young. The habit of reading, established in early life, cannot fail to develop youth of both sexes into intelligent, useful citizens. Hence, reading, well chosen, becomes the duty of young people as really as going to school. They ought to choose it, as they would choose any other means of intellectual and moral improvement. It is really, in our day, one of the conditions of the highest success. Successful men and women have been readers, and they are readers now. To many of them, reading has been a school and college. They could not be college-bred, but reading gave them the equivalent of a liberal education on a certain line.

Daniel Webster said, "In my boyish days, there were two things I dearly loved, namely, reading and playing; passions that did not cease to struggle when boyhood was over."

He read and reread so carefully that he could repeat the contents of many books. He said, "We had so few books that to read them once was nothing; we thought they were all to be got by heart."

In early life, even, his conversation was proof of his reading—intelligent, graceful, and instructive. In this way he became versed in English literature. Frequent quotations from the British poets showed how thoroughly he read them. He loved to meet and converse with well-read men and women. Alluding to this class, he once remarked, "The man I like to converse with above all others is the man who can teach me something," and the reader was the only man who could do that.

At fifteen years of age, John Bright left school to assist his father in his business. He carried from the Quaker schools he attended a decided passion for reading, which converted leisure moments into profitable instead of idle ones. He selected the best English writers of both prose and poetry, seldom laying his head on his pillow at night without having read more or less from some favorite author. In this way he acquired that remarkable command of language for which he was known the world over. Though only a business man—a manufacturer—

he became a member of Parliament " first among the living orators of his country; more familiar with the dainty, outlying, recondite literature of the world than is shown by any other member of a house composed chiefly of college-bred men." Reading did it.

The relation of reading to practical education is appreciated by few. Dr. Johnson said, " The foundation of knowledge must be laid by reading." Lord Bacon wrote, " Reading maketh a full man; conference a ready man; and writing an exact man; and, therefore, if a man write little, he had need have a great

ONWARD TO FAME AND FORTUNE. 183

memory; if he confer little, he had need have a present wit; and if he read little, he had need have much cunning to seem to know that he doth not." Colton says, " By reading we enjoy the dead; by conversation, the living; and by contemplation, ourselves. Reading enriches the memory, conversation polishes the wit, and contemplation improves the judgment. Of these, reading is the most important, as it furnishes both the others."

It was his clear view of the relation of reading to culture that caused Fénelon to say, " If the riches of the Indies, or the crowns of all the kingdoms of Europe, were laid at my feet in exchange for my love of reading, I would spurn them all."

A course of well-selected reading introduces the reader to the brightest and best minds of all ages and countries.

Thomas Hood recognized his great indebtedness to reading for the distinguished place he occupied in the literary world. He said, "A natural turn for reading and intellectual pursuits probably preserved me from the moral shipwrecks so apt to befall those who are deprived in early life of their parental pilotage. My books kept me from the ring, the dog-pit, the tavern, and the saloon. The closest associate of Pope and Addison, the mind accustomed to the noble though silent discourse of Shakespeare and Milton, will hardly seek or put up with that sort of company."

FÉNELON.

In the most facetious way he described his intercourse with great minds, through the printed page, as follows:—

"It was my misfortune, with a tolerable appetite, to be condemned to lenten fare, like Sancho Panza, by my physician, to a diet, in fact, lower than any prescribed by the poor-law commissioners, all animal food, from a bullock to a rabbit, being strictly interdicted, as well as all fluids stronger than that which lays dust, washes pinafores, and waters polyanthus. But 'the feast of reason and the flow of soul' were still mine. Denied beef, I had Bulwer and Cowper; forbidden mutton, there was Lamb; and in lieu of pork, the great Bacon or Hogg.

"Then, as to beverage, it was hard, doubtless, for a Christian to set his face, like a Turk, against the juice of the grape. But, eschewing wine, I had still my Butler; and in the absence of liquor, all the choice spirits from Tom Brown to Tom Moore.

"Thus, though confined, physically, to the drink that drowns kittens, I quaffed, mentally, not merely the best of our own home-made, but the rich, racy, sparkling growths of France and Italy, Germany and Spain—the champagne of Molière, and the Monté Pulciano of Boccaccio, the hock of Schiller, and the sherry of Cervantes. Depressed bodily by the fluid that damps everything, I got intellectually elevated with Milton, a little merry with Swift, or rather jolly with Rabelais, whose 'Pantagruel,' by the way, is quite equal to the best gruel with rum in it."

Boys and girls without a love of reading, should cultivate it. They may have no love for grammar and arithmetic, but they must learn to love them. This is indispensable for their future good and usefulness. The same must be said of reading. Make it a habit. Persistent application thereto for a season will beget love of it, a love that will stay, assuring improvement from year to year. The lofty aim necessary to develop true manhood and womanhood may be the outcome of careful reading.

WHAT TO READ.

IT will not do to turn the average boy or girl loose in a miscellaneous library, for very likely the bad would be appropriated with the good. Their ignorance and inexperience, if not their love of the sensational and corrupt, would be almost sure to mislead. Books are companions, and should be carefully and wisely chosen. The counsel of guardians and superiors should be sought, in order to make a wise choice. It is a matter too important and serious to be disposed of thoughtlessly. Carlyle said, "Readers are not aware of the fact, but a fact it is of daily increasing magnitude, and already of terrible importance to readers, that their first grand necessity in reading is to be vigilantly and conscientiously select; and to know everywhere that books, like human souls, are actually divided into what we may call sheep and goats—the latter put inexorably on the left hand of the judge—and tending, every goat of them, at all moments, whither we know, and much to be avoided, and, if possible, ignored by all sane creatures."

Henry Ward Beecher wrote: " Books are the windows through which the soul looks out. A home without good books is like a room without windows. No man has a right to bring up his children without surrounding them with books, if he has the means to buy them. It is a wrong to his family. He cheats them. Children learn to read by being in the presence of books. The love of knowledge comes with reading and grows upon it, and the love of knowledge in a young mind is almost a warrant against the inferior excitement of passions and vices."

But to select the books —that is the difficulty. Their number is legion. Several thousand new ones produced in our country last year, and as many in England! Nearly as many brought out the year before, and only a few less the year before that. The number soon runs up to fifty thousand different volumes we may call *recent* publications. In our largest public libraries, one hundred thousand different volumes, two hundred thousand, even four or five hundred thousand, bewilder the reader.

MARIE ANTOINETTE.

Thousands of them are "wretched stuff" that young or old should never read. But there are a thousand times more good books, which are food for the mind, than the greatest reader can peruse in his lifetime. Is it a small matter to select the few he can read from the great multitude he has no time to examine? To select twenty-five or fifty books from the five thousand produced in our land last year is not an easy task. It is more difficult still to choose them from a library of two or three hundred thousand volumes.

Here is an opportunity to exercise judgment, wise discrimination, and criticism, supplemented by all the good advice parents, guardians, and other friends can bestow. Under these circumstances the choice of books is not easy.

but is one of the most important and difficult duties imposed upon the young or old. Yet it must be done, or reading will prove a curse.

Allison says of Marie Antoinette, "She had little education, read hardly anything but novels and romances, and had a fixed aversion, during her prosperous days, to every species of business or serious employment." All girls, and boys, too, who read hardly anything but novels and romances, "will possess little education," and the longer they read the less they will know.

Frederick the Great, one of the busiest and brightest rulers of past ages, regarded books as so indispensable to a successful reign, that he devoted two hours each day to reading. At each of his five palaces he had a well-chosen library, the libraries being alike, that his course of reading might be continued at either palace at which he was stopping. He bought and read only those books that furnished food for the mind. Professor Samuel Lee, late of the University of Cambridge, England, was a day-laborer in his youth. His love of reading the most instructive volumes made him remarkable before he was out of his teens. He never read novels; he had no time for that. He had not half the time he wanted for works that made him strong mentally. In his reading he found Latin

MARIE ANTOINETTE LED TO EXECUTION.

ONWARD TO FAME AND FORTUNE.

and Greek words, to understand which he learned those languages. Thence he passed to Hebrew, Chaldaic, Syriac, and other languages; and finally became a distinguished professor in the aforesaid university. Reading was an education to him.

John Foster said, "A man of ability, for the chief of his reading, should select such works as he feels are beyond his own power to have produced. What can other books do for him, but waste his time or augment his vanity? . . . Useless books we should lay aside, and make all possible good use of those from which we may reap some fruit."

We have in our midst an eminent illustration of what a wise choice of books in early life will do for one, in the success of that distinguished journalist and author, Charles Carleton Coffin. He had ordinary school advantages in his boyhood and youth, but he was a voracious reader, not of novels, but of history and biography, especially the former.

FREDERICK THE GREAT.

A book was his constant companion, and his wise choice in their selection led him up into the literary sphere, where he has distinguished himself. In his youth he began to write for the newspapers of Concord, in his native State, and before he was out of his teens, several of his fugitive pieces found their way into *Littell's Living Age*. No doubt he was born with a talent in the direction indicated, but well-chosen reading inspired that talent, and gave it direction. His signal success has been on the line of his early reading and composition, and it is easy to trace the connection between the two. To-day, Mr. Coffin is second to no writer in this country in the department which he has chosen. His industry, application, and observation have made the most possible out of his early reading. He never enjoyed a collegiate education, but Amherst College conferred the degree of A. M. upon him some twenty years ago in recognition of his literary triumphs.

HOW TO READ.

IF a person reads for amusement alone, it is of little consequence how he reads. He may read by the yard, ton, or acre, and the result will be the same—intellectual dwarfishness; but if he reads for culture, as he should, his method of reading is of the greatest importance. Wirt said, "Get a habit, a passion for reading: not flying from book to book, with the squeamish caprice of a literary epicure, but read systematically, closely, thoughtfully, analyzing every subject as you go along, and laying it up carefully and safely in your memory. It is only by this mode that your information will be at the same time extensive, accurate, and useful." The omnivorous reader rushes from one book to another, so that there is no time for mental digestion. Even if there is food in his reading, it is neither masticated nor assimilated.

Coleridge divided readers into four classes: "The first may be compared to an hour-glass; their reading being as the sand, it runs in and it runs out, and leaves not a vestige behind. A second class resembles a sponge, which imbibes everything, and returns it nearly in the same state, only a little dirtier. A third class is like a jelly bag which allows all that is pure to pass away, and retains only the refuse and the dregs. The fourth class may be compared to the slaves in the diamond mines of Golconda, who, casting aside all that is worthless, preserve only the pure gem." The fourth class alone is respectable. How to read so as to belong to it is worthy of the closest attention.

Benjamin Franklin belonged to the fourth class of readers, pre-eminently so. He became a reader when a mere child, always reading slowly, critically, and, therefore, profitably. Beginning with "Pilgrim's Progress," he read "Burton's Historical Collections," "Plutarch's Lives," "Defoe's Essay on Projects," and Dr. Mather's "Essay To Do Good." In his manhood, Dr. Franklin wrote to a son of Dr. Mather: "I have always set a greater value on the character of a doer of good, than on any other kind of reputation, and, if I have been, as you seem to think, a useful citizen, the public owes the advantage of it to that book."

He was not more than twelve or thirteen years of age, when he read with pen in hand, and a note-book in which he jotted down references to particular facts and statements, and thoughts inspired by the book read. He continued this practice through life. In his mature years, he wrote to a young lady as follows:—

"I would advise you to read with a pen in your hand, and enter in a little book short hints of what you find that is curious, or that may be useful; for this will be the best method of imprinting such particulars on your memory, where they will be ready, either for practice on some future occasion, if they are matters of utility, or, at least, to adorn and improve your conversation, if they are, rather, points of curiosity; and, as many of the terms of science are such as you cannot have met with in your common reading, and may, therefore, be unacquainted with, I think it would be well for you to have a good dictionary at hand, to consult immediately when you meet with a word you do not comprehend the precise meaning of."

The foregoing advice was given one hundred and fifty years ago, but it is just as good counsel for readers to-day as it was then. Indeed, change of circumstances, which we have partially considered, adds force and value to the advice. It is the only way of reading to the best advantage, for it fixes the attention, assists method, strengthens purpose, and charges memory with its sacred trust.

Rev. Joseph Cook writes: "I have learned to rely on the margins of the books that I read as being themselves my best note-books. Of course I am speaking now only of the volumes which are my own property. These I am, perhaps, scandalously free in marking, and so every ordinary volume that I have in my library becomes a note-book. Let young men—and, we would add, young ladies, too—be taught to keep commonplace books, and especially to converse concerning what they read."

This counsel of Mr. Cook should have great weight, coming, as it does, from one of the most remarkable men of our age, or any age. He was a great reader even before he abandoned short clothes. He read science, literature, history, biography, and even metaphysics, in his boyhood. In academy and college he kept up his habit of systematic reading. The thorough manner in which he read made him master of every subject. Even now, reading is scarcely second to what is called study in his method of public instruction. He is a lecturer, known the world over. But for reading he would not have dreamed of his present field of labor, and, but for it, he would not continue now to be a public instructor.

The advantage of note-books over marginal references is so great that the latter can scarcely be recommended to young people who own few of the books they read. But the excellent habit of reading critically, with pen, or pencil, and note-book in hand, should be insisted upon everywhere; for it is good for both young and old, male and female, learned and unlearned—all classes who read.

The author once recommended this careful method of reading to a youth of fourteen years. He was a farmer's son, at that time expecting to be a farmer through life. In addition to reading with pen and note-book in hand, he was advised to write at least one short sentence in his note-book each day, upon some subject uppermost in his thoughts. He adopted this whole method of reading heartily, and, within a few months, his desire for learning became irrepressible.

He began to talk about a liberal education, even when he had no idea that his father would ever consent to such a measure. At the end of two years, his desire for a collegiate and theological course of study was too strong to accept denial. His father consented, fearing to take the responsibility of saying no. He prepared himself for his life-work, was an able and popular preacher at the outset, became a doctor of divinity at forty years of age, and is now one of the most popular preachers in our country, the pastor of a large church in a New England city. The right way of reading laid the foundation of his remarkable career.

WHAT ONE BOOK MAY DO FOR A YOUTH.

A BOOK that starts a young person off in a life career, good or bad, is a power. Nothing is more to be coveted or dreaded. The inspiration of a single book, or a few, has made preachers, poets, philosophers, authors, and statesmen. On the other hand, the demoralization of a book has sometimes made infidels, profligates, and criminals.

Benjamin Franklin read an infidel book, by Shaftesbury, at fifteen years of age, and it demoralized his religious opinions for years. But for the excellent books he read before, his infidelity would have blasted his life. As it was, his influence became baneful over two associates, whom he made as thorough skeptics as himself. One of them became a drunkard, and died in disgrace; the other lived without moral principle, holding the Christian religion in contempt. In ripe manhood, the good lessons of his boyhood, in a Christian home, asserted themselves, and Franklin confessed his grave mistake, and became a defender of Christianity.

In his early manhood, Abraham Lincoln had several boon companions, who were infidels, and they influenced him to read Paine's "Age of Reason," and

Volney's "Ruins." The reading of these two books caused him to doubt the truth of the Bible, so that, for a time, he was at one with his companions in their hostility to religion. He even wrote an essay upon the unreliability of the Bible, which he read to his associates. But, after a few years, he saw his folly, renounced all skeptical opinions, and returned to his early familiarity with, and confidence in, the Scriptures. Those two books well-nigh unsettled his moral character, and robbed the republic of a good president.

In his youth the late President Garfield worked for a "blacksalter," a few miles from his home. His employer owned "Marryat's Novels," "Sinbad the Sailor," "The Pirate's Own Book," "Jack Halyard," "Lives of Eminent Criminals," and, perhaps, one or two other books of the same character. Young Garfield read them with avidity. He read them over and over. They opened a new and untried world before him. The life of a sailor fascinated him, and he resolved to go to sea, but his wise and tender mother put obstacles in his way. The books had made an inroad upon his love of mother and home, and he was fully determined to try a seafaring life. His mother saw that the books had sowed the seeds of evil in his heart, and that he had started on the road to ruin. With wise management and the aid of a mutual friend, when a serious illness had prostrated him, his mother induced him to go to school and not to sea; and here was the turning point of his life. Two or three years before his death, he declared, in public, that the influence of those few books were never wholly eliminated from his mind.

On the other hand, a single good book has often conspired with good counsels and good principles to make life a success. It has started the reader off upon a career of honor and usefulness. Rev. John Sharp said, "Shakespeare and the Bible have made me Archbishop of York." John Wesley claimed that "The Imitation of Christ," and Taylor's "Holy Living and Dying," determined both his calling and character. Henry Martyn was made a missionary by reading the lives of Brainard and Carey. Pope was indebted to Homer for his poetical inspiration, it being the origin of his English "Iliad," as he said. Bentham read "Telemachus" in his youth, and, many years afterward, he said, "That romance may be regarded as the foundation of my whole character." Goethe became a poet in consequence of reading "The Vicar of Wakefield." Cary was moved to go on a mission to the heathen by reading the "Voyages of Captain Cook." Samuel Drew said that reading Locke's "Essay on the Understanding," decided the aim and achievements of his life. The lives of Washington and Henry Clay awakened aspirations in Lincoln's soul that "led him on to fortune." Joseph Lancaster read "Clarkson on the Slave Trade" when he was fourteen years of age, and it fired him with enthusiasm to teach the negroes in the West Indies. Without the knowledge of his parents he went there and commenced labors for their mental and moral improvement. His parents learned where he was and sent for him; but his heart was thoroughly in sympathy with benevolent work, and he opened a school for the poor at home. So great was his success, that the town, after a few years, erected a commodious building for his school; and here was the foundation of the system of education known as the Bell and Lancaster system.

Blount says, "The gifted men of to-day, who are prominent in all positions of life, read a far less number of books than do their sons and daughters. Look back over the history of the past. Did Shakespeare have many books to read? Did Spenser, Chaucer, Homer, Plutarch, read a hundred novels every year? Take the signers of the Declaration of Independence in our own country. What were they in a literary way? Men who were fed mentally upon the Bible, Pilgrim's Progress, and Josephus; men descended from a hardy Christian race, whose one book for study and recreation contained the Divine Revelation and the Psalms of David; and could there be a set of men collected the wide world over, of finer dignity, of nobler sense, of truer heart?"

DR. SAMUEL JOHNSON.

Dr. Johnson has been quoted as saying, "Beware of the man of one book," as if he were putting in a plea to read many books. But Johnson did not say or mean that. What he did say was, "Beware of the man of one book. Beware of the man who knows anything well. *He is a dangerous antagonist.*" The reading of a single book thoroughly is better than the superficial reading of many, was really what he said. He who knows one book well is better equipped than he who reads many in a cursory way. Demosthenes was a great admirer of the history of Thucydides. He fell in love with its plan and style, and resolved to be benefited thereby. He recopied the work eight times in order to make himself master of the style. That persistent effort to improve his own style proved of greater advantage to him than the reading of a hundred volumes in the usual way.

The foregoing does not commend the student of a single book at the expense of all others; by no means. In showing what it is possible for one book to do, the wise use of a few or many is not questioned.

ART OF THINKING.

READING without thinking is as unwise as it is prevalent. It is thinking that appropriates the knowledge a book contains for the reader's use. Indeed, it is the book's knowledge that inspires thought. The reader cannot think, unless the book furnishes something to think about. Thousands of books are "trashy," and provide no useful knowledge, and, therefore, are not suited to make readers think. They are wonderfully adapted to prevent thinking. Reading for amusement only does not require thought, and there is the trouble; it forestalls thinking, and thereby hinders mental growth. It is only by thinking that mind grows. If a book is too light and useless to inspire thought, it can contribute nothing to intellectual advancement.

Air and exercise promote physical health and strength, by assisting the digestion and assimilation of food, so that food actually becomes muscle, and bone, and blood—a part of one's self. In this way beef and bread become a part of the body's composition, so thoroughly are they assimilated. Our bodies may change every seven years, so that we may have new bodies; but it is only because other beef and bread have made other bone, blood, and muscle. They are our own bodies as really as ever. It is precisely so with the mind. What air and exercise are to the body, such is thinking to the intellect. The more critical thought, the more mental growth and strength; the less thought, the less growth and power. The mind was made to think with, as feet were made to walk with; and as failing to use the feet will leave them useless, so failing to think the best we can will enervate and dwarf the intellect. Thinking is the soul of intellectual life.

Sidney says, "Thinking nurseth thinking;" that is, thought propagates itself. Write down one thought upon paper, and another treads upon its heels; then another, and another, until the article, essay, or book is complete. The thinker wonders. His mind is deeper than he supposed. As another says, "There is a well of thought there which has no bottom; the more you draw from it, the more clear and fruitful will it be. If you neglect to think yourself, and use other people's thoughts, giving them utterance only, you will never know what you are capable of. At first, your ideas may come out in lumps, homely and shapeless, but no matter; time and perseverance will arrange and polish them. Learn to think, and you will learn to write; the more you think, the better you will express your ideas."

Thinking while reading is the only way to separate the chaff from the wheat. It is the only mental winnowing process known to man. It sifts knowledge, separating the good from the bad. Reading systematically and critically, with pen and note-book in hand, assists the sifting process essentially. These helps are important because thinking is possible. Were there no thinking, there would be no need of analysis and note-taking.

Reading for culture fosters the art of thinking; and then the latter magnifies the former. It is retroactive; it both gives and takes. Patrick Henry thirsted for knowledge, but saw no way of satisfying his desire except by reading. Reading promoted thinking, and thinking kept him reading. In this way he went on and up until his eloquence electrified the nation, and his statesmanship became a prominent factor in founding the republic.

Strong convictions, with courage to express and defend them, promote the habit of critical thinking. Luther was an excellent example of this truth. He believed with all his soul, and would stake his life on what he believed, at any time. He would appear before the august tribunal at Worms, though "as many devils as there were tiles on the houses" should oppose his way. This spirit made him a great thinker. A look into his eyes showed a great mind behind them. It was a thought from his glowing intellect that shot like a meteor across the world, illuminating it with the light of the Reformation. He was a strong thinker because he had strong convictions and courage to maintain them.

It promotes thinking to read and study what is greater than we are now. It is good for the mind to be kept on the stretch; to be obliged to labor and struggle to master a subject, book, or enterprise. Intellect strengthens by surmounting obstacles; it is the only way it can grow. To dwell upon studies that are below our present abilities, is the way to suppress thought, and dwarf the mental faculties. The author who does better thinking than is possible for us is the author to read. If he is original, so much the better. Emerson says, "It makes a great difference to the force of any sentence whether there be a man behind it or no." But "mind makes the man," so that we may well change the sentence to read, "It makes a great difference to the force of any sentence whether there be a thinker behind it or no." The author is no greater than his book or essay. His book is himself, whether valuable or poor, for he has emptied his mind into it. If it be little, it is because his mind is little. A great thinker makes a great book, which is always improving and elevating to read.

Close observation promotes thought also. The habit of critically examining inventions, enterprises, machinery, documents, books, and other things, so as to understand them, sets one to thinking. Here, again, observation inspires thought, and thought improves observation. The most observing men and women are the best thinkers. The closer their observation, the clearer their thoughts; the sharper their discrimination, the more original and crisp their ideas.

Edwards well said, "Think, as well as read; and when you read yield not your mind to the passive impressions which others may please to make upon them. Hear what they have to say; but examine it, weigh it, and judge for yourselves. This will enable you to make a right use of books; to use them as helpers, not as guides, to your understanding; as counsellors, not as dictators, of what you are to think and believe."

Forty-three years ago a Scotch lad emigrated, with his parents, to Pittsburg, Pennsylvania, and settled there. The boy was penniless then, but is worth from fifteen to twenty million dollars now, and his character is worth more than his money. His name is Andrew Carnegie. He had few school privileges, for at the early age of fourteen he was compelled to quit school forever, to earn his daily bread. He could read more or less every day, however, as he had been accustomed to do from childhood; but most of all, he was a close thinker for one of his age. He was never satisfied without knowing the reason of things. On this account he made rapid progress in learning the art of telegraphy at fourteen years of age. Two years after his father died, and Andrew became the sole support of his mother and brother. He rose higher and higher, and before he was twenty-one years old he became superintendent of the Pittsburg Division of the great Pennsylvania Railroad. It was done by thinking. His achievements were masterful because they were born of thought. He is the chief owner of steel and iron works in Pittsburg that have a capital of twenty million dollars. He makes speeches and writes books as readily as he makes steel and iron. His "Triumphant Democracy" is one of the best books published in our country. In a recent address to the students of a commercial college in Pittsburg, he advised the young men out of his own experience, thus:—

"Avoid drink, avoid speculation, avoid endorsements. Aim high. For the question, 'What *must* I do for my employer?' substitute 'What *can* I do?' Begin to save early. Capitalists trust the saving young man. Concentrate your energy, thought, and capital. Fight it out on one line."

That is his own brief biography. Only he who understands the art of thinking could live such a life; there are as many thoughts as deeds in it. Books did much for him, and he has shown his estimate of reading to the world by giving forty thousand dollars to his native town, Dunfirmline, Scotland, for a free library; five hundred thousand dollars for another library in Pittsburg, where he lives; two hundred and fifty thousand dollars for another in Allegheny City, and two hundred and fifty thousand dollars for still another in Edinburgh, Scotland—all of which show that he has not ceased to think. His heart is as large as his purse, for he is a genial, thoughtful, Christian gentleman.

READING NEWSPAPERS.

A FIRST-CLASS newspaper is a marvel of the age. It is as indispensable to modern civilization as school or college. Both old and young need it. It is found everywhere—in shop, store, office, family, school, restaurant, hotel, and on the train, steamer, and vessel. It commands attention, and gets it. Intelligent men and women welcome it. As it is a fruitful source of knowledge to every careful reader, no youth of either sex can afford to neglect it. To discard it would be to neglect one important element of success.

There are over twenty thousand journals and magazines in our country, about twenty-five hundred of which are daily papers, having a circulation not far from ten million copies. The aggregate circulation of all these periodicals annually must reach the enormous amount of three billions, or fifty copies to each man, woman, and child in the nation. Hence the great power of journalism in our land to-day. Dr. Porter, of Yale College, says that journalism "is very largely the educator and controller of public sentiment, and hence has become a most potent instrument and depository of power. The editor is at this moment, apparently, more influential than preachers, judges, or legislators. He is mightier than all these united." If this be true, the sooner it is recognized as an important element of American culture, the better it will be for the young of our day, and the better, also, for the future of our growing country.

But there is much that is "trashy" in our periodical literature, it is said. Very true; and much that is "flashy," also; but such should be avoided. The care and discrimination that will select suitable books from the thousands that fill our libraries, will readily choose a first-class journal for the family, school, or office; and only such should be selected for instruction and culture.

Experience and ability have conspired to make journalism the vehicle of knowledge and mental discipline that it is. Talents of the highest order have been, and still are, employed upon the newspaper. The names of Franklin, Otis, Adams, Hancock, Warren, Buckingham, Bryant, Greeley, Raymond, Leavitt, Beecher, Wilson, Prime, not to mention the renowned among living editors, prove that the ablest scholars and statesmen have consecrated themselves to this method of elevating the human race. For this reason there is much information and literature in the newspaper as valuable as any that is found in books. Indeed, at the present day, book after book appears, the contents of which were first published in the newspaper and magazine. So valuable has the newspaper become in

ONWARD TO FAME AND FORTUNE.

this regard, that it, instead of the treatise, is the guide of thousands in special directions. The clergyman, lawyer, physician, surgeon, merchant, teacher, salesman, mechanic, farmer, and so on, depend upon the periodical instead of the book for instruction in their respective lines of work. The literary men and women of our land, as well as statesmen, make great use of newspapers. It is said that President Garfield left, at the time of his death, several large volumes of scraps from newspapers, so carefully and systematically arranged that he could turn at once to any subject required, and find what he had on that topic. The same was true of Charles Sumner, Henry Wilson, and other public men. The journals discuss the questions and issues of the times, giving the labors and opinions of experts thereon, becoming, thereby, indispensable for reference.

It is a valuable practice for youth of both sexes to adopt, pasting in scrap-books such articles, facts, and discussions from newspapers as may prove of real value in after years. There is discipline and improvement in the habit itself, even if the scraps should not be available hereafter. The earlier young people adopt the plan, the richer will be its contribution to age.

JOHN GREENLEAF WHITTIER.

But a more important use of the newspaper is to learn what is doing in all the nations of the earth. Books treat of the past; history is the record of past events; but newspapers disclose what is transpiring now in the world. With the aid of telegraph, telephone, and cable, the first-class newspaper, morning and evening edition, furnishes a bird's-eye view of what the different people of the world are doing to-day. We sit in our homes, and from north, south, east, and west there pours in to us a current of information daily, that can be obtained in no other way. It is such information as no one can afford to do without. They cannot rank in society as intelligent, influential citizens without it. Young people overlook one important means of preparation for their life-work when they neglect this source of information. They must regard the newspaper as a means of education. Many schools and higher seminaries of learning in the United States have introduced it as a branch of study. History, geography, biography, political economy, and other things are taught in this way, and it is proving a very valuable method of equipping youth for their life-

Whittier's birth place

work. "Shall girls read newspapers?" some one inquires. Yes. Unladylike as it may appear to some, girls ought to read newspapers as much as boys. The knowledge to be gleaned therefrom is as good and inspiring for one as the other. That girls do not read the papers, especially daily papers, as much as the boys, is too true; and it is equally true that they are not as well posted as boys are on the condition of the world. Perhaps fifty dollars annually are spent in some families in secular and religious journals, without even a thought that they may contribute to the education of daughters. Possibly some parents prefer that daughters should not read the daily journal; but they should, nevertheless. As Dr. Porter says, "The comprehensive survey which the morning news gives us of what happened yesterday in every part of the world enlarges immensely the intellectual

ONWARD TO FAME AND FORTUNE. 199

vision," and girls ought to share this enlarged vision with the boys. If that city belle had read the daily papers carefully, she would not have asked her country cousin, on visiting her, "Which cow gives the cream?" Reading newspapers fortifies common sense. The reading of a newspaper—the *Newburyport Free Press*—did much to shape the career of our beloved New England poet, John G. Whittier. His humble Christian home provided him in boyhood with choice reading, and thus nurtured a literary taste; but the newspaper under the management of William Lloyd Garrison brought his young, quiet life into connection with the human race in the interest of liberty. Besides, the journal had an excellent poet's corner, where the poems of Bryant, Willis, Moore, and others, appeared. In this he became so intensely interested that he read the poems again and again until he had them by heart.

That the poetic corner exerted a decided influence upon his mind and heart, appears from the fact that he soon began to write poetry, and, at seventeen years of age, one of his poems appeared in that delightful poet's corner. That the prose part of the paper, also, had a moulding influence upon him is evident from the fact that he imbibed its anti-slavery sentiments, and became in early manhood, not only an abolitionist, but America's "Poet of Freedom."

Best of all are the moral results of well-chosen newspaper reading. It is the only reliable way of tracing the providence of God in our day. To the Christian, the newspaper is the record of God's doings on the earth. With the Bible in one hand, and the able daily journal in the other, he has such proof of the fulfillment of prophecy and the progress of truth, as the best commentaries cannot furnish. The newspaper is our commentary upon divine providence, recording events, discoveries, inventions, advances in science and art, the triumphs of industry and genius, and a host of other things that explain providence beyond what our forefathers ever dreamed of. So we claim that the best newspaper is a providential record for Christians to study. Nothing can be a substitute for it. It stands by itself, a remarkable institution in an age of wonderful inventions and discoveries, commanding attention, and challenging respect as the moulder of public opinion.

XXI.

HONESTY.

THERE is a distinction in the use of the four words, honesty, uprightness, integrity, and probity; and yet, in their popular use, they embrace the same correctness of principle and conduct. "We look for *honesty* and *uprightness* in citizens; it sets every question at rest between man and man. We look for *integrity* and *probity* in statesmen, or such as have to adjust the rights of many." Yet all of these persons are alike in moral *soundness* and virtuous living. So we select honesty from the four words as the more common, though homely, using it in the highest sense as the poet has it:—

"An honest man's the noblest work of God."

When Lamartine introduced the honored De l'Eure to the tumultuous populace of Paris in 1848, he said, "Listen, citizens! It is sixty years of a pure life that is to address you." Whatever more and higher De l'Eure might have been, he was *honest*. Such ought to be every son and daughter of Adam. Sir Benjamin Rudyard once said, "No man is bound to be rich or great—no, nor to be wise; but every man is bound to be honest." Therefore, honesty is more important than money, greatness, or wisdom. A valuable possession, surely!

A merchant engaged in an extensive wholesale business pointed a customer to a young man in his store.

"That young man," said he, "is my banker."

Perceiving that his friend did not comprehend the drift of his remark, he added, "He has the entire control of my financial matters. I have too much on my mind to be perplexed with them."

"Do you not fear to commit such a trust to a youth?" responded the customer. "No business man ought to run such a risk in these days of embezzlement and defalcation."

The merchant replied: "I have no fears; James came into my store when he was not more than twelve years of age, and he has proved to me that he is strictly honest. I would trust him as quick as I would my minister. He could defraud me of fifty thousand dollars if he were disposed, and make his escape before I could help myself. But I have no fears."

That young man was rich without having money. Such a character was worth more to him "than gold, yea, than much fine gold." It was something to get wealth with. Even Mirabeau said, "If there were no honesty, it would be invented as a means of getting wealth." We know that some business men deny this, and say that success cannot be achieved by strict honesty, but we scout such a conclusion.

No! Such a reign of immorality is not necessary. The solid and useful virtue of honesty is highly practicable. "Nothing is profitable that is dishonest," is a truthful maxim. "Virtue alone is invincible." "I would give ten thousand dollars for your reputation for uprightness," said a sharper to an upright tradesman, "for I could make a hundred thousand dollars with it." Honesty succeeds; dishonesty fails. The biographer of Amos Lawrence says, "His integrity stands absolutely unimpeached, without spot or blemish. He seemed ever to have a reverence for right, unalloyed, unfaltering, supreme; a moral perception and moral sensibility, which kept him from deviating a hair's breadth from what he saw and felt to be his duty. It was this that constituted the strength of his character, *and was one of the great secrets of his success.*"

The biographer of Samuel Budgett speaks of his transparent truthfulness throughout his business career, and among many incidents, he relates the following: "In Mr. Budgett's early days, pepper was under a heavy tax; and, in the trade, universal tradition said that out of the trade everybody expected pepper to be mixed. In the shop stood a cask labeled 'P. D.,' containing something very like pepper dust, wherewith it was used to mix the pepper before sending it forth to serve the public. The trade tradition had obtained for the hypocritical P. D. a place among the standard articles of the shop, and on the strength of that tradition it was vended for pepper by men who thought they were honest. But as Samuel went forward in life, his ideas on trade morality grew clearer. This P. D. began to give him much discomfort. He thought upon it till he was satisfied that, when all that could be said was weighed, the thing was wrong. Arrived at this conclusion, he felt that no blessing could be upon the place while it was there. He instantly decreed that P. D. should perish. It was night; but back he went to the shop, took his hypocritical cask, carried it forth to the quarry, then staved it, and scattered P. D. among the clods, slags, and stones. He returned with a light heart."

Such examples, which might be indefinitely multiplied, disprove the unfounded plea that strict honesty cannot achieve success in this wicked age of the world. They illustrate, also, the declarations of Holy Writ:—

"The integrity of the upright shall guide them; but the perverseness of the transgressors shall destroy them."

"He that walketh uprightly, walketh surely; but he that perverteth his ways shall be known."

A few years ago a lady entered a store in Boston, looked at some goods, and walked out without making a purchase.

"Why did not that lady purchase those goods?" inquired the proprietor of his clerk.

"Because, sir, she wanted Middlesex cloths," the clerk answered.

"And why did you not show her the next pile, and call them Middlesex?" continued the unprincipled trader.

"Because, sir, I knew they were not Middlesex," was the emphatic answer of an honest young man.

"Young man," said the merchant, "if you are so particular, and can't bend a little to circumstances, you will never do for me."

The clerk's response is worthy of a high place in history:—

"Very well, sir; if I must tell falsehoods in order to keep my place, I must lose it; that is all."

He left the store, and that God who requires as strict honesty in the warehouse as in the church, led him forth to prosperity. He became a leading merchant in a western city, while his dishonest employer became a bankrupt, and died in poverty.

Society never needed uncompromising honesty more than it does to-day. Young people never needed it more in going out into the great world than the young people of our day, for they will meet temptations to dishonesty everywhere. Designing and intriguing men who "have an eye to the main chance," and who claim that "every man is for himself," will press their way clear to the front.

Mean, brazen, unscrupulous, licentious, desperate, despicable men and women will be met on life's great thoroughfares, but if thoroughly mailed with unyielding honesty, having a conscience void of offence, these tempters will be powerless, for the highest authority declares, "Every man is tempted when he is drawn away of *his own* lust, and enticed." If they are right inside, the temptations outside will be as though they were not.

The honest man may be unfortunate. In the ups and downs of business he may become embarrassed, and even ruined financially, but he cannot be ruined morally. His unbending integrity is a guarantee against that; and, at the same time, it gathers a host of sympathizing friends around him in the hour of his adversity. A conflagration may sweep away his last dollar, or a sudden financial crash may leave him penniless, but all is not lost; the best survives the wreck.

Honesty will never perish; and noble hearts bring their loving tributes of respect in the dark hour of misfortune. *Honesty triumphs.*

WHAT HONESTY DID FOR ABRAHAM LINCOLN.

HE was called "Honest Abe." This *sobriquet* was given to him at New Salem, Illinois, whither he went to take charge of the "country store" of one Orfutt, in 1831. He was about twenty-two years of age, awkward, bashful, but strictly upright. He took no advantage of the ignorance or necessities of customers, but represented goods just as they were, gave scripture measure and weight, and always hastened to correct mistakes.

One day he sold a bill of goods, amounting to two dollars and six cents, to Mrs. Duean, living more than two miles away. On looking over the account again in the evening, before closing the store, he found that Mrs. Duean paid him six cents too much. "That must be corrected to-night," he said to himself; so, as soon as he had closed the shutters for the night, he posted away with the six cents surplus to her house. She was preparing to retire when he knocked at the door, and was very much surprised, on opening it, to see Orfutt's clerk standing there. Apologizing for the mistake, Lincoln deposited the six cents in her hand, and slept all the better that night for having corrected the error.

At another time, a woman came to the store late in the evening, when Lincoln was closing it, for a half pound of tea, which was weighed in haste. Immediately after she left, Lincoln locked the store and went home. On returning the next morning, his attention was called to the scales which had a four-ounce weight, instead of eight in them. He knew at once that he must have given the woman a quarter instead of a half pound of tea. Weighing another quarter of a pound, he closed the store and delivered it to the customer, asking her pardon, before commencing the labors of the day.

Such examples of honesty were not overlooked by the public. Men and women talked about them, and extolled the author of them. They led, also, to something more. In that part of the country, at that time, various games prevailed in which two sides enlisted; and it was the custom to appoint an umpire for each game. Lincoln became the universal umpire, both sides insisting upon his appointment on account of his fairness. His honesty won the confidence of all.

One Henry McHenry planned a horse-race, and applied to Lincoln to act as judge.

"No; I've done with that," answered Lincoln.

"But you must," urged McHenry.

"I must not, and I *will not*," responded Lincoln, with much emphasis. "This horse-racing business is all wrong."

"Just this once; never will ask you again," continued McHenry.

"Well, remember, 'just this once' it is," was Lincoln's conclusion, thinking it might be the best way to make a corrupting practice of "wild western life" unpopular. He acted as judge, and the party against whom his judgment weighed, said, "Lincoln is the fairest man I ever had to deal with. If he is in this country when I die, I want him to be my administrator, for he is the only man I ever met with that was wholly and unselfishly honest."

Dr. Holland said, "When Lincoln terminated his labors for Offutt, every one trusted him. He was judge, arbitrator, referee, umpire, authority on all disputes, games, and matches of man-flesh and horse-flesh; a pacificator in all quarrels; everybody's friend; the best natured, the most sensible, the best informed, the most modest and unassuming, the kindest, gentlest, roughest, strongest, best young fellow in all New Salem and the region round about."

This is a just encomium; but it never could have been said of him but for his unbending honesty, a quality for which he was known from his boyhood. The honest boy makes the honest man.

When Lincoln became a lawyer, he carried to the bar this habitual honesty. His associates were often surprised by his utter disregard of self-interest, while they could but admire his conscientious defence of what he considered right. One day a stranger called to secure his services.

"State your case," said Lincoln. A history of the case was given, when Lincoln astonished him by saying:—

"I cannot serve you; for you are wrong, and the other party is right."

"That is none of your business, if I hire and pay you for taking the case," retorted the man.

"Not my business!" exclaimed Lincoln. "My business is never to defend wrong, if I *am* a lawyer. I never undertake a case that is manifestly wrong."

"Well, you can make trouble for the fellow," added the applicant.

"Yes," replied Lincoln, fully aroused; "there is no doubt but that I can gain the case for you, and set a whole neighborhood at loggerheads. I can distress a widowed mother and her six fatherless children, and thereby get for you six hundred dollars, which rightly belong as much to the woman and her children as they do to you; but I won't do it."

"Not for any amount of pay?" continued the stranger.

"Not for all you are worth," replied Lincoln. "You must remember that some things which are legally right are not morally right. I shall not take your case."

"I don't care a snap whether you do or not!" exclaimed the man, angrily, starting to go.

"I will give you a piece of advice without charge," added Lincoln. "You seem to be a sprightly, energetic man. I would advise you to make six hundred dollars some other way."

He undertook the celebrated Patterson trial, a case of murder, supposing the accused was innocent. Before the evidence was all in, he became satisfied that the man was guilty, and withdrew from the case, leaving his partner to conduct it. The accused was acquitted, but Lincoln would not take a cent of the one thousand dollars paid to his partner for services.

Lincoln's professional life abounded with similar incidents, leading Judge David Davis to say, "The framework of his mental and moral being was honesty. He never took from a client, even when the cause was gained, more than he thought the service was worth and the client could afford to pay."

The time came, in 1860, when Lincoln's honesty was needed to save the nation. Slavery threatened to overthrow the Republic unless it was allowed to become universal. North and South there was distrust, alienation, and apprehension. The retiring President had governed for the South, in the interest of bondage. Loyal citizens had lost confidence in public men. The next President must be one whose character would challenge the respect and confidence of loyal people, or the ship of state would go under in the fearful storm gathering. Abraham Lincoln was the man. He could be trusted. Friends of the Union gave him their implicit confidence, and became a unit. His honesty had reached its highest value, and saved the Republic by destroying slavery.

POWER OF CHARACTER.

CHARACTER must not be confounded with reputation. Character is what a man is; reputation may be what he is not. Character is one's intrinsic value; reputation is what is thought of him—his value in the market of public opinion. Hence, character is stable and enduring; while, as another has said, "The reputation of a man is like his shadow; it sometimes follows and sometimes precedes him; it is sometimes longer and sometimes shorter than himself."

Character is indispensable. Every one is in duty bound to possess it. It is not optional with us to cultivate it or not, as we please: it is a solemn obligation. Professor Blackie, of the University of Edinburgh, said to a class of young men: "Money is not needful; power is not needful; cleverness is not needful; fame is not needful; liberty is not needful; even health is not the one thing needful; but character alone is that which can truly save us, and if we are not saved in this sense, we must certainly be damned." Smiles urges the same truth: "Everyone is in duty bound to aim at reaching the highest standard of character; not to become the richest in means, but in spirit; not the greatest in worldly position, but in true honor; not the most intellectual, but the most virtuous; not the most powerful and influential, but the most truthful, upright and honest."

Character is greater, even, than intellect. It is the most valuable possession a youth ever acquires. Without it he is poor, though he may have amassed a million dollars. The most abject pauper on earth is the man without character. He may live in a stately mansion and flourish his magnificent turn-out, and obsequious fools may applaud him, but he is a moral tramp, nevertheless, more perilous to society on account of his money, and to himself also.

Every youth, then, should know that it is his and her sacred duty to make unblemished character; that is an obligation they cannot shirk. It may not be their duty to be wise and learned, or to be senators or senators' wives, but it is their duty to possess spotless characters. Anything short of this cheats society and robs God. The youth who denies this truth, and lives indifferent to the worth of character, will probably drift along with the current of events until the star of his destiny reaches its zenith on the meridian of Sodom.

MARTIN LUTHER.

Character is also power, and it is this thought that we specially emphasize now. It is said that "knowledge is power," but knowledge may exist without character. Add character to it and we have invincible power. Luther said, "The prosperity of a country depends, not on the abundance of the revenues, nor on the strength of its fortifications, nor on the beauty of its public buildings; but it consists in the number of its cultivated citizens, its men of education, enlightenment and character. Here are to be found its true interests, its chief strength, its real power."

When Jonathan Goodhue, of New York City, died, the din of traffic was hushed in the streets. Commerce felt the loss keenly, and merchant and artisan crowded around his bier at the funeral. The mayor and other officials were there. The poor and unfortunate were there, too. None were so high and none so lowly as not to do him reverence. His character drew them there. The preacher said, on that occasion: "It is the recognized worth of private character which has extorted this homage. It is the man himself, the pure, high-minded, righteous man who adorned our nature, who dignified the mercantile profession, who was superior to his station, his riches, his exposures, and made the common virtues more respected and venerable than shining talents or public honors. This was the power of his life."

It was Washington's personal character, more than his skill as a general, or his ability as a statesman, that enshrined him in the hearts of his countrymen. John Adams was President in 1798, when it was expected that France would declare war against the United States, and he wrote to Washington, saying, "We must have your name, if you will permit us to use it; there will be more efficacy in it than in an army." This was a greater tribute to his character than that of a general in the War of the Revolution, who declared that Washington's presence "doubled the strength of the army." Moral qualities live longer than intellectual ones because they have more power over the hearts of men, and for this reason the name of Washington is connected with more places and events, in this country and Europe, than that of Napoleon or Cæsar.

Smiles says, "Character is one of the greatest motive powers in the world. In its noblest embodiments, it exemplifies human nature in its highest forms, for it exhibits man at his best."

CHARACTER AS CAPITAL.

CHARACTER must not be undervalued as capital. It has been said, "When poverty is your inheritance, virtue must be your capital," and many young men have learned the truth of this maxim from personal experience. They have found that they started in business just as well without money as they could have done with it. Some years ago, a youth of sixteen years was advised to sell bread on commission, because it would be more profitable to him than to drive a bread cart on monthly wages. He had learned the business of a baker, and had sold bread from a cart for several months.

"But I have no money to invest in horse and wagon," he replied; "every dollar of my earnings I have given to my mother for the support of the family."

"Buy a horse and wagon on credit," advised the friend. "A dozen men in town will sell you an outfit on credit because they know you. Poverty, with such a character as you have, is better capital than ten thousand dollars would be to some young men."

Encouraged by this counsel, he found no difficulty in purchasing a horse and wagon, for which he paid in less time than he promised. He succeeded in business, established a bakery of his own, became a prominent citizen of his town, represented it in the House of Representatives, was chairman of its school committee, subsequently represented his senatorial district in the Massachusetts Senate; for twenty years presided over more political, temperance, anti-slavery, and religious conventions than any other citizen of his county because of his ability in that line; was presidential elector to one of the most important national Republican conventions ever convened; and more than twenty years ago was Massachusetts commissioner to the International Exposition at Paris, France. Character did it. It was better capital for him than money. Had he possessed only money, he might never have got beyond the bakeshop. It was capital that did even more for him out of his business than in it. Money could only have aided him in the bakery business; it would not have made him an enterprising, useful, and honored citizen. But character did all this, and even more, for him.

Money capital will not secure confidence, or, at least, not the confidence requisite in the transaction of business. Enough money will beget confidence in the pecuniary ability of a trader, but that alone will not beget confidence in his moral ability. It is not a guarantee against lying, cheating, or other forms of overreaching; but character is. Hence, it is a peculiar kind of capital, constantly increasing in value, introducing the possessor to channels of influence and power he had not thought of. It was said of that famed New York merchant, Gideon Lee: "It was his misfortune—if, indeed, it be one—to be born poor; it was his merit, by industry and perseverance, to acquire wealth. It was his misfortune to be deprived of an education when young; it was his merit to force it in maturer age. It was his misfortune to be without friends in his early struggle, to aid him by their means or counsel; it was his merit to win them in troops by a character that challenged all scrutiny."

It is not the sight of money that makes the creditor feel easy, but it is the sight of character. The "sound of the hammer at five in the morning" satisfies him that industry is only one virtue of many in the heart of the toiler whose hammer is heard so early in the morning. Even the money capital of the debtor who is seen in the play-house, or heard in the bar-room, does not make the creditor easy, for he knows that these and kindred resorts have exhausted the pecuniary resources of many a trader.

A young man was serving as clerk on an annual salary of five hundred dollars. He was as efficient, reliable, and painstaking, however, as he would have been on a salary of five thousand. Customers liked him, his employers confided in him, his habits were correct, and his character was without a stain. He was surprised, one day, by an offer from one of their best patrons to become his partner in an extensive jobbing business. "Put your character against my money, and we will share the profits equally."

The modest young man scarcely knew what to say, at first. After recovering from his surprise, however, the subject was canvassed with the customer, and a speedy conclusion reached. The partnership was consummated, and it proved harmonious and successful. The character of the young merchant was worth more to the concern than the capital of his confiding friend. It gave the firm standing at once. Its value grew, also, from year to year, giving the company a firmer grip upon the public confidence. He who had only character to invest, found himself, in a few years, among the leading men of the city, not only one of its merchant princes, but one of its counselors, officers, and benefactors. The money invested at the outset had been long forgotten, but the character which the young man put in had grown fairer, richer, and more influential.

Louis XIV. ruled large France, but he could not conquer little Holland. The reason was not quite clear to him, and so he asked Colbert, his minister. The latter replied, "Because, sire, the greatness of a country does not depend upon the extent of its territory, but on the character of its people. It is because of the industry, the frugality, and the energy of the Dutch that your majesty has found them difficult to overcome." The war capital of France was a standing army; that of Holland was character.

XXII.

GREATER THAN ONE'S BUSINESS.

SOME men are greater than their business. Garfield once said to young men in a public address, "To carry on the business of life, you must have surplus power—be fit for more than the thing you are now doing. Let everyone know that you have a reserve in yourself; that you have more power than you are now using. If you are not too large for the place you now occupy, you are too small for it."

When the late Isaac Hopper, the distinguished Quaker philanthropist of Philadelphia, was the guest of a noted family in London, he received an invitation to visit another family, whereupon his host remarked, "Those people are very respectable, but not of the first circles. They belong to our church, but not exactly to our set. Their father was a mechanic." "Well, I am a mechanic myself," replied Mr. Hopper. "Perhaps if thou hadst known that fact, thou wouldst not have invited me."

"Is it possible," exclaimed his astonished host, "that a man of your information and appearance can be a mechanic?"

"Yes. I followed the business of tailor for many years. Look at my hands. Dost thou not see the marks of the shears? Some of the mayors of Philadelphia have been tailors. When I lived there I often walked the streets with the chief justice. It never occurred to me that it was any honor, and I don't think it did to him."

Mr. Hopper had made the most of himself, so that his culture hid the evidence of his trade. His refinement and manly bearing excluded thoughts of his origin and employment. From his start in life, he was greater than his business. In the end, he was greater than all business. His most intimate acquaintances felt, as they met him from day to day, that he was equal to any emergency, fitted for almost anything that was higher and nobler.

Benjamin Franklin was greater than his occupation. In admiring the statesman and philosopher, we lose sight of the tallow-chandler and printer. Miss Read supposed she had captured only a printer when she married him, but in process of time, she found that her husband was one of the fathers of American independence. Her first view of him was on one Sunday morning when he passed her father's residence with a baker's roll under each arm, and a third one, which he was devouring, in his hand. He cut a comical figure over which the young girl made herself merry, little dreaming that she was making fun of her future husband, who was altogether greater than his appearance indicated. Could she have seen the "Minister to the Court of England," one of the "Framers of the Constitution of the United States," "Minister Plenipotentiary to France," and the "Nestor of America," as the French Assembly called him, in the shabby and awkward young man devouring his roll on the street, surprise and wonder would have taken the place of ridicule. But true greatness hides often under very poor jackets. The youth who turns out to be greater than his business, begins life with his business appearing to be greater than himself. Franklin's remarkable career was the product of his wise maxims in practice which he expressed as follows:—

"If time be of all things the most precious, wasting time must be the greatest prodigality. Let us, then, be up and doing, and doing to the purpose. Sloth makes all things difficult, but industry all easy; and he that riseth late must not rest all day, and shall scarce overtake his business at night, while laziness travels so slowly that poverty soon overtakes him. Drive thy business, and not let that drive thee. There are no gains without pains. Diligence is the mother of good luck, and God gives all things to industry. Work while it is called to-day; for you know not how much you may be hindered to-morrow. One to-day is worth two to-morrows; and never leave till to-morrow what you can do to-day. Handle your tools without mittens; remember that the cat in gloves catches no mice. It is true there is much to be done, and perhaps you are weak handed; but stick to it steadily, and you will see great effects, for constant dropping wears away stones; and by diligence and patience the mouse ate in two the cable; and little strokes fell great oaks."

General Grant is another illustration of our theme. From the time he beat the pony in the circus, to the time he fought his way through the Wilderness to Richmond, he was continually showing that he was fit for something more than he was doing. He was but eight or nine years old when the proprietor of the circus called for some boy in the audience to come forth and ride the pony. A monkey had ridden him around the course and had been thrown, and throwing the boy was part of the programme. Ulysses responded to the call, when a shout of applause went up from those who had seen him ride a vicious colt around the public square, when the feet of the fractious animal in front and rear were alternately in the air.

"You are not afraid of being thrown, I suppose," remarked the manager, with a roguish smile in his eye.

"No, sir," promptly answered Ulysses, and mounted. Away flew the pony under the crack of the driver's whip, over the course, round and round, faster and faster, finally leaping and kicking to throw the young rider, who stuck his little feet into the sides of the pony, and clung to his mane with a grip that said as plainly as words, "You can't do it." The audience shouted in wild excitement, and some cried out, "Stick, Lyss, stick! good! good!" He did stick, and the pony was beaten. The vociferous applause that followed proved that the audience appreciated the boy's triumph.

At twelve years of age, Ulysses hauled the logs two miles for the new county jail which his father contracted to build. He hauled them with a pair of fine black horses which his father owned. Each log was one foot square, when hewn, and fourteen feet long. It was the business of the hewers to load the logs, and it took three or four of them to accomplish the feat. One dark, cloudy morning, when a drizzling rain was falling, he went to the woods as usual, but the hewers were not there. The threatening weather made no impression upon him, but it kept the men at home. What should he do? Strange as it may seem, he resolved to load the logs himself, instead of enduring the mortification of returning without them. He saw a half-fallen sugar maple, with its top lodged in another tree. Its trunk slanted just right to form an inclined plane on which he could haul the butt end of the logs up to the necessary height, which he did with the help of one of the horses. Then backing the wagon up and hitching a chain to one of them, the horses easily drew it into the wagon. In this way the usual number were soon loaded. His father was not only surprised at the result, but he was delighted with the boy's method of loading logs, and instructed his men to adopt it thereafter.

We have cited these two incidents among many to show that young Grant was greater than any business to which he was called in early life, and that "the boy was father to the man." At the outbreak of the late Civil War he was made captain of a volunteer company, but the place was too small for him or he was too big for the place. He became colonel, and soon proved himself too large for that position; so he was made brigadier-general, and soon after major-general. A grateful, loyal people looked on, and said, "You can do better still." He reduced Forts Henry and Donelson, and the nation said, "On to Vicksburg; you are equal to it!" Vicksburg conquered, and the Government had found the general to command all the armies of the United States, and to capture Richmond. "Fit for something more than he was doing," the people made him President—their greatest gift. At every step, he proved himself greater than what he was doing. He appeared to have reserves to bring up in every emergency; resources inexhaustible on which to draw in every crisis.

So the youth who is greater than his business is superior to reverses and greater than vicissitudes.

MAKING THINGS HAPPEN.

THE "Country Parson" says: "What you are prepared for rarely happens. The precise thing that you expected comes not once in a thousand times. A confused state of mind results from long experience of such cases. Your real feeling often is, such a thing seems quite sure to happen. I may say I expect it to happen, and yet I don't expect it, because I do; for experience has taught me that the precise thing which I expect, which I think most likely, hardly ever comes." This is true of that limpsy, go-easy, irresolute class of youth, who never determine what they will be thirty years from now, and therefore never do or dare. But it is not true of the class who strike out for themselves, and by pluck, industry, and persistent efforts, hew their way to success. They make things happen. It is the all-engrossing purpose of their lives to make definite things happen. Certain things must happen to make their life purpose triumphant. "Where there's a will there's a way," but it is not that sort of a will which says, "The precise thing which I expect hardly ever comes." It is the will which grows taller and stronger before mighty obstacles, and exclaims with another, "Impossible? Impossible is the adjective of fools!" "The precise thing which I expect" happens when such a will goes forth to its life-work. There is no waiting for "something to turn up;" such a will proceeds to turn things up. That is what it is for. It fills valleys, and levels hills; it surmounts obstacles royally, and overcomes difficulties like a conqueror. A youth with such a will is never the "creature of circumstances;" he is the master of them.

Said the late President Garfield, in a public address. "To a young man who has in himself the magnificent possibilities of life it is not fitting that he should be permanently commanded, he should be a commander. You must not continue to be the employed, you must be an employer. You must be promoted from the ranks to the command. There is something, young man, which you can command; go and find it, and command it. Do not, I beseech you, enter upon any business which does not require and compel constant intellectual growth." This is ringing counsel because it is right counsel; and President Garfield himself was an illustration of what he meant. He was not content to be "commanded" all his days; he became a commander. He was not content to be among "the employed;" he became an employer. To accomplish this he made things happen, such things as he wanted to happen, and which must happen, to achieve his purpose.

Singleness of purpose, untiring work, ceaseless application, undaunted courage, and inspiring hope, all fell into line, like so many warriors, under the command of his heroic spirit, and moved forward to victory. "Accomplish, or never attempt," was his motto. He wanted money to pay for a term at school, and he cut one hundred cords of wood in fifty days at fifty cents a cord, for it. He desired to enjoy the opportunities of Hiram Institute, and he became the bell-ringer and sweeper-general for the prize. He longed for a collegiate education, and, to get it, he crowded six years of hard study into three, wearing old clothes and accepting the poorest fare. Pride, ease, and pleasure went down under the kingly tread of his career. He was the unconscious illustration of what he wrote, at twenty-six years of age, to one of his discouraged pupils. "Tell me, Burke, do you not feel a spirit stirring within you that longs to know, to do, and to dare; to hold converse with the great world of thought, and hold before you some high and noble object to which the vigor of your mind and the strength of your arm may be given? Do you not have longings like these, which you breathe to no one, and which you feel must be heeded, or you will pass through life unsatisfied and regretful? I am sure you have them, and they will forever cling around your heart till you obey their mandate. They are the voices of that nature which God has given you, and which, when obeyed, will bless you and your fellow-men."

It was this "spirit stirring within him," which, when he wanted money to pay for schooling, made it happen; when he coveted the opportunities of a higher and better school, caused that to happen; and when he earnestly desired a college course, commanded that also to happen. He was never small enough, nor flabby enough, to say, "Experience has taught me that the precise thing which I expect hardly ever comes;" for his experience was exactly the opposite. What he wanted he made happen—the ineffaceable mark of victorious manhood. Study his life record, there is a good lesson in it. Farming at ten years of age, a wood-chopper, blacksalter, and amateur carpenter at from twelve to sixteen; a mule-driver on the canal at seventeen; student and pedagogue from eighteen to twenty-one; college boy, professor, and principal of institute at twenty-eight; a state senator at twenty-nine—the youngest member; at thirty a colonel in the War of the Rebellion; at thirty-one a brigadier-general; at thirty-two a major-general—the youngest in the Union army; at thirty-three a member of the national House of Representatives—the youngest of all—and most of the time for eighteen years, an acknowledged leader; at forty-nine elected United States Senator; and at fifty inaugurated President of the United States.

> "The heights by great men reached and kept
> Were not attained by sudden flight;
> But they, while their companions slept,
> Were toiling upward in the night."

There is no "luck" or "chance" in such a life. It was made to order; and every true, noble life is made in the same way. If men stumble into greatness, why should there not be more great men? Is not B as likely to stumble into it as A? What has talent, industry, perseverance, tact, and push to do with success that comes of luck? Such qualities are of no earthly use in a world of chance. There is no "flaming forge of life," where hewing one's way to success is unnecessary, and it is unnecessary if luck settles destiny instead of pluck.

ROOM AT THE TOP.

A LAW student once complained to Daniel Webster that the legal profession was so overcrowded as to discourage young men preparing for the bar. Webster's laconic reply to him was this: "Young man, there is room enough at the top." The student was not looking so high. If he had been, he would have overlooked the mass of contestants who jostle each other lower down. The need of elbow room is not half way up.

No doubt Webster meant to rebuke him for not looking at the top. A lofty aim is inspiring. It is better to aim high even if one does not reach the mark. He will go higher by aiming high than is possible by aiming low. The copy should be perfect, if possible, though the imitation be very poor. The painter must provide his pupil with the best model; the latter may never attain unto it, but it is the best test of his faculties. It is the only law of development that is practical.

Sir Robert Peel, so long a leader of the British Parliament, illustrious the world over, was trained for the highest statesmanship. From his boyhood, his father had his eye upon that renowned public service which the son rendered to his country in manhood. He was a bright, observing, aspiring boy, and his father accustomed him to extemporaneous speaking. On going home from meeting, when a child, his father would set him on the table, and require him to repeat as much of the sermon as possible. By persistent practice he was able, at last, to repeat the whole sermon, almost verbatim; and so of a lecture. He acquired such command of language that he was able to express his thoughts with remarkable facility, even in his youth. His course of study was marked out with reference to the highest position at a future day. The father's high ideal was kept before him constantly, so that he could not lose sight of it if he would. Of course, he was subjected to a severe discipline. The noblest qualities were constantly appealed to. He started for the best, and nothing less could be accepted.

One of his biographers says: "During the forty years that he held a seat in Parliament, his labors were prodigious. He was a most conscientious man, and whatever he undertook to do, he did thoroughly. All his speeches bear evidence of his careful study of everything that had been spoken or written on the subject under consideration. He was elaborate almost to excess, and spared no pains to adapt himself to the various capacities of his audiences. Withal, he possessed much practical sagacity, great strength of purpose, and power to direct the issues of action with steady hand and eye." It was done by his lofty aim, sustained by other noble attributes.

George Whitfield was a poor boy, and left his father early in life. To earn an honest penny for his widowed mother, he became bootblack in the University of Oxford. To the professors and students, he was an interesting boy. His whole appearance indicated that he did not mean to black boots for a living all his days. His eyes and ears were open to learn. Whenever he could catch up a book to read or study, his soul seemed on fire. One day a student found him poring over a Latin grammar. The student asked him how he would like to pursue a course of study in the institution. On receiving the reply that he could wish for nothing better, the student consented to become his teacher. That was the beginning of a marvelous career. Under the discipline of close application, industry, and perseverance, his intellectual faculties developed rapidly. Nothing was too hard for him; difficulties only increased his determination. Present attainments sharpened his appetite for the highest there was. So he worked, studied, conquered. He spurned mediocrity; the best he sought and found.

We scarcely understand how few persons reach excellence in their calling, until we go out into the world to ascertain. If we want to employ a first-class mechanic for a job, we are obliged to hunt for him; or a first-class agent or lawyer. A first-class reader in school, orator on the platform or in the pulpit, teacher, manufacturer, or merchant, is the exception. Even in the home, the best housekeeper, as well as the best servant, is exceptional. The masses are content with mediocrity, or less. We often find ourselves wondering that so many people are satisfied with the commonplace; that they are content to stand upon the lower round of the ladder when they might reach the top round, if they would only fulfill the conditions.

Perhaps the career of that great English statesman, Canning, is the most striking illustration of our theme. He was but a year old when his father died. In her poverty, his mother resorted to the stage for a living, so that the son, after a few years, became more or less familiar with the stage life, and showed marked tendency to dissipation. Moody, the actor, had already observed his remarkable talents, and predicted an illustrious future for him. But the boy was on the road to ruin. Moody was greatly troubled about him, and finally went to a wealthy uncle, and besought him to take charge of the boy and educate him. His uncle consented to do this, and he was sent to school at Eton at twelve years of age. At once he abandoned his waywardness, applied himself closely to study, saying, "I must work, if I would win."

By persistent application, he stood at the head of his class in every study. A literary society was organized among the students, conducted after the manner of the British Parliament, and the great public questions discussed by that body were discussed by this amateur legislative assembly. At once young Canning stepped to the front as debater and orator. His future fame began here; and he ruled that youthful parliament as, twenty years later, he ruled that more august parliament; "as a man rules a high-bred steed; as Alexander ruled Bucephalus, of whom it was said, that the horse and rider were equally proud."

At eighteen, he was a student at Oxford, one of the manliest of young men, declining to engage in college sports that he might have more time to devote to study. That he was striving for the top even then is evident from the following, which he wrote to a friend:—

"I am already too much inclined to aim at the House of Commons as the only path to the only desirable thing in this world; while, at the same time, every tie of common sense, of fortune, and of duty, draws me to the study of a profession."

Lord Shelburne predicted that "he would become prime minister to England," and he did. He took his seat in Parliament when he was only twenty-three years of age, and immediately commanded the attention of his countrymen, who thrust the honors of large public trusts upon him, as his public services multiplied, not satisfied, however, until they made him premier.

TACT.

THE great English merchant, Samuel Budgett, was once asked, "What is the secret of your success?" He answered promptly, "Tact, push, and principle." Perhaps this is the most concise and comprehensive answer ever given to the above question, when we consider that it covers the whole subject. It is a guide to success expressed in three words—Tact, Push, Principle. It is worth while to study them in order—the first in this paper.

Tact, what is it? Webster says it is "Peculiar skill or faculty." We should say that peculiar skill manifests itself in the use of faculties. Some people cannot use their powers to much advantage. They would accomplish vastly more, and enjoy a much higher reputation for ability, if they could. Common sense on the alert is tact. The more common sense, the more tact, usually. This is the most uncommon kind of sense; and hence many persons do not possess it.

ONWARD TO FAME AND FORTUNE.

The biographer of George Stephenson, the world-famed engineer, says, "There were many highly educated engineers living in his day who knew vastly more than he did, trained as they had been in all the science and learning of the schools, but there were none so apt in applying what they knew to practical purposes as he." Here we see it exactly. Other engineers had the talent. Stephenson had the skill; they knew what to do, Stephenson knew how to do it; they had talent, Stephenson tact; he could do the right thing at the right time, and in the right place; others, though highly educated, could not do that. Adam Smith wrote ably on the subject of finance. Indeed, in a sense, he became the world's instructor on financiering, and yet he could not manage the finances of his own family. He could tell other people how to use their money, but he did not know how to use his own.

There is no doubt that John Ericsson, of "Monitor" fame, was a born inventor, for he early developed extraordinary mechanical and mathematical genius. Before he was eleven years of age he made a saw-mill of ingenious construction, the frame of which was of wood, the saw-blade made from a watch-spring and the crank cast from a broken tin spoon.

JOHN ERICSSON.

We have not space to enumerate the long list of his inventions from that time until he produced the Monitor, which spread consternation throughout the Confederate navy and assured triumph to the loyal army. Nor can we stop to rehearse his achievements after his Monitor wrought a revolution in naval architecture to the time of his death, for they are counted by the score. They won fame for him in every civilized nation. Gold medals, titles, honorary degrees, and enduring tributes universities and crowned heads in different lands to his honor, testify to the appreciation of his great genius by grateful peoples. It was quite fitting that, when his remains were removed from New York, a few years ago, to his native land, Sweden, the American people should provide an escort for them elaborate and imposing as any that ever honored general or president.

But Ericsson's genius alone did not constitute him an example of success. He was a man of great tact and indomitable energy. Even in childhood he exhibited a strong determination to execute his own ideas. At one time he went about the house on all fours, in spite of persuasion and compulsion. When he had learned the Swedish alphabet—his native tongue—he saw that letters were only symbols; so he set himself about inventing other symbols to take their place; nor was he long in accomplishing his purpose. Then he demanded that his own

FIGHT BETWEEN THE MONITOR AND THE MERRIMAC.

alphabet should be substituted for the national one. It was this original, resolute, persistent element of his character that he carried with him into manhood. It planned not for defeat; it cowered before no opposition; it welcomed obstacles. Sleep, food, ease, were all sacrificed to his ruling purpose. Born in poverty, he was willing to remain poor if necessary to win his cause. His success was the outcome of his own tact and personal efforts that defied difficulties.

Sir Isaac Newton was pre-eminently a man of tact. From his earliest boyhood he was wont to search for the reason of things. A teacher called him " a sober, silent, thinking lad." At one time a windmill was erected near his home. It was a novel affair to him, and he went every day to examine it, until it was completed. He said within himself, " I can make one." Only a boy of tact would say that. Quietly he went to work, and soon produced the first toy wind-mill ever made, and put it up on the top of the house, where the wind set it to whirling at once, to the great joy of Isaac and several companions who were with him.

Next he invented the paper kite. Putting together the knowledge he had acquired from here and there, he concluded that he could make something that would fly on the air. "It must be light and of a certain shape and size," he thought. "It must have a tail, too, as a sort of rudder," he said, also. So he experimented until his ideas took tangible form, and his kite went sailing through the air. It was a memorable occasion for him and his boy associates, although they scarcely dreamed that the invention would go down through the ages to awaken the gratitude of the boys. Young Newton played a clever game to surprise his neighbors, by sending up his kite on a dark night, with a paper lantern attached to it. Beholders gazed in wonder at the strange phenomenon, supposing that a comet or meteor was lighting up the skies, until they learned that it was a device of the little philosopher Isaac.

SIR ISAAC NEWTON.

He also invented a curious timepiece. By carefully watching the movement of the celestial bodies, and observing their shadows on the wall of his room, as they moved slowly along, he made a dial for his own use. It was known as "Isaac's Dial" for many years, and was the origin of dials on window-sills which our forefathers used before the day of clocks.

Isaac cared nothing for hunting, fishing, and other sports that engaged the attention of the boys of his day. In so far as sport could be found in some ingenious device to satisfy his inquisitive mind, he courted sport, but no farther.

He could work on the farm with credit to himself, and go to market when necessary with the produce; but his active mind was not content with such humdrum duties. One day his uncle, with whom he lived, the good rector of a church, found him under a hedge so completely absorbed in the contents of the volume before him, that he did not observe the approach of anyone. Examination satisfied the uncle that Isaac was destined to fill a higher position than that of laborer on the farm. The boy was solving a difficult mathematical problem, to the surprise of the rector. This discovery closed his career on the farm, sent him to school, and finally introduced him into Trinity College. He became a most renowned philosopher of his day, in whose success tact played a conspicuous part.

PUSH.

"WHAT sort of an agent does J—— make?" inquired a friend of a Boston merchant.

"Good—not extra;" answered the merchant, adding, "his push makes him good; more tact would make him extra." The merchant meant to say that push alone will do much for a man, but will do more for him when coupled with tact. He stated a very important truth that demands attention; for push, which is another phase of energy, or force of character, is indispensable in every pursuit of life.

Buxton said, near the close of his life: "The longer I live, the more I am certain that the great difference between men, between the feeble and the powerful, the great and the insignificant, is energy—invincible determination: a purpose once fixed and then death or victory. That quality will do anything that can be done in this world, and no talents, no circumstances, no opportunities, will make a two-legged creature a man without it." This is putting it strongly, but the statement is substantially true.

Elihu Burritt, at sixteen years of age, was a poor, fatherless boy, apprenticed to a blacksmith. He was obliged to work at the forge twelve hours a day. In less than thirty years from that time he was known the world over as "the learned blacksmith." How was it done? Without tremendous push it never could have been done. He possessed that "invincible determination" to know something, in spite of his surroundings; and so he pushed on, slowly but resolutely. When busy at the forge, he studied mathematics. He solved mathematical problems in his own head. His biographer furnishes the following specimen: "How many yards of cloth, three feet in width, cut into strips an inch wide, and allowing half an inch at the end for the lap, would it require to reach from the centre of the earth to the surface, and how much would it all cost at a shilling a yard?"

With several of these problems solved in his head, he would go home at night and report them to an older brother, who had worked his way through Williams College. His brother would go through the calculations on a slate, usually finding that Elihu was correct.

It was during his apprenticeship that he took up the study of Latin and Greek, carrying first his Latin grammar in his hat, and afterwards his Greek grammar, to study at odd moments. During the evenings of one winter, he read the Æneid of Virgil and a part of Cicero. Often, at the forge, when he was waiting for his iron to heat, he would open his grammar and go through the conjugation of a Greek or Latin verb. At twenty-one, his apprenticeship completed, he went to his brother's school one term. Then he returned to the forge, working hard by day and studying hard by night. After laying by a little money, he resolved to spend a winter in New Haven, in study; not in college, but where he could breathe the literary atmosphere of that scholarly city. Without teacher or helpful friend, he began a course of study the next morning after his arrival. He took lodgings at a small tavern, where, at half-past four in the morning, as soon as the fire was built in the office, he studied German until breakfast, at half-past seven. After breakfast, when all the boarders had gone to their business, he studied Homer's "Iliad" until noon, with no assistance but his Greek dictionary. Just before the boarders came in to dinner, he laid aside his Greek and Latin, and took up Italian, thinking the latter would not attract the attention of the gaping crowd so much as the former. He returned to the study of Greek in the afternoon, but took up Spanish in the evening.

In this way he spent the winter; then, for a while, was a teacher. But his desire to become acquainted with Oriental languages was so great, that he finally resolved to visit foreign countries for that purpose. Not finding the necessary books in Connecticut, he concluded to visit the Orient to accomplish what he desired. Tying up his clothes in a handkerchief, he started for Boston, one hundred miles distant from New Britain, Connecticut, where he expected to find a vessel on which he could work his passage to a foreign port. But he found no such vessel. He learned, however, that there was an antiquarian society in Worcester, Massachusetts, with a library that contained the books he needed. Thither he hastened on foot, found the library in question, with all the advantages he was seeking. Immediately he secured a boarding place and work in a blacksmith's shop. The next morning he was early at the forge, and at night, to a late hour, was engaged in hard study.

For five years he continued these herculean labors in Worcester, without teachers, or even advisers, an illustration of push that is unparalleled, we believe, in American scholarship. He must have been surcharged with that "invincible determination" of which Buxton spoke.

It is no wonder that Edward Everett said, when speaking of him, "It is enough to make one who has good opportunities hang his head in shame." Rather, we would say, let every aspiring youth in our land study this example, and be encouraged to face difficulties like heroes, and overcome them like conquerors.

Alexander ascended the throne at twenty, and conquered the world before he was thirty-three. Julius Cæsar conquered three hundred nations, captured eight hundred cities, defeated three million men, and became a leading statesman and orator before middle life. But Burritt's push was equal to theirs, and his achievements were greater and better for the world, since he taught coming generations of youth what force of character can do; and, as the leading champion of peace, made war appear horrible and unchristian to the civilized world.

XXIII.

PRINCIPLE.

MRS. WESLEY wrote to her son Samuel, who was at school in Westminster, in 1709: "I would advise you, as much as possible, to throw your business into a certain method, by which means you will learn to improve every precious moment, and find an unspeakable facility in the performance of your respective duties. In all things act upon principle."

By principle, she did not mean character alone, nor conscience, nor honesty, nor benevolence, but all of these together.

Tact and push, without principle, are dangerous possessions. A practical turn at iniquity, accompanied by energy enough to make it telling, develops the scamp. But principle controls tact, and puts a check rein on push. It is the skillful driver of a mettlesome pair, having the grand team well in hand.

Mrs. Wesley knew that her boy Sam would never amount to much without principle, and she said so. The same is true of every other boy. To attempt to cross the Atlantic Ocean without a compass is no greater folly than to make the voyage of life without principle. There is no friendly port for either.

The late Ichabod Washburn, of Worcester, Massachusetts, was left fatherless when he was two months old, in a moneyless, but Christian home. At nine years of age poverty crowded him out of that humble home, and he went forth to battle with hardships; but he took with him the only capital his excellent mother could provide—principle. She taught him, as Mrs. Wesley did her Samuel, to "always act on principle," and he never forgot it. First, he lived with a soulless harness and carriage maker, who compelled him to sleep in the cold, desolate loft above the shop, to which he ascended by a ladder. He sent him to mill in mid-winter, horseback, without stockings or shoes, and paid no more attention to his intellect and soul than he did to his feet. Yet he served this wretch five years, patiently, uncomplainingly, and faithfully, because of his mother's lesson. Then he went to Worcester, Massachusetts, seeking work. He soon found it with a blacksmith, to whom he apprenticed himself for board and clothes. He began to attend public worship on his first Sabbath in Worcester. He hired a seat for which he paid fifty cents annually. To meet this expense, and provide himself pocket money, he made and sold pot-hooks, out of working hours.

At thirty-three we find him a manufacturer of wire in his adopted city, universally respected and trusted. He made first-class wire; his principle would not allow him to make any other. The Washburn wire soon became popular. It was the best wire in the market for pianos, telegraphs, and skirts. His business increased rapidly, until he employed seven hundred men. His profits became enormous. His benevolence was as large as his profits; his hand was open to aid every good cause. He gave away thousands of dollars annually, just as a rich man should; and when he died he left a large fortune, leaving in his will four hundred and twenty-four thousand dollars to objects of charity. Principle did it.

The apprentice who will cheat his employer out of time, or slight his work when it is possible, is devoid of principle. This is equally true of him when he profanes the name of God, or uses his Sabbath for pecuniary gain or pleasure. The farmer who puts the best apples on top of the barrel, the merchant who scrimps weight or measure, the taxpayer who conceals a portion of his property, and the laborer who will shorten his ten hours' work at both ends, are not actuated by principle.

A young man became clerk in a large warehouse of a New England city. After having served several months acceptably he hinted to his employer that he ought to be paid as much as a certain other clerk received.

"If you will do what he does, you shall be paid as much," replied his employer.

"And what is that?" the young man inquired.

"He takes customers to the theatre, and gives them a drink occasionally, that he may sell them a bill of goods."

Straightening himself up to his full height, and with the fire of indignation flashing in his eyes, our young hero answered:—

"I thank God that there is a poor-house in my native town, and I will go there and die before I shall do such dirty work;" and he left the store. That was principle.

Nicholas Biddle, president of the first United States Bank, found so much work on hand, at one time, that he asked a portion of his employes to work a few hours on the Sabbath. All but one consented; this one said, "I cannot conscientiously labor on the Sabbath."

"Then you must give up your place to some one who will," answered Biddle.

"Very well, I resign," said the young man, and withdrew. That was principle.

The following day a gentleman waited upon Biddle, saying, "I want a perfectly reliable private secretary, to whom I am obliged to commit great trusts. Can you tell me of one?"

"Yes," Biddle promptly answered; "I dismissed a young man yesterday because he would not work on the Sabbath. He has principle enough for you."

Victoria, the beloved Queen of England, from her coronation at eighteen years of age, shared the confidence of her subjects by her Christian spirit and honest, noble purpose. She was twelve years of age when her governess called her attention to the honors that awaited her. The modest girl could scarcely realize the fact at first, but when she fairly took in the situation she burst into tears and exclaimed, "I will be good. I understand now why you wished me so much to learn. . . . I will be good." She appears to have thought that, whatever other qualities she may have possessed, goodness was indispensable for the throne. Long after the crown of England was placed on her head, she said, referring to the time when her governess told her that she would be queen, "I cried much on learning it." It was this sense of personal responsibility, awakening the desire to become worthy of the British throne, that challenged universal confidence, and made her reign a model. Moral, rather than mental, qualities have made her the successful ruler of a mighty nation, on whose dominions the sun never sets.

NOT ABOVE ONE'S BUSINESS.

ALL necessary occupations are honorable. No disgrace can reasonably attach to them, except where the men or women who follow them are disgraceful. The truest dignity will crown the faithful in the humblest employment. They are entitled to a creditable passport into the best circles.

And yet this commonly accepted view of necessary pursuits is strangely overlooked in practice. Many people consider certain useful callings menial and degrading. Where they admit the necessity of such labors, they still regard them as ignoble.

Young people often catch this spirit. The store and learned professions attract them more than the shop and farm. The desire among boys to exchange country for city life arises, in a great measure, from this distorted view of manual labor. It is not popular to work on a farm or in a shop. It is more genteel to handle the yardstick than hoe or shovel. They will rank higher as ministers, doctors, or lawyers, than they will as mechanics or farmers.

Such are their false opinions, and they sacrifice everything to this delusion. Nine-tenths of all the youth who begin life on this line make a deplorable failure. Doctor Johnson well said, "He that feels his business is below him, will surely fall below it."

We risk nothing in saying that successful men, in all occupations, are the men who never feel above their business. Whatever their employment is, they consider that their occupation challenges respect. Illustrations of this statement abound in the business world.

The Boston millionaire and philanthropist, Amos Lawrence, employed a clerk, in his early business life, who was quite conceited. One day Mr. Lawrence asked him to take a package for a lady customer to her residence; but he declined, on the ground that the act would compromise his dignity. His employer rebuked him in the most cutting way, by taking the bundle himself to the lady's home.

It is doubtful, however, if a young man so ignorant of what true manhood is, can be profited by either rebuke or counsel. Conveying the package did not compromise the dignity of Mr. Lawrence, but magnified it essentially. It showed that there was nothing of the fop or dude about him, characters that are justly despised by the thoughtful everywhere.

When the celebrated Samuel Drew was becoming famous as an author, though still in poverty, he was carrying in his winter's coal without the least idea that it was beneath his position. A neighbor said to him:—

"Drew, that work compromises your dignity as an author."

Drew's reply is worthy of a place in the memory of every aspirant for real honors:—

"The man who is ashamed to carry in his own coal, deserves to sit all winter by an empty grate."

It was this spirit that enabled him to achieve remarkable success.

Peter the Great laid aside the robes of royalty, and entered the East India dockyard at Amsterdam, in disguise, to learn the art of shipbuilding. He took his place among the workmen, and became, in all respects, one of them; even wearing the same kind of dress, eating the same sort of food, and inhabiting equally humble lodgings. He possessed a strong desire to benefit his own countrymen by making them more familiar with the shipbuilding business, and he believed that the best way of accomplishing his purpose was to learn the art himself.

It never occurred to him that royalty would be compromised by the occupation of a ship-carpenter, nor did he care. He did not feel above doing anything that would prove a lasting good to his country. He deserved to be called "Peter the Great."

Washington was a man of this class. At one time, when several divisions of the army were engaged in constructing works of defence from Wallabout Bay to Red Hook, one of the parties, under the supervision of a subaltern officer, had a large timber to raise. While engaged in raising it, the officer doing nothing but shout, "Now, boys, right up, he-e-a-v-e," etc., a man rode up on horseback. "Why do you not help?" he inquired. The officer indignantly replied, "I help! Why, sir, I'll have you know that I am corporal!" The gentleman sprang from his horse, laid hold

PETER THE GREAT.

of the timber with the men, and very soon it was in the required place. Then turning to the corporal, he said: "Mr. Corporal, my name is George Washington. As soon as you have completed this work, meet me at your commander's quarters." There was no room in the army for a man who found so much dignity in a corporalship as to make him feel above lifting a timber. He was dismissed.

A pompous young merchant of Philadelphia purchased his dinner at the market one day, and gave a shilling to a seedy-looking man standing by to carry it to his house. He was somewhat mortified, however, to learn afterward that it was the celebrated millionaire Girard who played the rôle of a servant for him. Girard meant to show the young sprout what a fool he was, and cure him of his folly, if possible.

STEPHEN GIRARD.

In striking contrast with the last incident, a young man purchased a bag of coffee of Girard, who was always careful about whom he trusted. The buyer wheeled the bag to his place of business, and when he came for more Girard offered to trust him to any amount. The offer was accepted; the two men became firm friends, and the young trader amassed a fortune in time.

Benjamin Franklin wheeled his paper from the warehouse to his printing-office, when he set up business in Philadelphia; Daniel Safford, one of the wealthy, noble, honored business men of Boston, carried home on his back the iron which he bought when he commenced the blacksmith's business in that city; a New York millionaire earned his first dollar as a hod-carrier in the city of Troy, and he never became so proud as to despise a hod.

When Napoleon became a member of the military academy at Paris, he found that each student had a servant to groom his horse, and wait upon him generally. He addressed a remonstrance to the governor against this practice, maintaining that "a student of military affairs should learn to groom his own horse clean his own armor, and accustom himself to the performance of such duties as would be required of him for service in the field." Subsequently he established a military school at Fontainebleau, where this system was introduced, and proved the practical wisdom of its author. He who is too proud to wait upon himself is doomed to disappointment. Success will never wait on him.

> "Honor and fame from no condition rise;
> Act well your part—there all the honor lies."

SELF-POSSESSION.

BY self-possession we mean the faculties of the whole man well in hand. True self-reliance implies self-possession; the latter cannot exist without the former. He who would concentrate all his powers upon the accomplishment of an all-absorbing purpose, must be self-possessed. Interruption, surprises, and even surrounding confusion, will not throw him off his base. He keeps cool, labors on with a will, and never loses sight of the goal at the end of the race.

This is a valuable quality in the common walks of life. It is needed in all pursuits, and every day. For the want of it, both men and women, both old and young, become disconcerted, and fail when they ought to succeed. Unexpected experiences and startling casualties confuse them, and they know not what they do.

A woman, whose house was on fire, threw a looking-glass out of the window, and carried a pair of andirons several rods, to a safe place beside a stone wall.

A man, suddenly awakened from his sleep by the cry of fire, leaped from his bed to find that his own house was in flames. Instantly he proceeded to throw out of door and window, crockery, shovel, tongs, chairs, bed-clothes, mirrors, flour, meal, pies, etc., but forgot the trunk in which were deposited all his money, jewelry, gold watch, and valuable keepsakes, and it was consumed.

A mother, alone in her house with her little child, was so confused by the clothes of the little one taking fire, that she ran into the street, crying frantically for help, leaving the child to perish.

A self-possessed mother would have quenched the burning dress and saved the child.

A pleasure party on a small lake were enjoying themselves, when a young lady changed her position so suddenly that the boat dipped a little water. She uttered a scream, and sprang to the other side; others did the same, upsetting the boat, and drowning several of the party. Presence of mind would have averted all these disasters.

232   ONWARD TO FAME AND FORTUNE.

A schoolhouse in New York was discovered to be on fire by one of the teachers. At once she communicated the fact to the teachers in the other rooms, who announced the session closed, directing the pupils to leave the house orderly. Every room was emptied, and the pupils in the street, before the latter knew the cause of their dismissal. Had the teacher shouted, "Fire! fire!" when she made the discovery, there is no doubt that lives would have been lost in the general rush for the doors. The self-possession of the teacher prevented a catastrophe.

NAPOLEON.

A farmer's wife of our acquaintance was left at home on a Sunday with her three children, while her husband went to meeting. The latter had scarcely passed beyond the call of his wife, when a shout from one of the children told that the youngest, three years old, had fallen into the well. There was no man on the premises, and no neighbor near, as the mother well knew, and her first cool thought was, "If that child is saved, I must save her!" Running to the well, and seizing the windlass to lower the bucket, she called, "Nellie, darling! don't cry; mamma will lower the bucket."

Fortunately, the water was so low that the bucket could be dipped with difficulty, and it went down carefully, but quickly.

"Now, Nellie, dear, get into the bucket, and mamma will draw you up. Don't be afraid; mamma will draw you right up to her."

There was not the slightest appearance of alarm in the tone or words of the mother, for, in her remarkable self-possession, she meant to remove the child's fear, and encourage her to get into the bucket. Nellie obeyed her mother, crawled into the bucket, and in a minute more was locked in her mother's arms. Presence of mind saved the child. Maternal love, for the time being, held nerves, muscles, mind, and soul in complete subjection, in its indomitable purpose to save the child.

Courage is not self-possession. There may be courage without self-possession, and there may be self-possession without courage.

A gentleman of very nervous temperament, yet known for his great presence of mind in danger and emergencies, claims that he has cultivated this quality by much reflection. "I have planned what I should do if awakened in the night by my house on fire; how to dress quickly, what to do first of all, how to give the alarm, how to save my family, clothing, etc." He believes that similar forethought about burglars, accidents, and other surprises, begets coolness, and hence method and effectiveness of action.

We know a clergyman's wife who forecasted these possibilities to such an extent that on taking a journey, she supplied herself with bandages, court-plaster, and one or two remedies, in case of injuries by railroad accidents. Once her tact and efficiency were put to the test on the train, when an accident injured several passengers, and such was her coolness and success that her services became a matter of public record.

"Presence of mind and courage in distress
Are more than armies to procure success."

BEGINNING IN A SMALL WAY.

GREAT things begin small. The giant oak began with the acorn, the ocean began with the "little drop of water," and the continent with the "little grain of sand."

The Sunday-school enterprise, with which from twenty to thirty millions of people of all ages are connected in the United States and Great Britain, began with Robert Raikes teaching a few ragged street urchins on Sabbath morning; and the Christian church itself, having a foothold in almost every country, its membership numbering hundreds of millions, and its mighty influence dominating thrones and empires, began with a mere handful of believers in Palestine, despised, poor, and oppressed.

The first sixpence that Samuel Appleton, the Boston millionaire of forty years ago, possessed, was earned by assisting a cattle trader to drive his herd a few miles.

The first cent which Samuel Budgett, the wealthy English merchant of a former generation, ever had, was paid him by a blacksmith for an old horseshoe picked up on his way to school. The "village smithy" promised to add another penny to it at the end of two weeks if the boy would keep it so long. The promise and pledge were both kept, and two cents became the first capital of the future millionaire.

Sir Walter Raleigh introduced a single potato into Great Britain in the sixteenth century, and it has sustained the life of millions of people by its increase, conquered famine again and again, and contributed largely to the wealth, prosperity, and glory of England and America.

And so on through the whole range of race and lands. The actual of the young man and woman is inexperience, obscurity, ignorance, penury, hardship, and whatever else belongs to early struggles, while the possible is

SIR WALTER RALEIGH.

learning, renown, wealth, usefulness, and true greatness. Young people should learn wisdom from this lesson of history. They should be content to begin their life-work in a small way. They must not despise the lowest round of the ladder, nor jump it if they can; it is on the way to the top round. The youth who aspires to begin where his father left off is at war with history. He wants to break up the established order of things. He would begin great and not small. He does not want to pay the price of success: he expects to secure it cheaper. As if Providence would make him an exception to the rule!

Nothing would be more unwise and perilous. The sure experience of such a youth is to end smaller than he began.

Mr. Parton says:—

"Men destined to a great career, I have observed, generally serve a long and vigorous apprenticeship to it of some kind. They try their forming powers in little things, before grappling with the great. I cannot call to mind a single instance of a man who achieved success of the first magnitude, who did not at first toil long in obscurity."

Peter Cooper's attention was called, in his early manhood, to the manufacture of glue. He began in a very small way. With horse and cart he scoured the country round about for the hoofs of slaughtered cattle, conveying them to a small factory which he had extemporized, where he converted them into glue. He was quite successful from the beginning, working early and late, keeping his own books, selling his own goods, and practicing the most rigid economy. As his business increased, he enlarged his manufactory. Having no competitors, an extensive market for his wares was opened, and his profits grew to large proportions. But it required time in which to reach these results; and it was forty-five years before he reached the highest success. Had he commenced large and launched out in fine style at first, he would have made a failure of it in five years.

The manufacturer of the Rising Sun Stove polish now sends out to all parts of the world six tons daily, and he has realized a large fortune from his business, and, at the present time, it is more profitable than ever. But he commenced in the smallest of small ways. He carried his polish about in a carpet-bag, and retailed it from house to house, and after a time was able to purchase a horse and wagon, with which he enlarged his business. A few years later he could travel by rail to distant States and take orders, continuing this method until he had canvassed twenty-two States. By this time his business was large enough to satisfy his ambition, and his income large enough to warrant ample assistance. It was accomplished by beginning in a small way. In reply to an author who wished for information, he wrote: "I began business at the age of fifteen, with a capital of five dollars. My first factory was a one-story building, fifteen feet by twelve. My first product was a carpet-bag full of the articles I made, which I sold from door to door. I struggled with poverty and many obstacles. I worked half the night, and at two or three o'clock in the morning I crawled up into the little attic over my little shop, hardly large enough for a dog to sleep in, and after an hour or two of sleep, got up and went at it again. My factory has grown to cover three acres; my product has grown from a carpet-bag full to six tons a day, and the goods of my manufacture are sold in every civilized country. I never used tobacco, cider, or beer. I never gambled nor read low story papers or dime novels, but supplemented my meagre educational advantages with good reading."

The New York *Herald* is supposed to be one of the most valuable newspaper properties in the world, but the contrast between its present worth and influence, and its inferior beginning in a cellar on Nassau Street, is one of the marvels of our day. In that dark, damp abode, with a table extemporized by laying a wide board on two empty barrels, and one chair for the editor, Mr. Bennett began his work as a journalist. He was editor, reporter, book-keeper, manager, and salesman; working seventeen and eighteen hours daily; hoping, pushing, planning, waiting, but never moping or cowering before difficulties. "An intense desire itself transforms possibility into reality. Our wishes are but prophecies of the things we are capable of performing."

XXIV.

CHOICE OF COMPANIONS.

A GOOD companion is better than a fortune, for a fortune cannot purchase those elements of character which make companionship a blessing. The best companion is one who is wiser and better than ourselves, for we are inspired by his wisdom and virtue to nobler deeds. Greater wisdom and goodness than we possess lifts us higher mentally and morally. Says Feltham: "He that means to be a good limner will be sure to draw after the most excellent copies, and guide every stroke of his pencil by the better pattern that lays before him; so he who desires that the table of his life may be fair will be careful to propose the best examples, and will never be content till he equals or excels them."

"Keep good company, and you shall be of the number," said George Herbert, and nothing can be more certain. "A man is known by the company he keeps." It is always true. Companionship of a high order is powerful to develop character. Character makes character in the associations of life faster than anything else. Purity begets purity, like begets like; and this fact makes the choice of companions in early life more important, even, than that of teachers and guardians. When Sir Joshua Reynolds was a boy, he had so great a reverence for the character of Pope that he would press through a crowd to touch his coat with the end of his forefinger, as if he expected to be lifted higher by the act, and finally become more of a man. Somewhat of that feeling should rule in the choice of companions, selecting those whose nobleness challenges the touch of admiration.

It is true that we cannot always choose all of our companions. Some are thrust upon us by business and the social relations of life. We do not choose them, we do not enjoy them; and yet, we have to associate with them more or less. The experience is not altogether without compensation, if there be principle enough in us to bear the strain. Still, in the main, choice of companions *can* be

(237)

made, and *must* be made. It is not best nor necessary for a young person to associate with "Tom, Dick, and Harry," without forethought or purpose. Some fixed rules about the company he or she keeps should be observed. The subject should be uppermost in the thoughts, and canvassed often.

Companionship is education, good or bad; it develops manhood or womanhood, high or low; it lifts the soul upward or drags it downward; it ministers to virtue or vice. There is no half-way work about its influence. If it ennobles, it does it grandly; if it demoralizes, it does it devilishly. It saves or destroys lustily. One school companion saved Henry Martyn, and made a missionary of him; one school companion ruined John Newton, and made a most profligate and profane companion of him. Newton was sent away to a boarding-school. He was an obedient and virtuous lad, and his parents had no anxiety for his moral safety. But there was a bright, immoral youth in the school, who cared more for coarse fun than he did for books, and was profane, vulgar, and artful. He sought the companionship of young Newton, and the latter was captivated by his brilliancy and social qualities. He did not appear to be a *bad* young man. The two became intimate, their friendship strengthening from week to week. John Newton soon became as wicked as his companion, and finally ran away from home and went to sea—the worst school he could enter. On board the ship he found kindred spirits, and he waxed worse and worse. At last he was "the worst sailor on board the vessel," and many were the boon companions that he ruined. His end would have been fearful, had not a kind Providence interposed, after years of debauchery, and made him a Christian man.

The late Rev. Dr. Thompson, of New York City, published the story of a youth who came under his ministry at nineteen years of age. He was the son of pious parents, neither profane, idle, nor vicious, and had established a character for industry and sobriety. At twenty he united with Dr. Thompson's church, and at twenty-one was employed by a railroad company, where wicked companions beset him. He soon fell into evil ways, and, in less than one year, became too abandoned and reckless to be harbored by the church. The end came within three years, and Dr. Thompson shall describe it:—

"Two weeks ago to-day I knelt in that murderer's cell, in company with his parents, sister, and brother, who had come for their last interview with him on earth. That narrow cell was more solemn than the grave itself. Two weeks ago to-morrow I saw the youth, who had once been of my spiritual flock, upon the scaffold. It was an awful scene. He made a brief address. Oh, that you could have heard the warning of that young man from the scaffold! 'You know,' he said, 'how I was brought up. I had the best instructions a Christian father could give. Oh, if I had followed them, I should have been in my dear father's home; but evil companions led me astray, and I have come to this! I hope, now, as I leave the world, my voice will warn all young men. Our desires and passions are so strong that it requires very little to lead us astray. I want to urge it upon all young men, never to take the first step in such a career as mine. When the first step is taken in the paths of sin, it is very difficult to stop.'"

Beware of companions whose moral character is below your own, unless you associate with them only to reform them. Avoid those who depreciate true worth, and speak lightly of the best class of citizens, and sneer at reforms. They who sip wine, use profane and vulgar language, think that man cannot be successful in business and be honest, find their pleasure in the circus, theatre, or ball-room, instead of books, lectures, and literary society, are not suitable companions. They may not be bad young people, but their moral tone is below yours, and hence they are perilous associates for you. Rather choose those of higher and nobler aims, whose aspirations are to be true and useful, who would not, knowingly, risk a stain upon their life-work, with whom "a good name is better than great riches," and whose strong purpose is to make the best record possible.

Strength of character may successfully resist the worst companionship. The princess regent of Russia planned to destroy the claim of Peter the Great to the throne, by subjecting him to the company of a hundred profligate young Russians. Peter was a youth of sagacity, sobriety, and moral principle, so that his character withstood the test without a blemish. Instead of being lured into excesses of any kind, he beguiled his wayward companions into "the love of manly sports and military exercises." The evil spirit of the princess was rebuked by the failure of her fiendish plot.

MONEY NOT A SAFE IMPULSE TO EFFORT.

"THE love of money is the root of all evil," the highest authority declares; but few human beings appear to believe it, for they press on after it, continuing to illustrate the statement without heeding its warning. The rush of the world is for money. Money is power, money is happiness, money is everything. Henry Ward Beecher once said, "The whole air is full of gold dust, and men see everything through its haze." To be rich is the chief end of man.

In these circumstances it is not strange that youth of both sexes have a false view of riches. Young men want to make money; young women want to marry it. This desire is not only strong, but almost universal. Money is the one thing needful. Without it life is not worth living. Any sacrifice is not too great for it. Even morals may go if wealth may come. Young people need not be told that wealth is not found on this line; it is the way to poverty. There is no question that this inordinate desire for money is the cause of countless failures. Success is found on a higher plane. Meanness of disposition or aim is not embraced among the elements of success. True manhood and true womanhood are involved in true success.

The citizens of a New England city have just been startled and shocked by the fall of one of its prominent young men. A lawyer of marked ability and position for one of his years, the son of an illustrious sire, with riches and honor in his possession, is now pining in prison as a felon, disgraced and degraded by his false views of money. The seventy-five thousand dollars he married, the thousands he inherited, and the other thousands that he earned by his practice in law, all wasted by riotous living; and the crime largely aggravated by fraud and forgery. Evidently the young man's life is a failure, because of his false ideas of wealth. He did not know what money was for: he thought it was for luxurious living, for social splendor and éclat. Money for reasonable comfort and personal usefulness, was what he never dreamed of. His life was wrecked on this rock. Money was his perilous impulse to effort. Such examples are not few, but many. Together with less striking illustrations, found in the ordinary social and commercial relations of life, they show that the desire for money often becomes a perilous impulse. The purpose for which money is made is entirely overlooked, and it is sought as a means of gratifying appetites and passions. Its necessary and legitimate use is scarcely considered in the wild scramble for it, for there is no other object so generally coveted and sought after as this. Honor has its thousands of votaries, and pleasure its tens of thousands; but money is sought as the means of compassing the whole. It is wanted

HENRY WARD BEECHER.

not only for what it is in itself, but for what it will purchase. Yet money is not to be despised. It is not necessarily a curse—it is a blessing; a curse only when its legitimate use is disregarded. Another has said: "Money is bread; money is raiment; money is shelter; money is education, refinement, books, pictures, music; money is the society of the learned and accomplished." Is it less true than in Solomon's time that "wealth maketh many friends; but the poor is separated from his neighbor?" Money is science, invention, discovery, enterprise; money is the canal, the railroad, the telegraph, the steamship. This is strictly true, proving that money is as essential as light and heat to the world's progress, barbarism reigning where it is not. Scanty bread, scanty raiment, scanty shelter; no education, no refinement, no books, no enterprise, no canal, no railroad, no telegraph, no telephone, no steamship—such is the condition of society where money is not.

John Grigg was one of the exceptionally successful men of his day, in whose life money occupied just the place Providence intended it should. As a bookseller and publisher of Philadelphia, he became widely known for business ability and large wealth, yet he never sought money as an end. Indeed, he never appeared to think of becoming wealthy, or to plan for it. His only thought was how to serve his employer most faithfully and become master of his occupation. He entered the publishing house of Benjamin Warner, whose business was immense for that day. In three years Mr. Warner died, and he left a memorandum attached to his will that was worth more to young Grigg than any amount of silver and gold. With a view to the possibility of his business being continued, he said, "There are one or two young men in whom confidence can be reposed," referring to those in his employ. "I consider John Grigg as possessing a peculiar talent for the bookselling business. Very industrious, and from three years' observation, the time he has been employed in my business, I have found nothing in his conduct to raise a doubt in my mind of his possessing correct principles."

In consequence of this indorsement of his ability, energy, industry, and principles, the executors of Mr. Warner's estate intrusted its settlement to John Grigg. It was a great undertaking for one so young, for the business had been very extensive, and connected with it were numerous agencies and branches in the South and West. But in one year's time the settlement was accomplished to the entire satisfaction of all concerned.

This final disposition of the estate left Grigg without employment. Being in doubt as to his future work, he consulted Joseph Cushing, Esq., of Baltimore, who said to him, "Rely on yourself; you cannot fail to succeed. You will yet astonish yourself and the book trade of the whole country." The next day he hired a store and began a business career that finally "wrought a revolution in the book trade of the country." Riches poured in upon him without any plan or purpose to be rich. He planned and purposed to be true and faithful, upright and efficient, and wealth appeared to come as a reward of his good habits and unblemished character.

The career of John Grigg is a representative one, so far as money is concerned. It makes clearer than any description or plea just the place money should occupy in a man's career—a sort of side issue that is the direct result of striving for higher and greater things. With few exceptions, wealth has come in the same way to the rich men of our land and other lands. It is the fruit of powers well used, and service well rendered. It is just as true in the secular as it is in the moral world, that "whosoever will save his life shall lose it; and whosoever shall lose his life for my sake, shall find it." Sought for its own sake, money becomes a perilous impulse. Few survive the danger. The shores of time are strewed with the wrecks of lives that meant to clasp gold. They lost what they would have saved, while the other class found it.

Colton wrote, "Agar said, 'Give me neither poverty nor riches!' and this will ever be the prayer of the wise. Our incomes should be like our shoes: if too small they will gall and pinch us; if too large they will cause us to stumble and trip. But wealth, after all, is a relative thing, since he that has little and wants less, is richer than he that has much but wants more. True contentment depends not upon what we have; a tub was large enough for Diogenes, but a world was too little for Alexander."

MAKE ALL YOU CAN.

JOHN WESLEY put all that can be said truthfully about money into the following maxim: "Make all you can, save all you can, give all you can." This rule is so brief, exhaustive, and scriptural, that it would not be out of place in the Bible. Wesley himself never made a happier statement of truth than this; he crowded the whole subject into a nutshell. In this chapter we will consider the first clause, "Make all you can."

So far from wrong being attached to money-making, duty enjoins it. He who has the talent and opportunity to accumulate is under special obligation to make money. Some men and women are born money-makers; "they find a gold dollar under every stone they turn over." Their Midas-touch converts everything they handle into gold. They are called lucky, fortunate. But that is not it. It is simply their genius for making money. Matthews says of this class, "They have the instinct of accumulation. The talent and inclination to convert dollars into doubloons by bargains or shrewd investments are in them just as strongly marked and as uncontrollable as were the ability and the inclination of Shakespeare to produce a Hamlet and an Othello, of Raphael to paint the cartoons, of Beethoven to compose his symphonies, or Morse to invent an electric telegraph. As it would have been a gross dereliction of duty, a shameful perversion of gifts, had these latter disregarded the instincts of their genius and engaged in the scramble for wealth, so would a Rothschild, an Astor, or a Peabody have sinned had they done violence to their natures, and thrown their energies into channels where they would have proved dwarfs, and not giants.

"The mission of a Lawrence, equally with that of an Agassiz, a Bierstadt, or a Cornell, is defined in the faculties God has given him; and no one of them has a right to turn aside from the paths to which his finger so plainly points." Academies, colleges, hospitals, museums, libraries, railroads—none of which could have been possible without their accumulations—are the proofs of their usefulness; and though the millionaire too often converts his brain into a ledger, and his heart into a millstone, yet this starvation of his spiritual nature is no more necessary in his pursuit than in that of the doctor or the lawyer. The same law of duty that enjoins accumulation also prescribes the rules under which it must be made. If millions are made, under a careful observation of these rules, no sin can attach to the fortune. It is just as right to acquire a million as a dollar, if it be honestly done. Dishonesty makes the acquisition wrong, whether it be much or little. The wrong does not lie in the amount accumulated, but in the method. Therefore we say, without hesitation, that it is the duty of men who can to make money.

Others are not born with a genius to grow rich, any more than to paint or orate. They must cultivate a talent in this direction, as opportunity offers, as they would cultivate a talent for any work of the artisan. In this way, and in this alone, can they improve their God-given faculties as duty requires. With strict integrity of character any person can safely make the venture. The late Amos Lawrence wrote to a younger brother, "As a first and leading principle, let every transaction be of that pure and honest character that you would not be ashamed to have it appear before the whole world as clearly as to yourself. It is of the highest consequence that you should not only cultivate correct principles, but that you should place your standard so high as to require great vigilance in living up to it." It was under the rule of principle as high as this that Lawrence amassed his own fortune. Duty requires that others should observe the same rule in making money. There is no danger in the hardest struggle for riches under such a rule.

The acquisition of money becomes a valuable school of discipline when conducted upon Christian principles. It calls into exercise the best qualities of mind and heart, thereby developing true manhood and womanhood. To prove this statement, we have only to call the roll of honor, as it stands recorded on the page of history—Lawrence, Grant, Appleton, Spooner, McDonough, Allen, Peabody, Slater, Goodhue, Dodge, and others too numerous to mention. Their business did more for them than their schools. The wealth it brought them was the least important possession; the spotless characters coined in the process were more precious than gold. "A good name is rather to be chosen than great riches, and loving favor rather than silver and gold." This alone justifies the effort to make all you can. The process is not necessarily demoralizing, but uplifting and inspiring.

When Goodhue, of New York City, was buried, the din of traffic was hushed in the streets; and city officials, merchant princes, clergymen, lawyers, and scholars gathered to pay an honest tribute of respect to his memory. The character of the deceased drew them there, not his riches. The pastor said, "It is the recognized worth of private character which has extorted this homage. It is the man himself; the pure, high-minded, righteous man who adorned our nature, who dignified the mercantile profession, who was superior to his station, his riches, his exposures, and made the common virtues more respected and venerable than shining talents or public honors; who vindicated the dignity of common life, and carried a large, high, and noble spirit into ordinary affairs; who made men recognize something inviolable and awful in the private conscience, and thus gave sanctity and value to our common humanity. This was the power, this the attraction, this the value of Jonathan Goodhue's life. He has made men believe in virtue. He has made them honor character more than station or wealth. He has illustrated the possible purity, disinterestedness, and elevation of mercantile

LORD FRANCIS BACON.

life. He has shown that a rich man can enter the kingdom of heaven. He stands up by acclamation as the model of a Christian merchant." And all this under the rule " make all you can."

The real value of money was never so great as now. The progress of civilization has largely multiplied opportunities and enjoyments, so that money can do more good now than ever. " With this talisman, a man can surround himself with richer means of enjoyment, secure a more varied and harmonious culture, and set in motion grander schemes of philanthropy in this last half of the nineteenth century than at any previous period in the world's history." The proper use of money is better understood to-day than ever before; and there is a more general disposition to use it well. If some know better how to waste it, others understand, as never before, how to dispense it for the highest welfare of mankind. Organizations to spend money for the public good are legion now, and every form of suffering humanity finds relief. Another strong reason for the counsel " make all you can."

Lord Bacon's remark about riches will add force to the foregoing: " I cannot call riches by a better name than the 'baggage' of virtue; the Roman word is better, 'impediment,' for as the baggage is to an army, so are riches to virtue. It cannot be spared or left behind, and yet it hindereth the march; yea, and the care of it sometimes loseth or disturbeth the victory. Of great riches there is no real use, except it be in the distribution; the rest is but conceit."

SAVE ALL YOU CAN.

WHEN Wesley gave this counsel—" Save all you can "—he did not mean to inculcate stinginess, but a wise economy. There is a kind of saving that amounts to meanness; it ought to be avoided. " There is that withholdeth more than is meet, but it tendeth to poverty." If it fill the coffers, it empties the soul of all that is noble. Wesley was the sworn enemy of such saving as that. He meant what Dr. Franklin did when he wrote to a young man: " The way to wealth is as plain as the way to market. It depends chiefly on two words, industry and frugality; that is, waste neither time nor money, but make the best use of both. If you would be wealthy, think of saving as well as of getting. The Indies have not made Spain rich, because her outgoes are greater than her incomes." Again, Dr. Franklin wrote, " You may think that a little punch now and then, diet a little more costly, clothes a little finer, and a little entertainment now and then, can be no great matter. But, remember, many a little makes a mickle." Still, again, " A man may, if he knows not how to save as he gets, keep his nose all his life to the grindstone, and die not worth a groat at last."

Saving in this sense, is certainly a duty. It is the only way to prevent going behindhand in finances and to become forehanded. The author knew a farmer who was wont to do considerable business as a justice of the peace. A short time before his death, in old age, he told a neighbor that he was worth fifty thousand dollars. The neighbor was greatly surprised, and inquired:—

"How in the world have you done it?"

"By saving what other people waste," was the old man's reply.

Successful business men, whether merchants, mechanics, manufacturers, or farmers, claim that economy is absolutely necessary to success.

Richard Cobden, the noted English statesman, said to an audience of workingmen: "The world has always been divided into two classes: those who have saved, and those who have spent; the thrifty and the extravagant. The building of all the houses, the mills, the bridges, and the ships, and the accomplishment of all other great works which have rendered man civilized and happy, has been done by the savers—the thrifty; and those who have wasted their resources have always been their slaves."

Samuel Budgett claimed that the want of economy doomed "hundreds of business men to failure." Economy was one of the cardinal lessons he taught his six hundred clerks. He rebuked them for using too much twine in tying packages and too much paper in wrapping them, and required them to pick up the old nails about the premises, that they might be straightened for use. Some of the clerks called him penurious, because they did not understand him. He required these things more for their sake than his own. It was his way of teaching economy.

His numerous gifts to charitable objects proved that he was not penurious, but he was economical. One day he saw a lad who was following a load of hay pick up the locks that fell therefrom. He stopped to commend the boy, and recommended him to practice economy as a duty and advantage, and then gave him a shilling. At another time, he was walking with a female servant in the highway when he found a potato. He picked it up and presented it to his servant, accompanied with a practical lecture on economy. He promised to furnish land on which to plant it with its product from year to year. The pledge was accepted, and the potato planted. The yield was thirteen potatoes the first year, ninety-three the second year, and a barrel full the third year, and had the experiment been continued for fifty years Budgett could not have found land enough in England on which to plant the last crop. Here Budgett taught, not only the practical advantage of economy, but furnished a capital illustration of the law of accumulation that follows.

Many youth say, "Of what use is it to lay up a few cents a day? If it were a dollar, it would be worth the while." The small amount saved blinds them to the great value of the habit formed. Economy, as a habit of life, is of priceless worth. The amount saved, great or small, is nothing in comparison with the habit of economy. And yet the actual accumulation of small savings will astonish unthinking ones.

The habit of economy enables men to live within their means. They pay as they go, and thus keep out of debt. Smiles says, "Debt makes everything a temptation. It lowers a man in self-respect, places him at the mercy of his tradesman and his servant, and renders him a slave in many respects, for he can no longer call himself his own master, nor boldly look the world in the face. It is also difficult for a man who is in debt to be truthful; hence, it is said that lying rides on debt's back. The debtor has to frame excuses to his creditor for postponing payment of the money he owes him, and probably, also, to contrive falsehoods."

SIR EDWARD BULWER-LYTTON.

Sir Edward Bulwer-Lytton wrote: "Some of the neediest men I ever knew had a nominal five thousand pounds a year. Every man is needy who spends more than he has; no man is needy who spends less. I may so ill-manage my money that, with five thousand pounds a year, I purchase the worst evils of poverty, terror, and shame; I may so well manage my money that, with one hundred pounds a year, I purchase the blessings of wealth, safety, and respect."

Doctor Johnson claimed that debt was a "calamity." He said, "Do not accustom yourself to consider debt only as an inconvenience; you will find it a calamity. Poverty takes away so many means of doing good, and produces so much inability to resist evil, both natural and moral, that it is by all virtuous means to be avoided. Let it be your first care, then, not to be in any man's debt, for this destroys liberty, and makes some virtues impracticable and others extremely difficult. Frugality is not only the basis of quiet, but of beneficence. No man can help others that wants help himself; we must have enough before we have to spare."

Nature is frugal. The wisest economy is practiced throughout the entire domain. Nothing is wasted. Not a particle of matter is lost. The leaves fall and decay, the flowers wither and die, the rains sink into the earth, the snowdrifts disappear before the breath of spring, wood burns to ashes—but nothing is lost. In other forms all these contribute to the on-going of the universe; and without this economical arrangement we know not that the divine plan could succeed. Economy is one of the pillars on which the whole fabric rests.

"It is the savings of the world that have made the civilization of the world. Savings are the result of labors; and it is only when laborers begin to save that the results of civilization accumulate. We have said that thrift began with civilization; we might almost have said that thrift produced civilization. Thrift produces capital, and capital is the conserved result of labor. The capitalist is merely a man who does not spend all that is earned by work."

GIVE ALL YOU CAN.

SAVING to give is the highest and noblest motive. He who saves all he can is alone able to give as he should. There appears to be this natural connection between saving and giving, the secret of it being found in the disposition. Hence, too, the genuine satisfaction found in the act—satisfaction not only from giving, but, also, satisfaction of saving in order to give. It is the only way to enjoy money, and men who have it ought certainly to enjoy it as they enjoy other blessings. One of the last thoughts expressed by Peter C. Brooks, near the close of his life, was, "Of all the ways of disposing of money, giving it away is the most satisfactory." His experience confirmed the divine statement, "It is more blessed to give than to receive." "The liberal soul shall be made fat: and he that watereth shall be watered also himself." "He which soweth sparingly shall reap also sparingly, and he which soweth bountifully shall reap also bountifully."

Many men and women in our land of a past generation gave all they could in charity, and there are many of the present generation of philanthropists who are doing the same. In that bright galaxy which is just passing away, no name shines more conspicuously than that of George W. Childs, late founder and proprietor of the *Public Ledger*, of Philadelphia, the model newspaper of our country. He began his career as errand-boy in a bookstore in Baltimore, where he worked early and late with so much spirit and fidelity as to attract the attention of a publisher of Philadelphia, who secured him for his book-keeper. He served here until he went into the book business for himself. All these years he was as devoted to self-improvement as he was to business. He saved all the fragments of time for intellectual growth. While books were a coveted means of mental advancement in spare hours, his sharp observation became a source of his highest mental discipline. A stranger would have inferred from his appearance that he was a college graduate, but we have indicated how few intellectual advantages he enjoyed. He was strictly a self-made man, a millionaire philanthropist, more popular and widely-known, perhaps, than any other American. It was said of him: "Nobody in the United States has so many cordial friends; nobody in the world has befriended so many people."

His house was the home for public men. Irving, Emerson, Longfellow, Hawthorne, Motley, Prescott, Bancroft, Cameron, Farrar, Dickens, Grant, Garfield, and kindred spirits delighted to sojourn there, and yet Mr. Childs had no desire for public office. He might have been mayor of his city, governor of his State, and President of the United States, but he declined all these honors. Leaders of both parties united some years ago and offered to elect him mayor of Philadelphia if he would consent, promising that no other candidate should be in the field. In 1888, leaders of both parties urged him to become a candidate for the Presidency, two leading Democratic papers agreeing to contribute one hundred thousand dollars each to the campaign fund, and the president of a great railroad company offered his check for fifty thousand dollars; but he was firm in his declination of all such honors. "Your name will break the solid South," was urged. Mr. Childs answered: "Its use in that convention will break the heart of my wife." He had been so intimate with Presidents that both he and his wife knew what the trials of the White House were. General Grant said to him, "I would rather be proprietor of the *Public Ledger* than President of the United States."

Mr. Childs was happiest when he was giving all he could. Here his methods were as simple and unpretentious as they were in his business. He enjoyed using his great property to benefit his fellow-men. Giving was a calling with him. He said, "I believe that children should be educated to give away with judgment their little all; to share their possessions with their friends. If they are trained in this spirit, it will always be easy for them to be generous; if they are not, it will be more natural for them in the course of time to be mean, and meanness can grow upon a man until it saps his soul." He once said to a friend, "Nothing is harder than to prosper and to give away of your prosperity at the same time." But that is exactly what Mr. Childs did. He was as industrious and hard working a man as lived in Philadelphia, and he was as economical, too. To do good with his fortune was his chief study and aim.

Two men were conversing about the vast estate of John Jacob Astor some years ago. One asked the other if he would be willing to take care of the millionaire's property—fifteen or twenty millions of dollars—merely for his board and clothing. "No!" was the indignant reply. "Do you take me for a fool?" "Well," rejoined the other, "that is all Mr. Astor himself gets for taking care of it; he's found, and that's all. The houses, the warehouses, the ships, the farms, which he counts by the hundred, and is often obliged to take care of, are for the accommodation of others." "But, then, he has the income, the rents of the large property—five or six hundred thousand dollars per annum," responded the other. "True; but he can do nothing with that income except to build more houses, warehouses, and ships, or loan money on mortgages for the convenience of others. He's found, and you can make nothing else out of it," was the triumphant answer of the first speaker.

JOHN WESLEY.

We once heard a rich man say, "I was happier getting my wealth than I am spending it." We have heard of other rich men saying the same thing; but no man will say it who observes Wesley's rule, "Give all you can." That is the heaven-ordained condition of enjoying the spending of a fortune more than accumulating it. Cooper, Lawrence, and all that class of men, enjoyed spending their money far more than they did getting it, because a benevolent spirit controlled them. It is the liberal soul that is made fat; the stingy soul is made lean. They could almost say with Mark Antony, "I have lost all except what I have given away." What is dispensed by well-directed benevolence is not lost, it is invested. It will yield a constant income. "Give, and it shall be given unto you; good measure, pressed down and shaken together, and running over, shall men give into your bosom. For with the same measure that ye mete withal, it shall be measured to you again." It is good measure when we get that which is "pressed down, shaken together, and running over;" and that is what genuine benevolence receives every time. Therefore our charities should be reckoned as investments. The remainder of our property may "take to itself wings and fly away;" but this, never. Money judiciously given away is safe.

Opposers of the rule, "give all you can," plead "charity begins at home," and it usually ends there with those who make this plea. It has been styled "a neat pocket edition of covetousness," and really means that selfishness begins at home; and where selfishness begins, charity ends. Behind this maxim thousands have intrenched themselves against every appeal of benevolence, presenting a striking contrast with the noble-hearted man who was asked, " Have you not made yourself rich enough to retire from business?" "By no means," he replied: " I am not rich enough yet to give one leaf of the catechism to each member of my family." "How large is your family?" his interrogator inquired. "About fourteen hundred millions." This contrast presents the essential difference between selfishness and benevolence in practical life. "Self is Dives in the mansion, clothed in purple, and faring sumptuously every day. Benevolence is Lazarus lying at his gate, and fed only with the crumbs that fall from his table."

The spirit that gives all it can ennobles all other acts. In William Cary it manifested itself early toward companions and friends, and those who were poor like himself; and later in life it stood forth grandly in his great missionary labors in the East, where he literally spared not himself in toiling for the good of others. It is an interesting fact that he was the son of a very humble shoemaker, and the two men who supported him in the foreign missionary field were extremely poor in their boyhood—one of them was the son of a carpenter, and the other of a weaver—all three growing into manhood with this noble attribute beautifying their lives. The money of the two with the personal labors of the third, established a magnificent college at Serampore, planted sixteen missionary stations, translated the Bible into sixteen languages, and inaugurated a grand moral revolution in British India.

(252) BENJAMIN FRANKLIN.

XXV.

THE WISDOM OF SELF-HELP.

A MERCHANT of considerable wealth had two daughters, aged respectively sixteen and eighteen years. One day, when a financial crisis called his attention to the subject particularly, he said to them:—

"Daughters, suppose that I should suddenly become poor, as is the case with many wealthy men in the city now, what could you do?"

The inquiry was unexpected to the daughters, and, after some hesitation, one of them replied by asking another question:—

"Father, do you think that there is any danger of that?"

"I do not think there is any immediate danger," her father answered, "and yet I may lose all my property, as others have. Who would have thought, six months ago, that Mr. D—— would become a poor man?"

Much more was said, and the two daughters were very much impressed by the conversation. The idea was wholly new to them, but it was a reasonable suggestion. If their father should lose his property, there was no possible way for them to earn a livelihood. They discussed the matter, *pro* and *con*, and finally decided to fit themselves for some definite pursuit, as soon as the younger one had completed her school days. It was settled, too, with the consent of the parents, that the eldest daughter should learn dressmaking, and the younger millinery. At the proper time they put themselves under the instruction of a dressmaker and milliner, going daily to their tasks, until they were well qualified to undertake business for themselves, but their father was still prosperous, so that it was not necessary for them to ply the trades acquired.

Less than three years elapsed, however, when their father lost his entire property, and soon afterward a stroke of paralysis disabled him for life. The daughters were now prepared for the strange vicissitude. They opened a milliner's shop at once in the city, connecting dressmaking therewith, and easily succeeded in supporting the whole family. Their business increased so rapidly that twenty girls were employed in the establishment within three years after it was opened.

These daughters were accomplished. In school they were studious and fairly brilliant, and at home served in their well-appointed residence with grace and dignity. Yet there was no compromise of true womanhood in pursuing the course described. They did not descend to it; they ascended, in the spirit of genuine self-help, in which there is always wisdom as well as honor. These two young ladies developed character by their thoughtful and wise choice, and were more womanly in consequence. The result of their experience confirmed the remark, "The spirit of self-help is the root of all genuine growth in the individual; and exhibited in the lives of many, it constitutes the true source of mental vigor and strength. Help from without is often enfeebling in its effects, but help from within invariably invigorates. Whatever is done for men or classes, to a certain extent, takes away the stimulus and necessity of doing for themselves. . . . Even the best institutions can give a man no active aid. Perhaps the utmost they can do is to leave him free to develop himself and improve his individual condition."

Henry Laurens was an illustrious patriot and statesman in the time of the American Revolution. Through the uncertain fortunes of war, he found himself a prisoner in the Tower of London, where he wrote to his daughters, as follows: "It is my duty to warn you to prepare for the trial of earning your daily bread by your daily labor. Fear not servitude; encounter it, if it shall be necessary, with the spirit becoming women of honest and pious hearts, who have neither been fashionably nor affectedly religious." It might have been the first lesson in self-help the daughters had received from their illustrious father; if it was, we must say, "Better late than never" so wise counsel. Misfortune may be specially suited to magnify the virtue; but, surely, prosperity ought not to blind one to its great value as a discipline.

The following fact has just been furnished as an illustration of our theme. A boy of four years lost both father and mother by death. In consequence, the orphan was cared for by his grandfather, who was a business man. The best advantages for education were given to the grandson until he was sixteen years of age, when the grandfather suggested that it was time for him to be thinking of some definite life-work. One day he was somewhat surprised by his grandson's decision to strike out for himself. "I have considered the matter for several months," said the youth, "and there is no reason why I should be a dependent on you longer. With your consent, I will find a situation for myself in Boston, for I am confident that I can work myself into some profitable business. If I cannot do it, neither you nor anyone else can do it for me." There was so much real manliness in the boy's decision, and such a sensible view of true self-help, that the grandfather was delighted, and gave his consent without the least hesitation. Twelve years have passed since that day, and the grandson, not yet thirty years of age, is a prosperous business man of Boston. He is married, has two beautiful children, has built a fine residence near his grandfather, bids fair to be rich, and is the pride and joy of his relatives. His noble character is his largest fortune, and who can deny the real influence of self-help in forming it?

Dr. Arnold, the great English teacher, used to say, "Never do for a pupil what he can do for himself." We would say the same of any young person who is not in school. In the home, shop, business of any kind, "never do for him what he can do for himself," for such a course will hinder more than it will help. If a youth is to be made the most of possible, he must do it himself; no one can do it for him. Others can assist him to self-help, and that is all the really valuable assistance they can render. Dr. Arnold said of his work, "I do not work for, but with, my pupils, striving to guide them into efforts for self-education. . . . It is not knowledge that I teach, but the means of gaining knowledge. I desire not so much to impart information, as to prepare the minds of pupils to use to advantage subsequent acquisitions; to learn how to study, and how to start aright in the life-loving work of self-culture."

Emerson said of him, "Napoleon renounced, once for all, sentiments and affections, and would help himself with his hands and his head. With him is no miracle, and no magic. He is a worker in brass, in iron, in wood, in earth, in roads, in buildings, in money, and in troops, and a very consistent and wise master-workman. Anything he would do that was necessary; and he never looked down contemptuously upon a man who must work or starve. Once, when walking with Mrs. Balcombe, some servants carrying heavy boxes passed by on the road and Mrs. Balcombe directed them, in angry tone, to keep back; Napoleon interfered, saying, 'Respect the burden, Madam! Respect the burden!'"

EDUCATION NOT A FOE TO LABOR.

SOME bright people think that the higher education, at least, makes young men and women lazy. For this reason they discourage a thorough course of study, academic and collegiate, for those who engage in mechanical and mercantile business. "The time from sixteen to twenty years of age is worth more to a boy in his life-pursuit than it possibly can be in academy and college," they say. Hence, there has been actual embarrassment to college-bred young men in finding positions in the working world. Many business men believe that this educated class are less practical, and unable to render as valuable service as those who spend their time from sixteen to twenty years of age in becoming familiar with their chosen pursuit.

One of this cultured class sought a position in a Boston warehouse several years ago.

"You are too old for the place; we want a boy of sixteen or seventeen years," said the proprietor.

"I am willing to do a boy's work, for I want to learn the business," replied the young man.

"But we are not willing that you should. You would be subjected to trying annoyances by the clerks, who would poke fun at a college-bred young man of twenty-two doing a boy's work."

"That will not annoy me in the least, for I am determined to learn the business, and I know that my education will prove of great advantage to me."

"That may be," responded the merchant, "but the time you spent in college and preparation for it, was just the time that would have been most valuable to you in learning this business."

He did not secure the situation; and his case was one of a large class that illustrates the prevalence of an error in regard to education being inimical to successful business. There is no truth in the statement, and youth should beware of entertaining such a sentiment. Education does not foster laziness any more than it does pride; and surely it does not foster the latter, for the most learned men and women are the most modest and unassuming. The more they know, the less they see to be proud of. Learning modifies their estimate of self, and tends to make them humble. So of labor. Education dignifies it. The mere smatterer may feel above manual labor, but the real scholar never does. He knows that it is the source of wealth, and that it is promotive of health, affluence, and happiness; he knows that laziness is the source of poverty and misery, and he knows this much better than the uncultured man does. Hence, he honors hard work, and respects the man who is willing to put it into his daily life.

Young men or women cannot secure a good education without much labor. They must study more hours in twenty-four than the farmer or mechanic works. There is no movement among the literary class for eight or ten hours' work in a day; they must put in more than that if they would succeed. The question with them is not how few hours they can devote to the pursuit of knowledge, but how many. They must consecrate every moment of time at their command to their personal culture, whether it be ten or fifteen hours a day. Now, there is nothing in this practice that tends to cultivate laziness. On the contrary, it is well suited to cultivate industry, to attach the proper value to time, and to make labor honorable. A lazy boy or girl never gets much of an education. He prefers ignorance to mental labor, and poverty to manual labor. It is not culture that promotes his laziness, but the want of it. Introduce him into shop or warehouse, and he will be lazy there. If he knew more, he would be less lazy. True culture would diminish his laziness greatly. Education is what he specially needs. A dull, lazy scholar never becomes an expert in mechanics or trade, never! Unskilled labor is confined to the ignorant class. Sharpness of intellect and a degree of culture are indispensable to skilled labor. Experts are bright by nature and education.

Mr. Andrew Carnegie has not a good reason for the conclusion that "the almost total absence of the graduate from high positions in the business world, seems to justify the conclusion that college education, as it exists, is fatal to success in that domain." One of our prominent educators replies to him thus: "If this be true, why do self-made men so invariably send their sons to college? Is it that they may become unfitted for the positions their fathers now hold? On the contrary, these men are convinced that their sons will carry on their business better with the increased intelligence, and are, therefore, determined to give them the benefits of a college education." Chauncey M. Depew says, "I never saw a self-made man in my life who did not firmly believe that he had been handicapped, no matter how great his success, by deficiency in education, and who was not determined to give his children the advantages of which he felt, not only in business, but in the intercourse with his fellow-men, so greatly in need."

A few writers claim that our system of common school education creates an aversion to manual labor, and hence the rush of youth into mercantile life. The subject has created so great interest that the opinions of competent judges should be welcomed.

J. W. Dickinson, secretary of the Massachusetts Board of Education, says: "I believe that our system of public instruction is so organized and administered that it has a direct tendency to make intelligent, honest, and industrious men. The character of the people, their enterprise, and their great success in the affairs of private and social life, show that our educational institutions are accomplishing the objects for which they were established."

E. H. Capen, president of Tufts College, says: "I do not think the public school system has any tendency to create false notions as to the dignity of labor in the minds of our youth. I think it has decidedly the opposite effect."

Let the best discipline of our schools be enjoyed by the rising generation, and the dignity of labor will be more honored in the next century than it has been in this. As schools advance and scatter their blessings, farms and workshops possess new attractions.

PREPARED FOR POSSIBILITIES.

NO one can foretell the possibilities of a human life. In an age and country where the poorest boy may become the richest, best educated, and most influential citizen, and the humblest girl a model wife and mother, teacher and scholar, and mistress of the White House, it is presumptuous to prophesy the fortune a youth may command forty years hence. Providential changes may lift one into a position of honor and trust, or of hardship and trial, wholly unanticipated, and the fact should become a factor in the preparation for a life-work. It is certain that the faithful improvement of present opportunities to develop the whole man, will qualify a youth for any post of duty to which Providence may call him.

Forty years ago, a school-girl in Ohio resolved to acquire as much culture as her poverty would allow. She was the daughter of a farmer in humble circumstances, yet strongly desirous that his children should qualify themselves for usefulness. This daughter aspired to be a teacher, and she devoted herself to this commendable purpose with the closest application, going to school whenever money enough could be scraped together to pay the expenses of a term. She did not dream that any higher or nobler position than that of teacher in her own or some other town awaited her. She was too poor and humble to justify herself in building air castles of wealth or fame. The improvement of her time, however, and the discipline to which she subjected her powers, were as complete as they would have been if she had known that she would occupy the highest place in the land. Hence, she was prepared for any position to which a noble woman might be called. This Ohio school-girl, Miss Lucretia Rudolph, became Mrs. President Garfield, mistress of the White House at Washington. Little did she dream that such an exalted experience awaited her, when she modestly but persistently pursued her studies at Chester Academy and Hiram Institute. Indeed, when she became the wife of her teacher, James A. Garfield, such a heritage could not have seemed among the possibilities. But that was immaterial so long as her fidelity in youth fitted her for that, or any other sphere. The school-girl who is true to herself and her Maker is qualified to be, not only a teacher, but, also, wife of the President of the United States.

The foregoing proves that youth may acquire culture, mental and moral, that will adorn the highest position in womanhood and manhood. Should misfortune disappoint the hopes, such a one can take up the burden of poverty and personal sorrow, and bear it with royal dignity. Culture will not hinder the discharge of the humblest duties of every-day life, but will dignify them, and thereby magnify their importance.

A young lady who had scarcely been two years out of school, where her talents and application won for her the highest honors, was introduced by marriage to rapidly accumulating wealth. In fifteen years she was placed above the necessity of toil and care, moving in a circle where wealth and intelligence ruled. But misfortune overtook her husband; his wealth vanished in a single season, and finally, he himself went down to his grave under the calamity, leaving his wife and four children penniless. Although such a possibility had not been thought of, she was prepared for it. Her faithful self-culture in girlhood made it easy to fit herself for a medical practitioner. Soon she was settled in New York City, where her ability and skill rapidly increased her practice by winning public confidence. With business came money, and she gave her two sons a collegiate education, preparing them for the Christian ministry; and her two daughters, educated, like herself, to adorn any place of usefulness and honor, were introduced into affluent homes of their own.

The celebrated Dr. Parr was talented, studious, and trusty in his youth, though he did not indulge anticipations of greatness and fame. The latter were thrust upon

MICHAEL FARADAY.

him in due time, though he never would have shared them but for the industry and application of his youth. Here he laid the foundation of his future renown. Greatness easily followed early fidelity.

In early manhood Parr married a pert, pretty miss, his inferior socially and mentally. He might have made a better selection had he anticipated the possibility of great learning and wisdom, and if his wife had known that she was going to wed a learned man of the future she might have fitted herself for the position.

Put not even thinking of such a possibility, she became the wife of a man who was far, far above her thirty years thereafter. She could not appreciate his love of books, nor was she at all fitted to mingle in the literary circle to which he belonged. Consequently she became a perfect "thorn in the flesh." There was neither peace nor comfort in his home. The years in which an admiring public honored him were wretched years to him because life was embittered at the fountain. His domestic relations were a torture. Neither party was prepared for possibilities. Both got what they did not bargain for, or expect.

Michael Faraday was a poor boy, the son of a blacksmith, who apprenticed him to a bookbinder in London by the name of Reband, at the age of thirteen. Here the boy laid the foundation of his future greatness by making himself familiar with the contents of the books he bound. He remained in the bindery at night, after employer and employes had left, to read the volumes to which he had access. He became especially interested in "Mrs. Marcet's Conversations on Chemistry," and instituted a series of experiments, which made it necessary to invent and manufacture apparatus for his own use. Electricity, as well as chemistry, commanded his attention, absorbing every leisure moment, taxing his brain constantly, and often "turning night into day." There is no doubt that he was a born philosopher, but his natural gifts would not have served him profitably without those early habits of thoughtful inquiry, industry, and indomitable purpose, that made his youth remarkable.

These facts confirm the remark, "Youth is the springtime of life," the season of seed-sowing. "What shall the harvest be?" All that the most exacting could ask, if it be the real preparation for the possibilities of mature life.

ADAPTING ONE'S SELF TO CIRCUMSTANCES.

VERY few men and women can adapt themselves to all circumstances. They may adapt themselves to *some* circumstances, but not to all. Lazy, shiftless people have the poorest faculty to do this; enterprising, successful men and women can do it readily, for it is one of the conditions of success. They are obliged to make the best of things, bitter though the experience may be, and so they must accept the situation day by day. To sit down and lament and lose heart under any circumstances is to give up the race of life.

There lies before me a Maine woman's description of her pioneer life in the valley of the Penobscot. She says:—

"Trees were big ones in those days, and husband could not pile them alone, and we had no neighbors with whom we could exchange works, so he used to help me in the morning about the house, and then we went out into the clearing.

Husband would get one end of a log well up on the pile and then I used to put a handspike under that and hold it until he could pry up the other end. I made all the cloth we had; made a year's sweetening from maple syrup. I knit mittens, socks, shirts, and drawers, and even made cloth caps and my own bonnet." She was happy, with all the privations of her pioneer life, but she might have been otherwise, and she might have made her husband wretched, too; she had a capital opportunity to accomplish both. Many women would have been miserable in the circumstances, for the want of this excellent faculty of adapting themselves to circumstances. She possessed this quality in a high degree, and her humble home in the woods had as much real enjoyment in it as was ever found in a palace, and probably more.

But the mass of young people, and older ones as well, are not living pioneer lives. They dwell where society is settled, its manners and customs fixed. And yet they have as much need of the quality under discussion as pioneers in order that social life may be enjoyed at its best. There is no day when its possession will not result in good. In the most common walks of life as well as in the most select, its use is constantly demanded. For example, a Christian woman was in affluent circumstances. Her husband was able to provide her with all the servants she desired, and with all the comforts and even the elegances of a city home. But unexpectedly and suddenly he lost his property, and his business, too. "I can support the family by keeping boarders," suggested the lady. Her husband interposed objections to that, as it might impair her health. "I have no doubt that it would do me good," she replied, laughing. "Well, you take a philosophic view of the matter, I must confess," continued her husband; "you do not seem to be very much troubled with your new experience." "Why should I be troubled?" responded the wife. "I have no doubt that it will all turn out for the best in the end; that is the way things do when we endeavor to make them turn out for the best." Such a disposition is a fortune to a man or woman; it is really success itself, at least on one line.

Perhaps the need of this quality is most apparent among public men. Few of them accept the inevitable vicissitudes of public life with much grace. Dom Pedro II., late emperor of Brazil, is a notable exception. He belonged to a royal family, and was only five years of age when he became nominally the emperor of Brazil. He was a close observer of men and governments all of his life, as well as an accomplished scholar and philanthropist. From boyhood he was annoyed by the existence of slavery in his own land. He believed that it was wrong to hold property in men, and that God would not prosper a government that sanctioned it. So he adopted measures for the gradual emancipation of the slaves, its final abolition being secured in 1888. He was in Europe at the time, his daughter, Princess Isabella, acting as regent in his absence. At Nice he received a telegram from his daughter, saying that "she had that day signed a decree, totally, universally, and forever abolishing slavery in Brazil." With tears of joy coursing down his cheeks, he exclaimed, "Lord, now let Thy servant depart in peace, since mine eyes have seen Thy glory and Thy salvation." He was seriously sick when the telegram was received, but at once he began to improve, and was soon restored to perfect health, and restored to Brazil.

He was emphatically the friend and patron of free institutions. He always admired the government of the United States, and the institutions thriving under it. He visited this country several years ago, and became personally acquainted with its best things, and said, frankly, that he hoped to see the day when his own loved Brazil would be like the United States. He did live to see it, although he lost his throne before this consummation was reached. Neverthless, it was through his influence and by his plans that we now have "The United States of Brazil." It was, of course, a severe trial for him to abdicate before his beau ideal of a country was realized, but that he accepted the inevitable with good grace, if not good cheer, appears from his own words. In exile he addressed a proclamation to his late subjects, assuring them, in the most tender language, of his great love for them, and that his heart would never cease to pray for their prosperity and happiness; and still more, that he should live in hope of returning at a future day to his own land that he loved above all others, there to die and to be buried with their kindred. Few rulers ever had more unexpected and severer trials than he. He was greatly beloved by most of his people, and only an unforeseen combination of circumstances robbed him of his throne; and yet he lost not a whit of his old love of country, but continued the same thoughtful, loving, well-wishing friend of the people he had ruled.

There is much disappointment, chagrin, and failure among men for the want of this ability to accept the situation. We see it in the common walks of life, among all classes and conditions of men. A few adapt themselves to circumstances, while the many are out of sorts with their surroundings and accomplish nothing because they cannot have everything to their liking. "It is a great blessing to possess what one wishes," said one to an ancient philosopher, who replied, "It is a greater blessing still, not to desire what one does not possess."

John Newton once said, "If two angels were sent down from heaven, one to conduct an empire, and the other to sweep a street, they would feel no inclination to change employments." That is, the higher and purer the nature, the more readily do men adapt themselves to circumstances and rest satisfied. Angelic natures do it best. So that the human quality in question is not small or mean, but high and noble.

Youth needs it as much as age, yea more; for in youth both male and female are doing things for all time, and even for eternity. The earlier the disposition to be content with the allotments of Providence is established, the better will it be for all the future, here and hereafter. In the home and schoolroom, on the playground, and in social life, its beneficial influence will be enjoyed. Addison said that "it destroys all inordinate ambition, and every tendency to corruption with regard to the community in which we are placed. It gives sweetness to the conversation, and serenity to all the thoughts. It is the greatest blessing a man can enjoy in this world; and if in the present life his happiness arises from the subduing of his desires, it will arise in the next from the gratification of them."

GEORGE WASHINGTON.

XXVI.

HABIT.

"MAN is a bundle of habits," Paley said. This is true even of those who are a "bundle of prejudices;" for prejudice may become a habit by repetition. "Habits are second nature," says another, which is not putting the case so strongly. They are so readily formed, and formed so early, that they often seem to be born with the person. Yet habits are acquired; they may be taken on unconsciously, but it is done by repetition. The pianist thrums the instrument "six hours a day for twenty years," until it is more than "second nature;" it seems almost as if he were born for that special business. A popular teacher, writing upon habit, and speaking of spelling words as we write, says:—

"Spelling a word involves a combination of muscular movements of the hand, which, by repetition, becomes registered on the nerves and muscles of the hand so thoroughly that the hand spells correctly from habit. The eye guides the hand only at the start; afterwards, it is the muscular sense that guides the movement. We never unintentionally misspell our names; we have written them so often that the hand writes them without any conscious oversight of the mind." A good illustration of the power of habit.

The divine injunction, "Train up a child in the way he should go, and when he is old he will not depart from it," is true to the letter. It is equally true, also, that if he is trained up in the way he should not go, "he will not depart from it." The power of habit pertains to evil as well as good. The only difference is, that he who walks in the way of good, has a good habit, while the bad habit has him who walks in the way of evil. Another says, "A habit is something which we have; that is what the word means. As some one has wittily observed, it often becomes something which has us. Sometimes men shorten distance by 'cutting across lots,' as it is termed. Where they do this, a narrow strip of grass about a foot or fourteen inches wide will soon be destroyed, and a narrow strip of ground about the same width beneath it will be trodden hard, and that is a path. In the same way men form habits."

Habits begin to form with birth. The new-born child begins at once to show that he is a creature of habit. Let him sleep in a room with a light burning a few days or weeks, and he will protest against its removal by crying when it is extinguished; rock him to sleep at night until he is a few months old, and the mother must continue to rock him to sleep, as he has formed the habit of depending upon the rocking. On the other hand let him begin life without a lamp, and go to sleep as the birds do, without rocking, and he will never know enough of light or rocking-chair to depend upon them. It is wholly a matter of habit. Mothers endeavor to establish in their infants the good habit of receiving nourishment and sleep at stated intervals, instead of the evil habit of receiving them at any time without regard to system or health. It is the education of habit which they employ, and this continued through early life up to manhood and womanhood will secure the full benefit of the promise, "Train up the child," etc. Filial love, obedience, truthfulness, and other virtues, will follow, and when children become old they "will not depart from them." Shakespeare has it, "How use doth breed a habit in a man."

Scholars may form the good habit of obedience, improvement of time, systematic study, punctuality, thoroughness, and accuracy; or they may form the bad habits of inattention, disregard of rules, idleness, tardiness, and whatever else belongs to poor scholarship. It should not take them long to choose which class of habits to form. The highest aims of life impel them toward one, and the lowest aims toward the other. One course leads to certain success, the other to inevitable failure.

The law of habit governs the brute creation as well as the human race. The story of the blind old horse that went round and round in the bark-mill for years, grinding bark, fairly illustrates the power of habit over brutes. The beast had fulfilled his mission so well in the tanyard that he was turned out to eat grass and die. After cropping the grass a while the faithful animal would travel round and round, from force of habit, as if still at work for his kind owner in the mill. So men are likely to continue to move in the grooves which the habits of early life wore smooth and hard.

Lord Brougham said: "I trust everything, under God, to habit, upon which, in all ages, the lawgiver, as well as the schoolmaster, has mainly placed his reliance; habit which makes everything easy, and casts all difficulties upon the deviation from the wonted course. Make sobriety a habit, and intemperance will be hateful and hard; make prudence a habit, and reckless profligacy will be as contrary to the nature of the child grown an adult as the most atrocious crimes are to any of your lordships. Give a child the habit of sacredly regarding the truth, of carefully respecting the property of others, of scrupulously abstaining from all acts of improvidence which can involve him in distress, and he will just as likely think of rushing into the element in which he cannot breathe as of lying, cheating, or stealing."

Lord Brougham was himself an eminent illustration of the power of habit in his remarkable life. In his very boyhood he trained his mental faculties to habits of thought and study which bore excellent fruit through his whole life. He was not eighteen years of age when he wrote a treatise on the "Refraction and Reflection of Light," that was adopted by the Royal Society as an able paper for their "Transactions." Not a member dreamed that the author was a youth; and none of them knew the fact until his paper had reached its destination in the "Royal Transactions." He was so thoroughly trained to the habit of thought and labor that he excelled all cotemporaries in having his gifted powers well in hand for all emergencies. He was a mighty man before his head was sprinkled with gray. He was highly and widely honored in his life, and his memory all nations delight to cherish.

THE DRINK HABIT.

THE prophet vividly portrayed the growth and power of the drink habit when he said, "Woe unto them that draw iniquity with cords of vanity, and sin as it were with a cart rope." The beginning of an evil habit is small— "a cord of vanity" so weak and frail that it can be broken as easily as the web of a spider; but in the end it has the strength of a cart rope. This is especially true of the drink habit. Beginning with an occasional indulgence in the use of the weaker intoxicants—cider, beer, and wine—which so many consider harmless, an appetite for stronger liquors is created before the drinker is aware of it, and he finds himself a slave to the habit. One of this class exclaimed, out of the depths of his bondage, "I would give a world, if I had it, to be a true man; yet, in twenty-four hours I may be overcome and disgraced by a shilling's worth of sin."

Alcohol is the only thing that can make a drunkard, and it is the intoxicating element of all liquors that inebriate, from whiskey down to cider and beer. A smaller per cent of it is found in cider, beer, and wine, but there is enough of it even in these beverages to create the "drunkard's appetite," and form the worst habit that ever enslaved a human being. Nearly all intemperate men and women began their drinking career by the use of the weaker intoxicants. The writer once put the following question to seventy reformed drunkards assembled in the hall of Washingtonian Home: "When did you begin to form the drink habit, and by the use of what beverage?" The answer from all but one was, "In boyhood, by the use of cider and beer." That one fact is a stronger appeal for total abstinence than any argument possible. The greatest danger lurks in the weaker beverage, because it is thought to be comparatively harmless, when it is as potent as stronger liquors to create the drink habit. Two or three per cent of alcohol will create the appetite for strong drink as surely, and perhaps as quickly, as thirty or forty per cent. This fact should stamp cider and beer with the brand of condemnation as plainly as it does whiskey or brandy.

The real philosophy of the evil is this: Alcohol does not quench thirst nor satisfy the drinker. The more he drinks, the more he wants. One glass a day this month or year will be followed by two glasses a day next month or year. In this way, more and more is drunk, in larger quantities and more frequently, until drunkenness becomes a habit. It is not so with other drinks and foods. When thirsty we drink water and are satisfied. One glass satisfies us this year just as well as it did last year. A quart or a gallon in a given time will be ample one, ten, or fifty years hence. When hungry we eat bread and meat and are satisfied. If we eat one loaf of bread each day this year, we shall not be obliged to eat two loaves a day next year to appease our hunger. A loaf a day for life may be the rule, and it is because the natural appetite is gratified. On the other hand, alcohol, in large or small doses, creates an unnatural appetite which is never satisfied, but cries continually give, give, give.

With such undeniable facts before men, it is strange that young or old should dally with this tempter. Knowing that the victims of intemperance outnumber those of war and pestilence combined, it is inexplicable that the procession on the road to ruin continues its doleful tramp. Men see their fellows drink and perish, and yet they drink on, and perish also. In no other matters do they act thus. They avoid all other dangers if possible. They are loth even to take their chances amidst other perils. They give the unseaworthy vessel a wide berth. They refuse to ride on the train that is run by a drunken engineer. They keep as far away as possible from other dangers.

A wealthy lady of New York City advertised for a coachman. She was very timid, and desired a careful driver. So she asked the first applicant, "If you were driving near a precipice, how would you drive?" The man answered, "I would drive within two inches and not drive off." He thought that would be skillful.

Other applicants for the place answered in a similar way. At length, however, one applied to whom the same inquiry was put, and the answer came promptly, "I would keep as far away from it as possible," and he was hired. That was sensible treatment of physical danger. When old and young are as sensible about the drink curse, they will keep as far away from it as possible. "Touch not, taste not, handle not."

It is equally strange that government should allow the sale of that which creates this fearful drink habit. It sanctions the traffic, and builds almshouses and prisons for the men that traffic ruins. This is neither wise nor reasonable. Were a trader to sell grain that poisoned cattle and swine, he would be punished severely and his business prohibited. Is not a man better than a cow? Is not a boy better than a calf? Yet government tolerates the traffic that poisons and kills men and boys. It is no wonder that "vice has more martyrs than virtue."

Said the late John B. Gough, "Oh, it is pitiful, it is pitiful—the appetite for intoxicating liquors when it becomes a master-passion! one of the most fearful that man was ever subject to! And not only is it amongst the low, as we call them, and the illiterate; not only amongst those whose first words they heard were words of blasphemy, whose first words they uttered were words of cursing; but it also holds the man a slave who stands in front of the counter and pleads for drink: 'Give me drink. I will give you my hard earnings for it. I will give you more than that. I married a wife, and promised to love and cherish her, and protect her—ah! ah! and I have driven her out to work for me, and I have stolen her wages, and I have brought them to you—give me drink, and I will give you them! More yet: I have snatched the bit of bread from the white lips of my famished child—I will give you that if you will give me drink! More yet: I will give you my health! More yet: I will give you my manliness! More yet: I will give you my hopes of heaven—body and soul! I will barter jewels worth all the kingdoms of the earth—for "what will a man give in exchange for his soul?"—for a dram. Give it to me!' As one man said to me not a week ago: 'I felt under the power of the appetite as Dives must have felt when he longed for the drop of water: I longed for the stimulating influences upon my system, until I shrieked in my agony.'"

THE TOBACCO HABIT.

THE tobacco habit, like the drink habit, is mental, physical, and moral slavery. The victim is an abject slave to the weed, whether chewed, smoked, or snuffed. The appetite for it is formed in much the same way as the appetite for strong drink. In the beginning, the indulgence can be readily resisted, but in the end the victim is bound with fetters of iron. The best way to escape the bondage is never to begin the indulgence.

The habit is not only expensive, but it often undermines the health, where it does not lead to immorality and vice. It is a filthy habit, too; especially the chewing and snuffing forms of it. It is so filthy that railroad corporations provide a special car for travelers who are slaves to the habit, as farmers provide special pens for their swine.

The late Amos Lawrence was wont to refuse tobacco users who applied for positions in his large mercantile house. He once wrote to the president of Williams College, an institution that shared his benefactions, "I have always, for more than forty years past, given the preference, among such persons as I have employed, to such as avoided rum and tobacco, and my experience has confirmed me in the belief that it is true wisdom to have done so." He stipulated that his gifts to the college should be used to assist students who were not victims of the drink habit or tobacco habit.

Mr. Lawrence founded four free scholarships in Wabash College, Indiana, and wrote, when he conveyed his donation, "I would recommend that candidates for the scholarships who abstain from the use of intoxicating drinks and tobacco always have the preference." He believed, what every successful teacher will affirm, that the tobacco habit is inimical to good scholarship, as well as injurious to health and morals. Were he alive to-day, he would join the medical faculty in denouncing cigarettes, which so many boys in our land smoke, as extremely perilous, mentally, physically and morally. Another says, "The educators in Europe and America are agreed that the use of tobacco impairs mental energy. Life insurance companies are shy of its peculiar pulse. Oculists say that it weakens the eyes. Physicians declare it to be a prolific cause of dyspepsia, and hence of other ills. The vital statisticians find it an enemy of virility. It is asserted by the leading authorities in each department, that it takes the spring out of the nerves, the firmness out of the muscles, the ring out of the voice; that it renders the memory less retentive, the judgment less accurate, the conscience less quick, the sensibilities less acute; that it relaxes the will, and dulls every faculty of the body and mind, and moral nature, dropping the entire man down in the scale of his powers, and so is to be regarded as one of the wasters of society."

The wastefulness of the habit alone ought to condemn it. One who was a slave to the habit many years, wrote as follows after he had reformed: "Having often thought upon this subject, I concluded to go over the figures of the problem of the direct cost of smoking at one dollar per week, the amount, twenty-six dollars, being brought in as capital at the end of every six months, at seven per cent per annum, compound interest. The result is as follows:—

At the end of five years it amounts to	$304.96
At the end of ten years it amounts to	735.15
At the end of fifteen years it amounts to	1,341.97
At the end of twenty years it amounts to	2,197.94
At the end of twenty-five years it amounts to	3,495.37
At the end of thirty years it amounts to	5,108.56
At the end of thirty-five years it amounts to	7,511.08
At the end of forty years it amounts to	10,900.07
At the end of forty-five years it amounts to	15,680.59

At the end of fifty years it amounts to $22,423.98
At the end of fifty-five years it amounts to 31,939.19
At the end of sixty years it amounts to 35,454.44
At the end of sixty-five years it amounts to 64,281.41
At the end of seventy years it amounts to 96,980.22
At the end of seventy-five years it amounts to 128,641.56
At the end of eighty years it amounts to 181,773.12

A fortune is wasted in eighty years, and a great deal worse than wasted. There is nothing to show for it but ashes, quids, filthiness, and shattered health. It is not strange that so many poor men are living to-day. Tens of thousands of them have smoked, chewed, and snuffed enough tobacco to make them poor. Had they saved and improved their pecuniary resources as above, they might have been well-to-do at this time. The tobacco habit has actually entailed poverty upon them for life.

Despise and avoid the habit. Label it expensive, filthy, and immoral. Not one honest, reasonable plea can be made in its defence, for it is of no earthly use to anybody. No one is wiser or better for it; all are wiser and better without it. Taboo it, and ticket it "for its own place."

SEIZING AN OPPORTUNITY.

PLINY once remarked, "No man possesses a genius so commanding that he can attain eminence, unless a subject suited to his talents should present itself, and an opportunity occur for their development."

These were wise words. No matter what the talents are, the opportunity to develop them must offer, and the possessor of the talents must appreciate his chance.

For this reason, Dean Alford wrote:—

"There are moments which are worth more than years. A stray, unthought-of five minutes may contain the event of a life. And this all-important moment —who can tell when it will be upon us!"

No man knows his opportunity better than Edison, the famous electrician. It is related of him that, one afternoon in the summer of 1888, he chartered a train, shut down his works, and took his employes —over three hundred of them— to New York, to witness a ball game. They had not been upon the ball-grounds over fifteen minutes, when the thought of a new invention flashed upon Edison's mind, like a revelation, and he called to the "boys," "We must go back at once to Menlo Park; I have a new idea." And back they went to their work, that their employer might not lose his opportunity to add another invention to his achievements.

It is not every "new idea" that is worth chartering a train for, but Edison's ideas have been his fortune. They were too good to be lost; and he has made them available by reducing them to practice at once. All else becomes subservient to his opportunity for the time. The miller must grind the grist with the water that is running through the mill-race; if he waits till the water has passed, his opportunity has gone.

For young people to live in expectation of golden opportunities is inspiring. Some writers call these occasions emergencies; we call them opportunities. Living in anticipation of them leads to looking for them. He who is looking for them is more likely to know them when they do come.

The young man or woman best equipped by industry and application for life-work, is quickest to discover opportunities. Improvement of present time and privileges, therefore, is urged by the highest consideration—preparations to see and use opportunities for one's greatest good.

A writer says, "It matters not what sea a ship is to sail; its keel must be securely laid, its masts firmly set, its rigging of the toughest fibre, in order to sail any sea in safety. One hour's tussle with the tempest will test the fibre of its timbers which were toughened by a hundred years' wrestle with Norwegian blasts." So it is with preparation for wrestling successfully with great opportunities. The keel must be well laid. Manhood and womanhood must be firmly set. Mental and moral fibre must be tough. Then, all hail an opportunity! It is the golden gate that opens into a noble life!

A visitor to the studio of the noted sculptor, Story, at Rome, said, "Around the walls were shelves filled with small clay models, single figures and groups. The sculptor explained that often as he worked, some splendid subject for a marble figure or group would suggest itself. There was little or no use in trying to remember it; so he would at once turn aside from the work in hand, and put his idea into a model, small indeed, and hastily shaped, but he had all that he then needed, namely, the conception. At any time it could be worked up."

Story's experience was not an exception. All readers, students, and workers understood it. A valuable idea is suggested by a book, or piece of work, and it vanishes forever unless it is jotted down at the time in a book kept for the purpose. Putting it off to a more convenient season is practically treating it as being of no value. Conceptions slip away as quickly as they appear, unless they are secured by promptly embodying them in script or models.

Paxton, the architect of the Crystal Palace of 1851, was a gardener in the service of the Duke of Devonshire. Several years before, he conceived the idea of an immense building of glass, and he studied the subject, made his plans, and experimented, repeating his studies and efforts again and again.

When the committee advertised for plans of a building for the famous exhibition of 1851, Paxton saw his opportunity, and embraced it. He drew and forwarded plans so novel and suitable that they were adopted at once. Professional architects and engineers failed to meet the requirements, while this gardener, wholly unknown to fame in this line, won the prize. By close study and persistent trial, in leisure moments by night and day, he prepared himself to seize this opportunity, and make the most of it. It made him Sir Joseph Paxton.

It was when the attention of some philanthropic Americans were turned to the horrors of slavery, that William Lloyd Garrison engaged in editorial work in the city of Baltimore. He was not then an abolitionist, although he was opposed to slavery. He was in favor of colonization, so popular with many at that time. But living in the midst of slavery, where the terrible nature of the slave power and slave traffic was revealed to him, he became a resolute abolitionist, in favor of immediate emancipation.

"Now is the time to attack the system, or never," he said. "Slavery will destroy the nation unless we destroy it."

WILLIAM LLOYD GARRISON.

At once he entered upon the most vigorous assault upon the system. Friends endeavored to dissuade him from his purpose, but he resolutely answered, "Now or never. Ten years from now it may be too late!" Even some of his anti-slavery sympathizers reasoned in vain with him, to modify his views and methods. He was thoroughly aroused by the conviction that it was "God's opportunity" to inflict telling blows upon the monster evil; and this conviction braced him to defy opposition, persecution, and even death itself. Dragged through the streets of

Boston by a mob, with a rope about his neck, he accepted the experience with a coolness that astonished both friend and foe; and he still persisted in speaking and writing what he pleased, perfectly satisfied that the right would win in the end. "I am in earnest; I will not equivocate; I will not excuse; I will not retreat an inch; *and I will be heard,*" he exclaimed.

Subsequent events proved that Garrison was right. The conflict with slavery did not begin one day too soon. It was truly "God's opportunity," involving self-sacrifice, suffering, mighty contests, and harrowing personal experiences. Garrison lived to witness the overthrow of slavery; and he was never more convinced of the importance and necessity of seizing the favorable opportunity, than he was when the Emancipation Proclamation of President Lincoln set the whole slave population of the country free.

LETTING OPPORTUNITIES SLIP.

NOTHING slips by more easily than an opportunity, and, once gone, it is gone forever. The same opportunity comes but once in a lifetime. If not improved when it appears, it becomes a lost opportunity, leaving disappointment and pain behind, as loss always does.

In one of his poems, Whittier says:—

"Of all sad words of tongue or pen,
The saddest are these: It might have been."

To see what one might have become, what achievements he might have made, after it was too late to retrieve the fortune, is sorrowful indeed. To have the chance, yet lose the prize! To see the offer, and let it slip! Here is ground for lament when the fact is appreciated.

There lies before me the confession of an American author of "trashy stories," as he calls them, written for the "blood-and-thunder" papers of the land.

He possesses both a natural and acquired ability as a writer, and might have won fame for himself in the higher walks of literary life, but far better pay was offered him for trash than for truth, and he let the opportunity for usefulness and honor slip. His pen has brought him a fortune of two hundred and fifty thousand dollars, but that is all. No self-respect, no pleasant reflections, no peace!

A few months ago he said to the New York correspondent of the Boston *Journal*:—

"I count my life almost a failure. This trash which I have been writing has brought me returns upon which I can live comfortably, but look at the other side! I have no peace of mind when I think of the havoc I have undoubtedly wrought upon young and innocent minds. I can point to nothing with any pride of authorship. I am ashamed of it all. Even my children would hang their heads in shame did they know their father was the author of this trashy stuff."

The listener interrupted with the question, "Do not your children know it?"

"Bless your soul, no; and God forbid that they should ever discover it, at least during my lifetime. Why, there are only five persons who know that I am the author of the stuff I have put out, and they are pledged to secrecy by their friendship for me."

"Why did you start on that line of writing, when you might have taken up something better?" the listener inquired again.

"Because it paid me better to write a murderous story than a clean one; and, once begun, I have kept right on. My first proved so appetizing to its readers that the editor offered me nearly double the price he paid for the first, if I would write a second one. Now I hate to think of the number I have written. I have published my stories under fifteen or twenty different names, male and female, and if I have written one I suppose I have written two hundred of these beastly serial novels. They are all in the same vein, and there is not one which hasn't a lot of robberies or murders in it. How people can read them, I cannot tell. If they despised their reading, as I do their writing, I would be a poor man now. But it is now a thing of the past; I have written my last story."

He let slip the one opportunity of his lifetime to make himself a name for the right and good, and his lamentation shows what a fearful mistake it was. Such an example enforces the divine counsel, "Therefore, we ought to give the more earnest heed to the things which we have heard, lest at any time we should let them slip."

A prominent business man of New York City let the opportunities of his school-days slip, without improving them as he might have done. He possessed remarkable executive abilities, was very successful in business, and amassed a fortune; but he was often embarrassed, and even mortified, in the company of other business men, because of his limited education. He did not think of writing an important letter himself, for fear that bad spelling and bad grammar would expose his ignorance. He employed a private secretary for all that sort of work.

"I was like too many other boys," he said, "did not like school as well as I did work or play, and so I was never anything but a poor reader and speller—poor in most everything in which I should have been proficient, and might have been. But I did not value my opportunities; never stopped to think that they had anything to do with my manhood; and now I would give my present fortune for the acquisitions those lost opportunities would have given me. But, it is too late; regrets are of no avail now; I must carry the burden of that early mistake through life."

Conversation with a gentleman from Omaha, Nebraska, upon the remarkable growth of that city, elicited from him the following:—

"Four years ago I had three or four thousand dollars to invest, and I had a fine opportunity to invest it in real estate in that city. A piece of land in the suburbs, so near to the business portion of the town as to assure a rapid advance in value, was thrown upon the market. I was urged by interested friends to purchase it, and I thought well of the project, but delayed decision until one morning the papers announced that Mr. C. had bought the land. My opportunity was lost, and too late I saw my mistake. The land has just been sold for fifty thousand dollars, and it might have been mine, had I not foolishly let the opportunity slip."

Recently a lady in a Southern city saw a drunken youth of seventeen declaiming to a crowd of loafers on the street from English and Latin classics, showing that he was a young man of culture. While the woman was looking on with sadness the police arrested the young orator and lodged him in jail. Interested in his welfare, she sought an interview with him, and found that he was the son of a wealthy judge in Mississippi, and that he ran away from home.

"Were your parents unkind to you that you left them?" she inquired.

"Unkind!" he repeated, bursting into tears. "Oh, I wish I could remember a single unkind word from them! There would be a little excuse. No, they were only too indulgent. I was wild then, and I've heard father say after I had sown my wild oats I would come out all right."

"But I can't understand why you left good parents and home," said the lady.

"Wait a minute, and I will tell you. You see, I had good school advantages, and was a great reader. For a time I read what was elevating and good, and I might have continued to read such works, but stories of adventure attracted and charmed me. My chances for a noble and successful life were good up to that time, but I swapped the opportunity for the best life for the worst. Bad books made me long to imitate the young heroes. They gave me a start downward, and the rest was easy. Warn young people to beware of such reading, for it does great harm; it has ruined me."

There was a crisis in his life. Two ways met. Had he chosen the best books, companions, and habits that offered, his brilliant talents and great advantages would have led him to usefulness and renown, but he spurned the opportunity, and let it slip. Then, ruin was speedy.

XXVII.

A SOUND BODY FOR A SOUND MIND.

A BODY for a soul is not more indispensable than a sound body for a sound mind. To develop the latter at the expense of the former is unfavorable to success. Mind and matter are so dependent upon each other that disease of one interrupts the functions of the other. Not that a strong mind is never found in a frail body, but this is the exception.

Johnson was in feeble health most of his life; Dr. Channing never knew the happy experience of having a sound body for his great mind; Cæsar was subject to epileptic fits, and usually celebrated the planning of a battle by going into one; Amos Lawrence was a confirmed dyspeptic many years, and only lived by carefully weighing his food; Pascal was always "sickly," and Pope was an invalid when he did his best work.

After citing all the exceptional examples possible, it is still true that brain power has a strong ally in muscular vigor. The Broughams, Peels, Palmerstons, Gladstones, Washingtons, Franklins, Websters, Lincolns, Garfields, and Grants, were as renowned for muscle as brain.

Nevertheless, there is a large amount of ignorance, even among educated people, concerning the laws of health; and there is more disobedience than there is ignorance. Here most men and women, including youth of both sexes, know better than they do. They violate physical laws knowingly and deliberately; they indulge in excesses, against which they know that nature remonstrates; they neglect their bodies, and overwork their brains, with nature's signals of distress flying before their eyes. Every day they disregard known laws of health, all the while knowing just what they do, and having an inkling, at least, that sure penalties will follow.

The late Dr. Edward Jarvis, of Boston, wrote: —

"If a weaver, when he has woven his web, should put into his loom a parcel of sticks and wire, and then set the loom in motion, just for the pleasure of seeing it move; or, perhaps, in the hope that the loom would, out of these hard materials, make cloth as well as out of cotton and wool, he would do a very foolish act; but not more foolish than when he has eaten enough for nutrition to eat indigestible and innutritious matters just for the pleasure of eating. No engineer would pour upon the gudgeons and pistons of his engine acids instead of oils, just for change, because this would be in opposition to his knowledge of the laws of mechanics, and spoil his machine. Yet he will pour wine, and brandy, and tobacco juice into his stomach, and tobacco smoke into his lungs, which are infinitely more delicate organs than anything of wood or iron."

Both ignorance and defiance of physical laws create this state of things, especially among the young. The latter class are too apt to undervalue health, and even to treat it with indifference, as if it had little or no claim upon their intelligence.

There can be few graver errors than this. What though they can repeat the names and number of the bones of the hand or foot, and not know how to take care of them; what though they can enumerate the functions of the stomach, and not know what they put into it; what though they can repeat all the text-books say about the lobes of the lungs, and still persist in denying them fresh air and full play; what though they can rehearse all physiological rules in respect to exercise and sleep, and then pursue their studies so as wholly to neglect the first, and scrimp the last; their knowledge is of no practical value whatever.

What is still more unaccountable is the fact that young persons of both sexes —and the same is largely true of older persons—appear to think that there is no moral obligation resting upon them to be healthy, when they are as really bound to observe physical as moral laws. We are in duty bound to do all we can for health, as we are to do all we can for honesty. There is no more excuse for neglecting the body than the soul. Spiritual laws have no better claim upon our regard than physical laws.

Mrs. Cheney, writing of schoolgirls, says, "Health is the holiness of the body, and every girl should have a high standard of perfect health set before her, and be made to feel that she has no more right to trifle with and disobey hygienic laws, than those of morality or civil society. She should be as much ashamed of illness brought on by her own folly, as of being whipped at school for disobedience to her teacher."

Matthews says, "We are discovering that though the pale, sickly student may win the most prizes in college, it is the tough, sinewy one who will win the most prizes in life; and that in every calling, other things being equal, the most successful man will be the one who has slept the soundest and digested the most dinners with the least difficulty."

Horace Mann declared that "the spendthrift of health was the guiltiest of spendthrifts;" and he went on to say, "I am certain that I could have performed twice the labor, both better and with greater ease to myself, had I known as much of the laws of health and life at twenty-one as I do now. In college I was taught all about the motions of the planets as carefully as though they would have been in danger of getting off the track if I had not known how to trace their orbits; but about my own organization, and the conditions indispensable to the healthful functions of my own body, I was left in profound ignorance. Nothing could be more preposterous: I ought to have begun at home, and taken the stars when it should become their turn."

"The laws of physical health are fixed and uniform; just as inexorable as any laws by which planets move, or plants grow."

"If we wish to be useful, happy, and capable of mental progress, we need a physical system well cared for, working without friction or disturbance."

Lord Palmerston, for fifty-seven years England's popular premier, may well be cited as an illustration of a sound mind in a sound body.

He entered Parliament at twenty-one years of age, with a vow in his heart to serve his country well. For sixty years he was identified with the nation's welfare, and performed an amount of work that would have utterly exhausted ordinary men. He was secretary of war when Napoleon was overthrown at the battle of Waterloo, and assisted in the vast operations of that conflict. When he died he was the most popular man in the British realm.

It was always a subject of inquiry how Lord Palmerston maintained a sound body under the burden of such enormous labors. The only explanation is that he took excellent care of his body. Exercise with him was a religious duty. He rode horseback, walked, hunted, fished, and studied in every way to preserve his health. It was a common thing for him to ride off thirty miles on the back of a fleet horse. In a word, he adopted such a course of living as he thought would maintain a sound body, and rejected all others.

THE SOUND BODY MADE AND KEPT.

IT is more important to know how to have and keep a sound body than how to get riches and keep them. A writer says: "There is this difference between the two temporal blessings—health and money; money is the most envied, but the least enjoyed; health is the most enjoyed, but the least envied; and this superiority of the latter is still more obvious, when we reflect that the poorest man would not part with health for money, but that the richest would gladly part with all his money for health."

A nutritious, generous diet is indispensable to a sound body. This is substantially correct, whether a person lives indoors or outdoors. Scholars need it no less than mechanics, because it is the only way to make muscle. Both sexes need it, because food makes feminine as it does masculine muscle. There is a singular impression abroad that girls require less substantial food than boys; many parents think so. So we have the spectacle of boys consuming beef and bread, baked beans and a boiled dish, while many girls nibble bread daintily, and eat "goodies," as if heaven had prescribed a different diet for them. A grave error, this. Girls require as nourishing food as boys. Let boys eat as girls do, and they would be no more robust.

A few years since, Miss Nutting, a teacher in Mount Holyoke Female Seminary, wrote:—

"Our physician attributes a great part of the ill health from which the young ladies suffer to errors in dress, tight lacing, long and heavy skirts dragging from the hips, and the great weight of clothing upon the lower portion of the back, and insufficient covering for the lower extremities.

"Another fruitful source of evil, for which parents are largely responsible, is the supplying of schoolgirls with quantities of rich pastry, cakes and sweetmeats, which are eaten between meals, and often just before going to bed. In one instance, a young lady, previously in perfect health, in the course of two years made herself a confirmed dyspeptic, simply by indulging, night after night, in the indigestible dainties with which she was constantly supplied from home."

Facts prove that girls must have as sensible, nutritious diet as boys.

A generous amount of sleep also assists in making a sound body. Nature will not be cheated out of sleep without protest, any more than she will out of food. Scrimp the hours of sleep, and the consequences may be even worse than those that follow a meagre diet, since insanity is more to be dreaded than starvation.

The celebrated Dr. Richardson, of London, maintains that adults, in middle life, require an average of eight hours sleep daily, summer and winter, and that young people require more, nine and even ten hours. Sleep is "nerve food," "nature's sweet restorer," and without it there cannot be a sound body, any more than a sound mind. Turning night into day, in frolic, study, or work, therefore, is abusing nature, for she demands sleep from nine o'clock in the evening to six in the morning, regularly and unalterably, as sure as clock can mark the time, as one of the conditions of a sound body. "Early to bed," in the old saw, is well enough; but "early to rise," if it means getting up a long time before breakfast for study or work, is poor counsel. It will not make a man "healthy, wealthy, and wise."

Air and exercise are indispensable. We can live longer without food and sleep than we can without air. Indeed, food and sleep fulfill their mission well only by the aid of pure, fresh air. People, old and young, deny themselves pure air and exercise, sleep, and rest, and then ache and battle with disease the remainder of their days, and charge the result to brain work.

It is of no consequence what the pursuit of man or woman may be, health and strength cannot be preserved without constant watch and care.

We often wonder that some men bearing the burden of millions in business are not crushed under its weight before they have lived half their days; but one reason is found in the good care they take of themselves.

Of one of them it is said, during office hours he is one of the hardest working men in the world; outside his office he never talks, and probably seldom thinks, of business. He is of abstemious habits, a total abstainer from intoxicating liquors and tobacco. His food is always plain. He usually arises before six in the morning, and is generally asleep soon after ten at night. His family relations have always been a model of purity and kindly affection.

At the present day there is much talk about overworked pupils in our schools. It is claimed that too close and protracted study breaks down scholars—that our system of education is hard upon the nerves and health of students of both sexes. We very much question the ground of this complaint. The average student, male or female, is not overworked. Other things are the cause of poor health among this class, such as improper dress and diet, late hours, bad habits, and general neglect of the laws of health. In other words, the real cause of the poor health of most students is found at home, and not in the schoolroom.

Miss Adelia A. F. Johnson, a professor in Oberlin College, wrote as follows of female students:—

"When mothers are able to send us strong, healthy girls, with simple habits and unperverted tastes, we will return to them and the world strong, healthy women, fitted physically and mentally for woman's work. We believe that more girls are benefited than are injured by the regimen of a well-regulated school, and our belief is founded upon years of observation. The number is not small of girls who have come to us, pale, nervous, and laboring under many of the ills of life, to whom the regularity that must be observed in a large school, but, most of all, the stimulus of systematic brain work upon the body, has proved most salutary."

Mrs. Mary E. Beedy, who has enjoyed superior opportunities to learn of English customs and schools, writes:—

"The importance of health is a dominant idea in the whole nation. Children are trained into habits of out-of-door exercise till they get an appetite for it, as they have for their food; and it is not unusual to hear an Englishwoman say, 'I would as soon go without my lunch as without a walk of an hour and a half in the day.' And the habits of the upper class percolate down through all ranks of life. The schools that expect to get the daughters of the best families must show the best results in health. My own experience would lead me most unhesitatingly to say that regular mental occupation, well arranged, conduces wholly to the health of a girl, and boy, too, in every way, and that girls who have well-regulated mental work are far less liable to fall into hysterical fancies than those who have not such occupation."

The attempt to make study responsible for ill health, which is the legitimate product of ignorance or defiance of physical laws, can be readily controverted by recurring to facts.

RECREATION.

AMUSEMENT and recreation are often confounded. One says, " Amusements are necessary for the health of body and mind." This is not true. Recreation *is* necessary for the health of body and mind. Another says that diversion is important for physical and mental health; and on this basis he defends theatre-going, card-playing, billiards, and the whole string of entertainments that are gotten up to amuse the people. It is a serious error to patronize all these sources of mere pleasure on the ground that recreation is indispensable, for recreation may not embrace one of them.

Clergymen, in common with students generally, need recreation more than almost any other class. But they do not find it in the theatre, ballroom, bowling alley, or at the card-table. It is recreation for them to scour the fields, take a journey, ride on horseback, saw wood, till the garden, or prosecute the science of music. The same kind of recreation will do equally well for others. Both body and mind will be invigorated more by them than they are by most of the popular amusements of the day.

We repeat: recreation is absolutely necessary. Neither body nor mind can be strained to its utmost tension for a long time without permanent injury. When the late Rufus Choate was remonstrated with for his excessive mental labors, and reminded that his constitution would break down utterly, he exclaimed, " Constitution! Good heavens, my dear sir! My constitution was all gone long ago, and I am living on the by-laws." But the " by-laws" were not so long-lived as the constitution, and he went down to a premature grave. Overwork did it. Proper recreation would have added ten years to his lease of life.

Not so with Daniel Webster, who was in the habit of taking absolute rest between great mental efforts. Hunting, fishing, tilling his farm, and journeying, were the chief forms of recreation he enjoyed. He said to a gentleman in Providence, Rhode Island, " It is a law of our natures that the body or mind that labors constantly must necessarily labor moderately. The race horse, whose full power is exerted by occasional effort, must have periods of entire rest, or it will soon wear out; besides, suitable rest, in time, adds largely to its speed. The great walkers and runners of our race, have, from small beginnings, when fifteen miles a day fatigued them, walked, in the end, fifty miles at the rate of five or six miles an hour, simply by observing proper seasons of rest. The London porter will stagger, at first, under a burden of two hundred pounds, but will, at last, walk off with five or six hundred pounds, by carefully observing the law of his being in regard to labor and rest. The same law governs the mind. When employed at all, its powers should be exerted to the utmost. Its fatigue should be followed by entire rest. Whatever mental occupation receives my attention, I put forth all my power, and when my mental vision becomes obscure, I cease entirely, and resort to some light business or recreation."

Rest is recreation to the exhausted faculties. Change of occupation for a brief season is recreation for some.

Students often unbend their mental powers by turning, for a few hours, from hard study to light reading. A social chat for an evening relaxes the mental and nervous strain, preparing the mind for another tussle with hard problems the next day. When the great burdens and cares of the late Civil War lay so heavily upon Lincoln's head and heart, a few friends were wont to watch for an hour when they could step in and engage his thoughts in social and friendly conversation, that his harassed mind might unbend, and not break. Burritt sought recreation by leaving the library for the forge, exchanging the book for the hammer. One of America's great divines kept his body in good trim at a work-bench in a room of his house, where for many years he found ample recreation in the use of a set of carpenter's tools.

GEORGE BANCROFT.

We must not confound amusements with recreation. They are entirely distinct. Recreation is not necessarily amusement. Confounding them has led to the waste of much valuable time, and much character, too, in the games and sports mentioned. Hundreds of young men and maidens might become renowned in letters, or in science and literature, by devoting only the time they waste in doubtful and dangerous amusements. The time that many kill at billiards, theatres, and clubs was the time that made Hugh Miller, Burritt, Wilson, and many others illustrious. It is not wise to seek recreation where moral perils lurk, when it can be found elsewhere with innocence and safety.

These remarks do not apply to the dull, slow, lazy class of people, young or old. Get all the work possible out of them, and it will not be too much. They need spur and whip to keep their faculties in healthful activity.

When the late William E. Dodge began business in New York City, he found his recreation out of business hours in the alleys and slums of the metropolis, caring for poor boys. He fed and clothed them, and preached the gospel to them in his humble way. He made the lives of many of them easier and better at the same time that he sought recreation for his exhausted powers.

The late George Bancroft, America's great historian, at ninety years of age was able to pursue his historic studies with considerable enthusiasm. His remarkable longevity, notwithstanding his life was one of close application in his study, was due, no doubt, to his correct views of recreation. He found it in horseback riding and the cultivation of flowers. Even at ninety he did not altogether forsake the saddle which, in his prime, he sat in twice a day. At his summer home in Newport, he had extensive grounds devoted to the cultivation of the rose, and there he found delight and health. An eye-witness says of his garden of roses at Newport. "It is one of the wonders of the world. His hours of recreation and pleasure were largely spent among the roses, or else on horseback, the latter being an exercise of which he was always fond, and which old age never prevented him from practicing daily, and that, usually, on a most spirited steed." To proper recreation must be attributed much of his success as a historian.

DUTY.

OF all the watchwords of life, duty is the highest and best. He who sincerely adopts it lives a true life; he is really the successful one. It pertains to all parts and relations of life. There is no moment, place, or condition where its claims are not imperative. The poet states it well—

> "I slept and dreamed that life was Beauty;
> I woke and found that life was Duty!"

ONWARD TO FAME AND FORTUNE.

A thousand years after an eruption of Vesuvius had buried Pompeii beneath its burning lava, explorers laid bare the ruins of the ill-fated city. There the unfortunate inhabitants were found just where they were overtaken by the stream of fire. Some were discovered in lofty attics, and some in deep cellars, whither they had fled before the approaching desolation. Others were found in the streets, through which they were fleeing in wild despair when the tide of molten death overwhelmed them. But the Roman sentinel was found standing at his post, his skeleton-hand still grasping the hilt of his sword, his attitude that of a faithful officer. He was placed there on duty, and death met him at his post—the fearless sentinel that he was. Not even the bursting of a volcano, with its deluge of fire descending upon him, could drive him from his post, or disturb his self-control. It was a sense of duty that kept him true, an example of fidelity to a sacred trust; and to-day his helmet, lance, and breastplate are preserved in Naples as a tribute to his memory.

LORD NELSON.

Mary Lyon, founder of Mount Holyoke Female Seminary, used to say to her pupils: "Go where *duty* calls. Take hold, if necessary, where no one else will." Duty, as a watchword and inspiration, she kept before them constantly. Personal obligation, instead of personal emolument or fame, she besought them to remember. At length a contagious and fatal disease broke out in the seminary, and the first victim was lying at the door of death. Pupils were filled with alarm; many hastened to pack their trunks, and leave for home. A scene of confusion and dismay followed. Miss Lyon, with surprising self-possession and serenity, called the pupils together to allay their fears, and impart lessons such as the occasion suggested to her mind. "Shall we fear what God is about to do?" she said. "There is nothing in the universe that I fear, but that I shall not know all my duty, or fail to do it." On the following day the dreaded malady prostrated her, and, in a single week, she passed to the spirit land. Her last lesson was on duty, and her last act was meeting its demand.

Unlike Napoleon or Alexander, Nelson's watchword was duty. He never fought for fame. His ambition was subject to personal obligation. "England

BATTLE OF TRAFALGAR.

this day expects each man to do his duty," were the words emblazoned upon his colors in the battle of Trafalgar. If each man did his duty the victory would be complete, and if each fought for fame the battle would be lost. Duty is so much higher than glory, and so much more inspiring, that victories hang upon it. At this last and crowning conflict at Trafalgar he was mortally wounded, but lived to know that his triumph was complete, and expired, saying, "Thank God, I have done my duty."

Of the same type was Wellington, who once said to a friend: "There is little or nothing in this life worth living for, but we can all of us go straight forward and do our duty." Whether serving at home in his family, or serving his country on the field, one high, noble purpose inspired him—duty. He did not ask, Will this course win fame? Will this battle add to my earthly glory? But always, What is duty? He did what duty commanded, and followed where it led. It was his firm adherence to what he thought was right that brought down upon him the violence of a mob in the streets of London, assaulting his person and attacking his house, where his wife lay dead therein.

When Sidney, the immortal English patriot, was told that he could save his life by denying his own handwriting, and thus tell a falsehood, he replied, "When God has brought me into a dilemma in which I must assert a lie or lose my life, He gives me a clear indication of my duty, which is to prefer death to falsehood." A higher sense of duty, or personal respect for it, is not found recorded. It hallows human life by making death a secondary consideration.

A fearful conflagration a few years ago licked up five million dollars in the heart of Boston, within a few hours. The heroic firemen found themselves engaged in an unequal contest with the fiery demon, and yet they staked their lives on the issue, and four brave fellows went down beneath crumbling walls in their efforts to conquer. They perished in the discharge of duty.

The foregoing facts, better than argument, show both the nature and place of duty in the work of life. We see it in practical operation, always timely, honorable, and attractive. It cannot be discounted or even smirched. It stands out in bold relief, supported by a clear conscience and strong will. It demands recognition, and gets it. Duty is something that must be done without regard to discomfort, sacrifice, or death; and it must be done in secret, as well as in public.

The doer is not a "creature of circumstances:" he is master of circumstances. The power of a trained conscience and invincible will make him superior to all surroundings, and the discharge of duty becomes at once inevitable and easy.

Luther was warned against appearing before one Duke George, because he was his bitter enemy, but he replied, "I *will* go if it rains Duke Georges all the while, for *duty* calls."

"I am ready not only to be bound, but to die at Jerusalem," replied Paul to weeping companions who besought him not to risk his life in that wicked city. Duty was paramount to all things else; it was second to nothing on earth.

In the daily affairs of life, whether the most important or the least, duty should command. Youth must come under its control as well as age. The earlier its demands are honored in the home, social circle, shop, school, or college, the easier will be its service, and the larger satisfaction will it yield. Obedience to the behests of duty, and the ruling desire to be useful, are cardinal elements of success. It is a trumpet call that duty sounds, at which all the nobler attributes of manhood spring into life.

Smiles says, "Duty is the end and aim of the highest life; it alone is true;" and George Herbert says, "The consciousness of duty performed 'gives us music at midnight.'"

KEEPING PROMISES.

MANY failures occur because of promise-breaking. Confidence is broken, and without that success is out of the question. A man's word must be as good as his bond, if he would have others confide in him. But this is never true of one who does not keep his promises. Another says, "A person who pays little regard to slight promises usually is somewhat careless of greater ones also. Defects of this kind, like flaws in machinery, never lessen, but always grow worse, until, finally, under the strain of a powerful temptation, they often break down a man's career forever. The most punctual men in keeping a trivial engagement we have always found to be the exactest in their business transactions. Washington was a memorable example of particularity in small things, as well as great, and his strict probity in the latter was unquestionably the result, in a considerable degree, of his fidelity in the former."

Many persons consider a slight promise of not much importance. In the common affairs of life they say that they will do this or that thing, and never think of it again. It may be work promised, or money borrowed, or an interview arranged. This sort of promise sits so lightly upon many men and women that it is no better than no promise. Within a week we have noted facts of this sort as follows:—

A laborer had promised to work for a neighbor on Thursday, but he did not put in an appearance. "This is the second time he has promised and failed," said the neighbor. "There is no more dependence to be placed on his word than there is on the wind." Yet thousands of employers experience kindred disappointment in consequence of broken promises.

Mrs. B. sent her large chair to the upholsterer's for repairs. "Now, don't you disappoint me again," she remarked to him on leaving the shop. She had reason to make the remark, for the man had never done a piece of work for her yet in the time promised. "I would not employ him if there was another upholsterer within twenty miles," she had been heard to say. "Your chair shall be ready in one week," the upholsterer promised as Mrs. B. turned away. But the chair was not ready until two weeks had expired, notwithstanding his emphatic promise.

Mr. H., a merchant, loaned a fellow-tradesman fifty dollars for "two or three days." He wanted it just for "pocket money." The "two or three days" grew into two or three months, until the loaner inquired of the borrower if his days were the geological days of Genesis. "I declare, I ought to have attended to that before, and I will," the latter replied. And he did, when it became convenient, though many days more elapsed. A business man assures me that kindred looseness about keeping promises prevails in the business world; that men promise to pay in two or three days, more or less, when they do not mean it; that often one business man sacrifices the confidence of another for the paltry sum of twenty-five dollars, and even ten dollars, by breaking his promise.

One tells me this: a minister became indebted to him to the amount of twenty-five dollars. They were personal friends, each having implicit confidence in the other. "I will see that you are paid in two weeks," said the minister. After his friend had waited two months, he wrote to the minister, setting forth his needs, and requesting that he should send a check for the amount of the debt. But no check came, not even a reply to the letter. Two more months elapsed, when the two parties unexpectedly met face to face, in the streets of Boston. "I have not forgotten that debt; I shall send the money within a few days." Eight months have elapsed since that casual meeting and last voluntary promise, and the debt is still unpaid, and no word of apology or explanation has been made. That minister sacrificed the confidence of an old friend for twenty-five dollars, and his ministerial standing with all who knew the facts. Evidently he does not believe that "a good name is better than great riches," or he never would have sold it so cheaply. If a man's word is not worth more than that, it is of too little value to receive any attention at all.

"I have not given him a job for a year," remarked a business man of the town printer; "he never has work done when he promises."

A fellow-townsman standing by responded, "That is a general complaint; the business of the office might be doubled if he would do as he agrees." So the printer was branded as a promise-breaker, and justly so. Very uncomplimentary remarks were made about him, showing decidedly a lack of confidence in the man, and very limited respect.

With many, promise breaking is but a thoughtless habit. They do not intend to falsify their word, neither do they mean to deceive or cheat. They simply promise, scarcely thinking that it is a promise. But whether an evil habit or purpose, it is inexcusable and wicked.

It indicates an absence of strict integrity, without which character exists only in name, and life is a failure. A business man writes: "We have learned to be cautious of those who are ready to promise. It is the individual who carefully considers before he makes a pledge who can be most surely depended on to keep it. A multiplicity of promises necessarily prevents the promiser from observing them all, for one conflicts with the other, and disables the best intentioned. A disregard of promises, finally, is like a fungus which imperceptibly spreads over the whole character, until the moral perceptions are perverted, and the man actually comes to believe he does no wrong, even in breaking faith with his warmest friends."

Young people can scarcely attend to a more important subject than this. A promise is a solemn pledge, in which personal character is involved, whether relating to important or unimportant matters. Of course it should be kept. Integrity of character demands it. A successful career is impossible without it. True manhood and womanhood require it. Keeping promises is one of the conditions of success in the mercantile world. As the race improves morally, keeping promises will become more general, until the millennium invests the duty with a sacredness that challenges universal respect.

A striking illustration of our theme is found in the remarkable business career of the late Horace B. Claflin, of New York City.

All the schooling he ever received was that of the common school and academy of his native town. At the same time he learned more by observation than he did from books, so that he was constantly going up higher. His unblemished character added charm and power to his executive abilities.

That such a boy as he should finally establish a business that amounted to seventy-two million dollars in a single year, and for twenty years before his death averaged a magnitude of traffic greater than that of any other warehouse in the world, was not strange. By his own indomitable perseverance and application he developed ability enough to readily manage this enormous business. And he never broke a promise! From boyhood to manhood he redeemed every pledge! The embarrassments of the late war forced him to ask his creditors for an extension; and long before the extension terminated every dollar was paid with interest. Again, the panic of 1873 embarrassed him, but he came out of it with every promise fulfilled. He stood by his convictions like a martyr, too. Before the late war, when his Southern patrons withdrew their large patronage, because of his avowed hostility to slavery, he met the test grandly by saying, "My goods, and not my principles, are for sale."

GETTING SOMETHING FOR NOTHING.

A PUBLISHER advertised extensively for agents, and he received a large number of answers—they reached several thousands. Of the whole number, less than a score took outfits, most of the applicants did not mean business. Why? The advertisement did not say that an agent must pay two dollars for an outfit, so that a large per cent of them concluded that the outfit would cost them nothing, while it might be worth something to them. "They had no intention of canvassing," said the publisher; "they wanted to get something for nothing." This feature of American society is not confined to the class spoken of above. It is found almost everywhere to some extent. A party in a New England city purchased an estate for twenty thousand dollars, without having a dollar to pay for it. By promises and false pretences he obtained a deed of the property, and held it until the original proprietor was satisfied that the buyer meant to get something for nothing, when he took legal measures to regain his estate. An acquaintance, who is called a shrewd business manager, was approached by a tonguey oil well operator with a bonanza for sale. The oil well was in the great State of Pennsylvania, in a certain locality, easy of access, and probably a dozen other wells would be found around it. My friend purchased the well for ten or twenty thousand dollars, and he had just paid over the money when he found he had bought a myth—there was no such well in existence. The oil well operator had literally obtained something for nothing. Such schemes are so common that

CHRIST TEMPTED IN THE WILDERNESS.

they scarcely awaken surprise. Another party purchased a gold mine in the New West. He interested several parties in the enterprise, who joined him in raising a few thousand dollars for the purchase. Before they were prepared to work the mine, however, their title to it was successfully contested, so that they were minus both mine and money. The gold-mine operator knew the state of affairs when he sold, but he wanted to get something for nothing; and he succeeded.

The business world is flooded with operations of this kind, so that men have to look sharp if they would get something for something. This is one of the features of business in our day that creates so much uncertainty, and thereby entails a lack of confidence.

But the evil is not confined to the world of traffic, neither is it confined to men and women old enough to engage in mercantile transactions.

Young people are even more inclined to get something for nothing whenever it is possible.

The father of James Atherton sent him to school to get an education. It cost him much money, thought, and anxiety, but the education of his son would more than repay him for all this outlay. Perhaps James wanted an education, too; but he did not want to pay anything for it. He was a thoughtless, idle boy, smart at doing nothing, and shrewd in shunning duties. Study was too much of a tax upon his disposition; he could not pay any such price as that even for knowledge. If he could go to bed at night and wake up in the morning educated, he would not object to an education. But to dig and delve for it, month after month and year after year—he could not think of that. What was the real trouble with James? Only this: he wanted to get something for nothing. He would be educated without the necessary application and labor. He gave nothing to speak of in this line, while he got something, though it was not much. James is a business man now, and long since learned his folly. He sees that trying to get something for nothing at school was the greatest mistake of his life; that he now suffers every day for the want of the discipline of early life which a hard struggle for knowledge requires. If he could live his life over again he would not attempt such a one-sided scheme in mental progress as that of giving nothing for it. He is not able to write a correct business letter, and he is ashamed of it. Often his ignorance exposes him to great mortification in the company of intelligent people. He understands now that the young person who would acquire an education must pay something for it—God's price, which is study, improvement of time, high aims, and persistent toil.

There is a manifest meanness in the desire to get something for nothing, no matter what it is. All persons should be willing to pay fairly for what they have. They must give, as well as receive, an equivalent in every transaction. He who does not want to give an equivalent for what he gets is a relative of the sneak

ONWARD TO FAME AND FORTUNE.

thief. He is too mean to enjoy an honorable standing in society; and, if this be true, he cannot be honest. He violates the law of integrity, by trying to palm off nothing for something. The devil did that to Christ. He offered the Saviour "all the kingdoms of the world" if He would bow down and worship him, and he did not own one of them to give. He was not honest. All who imitate him by acting on the same line are, like him, dishonest.

THE LAST DAYS OF POMPEII.

XXVIII.

THE FILIAL TIE.

THE duty of filial love is universally recognized, and its beauty charms all hearts. It is not strange that the Greeks and Romans erected magnificent temples to the honor of those who ranked high in the practice of this virtue. The heroic manner in which Æneas bore his infirm old father from the flames of Troy won for him the title of "the pious Æneas."

In all ages, filial love has been called filial piety, because it is so sacred and valuable. Even the inspired writer found it necessary to employ figurative language to express the true loveliness of this virtue:—

"My son, hear the instruction of thy father, and forsake not the law of thy mother, for they shall be an ornament of grace unto thy head, and chains about thy neck; bind them continually upon thine heart, and tie them about thy neck." What gems and pearls are for adornment of the body, such is filial devotion for the adornment of the soul.

When Washington was elected to the chief magistracy of the United States, he repaired immediately to the home of his youth, to pay a tribute of love to his mother. The historian describes the scene as follows:—

"His head rested upon the shoulder of his parent. That brow, on which fame had wreathed the purest laurels that virtue ever gave to created man relaxed from its lofty bearing. That look, which could have awed a Roman Senate in its Fabrician day, was bent in full tenderness upon the time-worn features of this venerable matron. The great man wept. A thousand recollections crowded upon his mind as memory retraced scenes long past, and carried him back to his paternal mansion, and the days of his youth; and the centre of his attraction was his mother, whose care, instruction, and discipline had prepared him to reach the topmost height of his laudable ambition; yet how were his glories forgotten, while he looked upon her from whom, wasted by time and malady, he must soon part, perhaps to meet no more." Washington sacrificed none of his greatness when he wept at parting with her who taught him, as she said, "the lessons of diligence, obedience, and truth."

In like manner, when Abraham Lincoln was elected President of the United States he paid his widowed step-mother a visit. An eye-witness describes the scene thus:—

"Their meeting was of the most affectionate and tender character. She fondled him as her own Abraham, and he her as his own mother. That they might enjoy each other's society still longer, she accompanied him to Charleston, Illinois. When the time arrived that Mr. Lincoln must leave, both he and his mother were deeply affected. The parting between them was very touching. She embraced him with deep emotion, and said she was sure she should never see him again, for she felt that his enemies would assassinate him.

"'No, no, mother; they will not do that. Trust in the Lord and all will be well; we shall soon see each other again.'

"Inexpressibly affected by this new evidence of her tender attachment and deep concern for his safety, he gradually and reluctantly withdrew from her arms, feeling more deeply oppressed by the heavy cares which time and events were rapidly augmenting."

When General James A. Garfield was inaugurated President of the United States, he insisted that his aged mother should be at his side when he took the

WASHINGTON AND HIS MOTHER.

accustomed oath and delivered his inaugural address. As soon as he had been invested with the powers of the high office, he turned to his mother and kissed her. And when, a few months later, the bullet of the assassin had laid him on a bed of great suffering, his mother, then necessarily at a distance, was often in his thoughts, and loving, comforting messages he often sent to her. The last letter which he ever wrote was to her. Bolstered up in bed, he addressed the following note to her:—

WASHINGTON, D. C., Aug. 11, 1881.

DEAR MOTHER:—Don't be disturbed by conflicting reports about my condition. It is true I am still weak, and on my back; but I am gaining every day, and need only time and patience to bring me through. Give my love to all the relatives and friends, and especially to sisters Hetty and Mary. Your loving son,

JAMES A. GARFIELD.

MRS. ELIZA GARFIELD, Hiram, Ohio.

Such recognition of the filial tie in high places, honors the sons and dignifies human nature. There is no compromise of statesmanship or greatness by these acts. Rather, they adorn statesmanship and make greatness greater.

In the late Civil War General O. O. Howard was called the "American Havelock," because his Christian character was continually at the front. His re'igion made him an uncompromising foe to slavery, and he was willing to fight and, if need be, *die* for its overthrow. Referring to his career, he remarked that he could not have well been otherwise, after the discipline and teachings of such a mother as God had given him. All through his public career, his visits and letters to her proved the honesty and depth of his filial love, and when, a few years since, at a ripe old age, she went down to the grave in triumph, no son in his teens was ever bowed with deeper sorrow over the loss of her who bore him than was General Howard for the mother who struck the keynote of his noble life.

When the statue of Franklin was unveiled in Boston in 1856, a barouche appeared in the procession, which carried several brothers, sons of Mr. John Hall, all of whom received Franklin medals in the Mayhew school in their boyhood.

As the barouche in which they rode came into State Street, from Merchant's Row, these brothers rose up in the carriage, uncovered their heads, and remained in that posture while passing a residence in a window of which sat their aged mother. It was an act of filial regard so impressive and beautiful as to awaken the admiration of every beholder. The sons honored themselves when they thus honored their mother.

True filial love in early life assures cheerful obedience, which is an important element of success. Sir Robert Peel claimed that here was found the secret of the renown of the Peel family. He gives a single fact to show that Providence prospers children who obey the command, "Honor thy father and thy mother," and curses those who do not.

Harry Garland was the son of a neighbor. He was bright and smart, and had his own way, choosing pleasure instead of work. He called one day for William, Henry, and Robert to accompany him on an excursion.

"No, no," said their father, "they cannot go; I have work for them to do, and in my family we have work before play."

The boys wanted to go; but their father's "no" meant "no" to them; and so it always was in the Peel family.

The three brothers, William, Henry, and Robert, became renowned in their country's history. Harry Garland became an idler and spendthrift, and finally filled a dishonored grave. The Peel brothers regarded the filial tie, and respected its law; Harry Garland broke it, and went to ruin.

THE FRATERNAL TIE.

DARIUS, King of Persia, sentenced Intaphemes, with all his children and his wife's brother, to death. His wife appeared before the king in inconsolable grief, and pleaded for mercy in their behalf. Her repeated visits from day to day finally awakened the king's sympathy, and he thus addressed her through his messenger:—

"Woman! King Darius offers you the liberty of any individual of your family whom you may most desire to preserve."

To this she replied:—

"If the king will grant me the life of any one of my family, I choose my brother in preference to the rest."

Her decision surprised the king so much that he despatched the following message to her:—

"The king desires to know why you have thought proper to pass over your children and your husband, and to preserve your brother, who is certainly a more remote connection than your children, and cannot be so dear to you as your husband."

Her answer was:—

"O King! if it please the Deity, I may have another husband, and if I be deprived of these may have other children; but as both of my parents are dead, it is certain that I can have no other brother."

The fraternal tie was too dear to be wholly sacrificed. The king granted her request without delay.

The ties of nature are reason enough for an indissoluble bond of union between brothers and sisters. Humanity revolts at a disregard of the bond which God has instituted between these two kindred hearts. Indeed, the feeling of

ONWARD TO FAME AND FORTUNE.

abhorrence is awakened toward those families among the lower order of animals which live and die in quarrels. It is so unnatural and heartless that every reflecting mind expresses profound astonishment at the sight. The fact that two individuals are children of the same parents, having kindred blood coursing through their veins, and common interest at stake, is sufficient basis upon which to rest all the fraternal obligations of which we may speak.

"That man," said a keen observer of human nature, "has been brought up in the society of intelligent and virtuous sisters."

"Whence do you infer that?"

The person addressed answered:—

"Because he exhibits that gentleness and delicacy of feeling which result from the influence of intelligent and virtuous sisters."

It was for this reason that Washington Irving wrote, "Often have I lamented that Providence denied me the companionship of sisters; often have I thought had I been thus favored, I should have been a better man."

There is no more interesting spectacle than that of a family of brothers and sisters dwelling together in uninterrupted harmony; their mutual affection, plans, and studies to please and benefit each other. No labor or sacrifice is spared to minister to one another's happiness. Brothers are held to the loving home circle so naturally and surely that the society of mere pleasure-seekers has no attraction for them, and the haunts of dissipation no lure; and sisters find therein more real satisfaction than the ballroom or Saratoga can furnish.

Here the language which Shakespeare put into the mouths of the devoted sisters finds complete fulfillment:—

WASHINGTON IRVING.

"So we grew together,
Like a double cherry, seeming parted,
But a union in partition,
Two lovely berries moulded on one stem;
So, with two seeming bodies, but one heart."

Mary Lyon wrote to a sister, "Oh, that I could fly over the hills and pay you a visit! Friends know best the strength of their love when they are separate. If possible, I think more of you now than ever. But should I fill a whole sheet in describing my desire to see you, and the delight which would be derived from an interview with you, it would be saying just nothing at all; therefore, I shall leave it all to be supplied by your imagination."

This language is expressive of just what the fraternal tie is wherever it exists true and strong. It is powerful as it is tender, and as commanding as it is beautiful. Her biographer said, referring

CHRIST AT THE HOME OF MARY AND MARTHA.

to the fact that her brother's family was her home in early life after death broke up the home of her parents, until he moved to the West: "Her friends that remained with her well remember her grief as they were borne away. For months afterwards, whenever that brother was spoken of in her presence, her tears would flow, and her silent and subdued feelings did not hinder her friends from seeing how deeply and tenderly she loved him. Little did she imagine that, in process of time, those daughters were to return to receive instruction from her lips in a seminary founded by her instrumentality; and, being better fitted to perform the duties of life, were to go forth, some to labor as teachers in our own country, and one to teach the benighted heathen under the shadow of a Chinese pagoda."

When observers behold fraternal love strongly uniting brothers and sisters, they conclude that other virtues also adorn the private lives of that circle. It is not the only excellence that thrives in and around that home. Virtues are found in clusters; one does not dwell solitary and alone; each one is a centre around which others revolve. This is as true of fraternal love as it is of any other virtue.

When clothed in flesh, and executing His merciful errand on earth, our Saviour honored an humble but united family of Bethany with a visit; and, probably, in all the land there was not another in which the fraternal duties were more faithfully discharged than in that same family, consisting of Martha, Mary, and their brother Lazarus. The incident may be regarded as a sacred symbol, pointing brothers and sisters to those spiritual visits which the Master vouchsafes to them when their attachments are strong and their harmony unbroken.

Beethoven, the most gifted composer of music in modern times, illustrated the sweetness of filial and fraternal love in his daily life. His father was a poor man in consequence of bad habits, and yet the son treated him with true filial devotion. When wealthy admirers had placed the gifted son under the tuition of a master of music at their own expense, the father's habits became so bad that the son was obliged to relinquish his studies, and return home to take charge of two brothers younger than himself. He made the sacrifice cheerfully, because of his genuine fraternal affection; nor did he return to his studies until his brothers were able to care for themselves. His passion for music was weaker than his love of kindred.

THE EXPENSE-BOOK.

"TAKE this book and keep an accurate account of your expenses," said Mr. H. to his son about leaving for Exeter Academy, New Hampshire, where he would prepare for college.

"What good will that do?" responded the son, as if his father were requiring him to do a "little thing" too small for an aspirant for college honors to be troubled about.

"What good!" exclaimed the father, somewhat surprised by the spirit in which his suggestion was received. "It is one of the things that will help make a man of you, if such a thing be possible. You may think it is a small matter to put down for what you spend every cent; but I assure you that it will have much to do with your habits twenty years from now. You want to know where your pocket money goes—a little matter, you may think; but it will do much to incline you to virtue instead of vice in manhood."

This father was not a fussy man; he did not attach too much importance to the expense-book; nor was the son an exception among boys in regarding it as unimportant—small. Young people of both sexes are apt to class it with the "little things" that are of no account. Hence, few of them know where the pocket money goes. The pennies vanish, and the nickels, and their allowance disappears much sooner than they expect. Where it is gone is well nigh a mystery to them.

An expense-book accurately and conscientiously kept helps young people to know themselves. Many have scarcely scraped an acquaintance with themselves. They do not see how prone they are to spend money for useless, and worse than useless, things; confections, goodies, knick-knacks, fun, and so on *ad infinitum*. The expense-book will show what they are on this line. They can see themselves in it as others see them. There is the unmistakable record of their weakness. It stares them in the face; there is no such thing as denying it, or getting around it.

A young merchant, who was doing a thriving business, was generous and jolly. He was wont to keep a box of cigars upon his desk for his own use and the use of his customers, and, perhaps, his employes. It was the duty of one of the clerks to keep the box of cigars replenished, and he took it into his head to keep an account of the number of cigars he put into the box in three months. At the end of this period he asked the merchant if he had any idea of the number and cost of the cigars used in three months.

"Not the least whatever," the merchant replied. "It is possible five or six hundred cigars have been used. Perhaps not so many."

"You will be surprised, then, if I tell you," added the clerk, "that over two thousand cigars have been put into that box in three months, at a cost of not less than one hundred dollars."

The merchant was surprised, and could scarcely believe the statement, for he kept no account of the cigars used, having never kept an account of these little expenses. He kept no expense-book when he was a boy, and so never thought about keeping one when he became a man. Why should he? Is not the boy "father of the man?"

Whether the young student, of whom we have spoken, was faithful to keep an account of his expenses or not, we know of one boy who was. His parents required him to keep an expense-book before he was old enough to go away to school. When he left home for the academy his father allowed him fifty cents a month for pocket money, with which he could do as he pleased. But his expense-book set him thinking. It would look better if it should show a balance in favor of his pocket from month to month.

This thought decided his course, and he spent but twenty-five cents a month, thus saving one-half of his allowance. The expense-book did it. The whole would have gone but for that accurate account. He became a noble, affluent man, and often said that the expense-book of his boyhood contributed largely to make him what he was.

The expense-book has often established the habit of economy, which has proven the foundation of a fortune; while, on the other hand, neglecting to note the method of spending money in early life has led to improvidence and want. "The ship which bore home the merchant's treasure was lost because it was allowed to leave the port from which it sailed with a very little hole in the bottom." "A small leak will sink a ship." The expense-book may stop the small leaks.

"For want of a nail, the shoe of the aide-de-camp's horse was lost; for want of the shoe, the horse was lost; for want of the horse, the aide-de-camp himself was lost, for the enemy took him and killed him; and for want of the aide-de-camp's intelligence, the army of his general was lost; and all because a little nail had not been properly fixed in a horse's shoe,"—a good illustration of the manner in which an evil habit of youth, though small in itself, may grow and curse the whole future life.

So far as money is concerned, the expense-book is designed to guard against such a result.

Amos Lawrence presented to one of his sons on his twelfth birthday, an expense-book, with the following written on the first page:—

My Dear Son:—I give you this little book, that you may write in it how much money you receive, and how you use it. It is of much importance in forming your early character, to have correct habits, and a strict regard to truth in all you do. For this purpose, I advise you never to cheat yourself by making a false entry in this book. If you spend money for an object you would not willingly have known, you will be more likely to avoid doing the same thing again if you call it by its right name here, remembering always that there is One who cannot be deceived. I pray God so to guide and direct you that when your stewardship here is ended He may say to you that the talents intrusted to your care have been faithfully employed.

Your affectionate father, A. L.

In 1822, Lawrence wrote to the father of a boy who came from Connecticut to serve in his store, "Will it not be well for him to furnish you, at stated periods, an exact account of his expenditures? The habit of keeping such an account will be serviceable, and, if he be prudent, the satisfaction will be great ten years hence, in looking back and observing the process by which his character has been formed."

The expense-book is an idea, and it suggests an idea to the owner. Nor is it an ephemeral idea. It takes possession of the mind for life. It comes to stay. It speaks of character—how to make or mar it. It lures to virtue and hinders vice.

KEEPING A DIARY.

MANY of the great and good men and women of the past have kept diaries. Washington, Jefferson, Garfield, Mrs. Adams, Mrs. Sigourney, Canning, Kitto, and a multitude of illustrious persons we need not mention, carefully pursued this practice. We infer that they regarded the habit as of substantial value to them, if not to their posterity, and we know that many of them recommended the practice to young of both sexes.

The benefit of the habit to them was reason enough for recommending it to others. We think it is generally conceded now by the successful class in all departments of human industry, that keeping a diary is of great importance, and that the earlier the practice is adopted, the better are its results.

Keeping a diary aids thoughtfulness. Indeed, it is only the thoughtful who are inclined to keep diaries. A certain amount of care and time are necessary to maintain the practice, and to this the unthinking and superficial ones are inclined to object. To record the daily experiences of life challenges attention. The act invests them with additional importance, for they cease to be commonplace as soon as they become a matter of record. They are worthy of more thought than most people bestow upon them.

Joseph Paxton, who planned the Crystal Palace of 1851, kept a diary. He was the gardener of the Duke of Devonshire at the time the committee of the great exposition advertised for plans of a building. The public very properly expected that the architects and engineers of the country alone would compete for the prize. Yet this gardener, Paxton, furnished a plan that was far superior to the dozens of them that came from engineers and architects.

How can this fact be explained? Paxton answered all such inquiries when he said that it was a subject upon which he had been thinking for years, although he had not dreamed that the time would come when his thinking would take on such tangible form. He was a man of thought, and these deeds of his mind had taken forms of beauty and utility in horticulture; but here was a new field for him, where thinking was equally victorious. For this thinking, which he could do as well as not, he was knighted, and subsequently was appointed architect of the larger and grander Crystal Palace at Sydenham, having entire charge of laying out the pleasure grounds, fountains, etc., of that remarkable enterprise. He was elected a member of Parliament, also, in 1854, and, withal, became one of the most honored men of his country.

We do not claim that Paxton's diary made him author of the Crystal Palace, but it was one of the causes of that *thinking*, which he said wrought out the plan of that wonderful structure. This daily record compels a person to pause in the rush of life, and note carefully what otherwise might be undervalued or forgotten.

The diary becomes a source of real pleasure and profit as a reference book. Said an educated gentleman who kept a diary through his college course of study: "I regret that I did not continue it when I entered upon my professional life. I find myself frequently reading that college diary. It discloses my habits of study and thought, my method of reading, companionship, and recreation. It revives the recollections of college days, and I live them over again. It required some self-denial and time to make the record, but both sacrifice and time were well invested." Similar testimony would be borne by all the men and women who have maintained the practice, and not a few will declare that there is real culture in it, as well as pleasure and profit—that such a daily record develops language and cultivates ease and grace of expression, while the tendency is to lead the mind onward and upward to higher attainments. Anything that stimulates thought, and breaks up indifference to the experiences of every-day life, must prove a blessing.

Two literary gentlemen were discussing a public question, when they found themselves at variance respecting the date of a certain event. After the dispute had continued for a while, one of them thought of his diary as a source of proof. "I think my diary will give us a correct clue to it," he said, and proceeded at once to look up the record, which showed that neither of them was correct. The record was accepted by both, however, and thus became to them of real worth. Similar benefits are liable to follow this habit of keeping a diary almost any day. For this reason, those who have tried it never discourage the young from undertaking it.

The diaries of distinguished men and women have been of great value to the world in making up a just estimate of their characters. Biographers have found them to be a prolific source of information. The diary of Washington was indispensable to his biographers, and to the public. Nothing could be accepted in the place of it. It furnished an insight into his character such as no other source of knowledge could have done. The same is true of many distinguished men. Their diaries disclosed points of interest in personal character that otherwise would have been overlooked. The world never could have known exactly what they did without these records. A multitude of deeds would have been lost to men without them, and deeds, too, in which their true spirit breathed as nowhere else.

The lesson to every youth of both sexes, is, *keep a diary*. Regard it as part and parcel of education, too important to be omitted. Like the expense-book, its influence is conservative, and prevents youthful powers from scattering. Other things being equal, the youth who keeps a diary ranks higher than he who does not.

ART OF CONVERSATION.

CONVERSATION is an art, and very few are masters of it. Although it is the most common method of conveying thoughts, it receives less attention than the written or printed page. Men study to appear well in print, but give little attention to appearing well in conversation. The latter is treated as of little consequence; hence men and women who might shine in this department are poor talkers. It ought to be otherwise, since they spend more time in talking than they do in reading. Besides, no personal attraction is more satisfactory than the ability to converse well.

Pythagoras esteemed elegant conversation so highly that he commanded his pupils to maintain silence during the first two years of their instruction. He would have their minds thoroughly furnished, that their conversation might be worthy of the pupils of so illustrious a teacher. He was wont to say, "Be silent or say something better than silence." Lacordaire, a French writer, said, "After speech, silence is the greatest power in the world;" and Mrs. Sigourney wrote, "In all countries where intelligence is prized, a talent for conversation ranks high among accomplishments. To clothe the thoughts in clear and elegant language, and to convey them impressively to the mind of another, is no common attainment."

There is no doubt that the art of conversation is born with some people, for they converse well without much preparation. They possess a good command of language and readily express their ideas. Burke, Fox, Garrick, Coleridge, and Carlyle were fascinating talkers. Coleridge employed diction so elegant that "his audience seemed wrapped in wonder and delight, as one conversation more profound, or clothed in more forcible language than another, fell from his tongue."

On the other hand, Dante, Chaucer, Milton, Gray, Southey, and Dryden were poor conversationalists. Dryden said of himself, "My conversation is slow and dull, and my humor reserved." Alluding to his inability to converse well, Baker said, "I am fit for no communion save with the dead." Thomas excused his inability to express his thoughts easily in conversation, by saying, "I received my intellectual wealth from nature in solid bars, not in current coin."

Excellence in conversation should be sought. Instead of being overlooked, it should command the attention as an important factor in education. No matter in what sphere a person moves, this is one of the acquisitions that will prove of great value. A good conversationalist adorns any circle, and invests it with a charm. On the farm, in the shop, by the way, as in the drawing-room and parlor, the art is alike attractive and useful. It challenges respect and admiration, and, therefore, is worth striving for. Without it youth should consider their education incomplete.

A well-disciplined and well-furnished mind is requisite to become a good converser. George S. Burleigh said, "Great capacity for expression, with nothing to express, like those immense Roman aqueducts that have been dry for centuries, may challenge the admiration of the curious, but will hardly satisfy the thirst of eager explorers." Having something to say, a well-disciplined mind will usually say it well. A more facile command of language is the inheritance of one more than another, but, barring this gift of nature, culture must contribute directly and largely to the art of conversation. Reading, alone, will do much in this direction. It furnishes the mind with subjects of thought, and familiarizes it with language with which to clothe them. "Practice makes perfect" here, as elsewhere. The poor talker may become a good one. "All can learn to sing," says an eminent professor of music; and so all can learn to converse well. All may not learn to converse with marked excellence, nor can all learn to sing skillfully; but all can learn, nevertheless. Given a tongue, fair intellect, and a thorough education, the conversation will be good, perhaps graceful, and even elegant. Where culture is wanting, the attempt to converse well makes ignorance more conspicuous. Silence becomes the uneducated better than speech. Cyrus once said to a man who maintained almost unbroken silence in company, "If thou art a wise man, thou doest foolishly; but if thou art a fool, thou doest wisely."

The acquisition of this art is not easy. Carlyle said, "In the way of writing, no great thing was ever, or ever will be, done with ease, but with difficulty." He might have said the same of conversation. It is one of the attainments that polishes all the faculties by the effort to possess it. This is especially true where there is little or no natural tact for the art, and proficiency depends wholly upon cultivation. Cowper wrote:—

> "Though conversation, in its better part,
> May be esteemed a gift and not an art,
> Yet much depends as in the tiller's toil,
> On culture and the sowing of the soil."

Harriet Beecher Stowe belonged to one of the most remarkable families in America. Her father was Dr. Lyman Beecher, a man of brain and power. Her mother was a good match for her father. The large family of children were talented, enterprising, and became influential, and all were, and are, literary and scholarly. From boyhood and girlhood they were reading, studying, progressing. The late Henry Ward Beecher was one of them. They were born students, always in love with learning; they were at home in composition and authorship; their thoughts dwelt upon great thinkers and great subjects. Why? Mrs. Stowe has said that in her father's house, the conversation at the table, and around the hearthstone in the evening, was about books, authors, reforms, and religion.

MRS. HARRIET BEECHER STOWE.

The children never listened to gossip there, or meaningless prattle; everything spoken was important and uplifting, suited to cultivate a love of letters. Mrs. Stowe records one incident as follows:—

"I remember hearing father relate the account of Byron's separation from his wife; and one day hearing him say, with a sorrowful countenance, as if announcing the death of some one very interesting to him:—

"'My dear, Byron is dead—gone.'

"After being a while silent, he said:—

"'Oh, I am sorry Byron is dead! I did hope he would have lived to do something for Christ. What a harp he might have swept!'

"The whole impression made upon me by the conversation was solemn and painful. I remember taking my basket for strawberries that afternoon, and going over to a strawberry-field on Chestnut Hill, but I was too dispirited to do anything, so I lay down among the daisies and looked up into the blue sky, and thought of the great eternity into which Byron had entered, and wondered how it might be with his soul." The incident illustrates the moulding influence of conversation in the family; and there is no doubt that the usually literary cast that it took on had not a little to do with the remarkable literary career of the household. The curse of slavery and the blessing of liberty was a common theme of discussion at the Beecher fireside, not only with members of the family, but also with educated guests, in the presence of the children; and to this sort of early culture, probably, was to be traced in a large degree the fearless, outspoken, anti-slavery sentiment of the Beechers forty years ago.

ANDREAS HOFER LED TO EXECUTION AT MANTUA.

XXIX.

THE MASTER-PASSION.

THE master-passion is the ruling spirit or purpose of one's life. History furnishes eminent examples of it, to three of which we will call attention.

An English boy, by the name of Michael Reynolds, aspired to be fireman on a locomotive engine, but he was too young for that, so he worked away willingly to help his poor father at any kind of a job that was available, always industrious, cheerful, hopeful, and faithful. In due time he was installed fireman on a locomotive, a place he cherished above all others. Now he could learn all about an engine, and, after a little, drive one himself, perhaps. His thoughts and his ambition ran in this line, as he toiled from year to year. To command a locomotive, and drive it over an English railway at thirty miles an hour or more, had more fascination for him than to own and rein the best pair of dappled grays in the British realm. He could ask for nothing higher.

Reynolds secured the prize sooner than he expected. He fell so in love with his work, and exhibited such great tact, efficiency, and fidelity, that he was rapidly promoted. He soon outgrew the engine, proved himself to be greater than the business, fit for something higher and larger—just the man to become "locomotive inspector on the London and Brighton Railroad," a position which he honored by his intelligence, ability, and virtue. How it was done can be best learned from a book which he wrote and published several years ago. The purpose of the book was, to use his own language, "to communicate that species of knowledge which it is necessary for an engine-driver to possess who aspires to take high rank on the foot-plate." There is "high rank" for even an engine-driver, and an aspiration for it is the first condition of success.

When he was an engine-driver he was always at the station a whole hour before the time for starting, in order that everything should be in readiness. There were twenty-two things to be looked after before steaming up, as inspecting his engine in every part, seeing to the fire, water in the boiler, quantity of water and coal in the tender, going into the pit under the engine to test every nut and pin, adjusting the oiling apparatus, examining the fire implements, machinist tools, lamps, flax, yarn, copper wire, time-table, etc., all of which must be in perfect order, and in the exact place designed for them, that they might be seized at a moment's warning.

Reynolds became so expert in his calling that he could detect a defect in the locomotive or rail by the sound and jar of the machinery. Indeed, he could tell whether the heat he experienced proceeded from the fire-box or friction. We need scarcely add that he became a highly honored citizen, influential and wealthy, and a public benefactor.

Chauncey Jerome, the Connecticut clock-maker, was born in Plymouth, of that State. His father was a blacksmith and nail-maker, and owned a few acres of land, which Chauncey helped to cultivate as soon as he could handle a hoe. He went to school the three winter months each year, until he was ten years old, when his father took him into the shop to make nails. One year thereafter his father died, and he was obliged to leave home to work for his board and clothes. For the same remuneration, at fourteen, he was apprenticed to a carpenter to serve until he was twenty-one. He was bright, honest, aspiring, and never shirked or became discouraged. Once, when only ten years of age, he cut a load of wood for a lazy boy in the neighborhood for one cent. He did it in the evening, and often he cut loads of wood for the neighbors for a few cents per load.

One thing in the neighborhood early attracted his attention—Eli Terry's wooden clocks. During the autumn and winter months Terry would manufacture fifteen or twenty of them, and sell them in the spring and summer, his customers making the cases into which the clock machinery was put. They were the old-fashioned clocks that used to stand in the corners of rooms, reaching nearly to the plastering, in our grandfathers' day.

Chauncey magnified the clock business. If he could make clocks like Mr. Terry he would be satisfied. Whenever he could command an hour of his own he was at Terry's. It was fun to see clocks made! If he could only make them! Some day he might! Clock was on his brain, and in his heart, too, but the nick of time had not come. It did come, however, when he was seventeen, and he told his employer that he would buy his own clothes if he would give him the three winter months of the four years remaining of his apprenticeship. The proposition was accepted. Those winters were spent at Waterbury, Connecticut, learning to make clocks. He was happy now; his master-passion had triumphed.

While living with the carpenter to whom he was apprenticed, he overheard two neighbors discussing "Terry's folly," because he proposed to make two hundred clocks that year. Chauncey set up the clock business for himself, and lived to manufacture and sell two hundred thousand clocks in a year.

One of the most illustrious examples of our theme that we have now is that of Henry M. Stanley. At three years of age he was an inmate of a poorhouse in

ONWARD TO FAME AND FORTUNE.

Wales, where he received sufficient education to set up as a teacher at Mold, in Flintshire, when he left that institution. But the master-passion began to stir his soul, and he was not content. He must go somewhere, he scarcely knew where. His adventurous spirit could not be tied down. He obtained a situation as cabin-boy on a ship bound for New Orleans. Reaching that city, he was employed by a wealthy gentleman by the name of Stanley. The youth proved to be so bright, enterprising, efficient, and reliable that Mr. Stanley adopted him as his son, and gave him his own name, Henry M. Stanley. His real name was John Rowlands. Not long after his change of name and relations, his spirit of adventure asserted itself, and he wandered off into the Arkansas wilderness, and lived in a hut on the banks of the Wichita River for some weeks. His adopted father knew not where he was, but supposed that he was dead, and mourned deeply for him. But he found his way back on a flat-boat, to the joy of the Stanley household.

The sudden death of Mr. Stanley left our hero again penniless, for his benefactor had made no will. So he started out again in quest of fortune among the mining camps of California, and the Indian tribes of the Pacific coast. At twenty-one he found himself face to face with the

DAVID LIVINGSTONE.

War of the Rebellion, dragooned into the Rebel navy, though he was for the Union. The next few years he served as correspondent for the New York *Herald*, at Crete, where an insurrection against Turkish misrule made spicy times; at Abyssinia, where England fought King Theodore; the next year in Spain, reporting the Civil War for the *Herald*. He was here when he was summoned by Mr. Bennett, to Paris, by telegram.

Reaching Paris late the next night, he proceeded directly to Mr. Bennett's room at the Grand Hotel, and knocked.

"Come in," responded Mr. Bennett, who was in bed. Stanley entered.

"Who are you?"

"My name is Stanley."

"Ah, yes; sit down. Where do you think Livingstone is?"

"Really, sir, I have no idea."

"Do you think he is alive?"

"He may be, and he may not."

"Well, I think he is alive; and I am afraid he may be in want. So I intend that you shall go to him. Take whatever you need for yourself and for him. Go as you please, and do as you please. *But find Livingstone.*"

Here was a capital field for his master-passion to operate. It suited him exactly.

"Yes, sir, but the cost," Stanley suggested after a little.

"How much will it be?"

"I am afraid it will be over $12,000."

"Very well; draw a thousand pounds now. When it is gone, another thousand; when it is gone, another; when it is gone, another; and so on as long and as often as necessary. *But find Livingstone.*"

Thus in a few moments was opened a field of operation for the great explorer, in which he has won an enviable name in every part of the habitable globe. We need not repeat the thrilling story. It is enough that the master-passion has wrought wonders. Commerce, science, history, learning, and religion, bear witness to the value of his achievements.

LETTER-WRITING AS A FINE ART.

A BEAUTIFUL letter, written by a high-school girl, suggested our theme. Evidently she had studied the art of writing letters until she thoroughly understood the business. Punctuation, capitals, chirography, superscription, everything about the epistle was first class. The most critical observer could find nothing to criticise adversely. We found, upon inquiry, that in her school, instruction was given upon letter-writing. And why not? It is one of the most common things done—usually very poorly done; so poorly as to indicate that in schools generally this art is neglected. There are few efficient letter-writers. There would be many more if the subject received but occasional attention in our grammar and high schools.

It goes without saying that the ability to write an excellent letter, with beautiful penmanship, is a very graceful accomplishment. That so few possess this ability is not because the art is very difficult to acquire, but because it is undervalued. Little importance is attached to it. Scribbling will do very well in writing to a familiar friend. Youth of both sexes see no particular need of excellence in writing letters to each other, or even to their parents. They dash them off as if it were of the smallest consequence whether chirography or the King's English suffer or not. Were they writing to a professor, governor, or president, they might select their words, and wish they had given more attention to penmanship, as well as to spelling, which is a valuable acquisition when it is perfect.

A good composer, penman, and speller will make a fine letter-writer. Application and persistent effort for a fractional part of the time which the expert pianist spent—six hours a day for twenty years—would qualify a young man or woman to write to the president or his wife. The commonness of letter-writing makes youth indifferent to it as an art to be acquired, when this fact ought to awaken their liveliest interest in it. What must be done so frequently, and with so many people, deserves to be well done. "What is worth doing at all is worth doing well," is just as true of correspondence as it is of any other business. The letter referred to in the beginning of this paper was more ornamental to the schoolgirl who wrote it than diamond earrings and necklace.

In letter-writing, the versatility of talents which the author possesses appears. However highly educated the correspondent may be, however large the acquisitions he or she has made, letter-writing calls into use the entire culture. The whole life discipline is poured into the epistle, so that the *character* of the writer is manifest. Disraeli claims that chirography reveals the character of the author. Queen Elizabeth's penmanship was very fine, having been taught by Roger Ascham; and a French editor said of her chirography, in connection with that of her cousin, Mary Stuart, "Who would believe that these writings are of the same epoch? The first denotes asperity and ostentation; the second indicates simplicity, softness, and nobleness. The one is that of Elizabeth, Queen of England; the other that of her cousin, Mary Stuart. The difference of these two handwritings answers most evidently to that of their characters." He said, also, of Queen Anne, "She wrote a fair round hand. That is the writing she had been taught by her master, probably without any alteration of manner naturally suggested by herself—the copying hand of a '*common character.*'"

Take the hint about a "common character," and couple it with the remark of Hannah More, namely, "To read so as not to be understood, and to write so as not to be read, are among the minor immoralities," and the claims of good letter-writing are greatly magnified. Mrs. Sigourney wrote, "Elegant chirography and a clear epistolary style are accomplishments which every educated female should possess. Their indispensable requisites are neatness, simplicity, grace, and grammatical correctness. Defects in either of these particulars are scarcely pardonable. You are aware that the handwriting is considered one of the talismans of character. Whether this test may be depended on or not, the fact that letters travel further than the sound of the voice, or the sight of the countenance can follow, renders it desirable that they should convey no incorrect or unfavorable impression. The lesser niceties of folding, sealing, and superscription are not beneath the notice of a lady," and she might have added, or gentleman. Mrs. Farrar wrote a small work on "Letter-writing," in which she said, "It is well to find out the best way of doing everything, since there is a pleasure in doing things *in the best way*, which those miss who think *any way* will do." Cicero, who was master of the Latin language as well as of eloquence, boasted that his epistles were as carefully constructed as his orations. And he said, also, "Whatever may be the subject of my letters, they still speak the language of conversation."

THE DISCIPLINE OF DEBATE.

WHEN Benjamin Franklin was a young printer in Philadelphia, he organized his intimate associates into a literary club, called "The Junto." The object of it was intellectual improvement. The members met weekly, and discussed social, scientific, political, and moral subjects. It proved an excellent discipline to all the members, especially to Franklin, who said of it, fifty years thereafter, "It was the best school of philosophy, morality, and politics, that then existed in the province, for our queries, which were read the week preceding their discussion, put us upon reading with attention on the several subjects, that we might speak more to the purpose; and here, too, we acquired better habits of conversation, everything being studied in our rules which might prevent our disgusting each other." The immediate fruits of debate were, much better command of language, readiness to express their thoughts, and general discipline of the mental powers. Of the original twelve members, two became surveyors-general; one the inventor of a quadrant; one a distinguished mechanic and influential man; and one a merchant of great note, and a provincial judge; and all but one or two, honored citizens of more or less celebrity.

Curran, the renowned Irish orator, always referred to a debating society that he joined in youth as of great value to him in awakening his dormant energies. He was a timid boy, with an impediment in his speech, and consequently without promise as a public speaker. His schoolmates called him "Stuttering Jack Curran." Determined to overcome the impediment of speech, and make an orator, he joined the debating society, and made his *début*, which was rather discouraging, for the first time he rose to speak, his timidity overcame him, and he sat down without saying a word. One boy whispered to another, "Orator Mum." But the discipline of debate developed self-possession, ready use of language, ability to express his thoughts, and thereby started him off upon that splendid career when he was known as the most eloquent man of his times.

The late Henry Wilson, Vice-President of the United States, joined the village debating society of Natick, Massachusetts, in his early manhood. He soon found himself able to express his thoughts readily, clothing them in well-selected language; and his improvement was rapid from week to week. In that society he laid the foundation, as he always claimed, of that facility in debate for which he was so widely known in Congress.

At seventeen years of age, the late President Garfield joined the debating society of Geauga Academy, in Chester, Ohio. He was about the last boy in school who would have been selected for an orator. But debate proved both a surprise and inspiration to him, developing in him an ability to speak of which he had not dreamed, and when he left the school for Hiram Institute, teachers prophesied a brilliant career for him as a public speaker. He continued this practice in the debating societies of the Institute and Williams College, always preparing himself thoroughly for each debate, and no one of his classmates was surprised that in his manhood he ranked in Congress and throughout the country as one of the finest orators known. The debating society did for him what teachers and books never could have done.

Over fifty years ago, eight young clerks in Boston organized a debating society at their boarding-house on Allston Street. At first they were in some doubt about a name for it. "The Allston Club," taking the name of the street; "Boston Literary Association," and the "Payson Debating Society," taking the name of their landlord, who kindly offered them the use of a room, were names suggested. But one member, noticing that the surname of five of the eight members began with "S," said, "Let us call it 'The Five S's Society';" and his suggestion was adopted. For months this society continued its weekly debates, soon drawing in all the boarders of the house, and attracting a good audience on the street outside. Hearers were surprised at the ability developed by discussion, and the members regarded the discipline as extremely beneficial. Each one of the eight members became a very intelligent, successful, and useful business man in the city.

A few years later, within a few miles of Boston, several youth obtained the use of a schoolhouse in which to hold the meetings of their debating society. Two or three of them worked in a factory. At first the public were not admitted; but after the practice of a few months their doors were thrown open, and friends crowded the room. At the same time a citizens' lyceum was supported at the town hall, in which the members of the schoolhouse society finally became deeply interested. The originator of the latter was so enthused by the debate at the hall one night, that he sprang to his feet, and before an audience of a thousand citizens discussed the question of the evening with an eloquence and ability that carried the listeners by storm. Subsequently this youth became governor of Massachusetts, speaker of the National House of Representatives at Washington, and has filled other positions of public trust to this day. Of his associates in debate one became a prominent lawyer, another an extensive and wealthy manufacturer, another the warden of a state prison, and still another a popular clergyman. The pastor of the boy who became governor told the writer that when Nathaniel was eleven years old, a bobbin-boy in the factory, the superintendent of a mill invited a group of boys to spend an evening at his house. The pastor was there, and Nathaniel also. The pastor thought the aristocratic superintendent slighted the bobbin-boy, and he said within himself, "The time will come when that boy will stand higher than you ever did." Thirty years thereafter the pastor and superintendent appeared before the governor of Massachusetts, who was no other than that same bobbin-boy, in behalf of a public enterprise in the town where all of them lived. The pastor's prophecy was signally fulfilled.

An account of this bobbin-boy and his debating society was published a few years ago, and was read by a youth of seventeen in a Massachusetts village. He had four brothers younger than himself, and as many more boys in the neighborhood, whom he organized into a debating society. At that time he was learning the trade of a wheelwright, and not one of the number ever expected to go higher than that. Yet, of the five brothers spoken of, the eldest became a popular preacher; another is superintendent of schools, in a large town in Massachusetts; another was recently graduated at a New England college; and the other two became successful and very exemplary merchants. The debating society did it.

So it comes to pass that the debating society is on the road to success. Its discipline cannot be overestimated. It inspires to nobler efforts. There is no substitute for it.

WORTH OF AN IDEA.

IDEAS, not gold, govern the world. Machines do much of the world's work, but machines are born of ideas. A human worker without ideas is only a machine. He is content to serve all his life, doing the same work over and over again, making the same thing year after year, without progress, ambition, or purpose. It is the thinking man who becomes master-workman, perhaps proprietor. Ideas become to him an inspiration and force. They rally his intellectual powers; and these control and develop his physical ability. Stupidity becomes a machine in the workshop of life, but ideas only can make a man.

It is no chance system that returns to the Hindoo citizen a penny, and to the American laborer a dollar, for his daily toil; that makes Mexico, with its mineral wealth, poor, and New England, with its granite and ice, rich; that bids the elements in one country become subservient to the wants of man, and in another, to sport idly, and run to waste; it is thought that makes the difference. Ideas do not stir the Hindoo and Mexican as they do the American. Here they beget enterprise and invincible courage that defy difficulties and surmount obstacles. They assure victory.

THE FIRST PROOF.

Young people should take in the worth of an idea, for this will exert great influence upon the occupation they choose, the methods they adopt, and the books they read. Idealess occupations, associates, and books should be avoided, since they are not friendly to intelligent manhood and womanhood. Ideas make the wise man; the want of them, the fool.

Roger Sherman was apprenticed to a shoemaker for his board and clothes. But early in life, the idea took possession of his soul, "I can become a lawyer."

That idea was the making of him. It rallied his latent faculties, and bent them to one end. To become a lawyer was the dream of his youth. Obstacles dwindled away before the indomitable spirit which that one idea nursed into stalwart life. Every leisure moment became a self-improving moment. A book was his constant companion. Spare time was the most valuable time of all, for it was used to improve his intellect, and fit him for the duties of a noble manhood. His occupation became a teacher to him, and the world a school. He learned from everything around him; and, at thirty-three years of age, he was admitted to the bar. The dream of his boyhood was realized.

Gutenberg was a thoughtful young man, familiar with manuscript volumes, of which the age in which he lived could furnish but few. One day, when he was in a meditative mood, a new idea flashed upon his mind namely, that letters might be invented with which to print books instead of writing and copying them. He unfolded his idea to his wife, and she endorsed the suggestion heartily, whereupon the inventor proceeded at once to reduce his idea to practice. His decided inventive genius soon triumphed, and the art of printing became reality.

Gutenberg, who had been a skilled lapidary, now turned his attention to book-making, since which time the value of his new idea to the world has been illustrated by wonderful progress in the art. In contrast with the slow, difficult, and very imperfect method of making books by Gutenberg's letters, the methods of our day, multiplying volumes like the leaves of the forest, are magical indeed. The art of book-making now is characterized by rapidity, elegance, and cheapness. With the latest improvement in the printing-press, it is possible to supply the demands of the world for books at a price that brings them within the reach of even the poor. The rapidity with which books are multiplied is a marvel of our times.

A roll of paper, containing a thousand yards, will run through a Hoe press with almost incredible speed, printing sheets enough for five thousand volumes in a single day. In printing newspapers, a roll of paper at one end of the press is turned out at the other end, printed on both sides, and folded ready for mailing, at the rate of five thousand papers an hour. Equally remarkable has been the progress in typesetting, both by hand and machinery, and it is all the outcome of Gutenberg's idea of making letters. The inventor set in motion a train of influences that has changed the secular and moral condition of mankind. We cannot estimate the value of Gutenberg's idea.

Nor can we compute the value of Morse's idea, that gave us the electric telegraph. Morse was coming from Havre to New York City on board the ship "Sully." Dr. Charles S. Jackson, of Boston, was on board, and was describing an experiment made in Paris with an electro-magnet, by means of which electricity had been transmitted through a great length of wire arranged in circles around the walls of an apartment. Morse, who was a painter, and had just completed a three years' residence in Europe to perfect himself in his art, excitedly said, when Dr. Jackson finished, "Then messages may be transmitted by electricity."

There the telegraph was born. It only remained to test the idea. This Morse did, surmounting great obstacles, overcoming the most discouraging difficulties, making progress slowly, but surely, until he had the real thing—the telegraph. Who can estimate its worth to-day? Ask the man of business who communicates by telegraph with the four quarters of the globe. The recent fire in New York which destroyed the headquarters of the great Western Union

ONWARD TO FAME AND FORTUNE.

Telegraph Company, interrupted the business of the whole civilized world for a day, or until the company renewed business in another place. Such is the importance of the telegraph in our day, and such is the value of Morse's idea on board the "Sully."

The worth of an idea is illustrated in the ordinary walks of life. In every place, and at all times, we are reminded that a single thought is the most valuable legacy bequeathed to us. In articles of furniture that make our homes comfortable, and the utensils of the kitchen that lighten labor and administer to human wants, we find much to magnify the worth of a thought. Once they were only ideas in the brain of the inventor.

So small an article as the watch which we carry in our vest pocket, involves principles of construction the discovery and development of which have brought the race out of ages of mental gloom. Yet how few note their indebtedness to ideas when they consult their watches. They keep time, and that is enough; and they would be just as good for that if they grew like acorns.

Says another, "What a miracle of art, that a man can teach a few brass wheels, and

GALILEO GALLILEI.

a little piece of elastic steel, to out-calculate himself; to give him a rational answer to one of the most important questions which a being traveling toward eternity can ask. What a miracle that a man can put within this little machine a spirit that measures the flight of time with greater accuracy than the unassisted intellect of the profoundest philosopher; which watches and moves when sleep palsies alike the hand of the maker and the mind of the contriver; nay, when the last sleep has come over them both." And the author of all this was a solitary idea in the mind of Galileo, when he stood watching the oscillation of a lamp in the Metropolitan Temple of Pisa. A clear, vivid idea of the correct measurement of time flashed upon his mind, and his name and fame became immortal.

Despise not an idea; for the smallest is better than none. A man of one idea is sometimes ridiculed. Garrison was persecuted for his anti-slavery idea; but it wrought a revolution. It made him a public benefactor. His idea was worth all that liberty was worth. The youth who is rich in ideas will never be poor in reputation.

REDUCING AN IDEA TO PRACTICE.

MANY authors of good ideas have failed to reduce them to practice. They lacked the practical talent necessary to reap the profits of valuable conceptions. Hence, many inventors have derived no pecuniary advantage from their inventions; other parties have stepped in and taken the profits. They were able to beat the bush, but others caught the bird. The discoverer of gold at Sutter's Mill, California, and the proprietor of the mill never got rich; both died poor. They could discover, but they failed to appropriate and keep. It may require less tact, industry, and perseverance to beget a valuable idea than to reduce it to practice; for greater difficulties may obstruct the way of the latter, and more complications, even, may attend its consummation. Almost without exception, the successful men, who have made the best practical use of their ideas, have been men of marked courage, application, tact, and determination. Ordinary difficulties did not cause them to hesitate for a moment; and extraordinary ones seemed to arouse their whole being to almost superhuman efforts.

An illustration of this point has been brought to the attention of the American people. Congress voted a gold medal to Mr. Joseph Francis, of Washington, for "his distinguished services in discovering and applying scientific principles to inventions for saving human life and other humane purposes." The medal cost six thousand dollars, and is ornamented with designs emblematic of the recipient's life-work. It was presented to him by President Harrison. This crowning act of his success came late in life, for Mr. Francis was in his ninetieth year. Nor was this distinction gained without heroic struggles with poverty, opposition, and ridicule, as the following brief sketch of his life proves:

Mr. Francis was a Boston boy, and served as page in the Massachusetts Legislature from eleven to sixteen years of age. In 1812, when he was twelve years old, there was an unprecedented number of destructive shipwrecks, and the terrible tales of horror wrought deeply upon the sensitive nature of this gifted boy.

The war had destroyed his father's property and broken up a family of seven children, so that Joseph's earnings were necessary, to the last cent, to aid in the support of his brothers and sisters. In these circumstances, it was the more remarkable that he should conceive the idea of a lifeboat, and proceed—a boy of twelve years—to produce a model. Every moment, when he was not required to be at the State House, he spent in a workshop on Clark Street, near Hanover. His progress was slow but sure. With pluck and hope he worked on, sometimes baffled and disappointed, and often laughed at, but never yielding to discouragement. He was eighteen years old when his lifeboat, with all its life-saving qualities, was completed, and was placed on exhibition at the fair of the Mechanic's Institute, in Boston, in 1819. He crossed the Rubicon when his lifeboat was complete. The battle of his life was won by that early struggle. What manner of stuff he was made of became manifest then. The thought, tact, resolution, and force of character necessary to produce the lifeboat were competent to produce more and greater results.

The author of "Thrift" accounts for the failure of some men to derive advantages from their valuable conceptions, by saying, "Some of the best and noblest of men are wanting in tact. They will neither make allowance for circumstances, nor adapt themselves to circumstances; they will insist upon driving their wedge the broad end foremost; they raise walls only to run their own heads against; they make such great preparations, and use such great precautions, that they defeat their own object—like the Dutchman mentioned by Washington Irving, who, having to leap a ditch, went so far back to have a good run at it, that when he came up he was completely winded, and had to sit down on the wrong side to recover his breath."

In contrast with this, we see how Francis went to work in the straightest and shortest way to accomplish his purpose. He was not only competent to conceive, but having cultivated those manly qualities that one must possess in order to win, he was equally well prepared to execute. He would give practical existence to a noble conception.

In 1838, another and grander conception engaged the mind of Francis—that of an iron ship. Although poor and needy, he hastened to reduce his idea to practice. Having provided a very humble home for his family in the country, he shut himself up in a workshop on Anthony Street, New York City, to produce his ideal iron vessel. It took him six years to put his conception into a real ship, and they were years of hard study and harder struggles with want and the indifference of friends.

In 1847, his famous metal life-car was completed; but Congress repulsed its author, and the Secretary of the Treasury said to him:—

"There is no means known under heaven, nor will there ever be, of saving life under circumstances such as you recount; besides, the Government cannot afford to try experiments. Try your life-car, and if it will do anything like what you represent, you may rest assured the Government will adopt it."

Francis was equal to the occasion. While protesting against the attitude of the Government, he spent the next two years in proving to the world, at his own expense, the great value of his invention; and his success spread his fame over both continents. From that time his life was a succession of triumphs in America and Europe. Subsequent to 1855, he spent several years in Europe, establishing immense factories for the manufacture of his iron boats, vessels, and life-cars, floating docks, pontoon bridges and wagons, for five of the leading European governments. Medals, diplomas, and royal honors were showered upon him from the highest authorities. Crowned heads recognized his services in the interests of humanity; and it is claimed that no American, except General Grant, was ever more kindly received and honored by nobles and monarchs than Mr. Francis.

This is a remarkable life, with its lessons for every reader. The conception of the great idea of his life was the easiest part of it. His trials and exhausting labors came when he attempted to reduce it to practice. Had he been no more resolute and invincible than the average American, his conception never would have attained a real form. He would have soon found excuse for abandoning his idea in the poverty that oppressed him, or the difficulties that beset his way. But his noble qualities of mind and heart served him better than wealth. They won success for him without private or public patronage.

AMONG THE REAPERS

XXX.

THE IDEAL AND THE REAL.

IT is not enough to appreciate the power and value of ideas; we must understand that they are real, and that they make other things real, also. The common opinion is, that material things which we can see are real, while the ideal and spiritual things we cannot see are unreal, and, therefore, uncertain. The multitude believe that material things, which they can see and handle, are more reliable than ideal or spiritual things, which elude both vision and grasp. It is a grave mistake. Is the body more real than the soul? Rather, is it not true that, in a sense, the soul is the more real? A real man walks, talks, works, reasons, sympathizes and enjoys; but take away his soul—the thinking, reasoning part of him that we cannot see—and he is not a real man. He cannot walk or talk, reason or enjoy. His body is a mass of lifeless, useless flesh and bone, unconscious as a stone. Without the immaterial soul it cannot be a "thing of life and beauty." So that the soul is not only as real as the body, but makes the body real to us. The part that was not born to die, makes the part live that was born to perish. The spiritual is the real. It is the material that wastes and disappears, while the spiritual endures. "The things that are seen are temporal,"—transitory, uncertain, perishable. "The things that are not seen are eternal,"—enduring, satisfactory, real. Most miserable should we be if the soul were no more reliable and true than the body. There would be no foundation for hope, no reason for faith.

At this point, thousands of young people, with older ones, are throwing away their chances of success. They undervalue immaterial things. They value money, which they can see and handle, more than ideas, which they cannot see. Hence, religion itself is to them vague and visionary. It is altogether too unsubstantial and unreal to satisfy them. Forms of public worship are well enough, for these appeal to the eye; but so-called religion is too visionary, in their estimation, to appeal to anything. So religion is given a wide berth on the ground that it is unreal. It is the same with other immaterial things—they are undervalued, misimproved, and often rejected, because they are considered unreal. This is all wrong, and must be righted, in order to make the highest achievements.

Old and young must know that the ideal and spiritual make the real. For example, there stands a costly and imposing edifice—man's creation. It is symmetrical and grand in appearance; as a work of art, worthy of admiration and imitation. It is real, of course; but what makes it real? Thought makes it real. It existed in the brain of the architect before it became the fine structure that it is. Its plan and quality were the immaterial before it became material. It was just as real in the brain when it was a thought, as when it became a thing of art. Indeed, its latter form was not possible until the ideal had made it so. There could have been no edifice to delight the eye until after its ideal existence. The ideal created the real; the former is no more a nonentity than the latter, and it is equally certain and reliable. The creator must be as real as that which it creates.

Mind is immaterial; we cannot see it. Yet the body is not more real than the mind. The latter rules; the former is ruled. Mental energy gives physical life substantial existence. Mind is the man; the unalterable condition of true manhood. The more mind, other things being equal, the higher manhood. It is the mind, and what it stands for, that commands public respect and confidence. It settles, also, the measure of human influence; without it, man is a fool, with as little influence as a stone statue. He must command thought if he would lead men, for men follow minds instead of bodies. And herein is found the measure of a good book; the more thought it contains, with which to feed the mind of the reader. the more valuable it is.

Hence, history and biography are more disciplinary and profitable than fiction. Novels, as a class, are deficient in thought; they do not stimulate and develop the mental powers of the reader. They may stir his heart and move his passions, but they do not strengthen his intellectual faculties. Twenty years of such reading will not increase his true manhood; he will be no more of a thinker than he was before, perhaps not so much of a thinker. The mental powers must be taxed in order to grow, but novel-reading does not tax them. It does not keep the mind at high tension enough to grow. It appeals to the imagination, and keeps it on the alert, but imagination is not life, nor the stuff life should be made of. Too much of it makes life a failure. There is more thought and real philosophy of life in a single scientific treatise or standard history, than there is in a whole cart load of novels. The former nourish the mind and make it grow, the latter starve it.

It is with a companion as it is with a book. The most profitable companion is he who advances ideas, whose conversation is enlivened and made instructive by thought. Many young people, not to speak of older ones are content with frivolous talk. Their conversation is barren of ideas, and they never rise above light, trifling views of existence. For this reason they are poor companions. By the most intimate companionship they cannot improve and ennoble another; for good thoughts, deep thoughts, practical thoughts alone can do this. Mental energy is indispensable in a boon companion.

But we need not particularize. It is true in general, as another says:—

"There is not a single work of man that was not originated, developed, and perfected in all its parts, and had not its purpose fixed in the ideal world before it could be tangibly presented in the material. Mental energy is the only source and power in man that can originate, create, and develop. It is in the ideal world that the mind prepares the models, and fixes the purpose of all man's work, perfects the arrangement for manifesting the hidden plan, and superintends the transformation of the ideal work into visible representations."

So with all human experiences. Nothing can be more real than hope and fear, but no one ever saw a hope or fear. The trader can see his capital and his merchandise, and he can handle them, but the hopes and fears that he carries into his business he can neither see nor handle. The mother can see the child that death claims, but not the grief that overwhelms her. But was anything more real than her grief? Is there any illusion about it? Is it not as certain as any material possession, as a house or money? What reason exists for calling it unreal? The Christian is on his death-bed, and he is reconciled. He has a good hope in Christ that comforts and sustains him. He has given up house and lands, father and mother, brother and sister, wife and children, and all else that he can see, for the everlasting inheritance, but his Christian hope is too real to be abandoned. It is the only real possession that he has now, and it is "eternal." No one would think of suggesting to him that he had given up the real, and was clinging to the unreal, for that would be trifling at the very gate of heaven. Truth is real— nothing can be more so. Religion is real, though spiritual; far more real than skepticism is.

FACTS, NOT THEORIES, TO BE FOLLOWED.

FACTS are of God, theories of men. We live in a world of fact; there is not a theory in it, except what man created. The Bible is a book of facts; from Genesis to Revelation it does not contain a theory. Death is as stubborn a fact as life. "Jesus Christ came into the world to save sinners," is the most remarkable fact of all. Both in the material and spiritual world facts reign; in nature, art, science, mechanics, trade, education, and religion. Therefore it is quite evident that God meant facts should be the foundation and source of human knowledge and progress; that from this material society, the state, church, commerce, education, and character should be builded. The first thing that a child learns, as well as the last, is fact—countless objects of fascinating beauty and wondrous use. He has come to see this museum of facts in "the palace of the great King," and every waking moment of his young life is filled with endeavor to become familiar with the marvelous display.

J. L. R. AGASSIZ.

It is singular that human beings, who are ushered into this world of fact, should expend so much of mature life upon theories. Theories are everywhere, on every subject, enterprise, and phenomenon —theories true and false, wise and unwise, audacious and crazy. Only those that rest on facts are true. True theories are evolved from facts, and never exist independent of them. Hence, facts furnish not only the materials for education, but also the groundwork for all reliable theories relating thereto. Surely, "facts are stubborn things," as the adage runs. They are "irrepressible," we cannot get rid of them. A single fact may upset a hundred theories.

A medical gentleman, discoursing upon the absolute necessity of alcohol to the highest physical development, asserted positively that the necessary mission of alcohol is a better physical development of man.

A clergyman inquired, "Do you believe the Bible, sir?"

"Certainly I do, as sincerely as yourself," was the prompt reply.

"If your position be correct," continued the clergyman, "what will you do with the fact, that when God would make the strongest man that ever lived, Samson, He commanded, not only that the son should be a teetotaler, but the mother, also, even before Samson's birth, lest some taint of physical weakness be imparted to his constitution. God discarded alcohol in giving to the world the best example of physical strength on record; what will you do with the fact."

The doctor was silent. That one fact upset his old, worn-out theory.

One or two years before the death of Professor Agassiz, he spent four weeks in summer at Cotuit Port, Massachusetts. His object was recreation, and the collection of specimens of fish in the waters of that vicinity for his grand museum at Cambridge.

One day the professor was asked by one of the several citizens present if he had seen a certain fish (the name of which we cannot recall), found in schools, swimming with one fin out of the water.

He replied in the negative, whereupon one gentleman inquired:—

"Which fin is out of water, the back or tail fin?"

Without the least hesitation, the professor answered:—

"Oh, the back fin, of course!" evidently settling the matter in his own mind by some general theory.

A lad ten years of age was standing by eagerly catching every word of the distinguished naturalist, one of the bright, keen, sharp observers we find among boys, and in his great earnestness he spoke out:—

"I think it is the tail fin; I've seen 'em."

The men laughed, and the professor smilingly patted the little fellow on the head, saying that he hoped he would know all about it when he became a man. But the boy was not satisfied that the professor was right, and he determined to find out who had the fact. The next day the lad went down to the wharf and laid himself down flat on his face, to watch the fish. Four hours he waited there for the fish, but none came; and the next day the persevering little fellow repeated his efforts, waiting in vain three or four hours more. But on the third day his perseverance was rewarded by the appearance of a school of the fish swimming in full view directly under the wharf. Judge of his excitement and satisfaction, when a good square searching gaze proved that the tail fin was out. The reader can imagine how quickly the lad bore the intelligence to the professor, "a school of them fish is in the harbor."

Down to the wharf Agassiz hurried, to see for himself, and, sure enough, the tail fin was out of water. His theory had gone down under the power of the boy's fact.

Here is a wide field for thought and hard, discriminating study. For, even in the realms of education and religion, theories are the most common of common things. Many people are so bewildered by the conflicting theories on this and that subject, that they frankly confess their inability to know what to believe. They are lost in the wilderness of speculation.

Stephenson was afraid to tell a committee of Parliament that his locomotive would run twenty miles an hour, although he knew it would, for the people were so wed to theories and old ways and methods, that he feared the real fact would arouse hooting and mobbing. Copernicus showed that the world is round, and a papal bull was hurled at his head; people preferred the old theory. Galileo taught the annual and diurnal motions of the earth; and a dungeon was his reward for the fact. Harvey announced the truth about the circulation of the blood, and for the deed, he lost the best part of his practice, and the good opinion of doctors and

THE FIRST RAILROAD TRAIN.

others over forty years of age. The Greenwich pensioners, looking out from their palatial home upon the first steamer on the Thames, said, "We do not like the steamboat, it is so contrary to nature." They did not dream that nature deals only in facts. In like manner, Fulton with his steamer on the Hudson, Morse with his telegraph, Field with his Atlantic cable, and Edison with his telephone, fought the battle of theories against fact, and won. The reign of theories is broken and fact is king.

There is not only more inspiration in facts than there is in theories, but there is more mental growth. The right use of them improves and fortifies the mind, begetting a practical turn, and leading into wider and safer fields of inquiry and labor.

Dr. Hooker says, "If the study of facts should be made as prominent as I claim that they should be in education, it would change to a great extent the intellectual character of intelligent society. The man of common intelligence would be put, in some measure, on a level with those who make study their business. He would be a scientific observer, although he has not passed from the school to the college. Having learned from childhood to study the phenomena of the animate and inanimate world around him, wherever he turns he would find something to observe, and, therefore, something interesting to talk about in the family and in the social circle. . . . He would find 'sermons in stones,' in a higher sense than was contemplated by the Bard of Avon."

CHOICE OF PERMANENT VALUES.

SAID a father to a son's teacher, "I want he should study what will be of service to him when he becomes a man."

That is the object of school, and all industrial preparations for manhood and womanhood. It is a waste of time to seek a good thing that will last only a day or a year. A transient blessing may be desirable in itself, but if a permanent one can be secured by like effort in its stead, it is a very unwise use of time to try for the former instead of the latter. We ought to measure good things by the length of time they will be good. What will help us far away in manhood, as well as now, is surely more desirable than what will help us only now. Its real worth must be altogether greater. Four years in college may be of some service to a young man who means to be a trader or manufacturer, but if the same four years in actual business will be a better preparation for his life-work, the latter is worth more than the former to him, and he ought to choose it.

Education is a good thing for anyone, for it lasts through life, and even serves manhood better than it does boyhood. Hence it is of the highest value, valuable for what it is to-day, more valuable for what it is to-morrow, and most valuable for what it is through life. Permanent values are always far more desirable than transient ones; and in seeking them there is higher discipline and more character.

Robert Bloomfield was a poor boy, but he wanted an education. Reading might lead to it; he would try it. His leisure moments became his most valuable time, a book being his constant companion. Thus animated by a lofty aim, he applied himself to self-improvement year after year, and at forty years of age he was a famous scholar. The fulfillment of his hopes was realized, and his soul was satisfied, for he had secured what would be to him the richest boon through the remainder of his life. Before his death he ranked among the most learned men of his day.

Robert Bloomfield sought and found what was good at the start, and what continued to be good to the end of his life. Such should be the aim of every youth, choosing things permanent rather than those of transient value. Herein lies the great worth of honesty, industry, benevolence, punctuality, and kindred virtues; time does not limit their practical use, for they are just as practical and valuable in age as they are in youth. It is not so with wealth. Riches take to themselves wings and fly away. They often vanish when men least expect it, and even if they remain, they may prove a snare and a curse. And the same is true of honor and fame; they are uncertain possessions. Unlike honesty, and the train of virtues mentioned, they may sadly disappoint us. Honesty is never disappointing, and it always stays where it is really wanted. Its market value is never fluctuating; it is always at par, or above, never below. We can say of it as the apostle did of charity, "it never faileth." If we could say the same of money and fame, their values would be vastly augmented. But we cannot, and so their real worth is materially impaired.

ROBERT FULTON.

Youth is the period of discipline; and discipline, true and thorough, is a blessing that lasts beyond this life. Whether it be an education that is sought, or a trade, or an art, discipline is the blessing that should result—discipline of the threefold nature, physical, mental, and moral. This pays well for the most self-

ONWARD TO FAME AND FORTUNE.

sacrificing and persistent effort in any and every pursuit; nobler manhood and womanhood is surer to be. It is this thought and aim that should be uppermost, whether a person be engaged in manual labor, reading, study, or other necessary effort; discipline should be the one grand acquisition sought, because, like the charity of inspiration, it will last forever. "Charity never faileth; but whether there be prophecies, they shall fail; whether there be tongues, they shall cease; whether there be knowledge, it shall vanish away."

WILLIAM HARVEY.

Horace Greeley possessed so many attributes of the successful man that frequent reference to him is indispensable. Few men illustrate the subject in hand so well as he. From his boyhood, he had an eye upon permanent values. All through his life that which was of general utility for the longest time won his support, whether it was a book, utensil, machine, coat, daily paper, or a virtue. He was a stalwart foe to pretentious display, the spirit of caste, fashion, and the undue deference paid to wealth and position. These were transitory things, and, therefore, comparatively valueless.

He once wrote of the man who has run the race of life, "Ask not whether he has or has not been successful, according to the vulgar standard of success. What matters it now whether the multitude has dragged his chariot, rending the air with idolizing acclamations, or howled like wolves on his track, as he fled by night from the fury of those he had wasted his vigor to serve! What avails it that broad lands have rewarded his toils, or that all has, at the last moment, been striken from his grasp! Ask not whether he brings into retirement the wealth of the Indies, or the poverty of the bankrupt, whether his couch be of down or of rushes, his dwelling a hut or a mansion. He has lived to little purpose, indeed, if he has not long since realized that wealth and renown are not the true ends of exertion, nor their absence the conclusive proof of ill fortune. Whoever seeks to know if his career has been prosperous and brightening from its outset to its close, if the evening of his days shall be genial and blissful, should ask not for broad acres, nor towering edifices, nor laden coffers. Perverted old age may grasp these with the unyielding clutch of insanity, but they add to his cares and anxieties, not to his enjoyments. Ask, rather, Has he mastered and harmonized his erring passions? Has he lived a true life?"

These words indicate the trend of the writer's life—to permanent values. That he may have carried his views to an extreme will not be denied. He might have selected a handsome coat instead of a homely one, when he chose the most durable; his manners might have been simple, sincere, and polite, without being awkward or odd. There is a permanent value with grace, as there is a transient value with it. The first should be sought and found.

XXXI.

EYE-SERVICE.

A CAPITALIST, who is a lawyer, is having the foundation of a large block laid near by. He is superintending the work himself, and is on the ground with the men in the morning, and he is the last one to quit at night. He has two objects to be secured by personal superintendence. The first is to make sure of more and better work; the second is needed recreation. "It pays to watch workmen," he says; meaning that as a class employes do their best only when the eye of their employer is upon them. It is eye-service which they render; they do well because their employer is looking on.

Another gentleman has purchased a residence near Boston, and is employing carpenters and masons in making extensive repairs. "I spent twenty-three days in May superintending the work," he said, "and I found that it pays to look after help." Another testimony to the prevalence of eye-service. These facts indicate that some people are faithful only when they are watched. None of this class are on the way to success. They may be able to keep soul and body together by their service, but they will never possess the highest type of manhood and womanhood. They may be respectable, but will never become influential.

A lady employed one domestic nineteen years, and would have employed her longer had not death broken up the family. "She is as much interested in our family as any of us," the lady remarked. "When I am away, she seems to be anxious lest the order and neatness of the house should not be kept up. If possible, she is even more diligent and watchful in my absence, that no one may discover the least trace of negligence or unfaithfulness." It was the opposite of eye-service that this servant rendered to her mistress. She was just as faithful and true when unwatched as when her employer was at home. For this reason she was a first-class domestic. As a servant she was a great success, and added dignity to her calling. It may not seem to be womanly to scrub floors, wash dishes, scour paint, and do many other things which good housekeeping enjoins, but all these things may be done in a manner that proves them to be honorable and elevating. When floors are scrubbed and dishes washed with the same fidelity that prayers are said, the work is womanly in the highest degree.

James Holford climbed the ladder of fortune to the topmost round. When he stood at the bottom, in his boyhood, he imagined how he could go up. One replied, "Why, my dear boy, it is all luck. I have gone part way up several times and fallen back, and I have given it up. Luck is against me." Another said, "It is not so much luck as it is scheming. In these times only the schemers get up." Still another answered, "It is patronage that does it. You must have some relative or friend to help you up, or you have no chance."

James had good sense enough to resist all such twaddle. He believed that there was no chance for a boy like him except by personal fidelity. With that conviction he served his first employer in a way that won his implicit confidence, doing the best he could each day whether his employer was at home or abroad. If anything, he was more alert when his employer was absent than when he was at home, for he realized that additional responsibility rested upon him. In a single year his services were indispensable to the business. His employer said, "I could not get along without him." In twenty years he was at the head of a large, profitable business of his own, and a little later he stood upon the

HORACE GREELEY

topmost round of the ladder. Eye-service never accomplished such a feat, and never can.

After the triumph was won Holford said to the young men: "The steps from the foot to the summit are not many, but each has a name which must be distinctly known by all who would seek to climb. The first step is faith, and without this none can safely rise; the second, industry; the third, perseverance; the fourth, temperance; the fifth, probity (and this latter quality made eye-service impossible); and the sixth, independence. Having obtained a position thus high on the ladder, the future rise is easy, for faith will have taught the climber never to doubt or despair, industry will have kept him from vice either in thought or deed, perseverance will have shown him how easily difficulties are surmounted when calmly met, temperance will have preserved both health and temper, probity will have insured respect and given stability to the character, and independence of spirit, while it will give dignity to the man, will certainly gain the admiration of the world."

More than one hundred years ago, the famous "master of finance" in France, known as Paris Duverney, was a boy at work on his father's farm at the foot of the Alps. He and his three brothers were so obedient and faithful that their good father's cup of joy was filled to the brim. At length a crisis came in French affairs, and trusty agents were needed to feed the army in the war then going on between France and Savoy. These four brothers were called from their humble vocation to the task, because they could be trusted whether the king's eye was upon them or not. Nor was the government disappointed in their efficient service. They accomplished more, even, than was expected of them.

Their tact and enterprise proved equal to their fidelity. They rose rapidly in influence and fame, all acquiring fortunes, and all winning what was better than wealth, the confidence and respect of the public. "By the time they were all grown to manhood, the eldest, a man over forty, and the youngest eighteen or twenty, they had become army contractors and capitalists, noted in army circles for the tact, the fidelity, and the indomitable energy with which they carried on their business." So great did their influence become that, in the last years of the reign of Louis XIV., when France suffered disastrous defeats from the allied armies commanded by the great English general, the Duke of Marlborough, they actually saved the independence of their country more than once. When the national treasury could not furnish them with a dollar, they supplied the army from their private purses. On several occasions, the great French banker, Samuel Bernard, loaned them immense sums on their personal security, in one crisis not less than three million francs. While all the brothers won wealth and honor, the eldest, Paris Duverney, achieved the highest success. The entire absence of everything that constitutes eye-service was the secret of their wonderful success.

Eye-service has no high standard. It is really aimless, since it is anxious to please only the observer. It is devoid of principle; it may be one thing, and seem to be another, and nothing can be said in its favor. It blocks the way to success.

GRATITUDE.

"GRATITUDE is the memory of the heart." This is a good definition of the virtue, and suggests at once the sweetness and value of it. Where there is no memory of the heart, there is an absence of grateful feelings. Thankfulness is the expression of a grateful feeling, while gratitude is the feeling itself. There can be no thankfulness where there is no gratitude; and a thankless person is out of his place in a world like this. Character is essentially defective without this element of gratitude.

It cannot stand at the front to challenge respect and homage. An ungrateful man is a travesty upon his race. Swift said, "He that calls a man ungrateful sums up all the evil that a man can be guilty of." He is not a noble specimen of manhood, and therefore he is a failure.

One Jack Armstrong and his wife befriended Abraham Lincoln in his youth, when their son William D. was a baby. They welcomed him to their home and table when he was without work, and Mrs. Armstrong mended his clothes, and looked after his welfare as his own mother would have done. Abraham felt very grateful for her kindness, so that when the time came to pay his debt of gratitude, he was prepared to do it with compound interest.

Soon after Mrs. Armstrong was left a widow, her son William was arrested for murder. She wrote to Mr. Lincoln, who had become a noted lawyer in Springfield, Illinois, for his services. On "the memory of his heart" were indelibly inscribed her deeds of kindness when he was homeless and penniless, and out of its fullness he replied, offering his services gratuitously, and urging her to come at once to Springfield. She responded, and had no difficulty in convincing Lincoln that her son did not perpetrate the murder. On a public occasion five or six intoxicated young men engaged in a free fight, and one of the number was killed. Young Armstrong was a dissolute fellow, and the other parties charged the murder upon him. Lincoln took in the situation readily, and set himself at work to learn the facts. He spent several months in investigation, sparing neither pains nor money to unravel the mystery and set free the son of his benefactor. His efforts were crowned with success, and the mother's heart well-nigh burst with joy. She showered tears and thanks upon Lincoln, and insisted upon paying him for his eminent services.

"Why, Aunt Hannah (the familiar name by which Mrs. Armstrong was known), I shall never take a cent of your money for anything I can do for you. If I can repay you for your kindness to me years ago, I shall be only too glad to do it."

Not long afterward Lincoln heard that some men were attempting to defraud her of land, and he wrote to her as follows:

"Aunt Hannah, they can't have your land. Let them try it in the Circuit Court, and then you appeal it, and bring it to the Supreme Court, and Herndon and I will attend to it for nothing." He saved her land, which helped him to pay another portion of his debt of gratitude.

During the late War of the Rebellion, when Lincoln was President, Aunt Hannah's son, whom he saved from the gallows, responded to his first call for seventy-five thousand volunteers.

After he had served two years, Lincoln received a letter from his mother saying that she wanted her boy. She did not speak of any disability, only expressed a wish that he might come home. But this was quite enough for Lincoln, who did not consider that he had paid his whole debt of gratitude. So he ordered the discharge of the son, and, at the same time, wrote as follows to the mother:

SEPTEMBER, 1863.

MRS. HANNAH ARMSTRONG:—I have just ordered the discharge of your boy William, as you say, now at Louisville, Kentucky.

Large pay for small kindnesses, the reader might say; but true gratitude is large-souled, and never forgets to compute and pay interest. No one can possess too much gratitude any more than he can have too much honesty or truthfulness. It was a "pearl of great price" in Lincoln's heart. He was truer and nobler for it.

When James A. Garfield, at seventeen years of age, consulted Dr. Robinson as to taking a course of study, he "was shabbily dressed in coarse satinet trousers, far outgrown, and reaching only half way down the tops of his cowhide boots, a waistcoat much too short, and a threadbare coat, whose sleeves went only a little way below the elbows. A coarse, slouched hat, much the worse for wear, surmounted the whole." "He was wonderfully awkward," said Dr. Robinson, "but his independent, intelligent, manly manner impressed me very favorably. After a thorough examination of the youth, I said to him, 'Go on, follow the leadings of your ambition, and ever after I am your friend. You have the brain of a Webster, and you have the physical proportions that will back you in the most herculean efforts. All you need to do is to work. Work hard, do not be afraid of overworking, and you will make your mark.'"

This hearty, friendly counsel settled the question of acquiring an education with young Garfield, for which he never ceased to be grateful. He was drawn to Dr. Robinson as a son is drawn to a father. In his ripe manhood, after his early ambition and efforts had been crowned with great success, he realized more than ever his debt of gratitude to Dr. Robinson. He honored and loved him as a benefactor. He lost no opportunity to manifest his deep sense of personal obligation to the man who so generously encouraged him to study. His praise was ever upon his lips, and his gratitude illuminated and magnified all the other virtues of his noble character. His success was more complete because of his grateful recollection of the man whose counsel made such a career possible.

The highest success is not attainable without gratitude. It is indispensable to the growth and symmetry of the other virtues. Character is stronger and more attractive because of it. To be the recipient of kindness and assistance without grateful emotions is weakness, if not meanness. To respond promptly to personal favors with an overflowing heart is strength and nobleness.

XXXII.

PATRIOTISM.

PATRIOTISM is a disinterested love of one's country. It is not devotion to "our country, right or wrong;" that is fanaticism. It is love of our native or adopted land, because it is the best land, and therefore *right*.

That virtuous hero of the English Revolution, Andrew Fletcher, exclaimed, "I would lose my life to *serve* my country, but I would not do a base thing to *save* it." His was true patriotism.

Smiles says, "Patriotism is a principle fraught with high impulses and noble thoughts. It springs from a disinterested love of country. Who does not sympathize with Arnold von Winkelried at Sempach, with Bruce at Bannockburn, and with Hofer at Innsbruck? Their deeds were noble; the very thought of their example has contributed to elevate the minds of their countrymen. They left behind them an idea of duty which can never be forgotten."

Such patriotism embraced decision, courage, enthusiasm, and daring, out of which our republic was born; and the offspring of those heroic fathers come into the world embued with a kindred spirit, from generation to generation. A halting, undecided policy with rulers and people would make a country of such growth, size, and thrift as ours impossible. The fathers, by their Declaration of Independence, rolled a burden of responsibility upon their descendants, which the latter have found could not be borne except by similar "firm resolve," and so this quality of the American character has been preserved and nurtured through all the vicissitudes of national progress to this day.

The American flag was born of patriotism.

The time came, in the long and perilous contest for liberty, when an emblem of the country's independence and honor was required. The inspiration of an appropriate flag to rally and unite the defenders of freedom was indispensable.

By a happy choice, the patriots of that early day created the "Stars and Stripes," now known and honored the world over. The national banner of "red, white and blue" bore thirteen "stripes" for the original colonies, and thirteen "stars" for the original States constructed out of the colonies. Provision was made that on its field of blue a star should be added for each State thereafter admitted into the Union. In the remarkable growth of the nation, this cluster of stars rapidly grew to thirty-eight, and now seven more are added to the group—forty-five in all.

A more significant and beautiful emblem of national honor was n e v e r conceived. Among the flags of different nationalities, the American citizen feels that it is the choicest of them all. Indeed, judging from the manner of saluting it by foreign nations, we conclude that the citizens of other countries share in this sentiment of admiration for our national ensign.

Some years ago an international gala day on Lake Geneva was participated in by representatives of nearly all the civilized nations of the world. Each craft bore aloft the national banner, presenting a scene of novel and picturesque beauty, such as no beholder had ever gazed upon before. But when our country's flag, with its stars and stripes, appeared upon the scene, there went up a spontaneous cheer, spreading from boat to boat, increasing in volume of enthusiastic acclaim, until the chorus of admiration embraced every craft on the lake; a tribute of respect to "the flag of the free." Partly, no doubt, for the singular beauty of the emblem itself, but more for the cause it represented, arose this hearty and honest salute to the flag of our free republic. The harmonious choice of such an ensign seems almost the marvel of inspiration, in view of which we may

NATHAN HALE

appropriate the words of the sweet singer of Israel, "Thou hast given a banner to them that fear thee, that it may be displayed because of the truth."

The flag cost blood and treasure. Men and money were sacrificed in the outset, and still more men and money have been required to preserve it. Hence it is dear to the patriotic citizen. In the capital of every loyal State are sacredly preserved to-day the battle-flags of the late War of the Rebellion, bullet-riddled and blood-stained, carefully hung and guarded behind glass plate and iron rail. They remind beholders of the heroism and fidelity of the men who went down in the storm of battle, and of the value of the Union which they cemented with their blood. We preserve them, not as relics of war only, but as sacred mementoes of the patriotism that gave us, and has preserved, our country. Unhallowed hands must not profane them by their touch.

Here, then, is a reason why patriotism should characterize the youth of our land. The unpatriotic citizen cannot be a good citizen. He lacks an essential element of citizenship that must modify his life-purpose. He cannot really become a component part of the body-politic, as he should if he would make the most of himself for his native land. He must honor the old flag for the love of country it inspires, the national unity it symbolizes, and the power for which it stands. Then he becomes assimilated with the patriotic multitude as he develops into manhood and age, and will join with them in the poet's beautiful tribute:—

> "Flag of the free heart's hope and home,
>   By angel hands to valor given!
> Thy stars have lit the welkin dome,
>   And all thy hues were born in heaven.
> Forever float that standard sheet!
>   Where breathes the foe that falls before us,
> With Freedom's soil beneath our feet,
>   And Freedom's banner streaming o'er us!"

LOYALTY.

LOYALTY is fidelity to a principle, home, institution, or country. We shall speak of it in the latter sense: loyalty to the old flag. As such, it is patriotism in practice. The patriotic citizen only is loyal to his country. The absence of this sentiment, in times of national peril, exposes one to indecision and cowardice, if not treason. Hence its great value and beauty. It is indispensable to good citizenship; indeed, there is no true manhood and womanhood without it. It is involved in the American idea of republican institutions. Loyalty makes them live.

Just now this subject is demanding attention throughout our land. The flag is flung to the breeze over schoolhouses, that American youth may not forget their allegiance to the government it represents. It is a beautiful spectacle to stir youthful hearts with loyalty to their native land, the stars and stripes floating over the temple of knowledge, wherein they are trained for usefulness and honor. It is a glad omen for them to hail it with speech, songs, and cheers.

Garibaldi, the great, grand, strong, pure, affectionate old hero, whose heart was set upon seeing his darling Italy free, independent, and happy, is an example of true loyalty. He was willing to endure hardships, persecution, starvation, and exile, to make his native land free. In his greatest troubles, his lofty spirit declared, "In times of trouble, I have never been disheartened, and have always found persons disposed to assist me." An exile in South America for fourteen years, and again in the United States three, his loyalty to his country's flag never wavered, and he continued to nurse the patriot's hope in his soul that Italy would yet be free; nor was his hope in vain. The war between Austria and Sardinia called him to the field again; and what glorious achievements await the irrepressible man! The bloody tyrant of Naples driven from his throne! Sicily delivered from oppression! Nine millions of subjects added to the dominions of a constitutional king, Victor Emanuel. All Italy one nation excepting alone the dominions of the pope and the province of Venetia. This was Garibaldi's work! "It was the magic of his name, the fire of his patriotism, and his genius for command, that wrought these marvels."

Refusing all rewards for his services, and declining all public honors, he said to his countrymen:—

"I am a Christian, and I speak to Christians. I love and venerate the religion of Christ, because Christ came into the world to deliver humanity from slavery, for which God has not created it. . . .

"Yours is the duty to educate the people. Educate them to be Christians; educate them to be Italian. Education gives liberty; education gives to the people the means and the power to secure and defend their own independence. On a strong and wholesome education of the people depends the liberty and greatness of Italy."

"Viva Victor Emanuel! Viva Italia! Viva Christianity!"

In like manner the loyalty of the great Magyar chief, M. Louis Kossuth, to his beloved Hungary, won the admiration of the world. Elected governor by a liberty-loving people, yet driven into exile, the Christian was ready to starve and die for his country.

When he was an exile in Turkey, and the government of the Sublime Porte promised him protection on condition that he would embrace Mohammedanism, his magnanimous spirit rose above the fear of imprisonment and torture, chains and death, and he replied: "Between death and shame, the choice can neither be dubious nor difficult. Governor of Hungary, and elected to the high place by the confidence of fifteen million of my countrymen, I know well what I owe to my country even in exile. Even as a private individual I have an honorable part to pursue. Though once the governor of a generous people, I leave no inheritance to my people. They shall, at least, bear an unsullied name. God's will be done! I am prepared to die!"

This true loyalty is charged with the spirit of martyrdom.

Illustrations of loyalty to American independence illumine the pages of history.

In the darkest hour of the Revolution, when it seemed as if the cause of the struggling colonies must be abandoned, Washington declared that, rather than surrender to the king, he "would retreat over every river and mountain in America."

And, again, after his famous crossing of the Delaware, when he stood face to face with the Hessians, rising in his stirrups, and waving his sword above his head, he addressed his troops:—

"There, boys!" pointing to the foe; "there are the enemies of your country. All I ask of you is to remember what you are about to fight for! March!" That was true loyalty.

When the brave General Wayne fell at the battle of Stony Point, at the head of his column, he promptly rose upon one knee, and cried out to his men:—

"March on! Carry me into the fort. If I die, I will die at the head of the column."

It was not long after Captain James Lawrence was appointed commander of the "Chesapeake," that he fell mortally wounded in a fight with the British frigate "Shannon." With the seal of death upon his brow, he encouraged his faithful soldiers to fight on by his dying appeal, "Don't give up the ship!"

Such is loyalty to the country and cause we love. "How sweet to die for one's country," exclaimed an ancient patriot, as his life went out in battle. It is a sentiment that dignifies manhood, without which a cluster of other virtues cannot exist.

WASHINGTON CROSSING THE DELAWARE.

XXXIII.

A REASON FOR PATRIOTISM AND LOYALTY.

A CITIZEN of the United States has more reason to love his country than the citizen of any other land; for it is "a government of the people, by the people, for the people." Each citizen counts one. Rich or poor, learned or unlearned, ruled or ruler, he possesses the right of a freeman, and his ballot counts just as much as that of any other citizen, and no more. He helps run the government. Its officers are his officers, its institutions are his institutions, its fame is his fame, and he is thoroughly identified with it if he be a true citizen. Youth of both sexes need to understand this, in order to serve their country well.

So much is said and written to prejudice both young and old against our government that the misrepresentation should be exposed. Sometimes speakers and writers represent the government as taking advantage of a class of its subjects, especially the poor. It is said that the rich and ruling class run the republic in their own interests, and that more or less oppression exists in consequence. Hence there are many of the common people who really think that the government is not conducted "for the people, by the people." They believe that "Uncle Sam," as they call the government, imposes upon them unnecessary and burdensome taxes, and cheats them out of many things which they ought to enjoy.

A very false view, this. It is true that some representatives of the government have proved false to their trusts, and the people have suffered in consequence; but we must not confound a good government with an unreliable representative. However untrue an agent may prove, the government means to bless the poorest and humblest class as much as it does the richest and highest. Indeed, its purpose is really to bless them more, as facts clearly prove.

The post-office, with which the common people have more or less to do, furnishes an illustration of what we mean.

The writer can remember when thirty-three cents postage was charged to carry a letter where now it is carried for two cents. Poor people could not write many letters at that time, but the rich could pay the high postage without feeling it, and, therefore, could write as many letters as they pleased. The republic was young then, and comparatively poor, and the cost of running it was much greater in proportion. But it existed "for the people," and the poor were more of the people than the rich; so, as soon as possible, its postage was gradually reduced, a little at a time, as the condition of the treasury would permit. From thirty-three to twenty-five, twenty, eighteen, twelve, ten, five, and finally, within a few years, two cents, anywhere in the country! and five cents will take a letter to any part of the world! It will not be long before letter postage will be reduced to one cent to any State or territory of the Union.

Surely this is for the "people;" it is done in the interest of the poor. They can write as often as they please now, and they show their appreciation of the privilege by writing ten times as many letters as they did when postage was high. Over two billion letters and postal cards were reported last year from all the post-offices in the United States. This use of the letter-writing privilege, too, is much better for the people, preserving instead of breaking the family ties, thereby strengthening citizenship by cultivating the virtues of the home.

Last Christmas, in a single week, more than seventy thousand letters, containing money-orders for a million dollars, went through the New York City post-office alone, from foreigners to their friends in Europe. The beneficent provisions of our government, through its postal arrangements, make such expression of family affection and remembrance possible.

Another national measure in the interests of the poor is the Homestead Act. The United States owned a vast amount of unoccupied land, a large part of which it has virtually given to the poor. On very easy conditions, the father of a growing family could select a farm of one hundred and sixty acres somewhere on this uncultivated territory, and there build him a permanent home, and lay the foundation of future competence.

Tens of thousands of homes have thus been planted in our great West, many of their proprietors becoming affluent in time, important factors of influence and power in the States where they are located.

Many of these pre-empted farms are owned by foreigners, who have flocked to our land because they could get a farm for almost nothing, on which to support and rear their families. This, in addition to a free country, was a great boon to them in comparison with the hardships, oppression, and degradation of the countries from whence they came. Hundreds and thousands of these families, whether native or foreign-born, have become identified with the social and public interests of the States and territories where their lot is cast. Their homes are so many new links in the chain of influence that binds one part of our country to another. Their farms are reclaimed from the waste of the wilderness to add to the nation's wealth, and the comfort of their households. But for the Homestead Law they might now have been numbered with the paupers of the Old World or the New, eking out a miserable existence, with no hope of a better experience, and no prospect of bequeathing anything but want and woe to their posterity.

In like manner, the government provides free schools, that the masses may be educated, and thereby become intelligent, useful citizens.

This arrangement is not so much for the wealthy, as it is for the poor and unfortunate. The former class can pay for the best education there is, but the latter class, which largely outnumbers the other, must have it without money and without price, or remain in ignorance. The government recognizes the fact, and kindly makes provision for this most important of human necessities. It is because of this provision for free schools, that some of the ablest and best men in American history emerged from poverty and obscurity into honor and power.

So, in times of public danger, when large expenses are incurred for defence, as in the late War of the Rebellion, the government has drawn its needed revenue largely from the wealthier class, by enacting that they only who had an annual income of two thousand dollars shall be taxed to meet the extra demand. Thus, it has sought to relieve the less fortunate citizens, while yet they might enjoy all the advantages of good government with those who paid heavily for them.

We might multiply illustrations. This feature of our republic is prominent in every department. It is its fundamental principle. It is "for the people" now and always; and every citizen should see it in this light. Seen in this light only, can it be appreciated and loved for what it is actually worth.

PERSONAL RESPONSIBILITY.

DANIEL WEBSTER was invited to dinner at the Astor House, New York City, when he was Secretary of State under President Fillmore. He was very weary on reaching the city, and could not enter into the spirit of the occasion with his usual vivacity. In fact, he was thought to be rather unsocial, until a gentleman rallied him with this unexpected inquiry:—

"Mr. Webster, will you tell me what was the most important thought that ever occupied your mind?"

Webster hesitated for a moment, and then whispered to a friend beside him:—

"Is there anyone here who does not know me?"

"No; all your friends," was the reply.

Thereupon he answered:—

"The most important thought that ever occupied my mind was that of my individual responsibility to God." So saying, he proceeded to speak upon that subject, and, for twenty minutes, both surprised and delighted his audience.

Next to this great thought is that of one's individual responsibility to man. The latter may exist without the former, but the former does not exist without the latter. A real sense of one's responsibility as a member of society is indispensable to a true life. He who counts himself a cipher among men cannot feel that he is responsible for much. Such an idea is inimical to the highest aims and noblest deeds. A true man or woman is impossible without a sense of responsibility so deep and strong as to control the whole being. A soul imbued with a sense of its own responsibility will defy toil and difficulties, and rise to honor and fame. It is this which makes "a handful of good life worth a bushel of learning," as George Herbert said. Without it, indecision and weakness of purpose are inevitable; and these are the precursors of failure. Thorough, earnest work, accompanied by efficiency and mastery of the occasion, are the outcome of this irrepressible sense of responsibility.

In 1819, Sarah Martin was an assistant dressmaker, at Caistor, England, serving in families at a shilling a day. Her heart was greatly moved one day by hearing of the imprisonment of a mother for beating her child. "Perhaps I may reclaim her," she thought. At once a sense of responsibility in the matter possessed her soul, and it impelled her to seek admission to the prison. But the jailer refused to grant her request. She was not disheartened, however, and the sense of duty grew upon her, and she repeated her request for admission until it was granted. She was ushered into the mother's presence, to whom she frankly stated the object of her visit. The guilty woman burst into tears, and thanked her for coming.

At length her whole time was absolutely required in prison work. She must give up her dressmaking, with the prospect of being reduced to want, but she was equal to the emergency. She said, "I had counted the cost, and my mind was made up. If, while imparting truth to others, I become exposed to temporal want, the privations so momentary to an individual would not admit of comparison with following the Lord in thus administering to others."

A sense of personal responsibility did it. This converted the unknown, uneducated, humble dressmaker into a ministering angel. It developed within her an ability and tact for philanthropic work which no one supposed she possessed.

We have never known a public man whose sense of personal responsibility was in excess of that of the late Governor Thomas Talbot, of Massachusetts. He had no desire for public office, and, consequently, had declined to be representative or senatorial candidate, but finally had consented to run for state councillor. On being elected, the committee of the district suggested to him that the fortunate candidate was expected to provide a supper for his constituents. "Very well," answered Mr. Talbot, "I will authorize you to arrange for the supper, and send the bill to me." The committee appeared to be highly gratified, and other conversation followed, when Mr. Talbot added, "I have only one condition to propose about the supper, and that is, no intoxicating liquors shall be provided. I have never paid for a glass of liquor in my life, and I do not propose to begin now." The committee were taken aback, and one or two of them expressed dissatisfaction, and intimated that a supper without the customary beverages would be a farce. "Perhaps you may think so now, but after sleeping over it, I think you will agree with me," said Mr. Talbot; "but I must insist upon that condition."

The matter was dropped, and so was the supper. A majority of the committee were too angry to arrange for the entertainment, and the plan was abandoned. Thinking that the supper might have cost him a hundred dollars, he sent a check for that amount to be expended in the temperance cause.

Such a sense of personal responsibility is what the public men of our land need to-day. Mr. Talbot weighed the consequences of his own acts. He did that in private as well as in public. It was one of the prominent factors of his very successful life. He worked in a factory at twelve years of age, taking turns with his brothers in attending school. Part of them must work while the others studied, or the family would starve. Between that time and the time he filled the gubernatorial chair of Massachusetts, he put in an amount of work that involved self-denial and hardship, an amount of reading and study out of working hours, such as would not have been possible but for the deep sense of personal responsibility that characterized him.

Yet multitudes of the old and young shirk responsibility. They seek to avoid responsibility for what they might do, as well as for the wrongs they have done. Adam attempted to shift the sin of Eden upon his wife, and from that day the average man is disposed to excuse himself in the event of an accusation, and put the responsibility somewhere else. Not a few credit their failure in life to the management of other parties, or to the intervention of unfavorable circumstances. They are not rich, honored, or widely influential, because they have not had the opportunity. If they had been as favorably situated as half a dozen persons whom they can name, they would have become millionaires, governors, members of Congress. A bad disposition and an appetite for strong drink are often charged to heredity. And so men seek to avoid responsibility—as unwise an act as it is unreasonable.

A true man or woman will court personal responsibility. He and she know that it is the making of them. It is what will ally them unflinchingly to duty, which keeps one at his post, to die there, if need be. A kindred spirit is necessary in the common walks of life, and it is born of a sense of personal responsibility. "If I had five hundred heads, I would lose them all rather than recant my belief concerning faith," exclaimed Luther at Ausburg, when hard pressed by his enemies. His sense of responsibility moved him to do, dare, and die.

XXXIV.

PERILS OF SUCCESS.

IN the military family of Washington was one, in the early part of the Revolution, whose great ability, courage, and social qualities commanded universal praise. He had no peer in the service of the court and the camp. Washington himself regarded his rich endowments of mind and person as the assurance of the highest and most valuable service to his oppressed and distracted country. But when, at the height of his success in public life, Aaron Burr allowed his baser passions to usurp the place of patriotism and purity, he died, "not as Adams and Jefferson and Washington sank into the grave, amidst the tears and prayers of a great nation, but in shame, solitude, and gloom this profligate, whose ambition it was to tread the fairest flowers into the dust, passed away to the bar of a just God."

A successful merchant of New York City retired from business at forty-five years of age, rich, honored, and satisfied. It is a mistake for men of forty-five to dream and plan for relief from business thereafter. To desire ease, with nothing to do, at that age, when the physical and mental powers are in their prime, is a mistaken view of one's life work. However successful a person has been up to that time, there is real peril in the idea that a fortune and a good character at forty-five entitles one to retire from business and live at ease. It proved so in the case of the wealthy New York merchant. After the care and labor of establishing a princely home on the Hudson were exhausted, and he had nothing to do, a few months sufficed to tell upon his constitution. He began to tire of the monotony, his health became impaired, sleepless nights made him miserable, and finally he became a confirmed invalid, whom physicians tried in vain to restore. His wealth yielded him no happiness, his beautiful home lost its attractions, and he would have parted with the last dollar of his riches could he have been transferred to his counting-room, with all its care, perplexities, and hard work. He died before his fiftieth birthday, an illustration, in his untimely death, of the perils of success. Had he been less prosperous, so that he felt the necessity of continuing in business, industrious, enterprising, and tireless, until the winters of threescore years and ten had frosted his head, he might have enjoyed an old age that is a crown of glory.

There are more men and women who are demoralized by success on certain lines than are made manlier and womanlier by it. The command of human praise, the ability to shine as a "bright, particular star," the worshipful attention of their fellowmen that falls to their lot, drift them away from their surroundings, until, upon a tempestuous sea, without chart or compass, they sink into unknown depths. Robert Walpole remarked, "It is fortunate that few men can be prime ministers, because it is fortunate that few men can know the abandoned profligacy of the human mind." However much exaggeration there was in the sentiment expressed, it certainly contains the unquestioned truth that peculiar perils lurk in the paths of those who share high honors, great power, and overflowing wealth. Wealth hoarded, honor used to inflate pride, and learning acquired for a name only, are mistaken notions of success, that make it the occasion of disgrace and failure.

AARON BURR.

One of the most successful members of the New York bar, a score of years ago, allowed his own life to illustrate our theme. He was talented, eloquent, and magnetic on the rostrum and in the parlor. His practice increased beyond his most sanguine expectations. On account of his abundant gifts, demands were made upon him outside of the legal profession, and he was brought largely thereby into public life. Money poured into his lap, his acquaintance and counsel were sought by the wealthiest class, and he shared general confidence because he was a man of moral and Christian principles. Few men of any profession were ever so successful as he at the time of his marriage. He married a society woman, who introduced him into a social life altogether new to him. Heavy drafts upon his time and purse multiplied in this new relation as the years rolled on. The enjoyment of his wife, and the bewilderment of social splendor, blinded him to the inevitable issue of affairs, until the pecuniary embarrassment stared him in the face. In this hour of temptation, the unlawful appropriation of trust funds to relieve his condition brought him into disgrace, and made his life a failure. But for his success at the bar, in social and political life, his career might have rounded into one of the noblest and best on record.

Success in the noblest enterprises and reforms, secular and moral, often brings achievers into great tribulation. True to their convictions, they are brought face to face with perils in the spirit of self-sacrifice. They go where duty leads. They stand where duty bids. They die where duty decrees. When Leonidas found himself besieged, in the Pass of Thermopylæ, by Xerxes with two million men, he thought only of the cause of Greece for which he was there. He had reached the pinnacle of fame among his countrymen, by heroic adherence to right for the public welfare; and now the crisis was on. He was counseled to flee while he could, but he declined. Advising all of his allied forces, who feared to stand in the deadly breach, to retire, he found himself alone with the three hundred brave Spartans; and they marched boldly out of the Pass to meet the enemy. In this spirit the morning of battle was hailed, "Eat your last meal," exclaimed Leonidas; "to-night we shall sup with Pluto." At sundown not one of the little Spartan army was alive; and twenty thousand Persians lay dead upon the field. The Spartans lost, and yet they won. For Aristodemus, who forsook Leonidas at the Pass, became so inspired by the latter's example, as he reflected upon it, that he redeemed Greece in the battle of Platæa.

Almost every day we read of events, in the daily journals, that illustrate our theme. True men and women, in the successful discharge of common duties, are forced into overwhelming perils. The faithful engineer, on Lake Erie, was congratulated upon both his skill and fidelity, to which he replied, "I have done only my duty." Not long after, his steamer took fire, and herculean efforts were made to reach the shore. The fearless man proved true to himself and the men and women on board, standing at his post until the cruel flames roasted him alive. He sacrificed his own life; but the passengers for whom he died were saved. So the moral reformer sees perils multiply as he becomes a power to overthrow slavery, turn back the tide of intemperance, suppress vice and crime, expose political corruption, and defend the right. But there is no discount on his success at whatever cost.

PLACE OF FAITH IN A TRUE LIFE.

FAITH in one's self and one's life-pursuit is indispensable, for it rallies all the faculties to endeavor. He who thinks he can, *can;* he who thinks he can't, *can't.* These are the two classes of persons we meet; one successful, the other a failure. A man must confide in his own ability to fulfill his calling, if he would win. He need not indulge in egotism, or be over-confident; but he must believe that he can do what he undertakes, else he will fail.

When Edison conceived the idea of the phonograph, he grew elated over the possibility. Further thought and study culminated in the belief that he was able to produce the wonder. He undertook the task under the settled conviction that he could make the instrument, and that conviction never wavered, though his progress was slow. Year after year he studied, experimented, and labored, sometimes encouraged, sometimes disappointed, but never despairing. It *can* be done! *I* can do it! This confidence in himself to achieve did not suffer his energies to flag, nor his expectations to waver. At the end of seven years, his phonograph would talk, but it would not talk as he desired. It would say *pecie* instead of *specie*. But it "*shall say specie,*" he resolved; and in three months more it spoke the word plainly and loudly as he wished. Faith in himself conquered, for it kept his courage alive and caused his faculties to do their best. Without it there would have been no phonograph.

Mr. Edison's phenomenal success with his electric light is known the world over. When scientists, editors, and scholars doubted, his faith never wavered. He was confident that electrical science was in its infancy, and that he could evolve from its hidden resources what would startle the world. Through faith he wrought mightily, adding patent to patent, until more than a thousand separate patents were involved in the production of his electric light. We now put it to a great many uses for which we are indebted to Edison, though we are only beginning to know its priceless value. It performs errands for us, carrying messages, closing bargains, and making business hum; it puts life and power into locomotives, and sets ponderous machinery in motion; it runs cars, lights streets and houses, rings door- and table-bells, writes letters, makes fires, and even cures and kills people; for we take it as a medicine, and with it execute criminals. What more will be done with it remains to be seen.

For the present development and use of the electric light, we are more indebted to Edison than to any other inventor. His faith in himself and electrical science has wrought mightily. An editor says, " His improvements in telegraphic apparatus, and in the working of the telephone, seem almost to have exhausted the possibilities of electricity. While Huxley, Tyndall, Spencer, and other theorists talk and speculate, he quietly produces accomplished facts, and, with his marvelous inventions, is pushing the whole world ahead in its march to the highest civilization, making life more and more enjoyable."

When Edison had labored two years in his own laboratory, he said, "Two years of experience proves, beyond a doubt, that the electric light, for household purposes, can be produced and sold," for which he was severely criticised, and even ridiculed. But long since he fulfilled his own prophecy, as the increased convenience and comfort of families bear faithful witness.

Charles Goodyear purchased an India-rubber life-preserver as a curiosity. He was told that rubber would be of great value for a thousand things if cold did not make it hard as a stone, and heat reduce it to a liquid. "I can remedy that," he said to himself. Experiment after experiment failed. The money he put into the research was sunk. His last dollar was spent.

THOMAS A. EDISON TRYING THE PERFECTED PHONOGRAPH THE NIGHT BEFORE THE PUBLIC ANNOUNCEMENT OF HIS SUCCESS.

His best efforts were baffled, and his best friends forsook him, because they thought he was partially insane. A gentleman inquired after him, and he was told, "If you see a man with an India-rubber cap, an India-rubber coat, India-rubber shoes, and an India-rubber purse in his pocket, with not a cent in it,—that is Charles Goodyear." But Goodyear was not a lunatic. It was faith in his ability to do that caused him to pursue the idea of vulcanized rubber with such persistency, and his efforts were crowned with success. Faith did it.

Columbus believed that there was a new world beyond the untraversed sea, and that he himself was able to find it. Year after year he sought in vain the patronage that would make his project possible. Though opposed, thwarted, ridiculed, and even persecuted, he pressed his suit over and over. Adverse circumstances seemed to strengthen his purpose, and make him invincible. In the darkest hour he never lost heart. Faith in himself and his great enterprise finally triumphed.

Franklin believed that lightning and electricity were identical. More famous scientific men than himself believed otherwise, but this fact did not modify his own opinion. His conviction deepened as he pondered the matter. He proceeded to prove what he believed, by the aid of a kite. He disclosed his purpose only to his son, lest he should be made the butt of ridicule. But he succeeded. Faith in himself overcame obstacles, adverse opinions, and current theories, and he won immortal fame. The same has been true of great statesmen, explorers, discoverers, inventors, and the world's best workers generally. Faith in their own ability and purpose made them persistent, and finally victorious. Our own land is a fruitful illustration of this truth, from the time the Pilgrims sought freedom to worship God on these shores. The eleventh chapter of Hebrews is a good record of the facts.

By faith the Pilgrim Fathers, warned of God of things not seen as yet, prepared the "Mayflower" to the saving of their households, and set sail for a place which they should after receive for an inheritance. By faith they took up their abode in the land of promise, which was a strange country, inhabited only by savages and wild beasts, and here they laid the foundations of this great republic. By faith they endured privations and hardships, not counting their lives dear unto themselves, if they could possess a country of their own. By faith they passed through the Red Sea of difficulty, in tilling the soil, establishing a government, planting churches and schools, until, out of their weakness being made strong, they waxed valiant and mighty, turning to flight the armies of the aliens. By faith Washington led the American army and achieved independence, whereby he became known as the "Father of his Country," securing for himself and his posterity the unexampled thrift of a free nation. By faith Lincoln came to his reign in a time of great darkness and peril, when slavery threatened to destroy the government; and he broke the chains of oppression and saved the land from overthrow, whereby he became known as the "Saviour of his Country." But time would fail me to tell of all those who, through faith, have builded a great nation, whose material, intellectual, and moral resources are without parallel. Without faith such an outcome was impossible.

Without faith in men and means, not one day of a true life can be lived. "I have no faith in editors," says the faithless citizen, as he takes up the morning paper only to lay it down again, for he cannot believe its news. "I have no faith in cooks; whole families have been poisoned by them," and he cannot eat his breakfast. "I have no faith in men," and so he declines to do business with them, lest he be cheated. "I have no faith in engineers; they are a drunken class," and he refuses to take the train for the city lest his life be sacrificed by a reckless engineer. Before nine o'clock in the morning, it is proven that a single day of real life cannot be lived without faith in men and enterprises.

COLUMBUS BEFORE THE DOCTORS AT SALAMANCA.

XXXV.

RELIGION IN BUSINESS.

MANY think that religion belongs to the church and its work. They concede that it is very well for the Sabbath, but rather hinders than helps the work of the other six days. "Keep it where it belongs," they say; and turn to their farms, shops, and stores, to run their affairs upon worldly principles, and leave God out of secular bargains. A greater mistake was never made, for religion requires the following very reasonable things in secular affairs, namely: that man should make the most of himself possible; that he should watch and improve his opportunities; that he should be industrious, upright, faithful, and prompt; that he should task his talents, whether one or ten, to the utmost; that he should waste neither time nor money; that duty, and not pleasure or ease, should be his watchword. And this is precisely what is demanded of employers and employed in shops and stores. Religion employs all the just motives of worldly wisdom, and adds thereto those higher motives that immortality creates. Indeed, religion demands success.

God's plan of spreading Christianity over the earth necessarily embraces both worlds. "Seek ye first the kingdom of God and His righteousness, and all these things shall be added unto you." What things? What we shall eat, what we shall drink, and wherewithal we shall be clothed, are the necessary things of this life. Christianity must use science, learning, commerce, skill, discovery, invention, labor, and capital—things that constitute the business of life—in order that it may go to the "uttermost parts of the earth." Men and women for preachers and teachers in every land, constitute but one in a multitude of agencies brought into requisition. Editors, authors, printers, manufacturers, scholars, engravers, merchants, binders, book-keepers, salesmen, porters, draymen, carpenters, sailors; warehouses, schools, colleges, and universities; the printing-press, railroad, telegraph, telephone, Atlantic cable, ships, and steamers; and thus on, until contribution is laid upon the mechanic arts, manufactures, and traffic, as well as upon the mental resources of society—all are used in the great plan of Providence to make the reign of Christianity universal. The printer, author, telegraph operator, railroad builder, and all workers in shop and field, are really doing their work more for God than man, for all that they plan and do is made subservient to His purpose to advance Christianity throughout the world.

So that religion is already in business, and has been from the start. Indeed, it creates business, rapidly increases its magnitude, and demands that it be prosecuted with enterprise. "Not slothful in business, fervent in spirit, serving the Lord." Hence it is that traffic, commerce, mechanical and industrial enterprise are the most prosperous and thrifty where the Christian religion is. Religion cannot perform its heavenly mission without impressing earthly business into its service.

The great warehouse of Samuel Budgett, of England, was conducted strictly

ARRIVAL OF THE MAYFLOWER AT PLYMOUTH HARBOR.

upon religious principles. One large room of his mercantile building was a chapel, where "master and men" assembled for prayers morning and evening. A religious atmosphere invested the establishment, as much so as a Christian family was ever invested by it. The men realized that they were under an exalted influence that demanded thoughtfulness, diligence, and fidelity. It was an illustration of religion in business of the highest type. If religion in a large mercantile house would interfere with its prosperity, it must have interfered there. If daily prayers could ever be an interruption to pressing business, it must have been there. But the reverse was true. "Of what use is it?" said a visitor to an employe of twenty years' experience with the firm. "The good of it! See for yourself: no such establishment for harmony, labor, and success, in England." Another employe was asked, "What is the secret of Mr. Budgett's success?" and he replied, "His true religion." When religion creates discontent and disorder among employes, and prayers make them lazy and unreliable, then, and not till then, will religion hinder business. Mr. Budgett pursued this course that order, peace, enterprise, efficiency, and fidelity might be secured, and he was not disappointed. There was not in all England another warehouse to compare with it in this regard.

Religion is often the primary cause of true self-knowledge, and the only impulse to self-culture. Dr. Jonas King was the son of a farmer in Hawley, Massachusetts, a steady, though not precocious lad. As soon as he became a Christian, a longing for an education sprang up in his soul. He was fifteen years

WATCHING THE DEPARTURE OF THE MAYFLOWER.

of age, with little education and no money, and no friends to render him assistance. On foot and alone, with an invincible determination to qualify himself for the ministry, he started for the Academy in Plainfield. The teacher inquired who he was. His answer was short and direct:—

"My parents live in Hawley, seven miles away from here; I am fifteen years old, and want an education, and I have come to see you about it." "Have you any acquaintances in town?" "No, sir." "Can your parents help you any?" "No, sir." "Have you any friends or relatives who can assist you?" "No, sir." "How, then, can you expect to get an education?" "That is what I came to see you about. I don't know how it can be done. As soon as I know, I will do it." That was enough. "I will see," responded the teacher.

From that time young King went forward. He had no more idea that religion could make a great man of himself than his father had. He was appointed professor of languages in his *alma mater*, but he declined the appointment, and subsequently became the renowned missionary in Greece. But for religion, neither this country nor Greece would have known such a man as Dr. Jonas King. John Foster said, "This that you call divine grace, whatever it may really be, is the strangest awakener of faculties after all."

It is a bad business that religion hinders. It facilitates a good one. If its elevating and transforming power could be thus concentrated upon every wicked business, converting its supporters and turning them against it, the world would soon be rid of enormous burdens of guilt.

When misfortune overtakes the religious man, and he is compelled to retreat from the marts of traffic, he faces every tempter to deceit and fraud, parts with his money, residence, style, and servants, and, laying aside every weight of sin that doth beset him, comes out of the perilous contest without a stain upon his character, or the smell of battle upon his reputation.

INFIDELITY A FOE TO SUCCESS.

SKEPTICISM is not evidence of smartness or strong-mindedness, as many youth of our day suppose. Christianity has exerted too great an influence upon men and nations to be treated with contempt, or spoken of with flippant insinuation. The best men are Christian men, and the best nations are Christian nations. The best of everything we call Christian. The best institution is a Christian institution, and the best enterprise is a Christian enterprise, and it is because these things are imbued with the Christian religion, which is the only religion that ever materially advanced the human race, as the facts of history prove.

On the other hand, infidelity never did one good thing for mankind; and by infidelity we mean, not only the skeptical, but also the deistical and atheistical views that antagonize Christianity. They are all manifestations of that hostility to religion which is popularly known as infidelity in our time. Men are no wiser for it, and society no purer for it. Human progress is no greater for it, and the human race was never in the least improved by it. Infidelity cannot point to an institution or enterprise, domestic, social, intellectual, or moral, of its own getting up, that has conferred a blessing upon mankind—not one! And this is saying the best thing that can be said of it; for the statement does not rehearse the painful demoralization of individuals and communities which its actual history records.

There is no reason in the world, then, why any youth of our day should cater to infidelity, even in its mildest form. As it never bestowed a single benefit upon a person, young or old, it deserves no favor. As it has proved a barrier to success in many instances, it deserves repudiation. By discarding the highest inspiration possible to a noble life, it is without the least claim upon our confidence and respect. The youth who rejects God and the Bible as His revelation, is, by general consent, disqualified to hold important trusts. The employer does not want him. There is no responsible position for him in store or bank. He has rejected the sure basis of moral principle, and hence is distrusted. The advertisement, "a young man who does not believe in God or the Holy Scriptures desires a situation in warehouse or bank," would not make an opening for him. He has advertised the best reason why thoughtful men should not employ him. The proclamation of his unbelief is inimical to a successful life.

It was in order for people, in the days of Christ, to doubt the truth of Christianity, and to ask for more evidence, another "sign from heaven." It was a new and strange revelation to them, in direct conflict with their customs, institutions, and religion. To embrace it would be to turn the world, of that day, "upside down." But it is not so with the people of our day. Christianity has been tried eighteen hundred years—longer than any system of education, finance, or government—long enough, surely, to establish its claim to universal confidence, if such a claim were possible. It has done this, by proving its adaptation to human wants in every age and clime, and by giving an impetus to human progress such as the world never had before. The highest civilization, the best manhood and womanhood, are found where the Christian religion is. For this reason, it is altogether too late for infidelity to set up any claim to respect. We have outlived the time when it was proper to doubt the practicability and great value of religion, as we have outlived the time when it was in order to doubt the fact and use of the telegraph. When Morse announced his discovery, it was received doubtfully by many, and with ridicule by some wise men; but we have outlived the time when to doubt the practicability of the telegraph is in order. It is too late in the day to doubt any of its claims now. It is proven worthy of public confidence and support. At first the author of it was thought by some to be a fit candidate for the asylum for the insane, but now the doubter would be adjudged as more fit for that institution.

Precisely so with Christianity. It has proved itself worthy of general confidence by practical operations, and by accomplishing what it promised. It has more influence in the world to-day than ever. It moulds institutions and governments, and has made our republic what it is. To deny this is to deny the plainest facts of history. Infidelity denies it, and so is no more worthy of our confidence than is the lunatic who swears that the sun is not shining at midday.

Can you doubt that the clock was made by human ingenuity? Who would say that it happened, or grew, or exists without design or plan? Yet, the proof of divine thought and purpose is more exact and overwhelming in the great planetary system than human thought and purpose are in the clock. We have to set our clocks and watches by Greenwich and Washington; and they get time of the sun. Astronomers and electricians who require exact time have to go to God for it. He makes time and gives it to us, minute by minute, and makes the human faculties that can tell the exact time on His celestial clock. So exact is this divine measurement of time that the planets move in their orbits a thousand years without the loss of a second, and even the eccentric comet comes around on the very nick of time. A clock is a poor imitation of this. And now, in view of such wonderful proofs of divine intelligence, skill, and plan, what biting sarcasm is there in the words of inspiration, spoken of the atheist, "The fool hath said in his heart, there is no God." He who denies the existence of God, in these circumstances, is found in the school for idiots.

In Mrs. Bird's interesting book on the Rocky Mountains occurs this fact: "Mountain Jim," as he was called, often served as guide to tourists, although he was a sort of desperado, whose hands had been stained with human blood. He guided a party of English tourists, of whom Mrs. Bird was one, through a portion of the Rockies. One night he announced to the party that they would take an earlier start in the morning than usual, in order to witness the sunrise at a given locality. Accordingly, they were earlier on their way, and reached the promised locality just as the orb of day was bathing the mountain peaks with light. Such a scene of splendor no one of the party had ever witnessed before. Not only the

S. F. B. MORSE.

mountain summits, but the sky itself was radiant with purple and gold. As the company stood in silent wonder and awe, "Mountain Jim," who stood with uncovered head, exclaimed, " I know there is a God!" How unreasonable, and even senseless, are the utterances of educated infidels in contrast with the honest words of this uncultivated " Mountain Jim."

The highest success is not possible without sincere belief in God and His Providence.

THREE CELEBRATED AMERICANS.

XXXVI.

THE BIBLE IN BUSINESS.

MANY young people suppose that the pulpit, the Sabbath school, and the Christian family are the only places where the Bible should be found. "The Bible in business!" they exclaim, with surprise. They have thought of the Bible in religion, but the good book is too sacred for the business world. In the shop and mill, in the marts of trade, and on the farm, in the forum and senate, its character would be compromised and business trammeled. But these are very superficial and erroneous ideas. Business is just the place for the Bible—all sorts of business; business of the hands or head; farming, trading, manufacturing, studying, teaching, preaching, and what not. It is a business manual or guide of exceptional quality. That is what it is for. True, it is to save men; but it is to save business as well.

The successful men of our country, in every department of labor, accomplished their purpose on principles derived directly from the Bible, or which were in harmony with it. Interview the most prosperous men of to-day, in mercantile or other business; ask them for the most important rule of life that has aided them in their pursuits; and whatever that rule may be, it will be found in full accord with the Bible. Doubtless, from one or all of these three sources—the Moral Law, the book of Proverbs, and the Sermon on the Mount—may be quoted the identical passage from which its sanction is derived. The fact is, there is not a rule fit for human conduct, in private or public life, that does not find its highest sanction in the Word of God. A rule that cannot bear the test of an appeal to the Bible is not worthy of a place in human affairs; it should not be tolerated in civilized society. Of course, this would condemn many of the maxims and customs that are current in social and public life; and they ought to be condemned. Youth should repudiate and avoid them. As they value unblemished character and the noblest achievements, they should regard them with unqualified repugnance.

Some years ago a "Business Guide" was published in Scotland—a "pocket edition"—consisting wholly of selections from the book of Proverbs. And why not? Neither the literature of Scotland, nor any other country, could furnish as complete a "code of morals" for the farm, shop, and counting-room as Proverbs. It has not a parallel in any language on the globe. This statement is easily proved. Successful men of the world, like Franklin, McDonough, Budgett, Appleton, Lawrence, Allen, not to mention others, announced the rules and maxims that gave them success. Let us test some of these.

"Remember that labor is a condition of of our existence." Fourth Commandment.—Ex. xx. 9. "If any would not work neither shall he eat."—2 Thess. iii. 10.

"Diligence is the mother of good luck." "The hand of the diligent shall bear rule."—Prov. xii. 24. "Seest thou a man diligent in his business? He shall stand before kings," etc.—Prov. xxxii. 20.

MOSES, BY MICHAEL ANGELO.

"Do unto all men as you would be done by." The Golden Rule.—Matt. vii. 10.

"Never covet what is not your own." Tenth Commandment.—Ex. xx. 17.

"Choose an occupation, and stick to it." "This one thing I do."—Phil. iii. 13. "Let thine eyes look right on, and let thine eyelids look straight before thee. Ponder the path of thy feet, and let all thy ways be established. Turn not to the right hand nor to the left."

"Perseverance conquers all things." "No man, having put his hand to the plough, and looking back, is fit for the kingdom of God."—Rom. xiv. 15. "Patient continuance," etc.—Rom. ii. 7.

"A penny saved is a penny earned." "Gather up the fragments that remain, that nothing be lost."—John vi. 12.

"Whatever is worth doing at all, is worth doing well." Parable of the Talents.—Matt. xxv. 14-31.

"Never use intoxicating drinks." "Look not thou upon the wine when it is red."—Prov. xxiii. 31.

"Never feel above your business." "Pride goeth before destruction, and a haughty spirit before a fall."—Prov. xvi. 18.

"Keep good company, or none." "He that walketh with wise men shall be wise, but the companion of fools shall be destroyed."—Prov. xiii. 20.

"Idleness is the parent of want and failure." "An idle soul shall suffer hunger."—Prov. xix. 15. "Through idleness of the hands the house droppeth through."—Ecc. x. 13.

"Drive thy business; let not thy business drive thee." "Whatsoever thy hand findeth to do, do it with thy might."—Ecc. ix. 10.

The foregoing is but a sample of the practical wisdom of the Bible especially adapted to the business world. We might enumerate each element of success known to men, and we should find that its foundation is in the Word of God. It was taught there before it was practiced by men. As a book of real genius, worldly wisdom, and pure morality, it surpasses anything to be found in the whole range of human learning. The book of Proverbs alone furnished the sages of the past, like Franklin, with the substance of their proverbial sayings that dropped as apples of gold from their lips. They embodied in their own language and repeated wisdom that was written long before in this wonderful book.

An infidel lawyer of New York City was induced by a brother lawyer to study the Bible so as to learn what the evidences of Christianity were. Some months thereafter the two met on the street, when the infidel said, "I have been studying the Moral Law." "And what do you think of it?" inquired the other. "I will tell you what I think of it. I have been looking into the nature of that law. I have been trying to see whether I can add anything to it or take anything from it so as to make it better; but I cannot do it. It is perfect. . . . I have been thinking. Where did Moses get that Law? The Egyptians were idolaters; and so were the Greeks and Romans. Moses lived at a period comparatively barbarous, but he has given a law in which the learning and sagacity of all subsequent time can detect no flaw. Where did he get it? He could not have soared so far above his age as to have devised it himself. I am satisfied where he obtained it. It came down from heaven."

This incident is instructive to youth, as showing that the Moral Law is a perfect rule of conduct everywhere—on the farm, in the mill and shop, at the counter, in the bank, in the Legislature, in Congress, and wherever duty calls men. There is no substitute for it, nor can it be improved. Any rule or regulation of human origin that is in conflict with it would be thrown out of every honest shop and warehouse.

Each youth must become "the artificer of his own fortune;" and the Bible will help him in this personal work. It will render him essential aid in self-culture, the acquisition of knowledge, the choice and pursuit of an occupation, the use of money and opportunities, and the discharge of public and private duties. Its history, literature, and learning, its purity, beauty of diction and grandeur of thought, make it a book worthy of the highest respect and profound study.

The Bible was John Quincy Adams' constant companion, not only in his private life, but in his public career as well. His words prove the value he set upon it for the business of life. He once said, "It is not so much praiseworthy to be acquainted with, as it is shameful to be ignorant of it." Again, "For pathos of narrative; for incidents that go directly to the heart; for the picturesque in character and manner; for copiousness, grandeur, and sublimity of imagery; for unanswerable cogency and closeness of reasoning; for irresistible force of persuasion and practical value, no book in the world deserves to be so unceasingly studied as the Bible."

THOROUGHNESS

TALKS TO YOUNG MEN

BY THAIN DAVIDSON, D. D.
Author of
" Brave and True," " Talks to Young Men," " A Good Start," Etc.

PREFACE

A RECENT magazine writer, contrasting England with America, says, "England is not a country for average men; every profession is over-stocked, and the only chance of success is for the man of signal ability and address to climb to a lofty position over the heads of a hundred others. America, on the other hand, is full of persons who can do many things, but who do no one thing well. The secret of their failure is mental dissipation, the squandering of the energies upon a distracting variety of objects, instead of condensing them upon one." The infirmity of character thus referred to is, we fear, only too true, and is becoming more apparent every year, the fierce competition which exists, and the more limited number of lucrative openings which now offer themselves, make it increasingly difficult for young men of spirit and ambition to find fitting spheres of occupation, yet the cases probably are few in which dogged earnestness of purpose, united with thoroughness of execution, does not meet with success. Too many youths enter upon the business to which they are assigned in a languid, half-hearted way, and do their work in a slipshod manner, the consequence being that they inspire neither admiration nor confidence on the part of their superiors, and cut off almost every chance of success. There is a loose, perfunctory method of doing one's work that never merits advance, and very rarely wins it. The good old Book gives many a fillip to practical energy, bidding us, "Whatsoever our hand findeth to do, to do it with our might;" and very notable are the words of the inspired sage, "Seest thou a man diligent in his business" (literally, prompt in his work), "he shall stand before kings." I have used the word "slipshod" as denoting a type of character too common in our day, and the word is singularly

PREFACE.

expressive. A slipshod man is a man shod with slippers, a man who rarely puts on strong boots, suggesting the easy country squire sauntering in his garden, rather than the vigorous workman harnessed for a tough day's toil. But this precisely answers to the impression which too many young men convey. Why, they seem to be half asleep! Instead of buckling to their task with all the force they possess, they merely touch it with the tips of their fingers, their rôle apparently being the *maximum* of ease with the *minimum* of work. Such lads have no right to look for anything else than failure. Ask any man who has been particularly prosperous in some line of business, and in all likelihood he will tell you that he largely owes his success to the fact that he started with the fixed resolve that, whatever he should take in hand, he would do it to the best of his power.

This was the principle of Strafford, the great minister of Charles I., who took for his motto the one word, "Thorough!"

Ben Jonson in one of his plays makes a character say, "When I once take the humor of a thing, I am like your tailor's needle—I go through with it."

A high-minded man will set his face against every form and phase of *shirking*, and will feel that whatever is worth doing at all, is worth doing well. The connection between thoroughness and success is well illustrated by the record given of good King Hezekiah, to whom the testimony is borne that "in every work that he began he did it with all his heart, and prospered."

It may be said that this case is hardly to the point, inasmuch as Hezekiah was born in a palace, and at twenty-five years of age was the occupant of a throne. It is easy, one may allege, at so high a level as that, to make one's mark upon the world, and command a certain measure of prosperity. I shall be told that when a young man has a nice little capital to start with, and good social influence to back him, it is comparatively easy to carry all before him.

But with most readers of this little book how different is the case! To this it may be at once replied, that the greater number of eminently successful men have commenced life under peculiarly unfavorable conditions. It is rather the exception than the rule, that a youth, brought up under all the advantages of wealth and rank and education, has, by dint of his own pluck and energy, forced his way to the front and reached an eminent position. Examples might easily be given, almost without number, of men whose brilliant career, starting from the lowest rung of the ladder, was due entirely to sheer thoroughness and perseverance. Let no one think that because his social position is humble, and his means small, he has but a poor chance in life. The quality I recommend is an article of the highest commercial value. Especially at the outset of life is it important to brace one's self to genuine hard work.

"It is good for a man that he bear the yoke in his youth." The young gentleman who, being in sound health, advertises for "a light situation," is not likely to prove of much use to his employer. Real hard work has an excellent moral influence upon a man.

Much of the nerveless, languid indolence that abounds is due to the want of a backbone of principle. So long as one's personal character is not solid, and permeated through and through by the grace of God, there can be little guarantee of a sustained efficiency. The following pages are written under the conviction, which has grown upon the author through long years of close intercourse with young men, that, as a rule, he is the best workman, and the best clerk, who is the truest Christian.

If a man's religion is of the right sort it will sharpen his faculties, quicken his energies, heighten his self-respect, give solidity to his character, and enhance both his usefulness and his prospects of success.

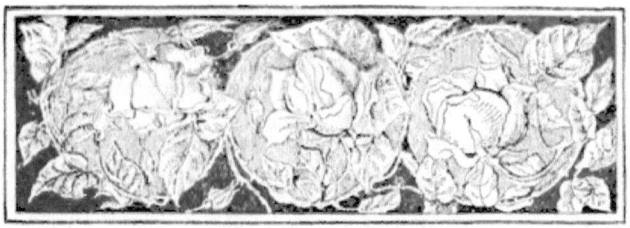

THOROUGHNESS.

I.

HEARTINESS.

THE word "heartily" occurs but once in the Bible. One could almost guess from whose lips or pen it dropped.

Never was man better entitled than was the Apostle Paul to give to all his fellow-Christians the exhortation, "Whatsoever you do, do it heartily." Himself characterized by the most intense earnestness of purpose, and his life both before and after conversion filled up with an almost vehement activity, the word comes from him with all the force of an unimpeachable consistency.

It is a bit of counsel very much wanted in these days, and especially by many of both sexes who are just entering upon the responsibilities of adult life; for there is too often an affectation of languor and *nonchalance* which is very offensive to a noble and generous mind. The advice admits of wide and general application; but it is clear to any one who looks into the passage where it occurs, that the inspired writer was dealing with the common and secular duties of life, and desired this heartiness to be infused into all the details of our daily calling. He speaks primarily to servants, to employes, to persons who are under the authority of a master; and his precept reminds one of the sharp, crisp word which the mother of our Lord addressed to the domestics at the marriage-feast in Cana, "Whatsoever He saith unto you, *do it.*" Don't intend it merely, or think about it, or dream over it; but do it.

Now, this age of ours needs practical people, who throw their whole heart and soul into anything they undertake, and determine to make a thorough good job of it. It demands men who do not content themselves with idle speculation or ingenious scheming, but who buckle on to real, solid work.

There is always a certain proportion of young men of a dreamy, high-flying order, and I am profoundly sorry for them, for some of them are good fellows too. They are eternally planning and inventing, but their plans and inventions come to nothing; and meanwhile they get beaten in the race.

I happen to know a few of these innocent wiseacres, who, if they have brains, have no hands; and the consequence is that they are to-day just where they were ten years ago, and are likely to remain for the rest of their natural lives. These gentlemen should have been born in the middle ages; this is not the time of day for them. Men now stand too thick on the ground, and mere dreamers must go to the wall.

In the keen struggle for life on every side of us, indolence is left behind at the starting. Competition demands whole-hearted purpose and determined energy, if you would not be beaten. Commercial life is now no "sleepy hollow." A feather bed and a long pipe are not generally associated with brilliant success. It is said that a lobster, when left high and dry upon the rocks, has not the energy to creep back to the sea, but waits for the tide to come back to it. If the tide does not rise high enough, it remains where it is and dies, though the slightest effort would enable it to reach the water. And, truth to tell, I am unlucky enough to meet with a good many human lobsters who are always waiting for some wave of good fortune to set them afloat.

I have met with young men who think that, could they only get abroad, they would be successful. But it is of no use going to Africa or Australia, if you carry a set of lazy bones with you. There is a living to be got in our own country yet at almost any trade, if a fellow will but give his whole mind to it.

But how many lads there are who try their hands at everything and accomplish nothing: reminding me of a pocket-knife I once saw, with half a dozen blades, a gimlet, a letter-balance, a cork-screw, a pair of pincers, and a toothpick, the whole thing costing two shillings, and not worth a copper.

No, no; the old proverb has much truth in it: *Non multa, sed multum;* that is, "not many things, but much."

Do one thing thoroughly rather than many things indifferently. One thing at a time, please; and make a thorough job of it. Stick to your present post, young man, till a better one opens up. Mind your business, or it will not mind you.

To look one way and pull another may do on water, but not on land.

The most successful men, after all, have been, in a sense, men of one dominant idea. The controlling passion with Luther was moral reform; with Newton, science; with Herschel, astronomy; with Humphry Davy, chemistry;

with Watt, mechanics; and so with a countless list of famous men. They found out their special gift, and bent their energies towards its cultivation.

How is it that some of your acquaintances are always unsuccessful? Because they have not steadily applied their powers in one direction. Like a young friend of mine who wished to be a musician, and took lessons on the pianoforte; then, tiring of that, he tried for a month or two to learn to play the violin; then he exchanged the fiddle for the flute; and now, for aught I know, he may be grinding a hand-organ on the street; for such indecision of character is the highroad to beggary.

It is just possible, no doubt, that a young man may, at the outset of life, mistake his calling; in that case, the sooner he change it the better.

It is no discredit to you, if you perceive you are in the wrong groove, to try to get into another. One of the most estimable clergymen I have ever known was for many years of his life an officer in the army; another friend was a total failure in the ministry, but is now a very successful physician.

It is surprising with what slender materials one may accomplish good work if only the whole heart is thrown into the business. In hundreds of instances of conspicuous failure the secret has been mental dissipation, the squandering of the energies upon a multiplicity of objects instead of condensing them upon one. The human mind is like a burning-glass, whose rays are powerful only when focused to a point. "Be a whole man at everything you undertake," was the sage advice of a celebrated Englishman to his son at school.

Yes, even in your recreations, if you go in for some athletic sport, or game of ball, or pedestrian trip, or row on the river, or should you take up some special line of study, whatever it be, go at it *con amore*, "with both hands earnestly," your very footstep having an inspiring ring; the grip of the hand, the tones of the voice, the expression of the countenance, all testifying that you have a heart, and a large heart too, and that that heart is thrown into everything you attempt. It is the men who act thus that

"Leave footprints on the sands of time."

II.

PROSPERITY AND PRESUMPTION.

OF a certain ancient Jewish king it is recorded that "he was marvelously helped till he was strong; but when he was strong his heart was lifted up to his destruction."

Unhappily, prosperity and presumption have often proved to be nearly related. Nothing tries a man's moral fibre so much as the favor of fortune and the flattery of the world. "I understand, sir, you are in a dangerous condition," said the godly Richard Cecil to a young man who had just become possessed of a considerable fortune. "I am not aware of it," was the reply. "Probably not," rejoined the other, "and, therefore, I have given you a call. I hear you have become rich. Take care; for this is the road by which many a one is enticed to his destruction."

As there are various kinds of prosperity, so there are different forms of presumption; and it is well for us to be on our guard against them all. For example, in the first place, there is the pride of *wealth*.

It does not require a large fortune to make some persons "purse-proud," and very disagreeable people these are. They have risen from nothing; they are the architects of their own fortunes.

Well, all honor to those whose skill and perseverance have carried them up from step to step of the social ladder, if they remain becomingly modest and unaffected. But, truth to tell, the cases are not unknown of persons who under such circumstances begin to toss their heads, and put on airs, as though it were the greatest condescension on their part any longer to associate with those who were once their playmates. I have known young men who came up from the country a few years ago with not more than enough money to pay for a week's lodging, but they got into a good niche, fortune smiled upon them, and already they are rich men; yes, but I observe they take good care not to tell us anything about their father's two-roomed cottage, or their mother's spinning-wheel; they are too fine now to belong to the religious body with which they were brought up; and as for their accent, it is the strangest conglomeration you ever listened to.

Now, that is very small, and very contemptible; but after all it is just poor human nature, and we are all prone to it, in some form or another. It is a common saying, that in Boston, where they worship literature, the main question is, in regard to any new arrival in the city, "How much does he know?" In Philadelphia, where they worship rank, it is, "Who was his father?" And in New York, where they worship the dollar, it is, "How much is he worth?" But if your estimate of a man is determined by his wealth, or by his birth, or even by his learning, it does not say much for your own judgment. "The *man's* the gowd for a' that."

We have it on the highest authority that "the prosperity of fools shall destroy them." Yet we must not imagine that a successful career of necessity involves moral deterioration; for many an instance happily may be pointed to in which, with money pouring like a flood into a man's lap, he has remained as humble and unostentatious as before, and has used his wealth to noble purpose.

Again, some are lifted up by the pride of *intellect*. You have need to be on your guard against a current which is running very strongly in our day, namely, the tendency to set up the reason against religion. I fear there is an increasing number of young men—clever fellows, perhaps, they are—who have given up Christianity altogether, alleging that their cultured understanding compels them to reject it.

It is distressing to find so many amongst the higher classes, as they are called, persons who enjoy the luxuries and refinements of life, and whose influence, if wisely directed, would be so wholesome, fancying themselves able to grapple with problems far beyond their reach, and in their bewilderment abandoning themselves to a dreary agnosticism. They think they ought to understand everything, and so, because they cannot, they will believe nothing. Doubt and unbelief once sprung are hard to eradicate. The saddest men I know are the men who in their pride of intellect have cast off the faith. Surely their position is one that is easily assailed. There is much more for revelation than against it. Truth shines by its own light; and even the internal evidence which the Bible affords to the ingenuous mind that studies it, is alone sufficient to silence the caviller. Never apologize to the doubter; it is he who owes you an apology. The man who attempts to rob you of your faith does you an infinitely greater wrong than he who tries to rob you of your purse or property. It is pitiful to see a Christian professor wincing before a blatant, egotistical scoffer, as though with a craven fear that the would-be philosopher is right, and the believer in Jesus Christ is without firm ground to stand on.

Thank God, the best intellect of our time is in favor of Christianity.

Some years ago, indeed, science seemed to threaten our religion. Startling discoveries were made, which many thought must necessarily subvert the teaching of the alleged divine revelation. Not a few trembled for the ark of God, and were ready like Uzza with presumptuous hands to bear it up. There was no occasion. The ark was safe enough.

The faith of the Christian still survives. Science bears toward it a more respectful attitude. It is not saying too much to aver that the direction of the best scientific thought of our time is toward the Bible, not against it. The reaction that has set in is unquestionable. The difficulties that face the skeptic are enormously greater than those with which the intelligent Christian has to deal. The manly believer will hold his ground firm, and not yield an inch to the foe; if he intelligently realizes his position it is impregnable. Taking even the lowest ground, it is easy to challenge any one with the question whether infidelity or faith most tends towards human happiness and moral development. Contrast the labors, say, of such men as Voltaire and John Wesley.

Can it, without a transparent untruth, be said of the former that he has made any man happier or better? Yet who will deny that, through the instrumentality of the latter, thousands and tens of thousands have had a brightened life and a peaceful death? A shallow and affected intellectualism assumes an air of pity toward those who firmly hold an evangelical creed; but it needs little more than a glance at the history of our land to show that it is the Christian religion in its purity that has supplied not only the loftiest motives, but the mightiest and steadiest impulse; and that whether a man be a king, a warrior, a merchant, or a ploughman, whatever work he takes in hand will be more effectively done if he is under the control of an earnest piety.

Indeed, the only guarantee that prosperity will not spoil a man is that he gratefully traces it to its divine source, and realizes the increased responsibility it involves.

III.

QUIET MEDITATION.

IT would be a good thing for many of our young men in this restless, bustling age, when there is so much hurry and feverish excitement, to contemplate the character of the gentle and retiring Isaac, who all through his life was a quiet home-loving man. His birthplace was in the extreme south of Palestine, a bare upland district between the Judean hills and the Arabian desert; and there is no reason to believe that he was ever many miles from the spot where he was born. When it is said of him in the sacred narrative that he "went out to meditate in the fields at eventide," the construction of the Hebrew sentence indicates not an isolated act, but a habit of life; and his practice may be commended to the youth of our day. No doubt to many men such a kind of existence would be insufferably monotonous. But not a few happy and fruitful lives have been spent far from the stir and din of cities; and Isaac shows how it is possible to serve one's generation and to honor God in a quiet, sequestered sphere, just as well as in a life of prominent action. Do not imagine that it is only brilliant philosophers, and orators, and statesmen, and warriors, and divines, that live for the good of their race; or that happiness is mainly found amid the excitement of courts and public assemblies. Ah! in some shady nook,

"Far from the madding crowd's ignoble strife,"

there may be found a serener joy, and a piety that shall for generations leave a blessing behind it. Some of my readers are the sons of parents now passed into the skies, whose retired and godly lives shed a fragrance around them, and whose names are never mentioned in the district without loving respect. No wonder you cherish their memory as your richest inheritance, though the big world never heard of them.

"Remote from towns they ran their godly race,
Nor e'er had changed, nor wished to change, their place."

It is by no means the star-decked chieftains and notables of earth that are most to be envied. A noiseless, meditative career like Isaac's may have the choicest benediction; and even Solomon in all his glory was ready to acknowledge that "better is he that ruleth his spirit than he that taketh a city." The quiet domestic life in the midst of which Isaac was reared, along with the pure example set before him by both his parents, served, under God, to mould him into a gentle, guileless, and religious nature. His character has been described as soft, and almost womanly; but is it evident there was no lack of firmness and courage, for few young men could have stood the ordeal which on a memorable occasion on Mount Moriah he had to endure. The fond love of mother and of home is not incompatible with a brave and manly character. I cannot recall a single instance of a young man going to the bad who was tenderly devoted to his parents. Depend upon it, next to the love of God, this is the noblest emotion.

An interval of three years elapsed between Isaac's loss of his mother and his marriage; but he had the happiness before her demise of introducing to her his future wife. I observe that all the charms of Rebekah did not weaken the bonds of filial affection. Not till three years after Sarah's death was he "comforted;" and the depth of his love as a son was a good omen of his devotedness as a husband.

There is something here for young people of both sexes to note: the youth who is considerate to his mother is the man whose love a maiden may safely rely on.

Isaac's peculiar relish for a quiet, uneventful, domestic life is not without its lessons for ourselves. Many a foreigner rallies our countrymen upon their too great fondness for their own fireside; but I think we may be proud of the reproach.

Sir Walter Scott expressed a true national sentiment when, on his return to Abbotsford for the last time, after a long stay on the Continent, he ordered himself to be slowly wheeled in his chair through the various rooms, and then said, "I've seen much, but nothing like my ain house; give me one turn more."

Nor does the remark hold good only in the case of lordly and well-furnished mansions; a lowly cottage may possess an equal charm. The Ettrick Shepherd touchingly addresses his humble cabin, when about to exchange it for a more pretentious structure:—

> "I lo'e ye weel, my wee auld hoose,
>   Though laigh thy wa's and flat thy riggin';
> Though roon' thy lum the sourock grows,
>   And rain draps gaw thy cosy biggin'."

Although that ever-popular song, "Home, sweet home!" was written by one who never had a home of his own, there are few lines that find a truer echo in every refined and virtuous heart; and the more that real religion exerts its benign sway, the more is such happiness intensified.

The love of private meditation is a feature of Isaac's character which we would do well to cultivate, and which is too little known in these busy, bustling times.

It would be a good thing for many people if they talked less, wrote less, worked less, and meditated more. They seem to be working at high pressure from morning till night, driven from pillar to post all day long, and then fit for nothing but the pillow; and so the days run on, and the years glide by, and they hardly know what it is to take a few moments for serious reflection.

We are left to make our own guess as to the themes which occupied Isaac's mind as he took his evening stroll in the fields of Beersheba; but without doubt they were of a pure and elevating character. I see in him not a morose and melancholy recluse, a morbid misanthrope who shuns society; not at all. Rather do I see the picture of a thoughtful saint, who is able to find true enjoyment in communing with nature and with God. The best of men have found pleasure in occasional retirement, and it betokens some moral defect when one has no desire to be sometimes alone. An hour of reflective solitude should not only be very profitable, but very enjoyable. Many of our sweetest poets have sung the charms of retirement from the world; and the saintly Dr. Love once observed, "I have found retired places to be the secret haunts of the Son of God." To speak thus is to offer no contradiction to that utterance of highest authority, "It is not good that the man should be alone;" and I fancy that in those quiet evening hours Isaac was only illustrating their harmony. For who can doubt that many of his thoughts were then given to the important change he was about to make in his condition, and to the new duties and responsibilities it would involve? It was whilst he was thus musing that the fair form of Rebekah broke upon his view, and the living answer to his prayers stood before him. The picture may seem to you to have a touch of the sentimental. None the worse for that. Our age is getting just a little too prosaic and utilitarian. There is a reaction from the ecstatic, rapturous, and rhapsodical style of half a century ago, and, like all reactions, it is apt to be extreme.

It is possible to make matrimonial arrangements too much an affair of convenience, or business, or money; but such unions are rarely suggestive of Eden.

Love, even in its most romantic forms, is a beautiful thing; and when combined with thoughtfulness and piety, is the fairest flower that has escaped the fall.

But I must not run into this vein. Every young man should seize a little time each day to be alone with God. The Bible is a sweet companion to one who has a new heart. Office hours may be long, but some part out of every twenty-four hours should be snatched for fellowship with Heaven. The flame of piety must be burning low, if you have neither desire nor time for quiet meditation.

IV.

CHUMS.

"TO be without friends," said Lord Bacon, "is to find the world a wilderness." No man can live in a state of isolation from his fellows! or, if he can, I may almost aver he is not a man; at least, the human element in him is nearly imperceptible.

Each of us yearns for a heart that beats in unison with our own, for an ear into which we can pour our confidences and our troubles, for a hand we can safely grasp, and for an arm we can always lean on. It was all very well for Cowper to sigh, "Oh, for a lodge in some vast wilderness!" but no one could better depict the pleasures of the cheerful tea-table; and, ridicule as he might the irksomeness of too much company, Charles Lamb dearly loved the chatty hour with a kindred spirit.

For it is not only when difficulties oppress us, and our back is to the wall, that we know the value of a trusted friend; but even in our most bright and prosperous hours we feel that joys have not half their sweetness unless we have a companion to share them with us. Whether our dwelling be a castle or a cabin, our trials will be lighter, and our comforts richer, if we have with us one so thoroughly in sympathy with ourselves, that what is a joy or sorrow to us will also be a joy or a sorrow to him. Point me to a man who has no choice friend, I know no one on earth less happy, unless it be he who has never sought one. If isolation breeds selfishness, it is no less true that only the grossest selfishness can tolerate isolation; and you may be sure of it, that if there be an individual who neither has nor cares to have associates, he is about the most wretched being you can anywhere meet with. A man's acquaintances may be numbered by the hundred; his companions he may probably be able to count upon the fingers of one hand; his friends, in the best sense of the word, may be two or three; but in the centre of all these he has in all likelihood one whom he specially delights to call his *chum*.

This is a singular word, and is derived from the Armoric root *choum*, to abide with or remain. A chum therefore, in the literal sense of the term, is one who is always with you; a chamber-fellow, one who shares the same room.

The conditions of city life in which thousands of young men live, naturally tend to the formation of such a relationship; and out of it have sprung some of the most delightful instances of sworn and life-long attachment.

It is impossible to overestimate the importance of the utmost care in the formation of such ties. Every youth who comes to take up his residence in a large town should be exceedingly cautious in the choice of a boon companion. It is always easy to secure friends *of a sort*. The stranger will generally find that the thoroughly bad fellows are the first to fraternize with him. They find out his weak points, and flatter him. They patronize him. They offer to take him all about town.

They generously volunteer to conduct him to any place he wishes to visit, he, of course, paying all expenses for both. I have invariably observed that if a good young man and a bad young man go together to some questionable entertainment, it is the former gentleman who has to pay the bill. The other, of course, plunges his hand vehemently into his pocket, and says, "Pray, allow me," but somehow the money is never forthcoming at the proper moment. We are constantly reading in the newspapers of some verdant stranger who has been taken in by what is called "the confidence trick," but the journals tell us nothing of the hundreds of well-disposed young men who are yearly caught in the net of an evil companionship, and who are snared to their eternal ruin. It is perfectly amazing what an ascendency a man of strong will and marked individuality may exert over another, whilst the latter remains unconscious of the influence. This subtle power may be either elevating or degrading in its effect; but the unwholesome friendships are generally the first to offer themselves. As a rule, it is much more easy to find a bad companion than a good one.

Men of high moral tone and intellectual superiority are more slow to offer their hand. They have to be sought for; they have to be picked out.

Therefore do not be in a hurry in the formation of friendship. Keep the man at arm's length till you know something of him. Acquaintanceship is one thing; intimacy is another.

You may be courteous without being confidential, and civil without being effusive. Do not suffer yourself to be unwittingly bracketed with an idler or a fool. Think twice or three times before you accept a friendship that is obtruded, almost forced upon you.

THOROUGHNESS.

> "The man who hails you Tom or Jack,
> And proves by thumping on your back
> His sense of your great merit,
> Is such a friend, that one had need
> Be very much *his* friend indeed
> To pardon, or to bear it."

Young men are often victimized by mean fellows who only want to get out of them all they can, and then throw them away like a squeezed orange.

So long as it is in their humor or to their advantage, they will be hand and glove with you, but when they find you can do them no more service, you are dropped at once. There is nothing more galling to a sensitive nature than to be suddenly deserted by one on whose constancy you had been led to rely.

A man has not lived long in the world before he finds that there is much professed friendship which looks like gold, but is only tinsel.

Beware how you let a man of loose character talk familiarly with you. When he gives you a hearty slap on the shoulder, return him a look that will make him pause before he does it a second time. Show him you mean to be select in the choice of your friends.

Remember your own character will be judged by the kind of persons you associate with. Be it a prince or a day-laborer, a man's favorite company is a pretty sure index of his own moral standard. Pythagoras, before he would admit any one into his school, made strict inquiry as to who his intimate associates had been; rightly judging that those who had been careless about their companionships were not the most likely to derive benefit from his instructions. A very brief acquaintanceship has been known to do a lifelong injury. The chemist will tell you that a single grain of iodine is sufficient to give color to a hundred gallons of water; and a week of unwholesome friendship may prove enough to poison your whole life.

The quality of a particular friendship may often be guessed from the mode in which it has originated. The companion whom you picked up in some place of vicious entertainment is not likely to turn out a blessing. The model chum is one whose character, moulded by religion, combines intelligence, purity, reverence, and self-respect. Such a man will do you good and not evil, all the days of your life. But when a friend of this kind is found, confidence must not be met half-way. Mutual trust is indispensable. Be as true to him as you would wish him to be to you.

> "The friends thou hast, and their adoption tried,
> Grapple them to thy soul with hoops of steel.
> But do not dull thy palm with entertainment
> Of each new hatched, unfledged comrade."

V.

ONE OR TWO FOOLS I HAVE MET.

MY album—I mean my photographic album of young men—has a few rare specimens of humanity that have come under my notice, studies in character that are worth looking at, if only in the way of warning: portraits of men who have been compelled to confess, as King Saul did to David at the hill of Hachilah, "Behold, I have played the fool."

I. The first on the list is the IDLER. If the world contains a genuine fool, it is the young man who throws away his time. Some things God gives often, others only once. Youth belongs to the latter category, and once wasted cannot be redeemed. No treasure so precious, no waste so ruinous.

Money lost may be recovered; health lost may be restored; friendships lost may be regained; even character lost may be redeemed; but time lost, *never!* The years, the months, the days—I might even say the hours—of early life are simply invaluable. There is not so much as one you can afford to squander.

A young idler is the worst of all; for no moments are so precious as those of youth. Unhappily, there are always a certain number of ne'er-do-wells loafing about, lazy, indolent fellows who would hardly take the trouble to hold up a basin to the skies, if the clouds were to rain down gold.

Professor Dugald Stewart tells of a bright youth of his acquaintance who spent fifteen years in training himself to balance a broomstick on his chin! Truth to tell, there are lads who seem born but to eat and sleep. They remind one of Tudham's dog, that was so lazy it had to lean its head against the wall before it could bark. Were St. Paul's rule carried out to the letter—"If any man will not work neither should he eat"—there would be plenty of skeletons about: but unfortunately, these lazy-bones generally contrive to get their mouths deep into the trough of other people. One of the most melancholy sights in the world is a young man with nothing to do. I speak not of one who is out of work, though that is bad enough, but of one who will not work, which is ten times worse.

Idleness is always demoralizing. You cannot be too careful as to the use you make of your leisure hours; for many is the young man who, to do him justice, is thoroughly assiduous in his office or place of business, but as soon as he shuts his books, locks his desk, puts on his hat, and turns his steps towards his home or his lodging, he abandons himself to indolence, and *then* comes the devil's chance. Almost all the moral havoc that is wrought amongst young men is effected after the office or shop door is closed. Few men go wrong when they are busy at work. The worst thing you can do of an evening is—to do nothing. You may almost predict what a man's future will be if you know how he spends his hours of leisure. All honor to those who take up some course of useful reading, some branch of literature, the study of French or German, or some practical form of philanthropy. But there are hundreds who never dream of such a thing, and when a few years have gone, will wake up to see how stupid they have been, and to exclaim, with the son of Kish, "Behold, I have played the fool!"

II. Another portrait my album contains is the BUFFOON. No wise man will say a word to the disparagement of mirthfulness. No, God has given us this faculty; and life is grave and sad enough without extinguishing this electric sparkle, which throws a little brightness into many a gloomy hour. Pity on the miserable soul that condemns all flashes of wit and humor, that frowns on joke and fun and laughter, and every form of merriment, as if it were unbecoming the Christian. Such a man is the greatest enemy to religion.

But it must be confessed there are silly fellows who seem to be incapable of a serious thought. They jest at everything. They treat life as if it were just a great farce. They have not a particle of gravity or good sense about them. They are only what bells are to horses, making plenty of jingle, but not helping to draw. What with stale puns and coarse jests, and threadbare stories, and slang of the streets, their one object in life is to keep the world a-giggling.

The true sparkle is wanting; they are but painted gems, gewgaw tinsel, everything but the real diamond. It is a poor ambition this; the habitual jester is an empty fribble, and suggests the lines of Dryden:—

> "A man so various that he seemed to be
> Not one, but all mankind's epitome;
> Stiff in opinions, always in the wrong,
> Was everything by turns, and nothing long;
> But, in the course of one revolving moon,
> Was chymist, fiddler, statesman, and buffoon."

Such men have not an atom of reverence in their nature. Levity is the very atmosphere they breathe. They have not a conception of the dignity of man. They have scarcely respect even for religion, and some brutally-profane quotation from Holy Scripture will set them in a roar. Thus they go giggling through life.

and illustrate the words of the prophet: "Ye shall conceive chaff, and bring forth stubble."

Such men might be admissible in a menagerie, but life is too serious to tolerate them.

III. The next character I light upon, who has ultimately to make Saul's confession, is the MAMMONIST. This gentleman has no time either for idleness or buffoonery; he is busy from morning to night, and there is no nonsense about *him*.

Life, he holds, is given for one great purpose, and that is to make money; so every other thought is tossed to one side. If he does not give himself to the theatre, and the ballroom, and the circus, and the gaming-table, and the midnight carouse, it is not because he has any scruple about these things, but because they demand money. If he rises early, and sits up late, it is not because he grudges his time on sleep, but because he is greedy of gain. If he rarely visits the House of God, it is not because he has anything to say against religion, but because his heart is so choked full of business, he cannot give his mind to higher themes. This gluttony of wealth grows on one, till it blinds the reason and dominates every faculty of the soul. Men forget that more than money is wanted, even for the enjoyment of money. Accumulated riches are in themselves powerless to secure real happiness.

> "They call thee rich, I call thee poor;
> Since, if thou darest not use thy store,
> But sav'st it only for thine heirs,
> The treasure is not thine, but theirs."

IV. There is yet another fool whose portrait my album contains: he is known by many an ugly name: libertine, prodigal, SENSUALIST. I shall not affront my readers by describing him further than by saying he is the slave of his baser passions, and wallows in the mire of bestiality. The pure shrink from his lecherous touch; his very breath blights every innocent thing. The stenchful ichor of his lustful life makes a Sodom of every place which he habituates. He leers in the face of virtue, and has only a sneer for every mention of purity. His literature is the refuse of Holywell Street, his haunts are the tavern, the casino, and places which I hardly dare to name. Ah! an awful Nemesis is at his heels. Rather would I see a son of mine laid in a pauper's grave than see him fall into the maw of this besotted devil.

The hour of retribution hastens, and generally arrives even in this life. A Day of Judgment verily antedates the grave, when the remorse-stricken reprobate, looking back on a blasted life and forward to a lost eternity, lifts up his hands in despair, and exclaims, "Behold, I have played the fool!" Well does Young say:—

> "Be wise with speed;
> A fool at forty is a fool indeed!"

VI.

HASTING TO BE RICH.

THE Old Book has not a word to say against the earning of money, but it is very plain in its warnings against eager impatience to acquire it. It is no sin to be rich, nor to wish to be rich, nor to try to be rich; the mistake is in being too eager after riches.

So far from being evil is a moderate desire for wealth, that if there be a man who is altogether free of it, who has no wish to possess, to whom gold and silver have no more value than dust, there must be some serious defect about such a person; his friends had better look after him, for he is clearly unable to look after himself. Placed as we are in this world, it is our duty to make gain, if it can be done by legitimate and laudable means. The wish to do so is a God-imparted instinct of our nature, and may, and often does, prove a healthful motive power. Without it the world would stagnate, and commerce would be paralyzed.

Some of the best and noblest of our race have been men of large fortune, who have known, not only how to acquire money honorably, but how to dispense it usefully.

Who can doubt that the Divine Father looks from heaven with pleasure and approval upon the busy hives of industry, and upon the eager crowds that every morning pour into the city to pursue their legitimate calling?

The activities of the mercantile world are a fence to virtue. From a large class of temptations young men are never more free than when they are closely occupied with the affairs of trade. From the moment you enter the office or the workshop in the beginning of the day, until you leave it in the evening, you are hedged by method, you run in a groove of occupation, and the Evil One has less purchase upon you. It is when the day's work is done, and you go out free to please yourself as you may, that your moral safety becomes imperiled. **Tell me how a young man spends his evenings, and I will have a very good idea of his character.**

Some men have too much and others too little time at their own disposal. Both extremes are evil; but probably amongst the readers of these pages there are not many who are exposed to the former snare. Not much danger of *you* having to try to "kill time;" the trouble is rather that want of time for leisure is like to kill *you*. Business, business, from morning to night, from Monday to Saturday, so that you have rarely the chance of a pleasant hour with a book, or of an evening stroll, or of a game at football or cricket.

Now, a man cannot work like that without incurring evil consequences. In the first place it will tell upon his health. Many of our city clerks are not the robust fellows they ought to be. They are too thin in the face. Their color suggests dyspepsia. Too early in life they understand what is meant by disordered livers, and languid circulation, and depression of spirits.

In this keen and competitive age it is pretty certain that your business, whatever it be, will demand all the vital force you can muster. One of the first conditions of real success in life is a good, hearty, wholesome body, a sound physical constitution. Not a doubt of it. The youth who has not this stands but a poor chance by the side of healthy men. Hundreds of our young men are not nearly so robust as they should be, and, I may add, as they *might* be. They do not have sufficient leisure and out-door recreation. Everywhere men are killing themselves by overwork. The wear and tear of nerve and brain is excessive. There is a fierce struggle going on in nearly all lines of business which makes life little better than a continued drudgery. Men will not be satisfied with reasonable profits; and rob themselves of sleep and rest till the system is able to bear it no longer. This worship of work is carried a little too far. Life in all the professions, and in many departments of trade, is literally a battle, and hundreds are prematurely falling on the field.

Man's physical organism, if taken care of, is a grand and serviceable machine; but it will not stand the strain which some unwisely put upon it.

Many of our city youths are in need of a word of warning, too, in relation to the hasty and uncertain meals which are often a mere apology for dinner. Not seldom the seeds of disease are laid by the want of nutritious diet at a period of life when plenty of nourishment is essential; but, to see how some young men take their midday meal, you would wonder they can hold out for six months. In a close restaurant or stuffy coffee-shop, where the table-cloth is changed once a week, and the knives are odorous of stale onions, and the meat is suggestive of leather, a lad is not likely to have the appetite that is essential to good digestion. He does not eat his dinner; he *bolts* it.

Again, this unwholesome haste to be rich is responsible for most of the dishonesty which exists in the commercial world. Men are determined by hook or by crook to get money; if they cannot get it in a fair way, then they must get it in a foul. Hence the deplorable prevalence of gambling in one form or another.

On every side we find financial adventurers who hope to better their position, not by the practice of industry and economy, but by clever speculations and sharp enterprises. By an unworthy use of their wits, they mean to make money for which they give no equivalent in honest toil. They go in for great risks and enormous profits; business with them is nothing better than a lottery. These men are the pests of the mercantile world; they destroy confidence, and lower the whole *morale* of the market-place. The best rule for the making of money is "slow and sure." Light gains make heavy purses. The saying that "one cannot be honest and live" is as old as the devil. It is much more true to say you cannot be *dishonest* and live, in any worthy conception of what living is. The mistake with so many who start in the race for riches is that they are not willing to creep before they walk, and walk before they run. The penniless man of to-day wants to be a millionaire to-morrow. A New York wit thus epitomizes his mad career:—

> "Monday, I dabbled in stock operations;
> Tuesday, owned thousands, by all calculations;
> We'n'sday, my Fifth Avenue Palace began;
> Thursday, I drove out a spanking bay span;
> Friday, I gave a magnificent ball;
> Saturday, *smashed*, with nothing at all."

VII.

"AS THE MAN IS, SO IS HIS STRENGTH."

I FANCY it was an old proverb which the two princes of Midian, Zeba and Zalmunna uttered, when finding their case hopeless, they prepared themselves for death, and asked the powerful Gideon to dispatch them quickly; "for," added they, as they looked upon his stalwart form, "as the man is, so is his strength."

Be it so, the ancient adage is true in more ways than one.

For example, first, as a man is *physically*, so is his strength.

Clearly, Gideon belonged to the order of nature's nobility. He was a man of splendid figure and bearing, of a tall and commanding presence.

That right arm of his could do mighty execution, whether it wielded the flail, or the sword, or the prickly branches of the thorn-trees at Succoth.

Whatever work it undertook, it would accomplish with thoroughness and effect. When two warrior-chiefs were questioned as to the appearance of the men they had slain at Tabor, their answer to Gideon was, "As thou art, so were they; each one resembled the children of a king."

Now it is perfectly true that we cannot give to ourselves a handsome mien, nor add one cubit to our stature; nevertheless, it is equally true, and of none more true than of young men, that you can do much to promote your health, to build up your constitution, and even to give dignity to your physical presence.

By a regular life, by moderation in diet, by scrupulous temperance, every one of us can do not a little in that direction; and in many a case it is easy to perceive on our first glance of a man, either on the one hand, that he is loose and slovenly in his habits, or, on the other, that he is orderly and regular.

This is of more importance than some of my readers perhaps imagine; and the rapid advance and conspicuous success of many a youth whom I have known, has been due, in no small measure, to his personal appearance, to his pleasing and manly bearing. Of course, there are walks of life where this will not show so much; but, as a rule, it is safe to say that, given a good address, a bright and gentlemanly, not slouching and clownish exterior, a young man's chances of preferment are decidedly greater; and the axiom generally holds good, that, as the man is, even in outward physique, so is his strength.

Or secondly, take it another way: as a man is *intellectually*, so is his strength. The familiar adage that "knowledge is power," is a truth to which a wiser than Bacon gave expression thirty centuries ago, for these are the words of King Solomon: "If the iron be blunt, and he do not whet the edge, then must he put to more strength; but wisdom is profitable to direct." Young men must remember that the day for stone hatchets and blunt axes is past; and that, from the humblest craft to the most exalted, in order to succeed, it is requisite to have intelligence and brains. I have heard some of our wealthy self-made city men say that, out of every hundred youths who come to them applying for a vacant post, not five have really got a head upon their shoulders; they want *gumption*, shrewdness, sound common sense. Of course, you must have education. In these days of free school and technical education, and evening classes of all sorts, a man is sadly handicapped without a thorough schooling; but mere schooling will never give a young fellow common sense. You want to have your eyes open and your wits awake; to be sharp, and ready, and active. The commerce of the world is not indeed in the hands of learned scholars; but it is for the most part in the hands of shrewd, clear-headed, practical men, who understand their business, and know how to push it.

There are many lads who come up from the country with the notion that they will be quite an acquisition to the metropolis, and that the moment they knock at the door of a merchant's office they will be eagerly accepted for some comfortable situation; but are chagrined to find they are not in such demand.

The fact is, that some of them are such greenhorns no one will accept their services *gratis*. They have moved from infancy in a certain narrow groove, and they cannot get out of it. They need pliableness and versatility.

This age of keen competition demands men of sound brains; and it is mind that conquers matter.

Intellect becomes an equivalent for strength, and a quick intelligence means money. In real power of work the skilled artisan leaves the mere laborer far behind, and the thoughtful clerk the mere mechanical penman; so that, as a man is in intelligence, so is his strength.

But, once more, the ancient proverb admits of a yet higher application: as a man is *morally* and *spiritually*, so is his strength. Faith and character, beyond anything else, determine your power of conquering difficulty and of accomplishing good.

"AS THE MAN IS, SO IS HIS STRENGTH."

This is the sure gauge of your personal force in society and in the world. Without a moral backbone you may as well be a jelly-fish for any real solid good you will do.

There must be a foundation of stern principle, or you will be as weak as water. A man with a resolute conscience will always be a power. No doubt conscience may be prejudiced and perverted; it may even be scrupulous to a fault. Sternly upright men not seldom have crochets at which other men equally good can only laugh. One's moral sense may be drugged by the air it breathes, as men get giddy in wine-vaults without tasting alcohol. It is a grand thing to have a conscience at once sensitive and sound, to have an acute moral faculty and a robust common sense combined.

There are no finer young men in the country than those who, to a clear, practical, all-round intelligence add "a conscience void of offence toward God and toward man."

Character, be sure of it, is the best capital. A youth of keen sagacity, and at the same time of high moral tone, is an article of great marketable value. I have known men—they are now no longer young—who never met with success, and insisted that Providence had an implacable spite against them; whereas the secret of their failure lay in the rottenness of their own character.

Unstable as water, they could never excel. When a man's life is wrong, and his heart is wrong, he must be weak. It cannot be otherwise. "As the man is, so is his strength."

Without high self-respect you carry no momentum with you. Mirabeau, the infidel, once said, "If there were no honesty in the world it would be invented as a means of getting wealth." Strict integrity will fetch a high price in the end. It is a truth worth reflecting on, that as a man is physically, intellectually, and morally, so is his strength for the work of life.

VIII.

THE DIVINE PLUMB-LINE.

STONEMASONS, bricklayers, and carpenters in the building of houses make use of a very simple instrument to secure that the walls are perpendicular. The instrument consists of little more than a cord, to one end of which a piece of lead is fastened. Standing on the wall, and letting the line drop beside it, the architect or workman can see at once whether the wall recedes or bulges, whether it leans inwards or outwards, or whether it is absolutely straight.

The instrument is called a plumb-line, and in vision the ancient prophet Amos saw one in the hand of God. The sight was solemn and suggestive.

No one looks with pleasure upon a building which is askew—at least, he would not choose to reside in it. In some parts of the "black country," where the ground is undermined with coal-pits, the houses appear to the visitor as if they were all in a state of intoxication.

Bending forward this way, or reclining that, they seem as if they were ready to tumble into ruin, and are only held up by strong, unsightly bands of iron, everywhere to be seen, binding them in a firm embrace. In the salt districts of Cheshire, too, owing to the incessant pumping up of the brine from below, the land undulates like the ocean after a storm, and not only private houses, but public buildings and churches are to be seen leaning this way and that, as if a gentle push would tumble them all into ruin.

It need hardly be said that in such instances there is nothing to be laid to the door of architect, contractor, or mason; it is through no fault of theirs that the houses totter as they do. This cannot be alleged in regard to certain structures in our large cities, which, despite a firm ground to stand on, lie at all sorts of angles, need propping up with unsightly beams, and sometimes come crashing down, burying their inmates in the ruin.

THE DIVINE PLUMB-LINE.

A few years ago some workmen were engaged in trying to remove a piece of the old London wall. It was no easy job. They tried with hammers, then with pickaxes; then they had to borrow the help of some stalwart railway laborers. But all to no purpose—the wall seemed only to smile at their endeavors. At last they were obliged to resort to the use of some explosive to blow it up, as they would a block of solid rock. That is hardly the way we build nowadays.

The famous Campanile, or Clock Tower of Pisa, in Italy, has for more than five centuries been reckoned, if not one of the wonders, at least one of the curiosities of the world. In height a hundred and eighty feet, so obliquely does it stand that the top projects not less than thirteen feet beyond the perpendicular; and though its long endurance might be enough to guarantee one's safety in ascending, yet many fear to climb, and I confess to have been one of those who are content to scrutinize it from the level of the grass below.

The tower of Pisa is visited by thousands, undoubtedly for the reason that it is probably the only instance in the world of a lofty structure, so far off the centre of gravity, still refusing to fall. But men cannot afford the risk of erecting towers after this fashion, and if there is one thing more than another on which the good reputation of a builder rests, it is that the walls he raises will bear the most rigid test which the plumb-line can afford.

Amos sees the Almighty with a plumb-line in His hand. It is not an edifice of stone, or brick, or wood that He is testing, but an edifice of character. All men are builders, and their workmanship shall be submitted to a rigid scrutiny. In a striking passage in one of his essays, Thomas Carlyle says, "Man is the architect of circumstance. Our strength is measured by our plastic power. From the same materials one man builds palaces, another hovels, one warehouses, another villas; bricks and mortar are mortar and bricks until the architect makes them something else. Thus it is, that in the same family, in the same circumstances, one man rears a stately edifice, whilst his brother, vacillating and incompetent, lives forever amid ruins."

The plumb-line is the most impartial of instruments. Indeed you cannot construct it, though you try, so as to make it tell false. The workman uses a great variety of tools, any of which may be more or less defective: his planes, saws, rules, squares, levels—any one of these may be faulty or imperfect, but a mere infant with a piece of cord and a bit of lead can make a plummet of unerring accuracy, for it is simply obedient to the great law of gravitation.

No builder can challenge its fidelity; more true than the magnetic needle to the pole does that pendant drop towards the centre of our planet. A balance can be tampered with, a foot-rule or yard-measure may be inaccurate, a spirit-level may be untrue; but the simplest plumb-line must of necessity be correct. And—there is no partiality with God.

His law, and no human whim or fancy, is to be the standard of conduct and character. Even the world demands a straight up and down religion. A great deal of modern piety is adapted to suit prevailing notions and imperfect codes of morality.

One is too ready to conclude that what society says must be right, and that what the newspapers applaud is good; whereas the only infallible test is God's eternal truth. Indeed, all religions but one begin at the wrong end. The religion of the Bible insists that a man's first business is to be right with God, and then keep according to line: "Do justly, love mercy, and walk humbly before Him." It is a popular notion in these days that a man may construct his religion of any fashion he pleases. As though a stonemason were to say, "Of what use is the plumb-line to me? That old-fashioned thing I have no need for; my own eye is sufficient for me." He would not be long in discovering his mistake. Remember, if the wall shows any bulge or deflection, it is not an easy matter to put it right when it is finished. Down the whole structure must come, and be commenced anew. There are those who built up the fabric of their religion years ago, but built it aslant, and they have never been able to get it right since. They had unbounded confidence in the correctness of their own moral vision; they kept looking at the edifice as it arose, and satisfied themselves that it was strictly vertical; whereas, the instant the divine plumb-line was applied, the whole structure was condemned.

The whole subject is instructive, and suggestive chiefly of two lessons. As we listen to those solemn words, "Judgment will I lay to the line, and righteousness to the plummet," we are thrown back for our eternal hope on the imputed obedience of One who has fulfilled all righteousness; and are reminded that if we profess this evangelical faith, nothing less must be our ambition than to bring up our common life to the divine and faultless standard.

IX.

A NOTABLE ELEVEN.

THE Old Book tells us of a band of young men from the hill country of Gad who rendered noble service to King David in a time of peril, and whose names, engraven on a tablet more durable than granite or marble, are worthy to be reproduced upon this page, as follows: "Ezer, the first; Obadiah, the second; Eliab, the third; Mishmannah, the fourth; Jeremiah, the fifth; Attai, the sixth; Eliel, the seventh; Johanan, the eighth; Elzabad, the ninth; Jeremiah, the tenth; Machbanai, the eleventh" (1 Chron. xii. 9-13). Splendid fellows they were, hardy sons of the mountains, "their faces like the faces of lions, and their feet swift as the wild gazelle's." These were all the descendants of Gad: every one of them was born to be a captain; the least of them was worth a hundred ordinary men, and the greatest of them was worth a thousand. Now, in times like our own, when so many of our youth are not worth their salt, so limp and nerveless that it would take a score or two of them to make one hero, it may not be amiss to look at these grand figures, whose names, we may be sure, are not without a purpose on the sacred record.

The incident with which they are associated occurred at a time in David's history when he was being pursued as an outlaw by King Saul, and had to flee for his life. He had taken refuge in the south country of the Philistines, in the fortress of Ziklag, where he resided for sixteen months.

Whilst there, biding his time, he was joined by successive detachments of men, who knew that his cause was a just one, and who cheerfully endured hardships and risked their lives to prove their loyalty. One of these companies was the eleven whose names have already been given.

I observe, first of all, they came from the country. They were stout, rough fellows from the mountains. Their home lay to the east of the Jordan, in that high tableland that stretched away towards the northern frontiers of Arabia.

They were highlanders indeed; born and bred among the forests and cattle pastures of the mountains of Gilead, accustomed to the dangers and delights of a free, roving Bedouin life, and but little acquainted with the higher civilization and softer manners of Judah. There is often something very attractive in the character of such men.

The dull conventionality, commonplace ways and matter-of-factness of lower regions are unknown to them; their spirit seems to catch the inspiration of the noble mountains, dark ravines, and lowering tempests; and the result is a fearless heroism and a patriotic fire, not unmingled with superstition, which make them invaluable as friends and terrible as foes. Possibly they are a trifle too warlike and keen for battle, just a little hot-headed and pugnacious; like some of the old Scottish clansmen that were never at peace unless they were fighting.

There was a shrewd farmer who had a great many sheep on the mountain and a great many in the valley; and when asked the difference between them, he said that those in the valley gave the best meat, but that those on the hills had the stoutest horns. If I come across a young man with strong horns, rough, bold, impetuous, and daring, I generally find he has some Highland blood in him.

I do not necessarily refer to Scotland. Many other lands have their highlands too, and can produce some veritable sons of the mountains. And, as a rule, these fellows have good stuff in them. It is not a bad thing to have two stout horns, they are often needed in the battle with sin; and if they are well used, they grow. "The horns of the righteous shall be exalted."

Do not be ashamed, William or George, of being a young man from the country. These smart town fops may laugh at some of your country ways, but it would be well for them if they had a little of your moral backbone. The fact is, I don't know what we should do in our large cities without the continual importation of fresh life from the country.

It is often a very fine type of character that is developed, as I may say, in the mountains of Gad. Where will you find in history a more scrupulous conscientiousness than that of Jephthah, a more genuine generosity than that of old Barzillai, or a sterner righteousness than that of Elijah? And each of these men belonged to the mountain tribe. Ah! this is just the stamp of men so much needed amongst ourselves; the least of them is worth a hundred, and the greatest of them is worth a thousand. Only let such free, enthusiastic natures be controlled by noble principles and inspired with lofty ideals, and grand will be their record in the world's work. The very impetuosity and spontaneity of such men will urge them to arduous tasks in God's cause from which weaker souls would only shrink in dismay.

But, secondly, we must not overlook their fine physical development. Splendid and imposing fellows were they, powerful athletes, these eleven of Gilead. "Men of might, men of war, fit for battle, who could handle shield and buckler . . . these are they that went over Jordan in the first month, when it had overflown all its banks; and they put to flight all them of the valleys, both towards the east and towards the west." Undoubtedly, a great soul is sometimes enshrined in a miserable body; all the same, we ought to regard these cases as exceptional, and strive to enlist in the cause of truth and of goodness the manifold powers and energies of man.

Given a young man of perfect health, whose pulses beat with unalloyed vitality, whose whole body, as Paul exhorts, is a temple of the Holy Ghost, and what wondrous possibilities for good are his! Admired by all for his fine physical powers, his influence as a sturdy soldier of Jesus Christ will be all-powerful, not only on feeble brethren in the faith, but on the careless and vicious.

The Christian Church in these days must not be open to the reproach of consisting largely of milksops, unmanly creatures, limp as blotting paper, soft as jelly-fish, men who almost need to be wheeled about in perambulators, and dare hardly speak above their breath. No, no, that won't do; it must be made clear that religion appeals to what is noblest in humanity, and tends to the invigoration, not only of the mental faculties, but even of the bodily powers. Not long ago a gentleman asked a friend of mine, " Do you know the youth I have a particular dislike to? He is what you call the Christian young man." "Do you mean a prig?" said the other. "Yes! that is just about it."

Well, you do occasionally meet such an objectionable specimen, a prim, self-conscious, narrow-souled individual, like the pharisaic lad who hoped his landlady would accept of his faultless Christian example in lieu of payment for his weekly bill; a youth of that sort wants to be put under the pump, and have the conceit taken out of him. The religion of Christ is essentially manly and invigorating; it is bracing, like the mountain breezes of Gilead. It is a true tonic for the mind and heart, entering into the recesses of our nature and imparting strength, courage, and endurance. It is intensely real—a safeguard to the tempted, an inspirer to noble life.

When I look at these eleven of Gad, courageous as lions, fleet of foot as roes, and nimble as fishes to swim the full-flooded Jordan; and when I see all their powers devoted to the service of David, I say, this is the type of men we want in our day to lead the van in the great conflict with iniquity and error. Give us bold, broad-chested, well-developed men to take the front, and victory is not far off!

X.

THE COMPENDIUM OF CHRISTIAN DUTY.

THE practical side of religion is well and concisely expressed by the ancient Morashite when he declares that what the Most High requires of one professing to be a worshiper of Him is, that he "do justly, and love mercy, and walk humbly with his God." Of course, something of the greatest importance is supposed to precede all this. The formula of duty here provided is not meant to cover all that comes under the head of religion; still less does it indicate where true religion begins: *that* has been already specified by the prophet.

To the soul that is uneasy and self-condemned, and whose passionate inquiry is, "Wherewith shall I come before the Lord?" or, "With what sacrifices shall I make atonement for my sins?" His reply is, "He hath showed thee, O man, what is good;" He hath already pointed thee to the true and only expiation, to the Divine Redeemer predicted in the former chapter (Micah v. 3, etc.). But when faith finds its resting-place in the great transaction of Calvary, then Christian duty begins; and it is succinctly set forth in this triple formula.

It is important to remember where such obligation begins. It starts with *justice:* "that thou do justly." No doubt this forms but a part of the duty binding upon a Christian; indeed, though his whole character and life be ruled by strictest equity, he may still be far short of the moral standard enjoined. But, unhappily, the case is not uncommon of a person attempting to compound for a certain looseness here by an exceptional measure of the mercifulness and devout humility which are equally inculcated by the prophet. We have met with men who were benevolent and sympathetic to a degree, and seemingly possessed of a deeply religious spirit, who were nevertheless rather *shady* in their commercial transactions, and could, without compunction of conscience, lend themselves to practices incompatible with a high sense of honor.

Such men must be sternly reminded that no amount of kindness to the poor, and no depth of spiritual feeling, can be held to compensate for the lack of absolute honesty in all their worldly transactions. Religion must first of all prove itself in the domain of secular and every-day life. "The kingdom of God is righteousness," before it can be "peace and joy."

Nowhere more than here is thoroughness indispensable. The scandal of Christianity to-day is that, as in Micah's time, so many who profess to "lean upon the Lord" are not square in their bargains. Their religion begins at the wrong end. Get money by any means, is the principle upon which they act.

The wise man has written, "He that hasteth to be rich shall not be innocent," and the mercantile world is full of evidence of the truth of this. Young men are tempted to imagine that they can obtain wealth by a swifter and easier process than the practice of industry and economy, and are fascinated by the idea of fortunate speculations and splendid enterprises. Too often in the eager race for riches conscience becomes blind, and methods of doing business are resorted to which ought to be abhorrent and hateful to every man of principle.

It is clear that so long ago as the days of Solomon it was the practice of buyers and sellers in the markets of Jerusalem to attempt to overreach one another. A purchaser would beat down an article, and insist that it was not worth the sum demanded, and then, when he had secured it at the lowest point, he would go and tell every one what a sharp bargain he had struck, and how he had outwitted the merchant. "It is naught, it is naught, saith the buyer, but when he goeth his way, then he boasteth." No severer terms of reproach are found in Scripture than those which Micah addressed to the merchants and tradesmen of Samaria and Jerusalem, who with "scant measures," and "wicked balances," and "deceitful weights," would nevertheless "lean upon the Lord," and seek the consolations of religion. Duty then, no less than charity, begins at home. Never can it be right to take unfair advantage of another. The ban of Heaven is upon all forms of dishonesty. And, thank God, this is recognized by thousands of mercantile men in this and other lands. Strict integrity is still an article of high commercial value. It never pays in the long run to have God against you.

Excellent is the testimony given by an epitaph which was carved on the tombstone of a deceased merchant:—

> "His nay was nay without recall;
> His yea was yea and powerful all;
> He gave his yea with careful heed;
> His thoughts and words were well agreed;
> His word was bond and seal."

The next requirement is that thou "*love mercy.*" This is a step in advance, but a step demanded of every man who would be a Christian.

He that stops short at even-handed justice, content with an even balance, may be but a poor creature after all: clearly he is not in touch with his Maker.

It has been said that to return good for good is human; to return evil for good is devilish; to return good for evil is divine. Our life is to be regulated, not by the old arithmetical rules of rigid justice, but by the law of love engraven on the heart. All selfishness is to be raked out of the heart, and a new and heavenly fire kindled within.

Young men do well to remember this; for the softer graces are not seldom lacking even where there is a high sense of honor, and a stern uprightness of character. To be hard and inconsiderate is never manly; nor are sympathy and kindness any token of weakness.

There is a mode of doing business in these days which violates the eternal law of brotherhood, and is simply ruinous to small traders. Certain classes of goods are sold at so extremely low a figure that it is impossible for a man to make a living unless he has an amount of custom which he is never likely to command. Strong men elbow weak men out of the field altogether.

Satisfying their conscience that they are sternly honest in their dealings, they carry on a style of business which shows no mercy to their fellows, and feel not an atom of compunction though this and that good neighbor be crushed and ruined. But the two commands must not be disjoined; though your weights and balances are correct, and your lineal measures quite thirty-six inches to the yard, you must not imagine you are necessarily above reproach, so long as doing justly you still fail to love mercy also.

The third requirement is, of course, the highest of all: "*to walk humbly with thy God.*" Of two at least of the saints of the olden time, the record is borne that they walked with God.

To Enoch and Noah belongs this rare and honorable distinction. Too ready are we to take for granted that this is an attainment far beyond the reach of common men. We think it a standard to be attained only by one or two in a generation, by a Janeway, a Haliburton, or a McCheyne—men of rare spirituality, who have held close companionship with Heaven.

There is quite a mistake. Nothing less is required of every one who bears the Christian name. It speaks of a glowing and high-toned piety. It speaks of a life of prayer and communion with the Eternal; each day begun with fresh self-dedication to Him, and ended in the serene consciousness of His love. Never be contented with a lower level. Never be tempted to imagine that even a life of honesty and benevolence will suffice. Never be satisfied to live a day without intercourse with Heaven. Strive to feed on the hidden manna, and to know the secret of the Lord, which is with them that fear Him. Show that it is possible to live in the world and yet above it. The literal rendering of the ancient prophet's words is remarkable: "that thou humble thyself to walk with God." It is only with the humble that He will consent to walk; and it is only the humble that can walk with Him.

It is a strange but suggestive paradox—for here the lowest is also the highest level—as Montgomery well sings:—

> "The saint that wears the brightest crown
> In deepest adoration bends;
> The weight of glory bows him down
> The most when most his soul ascends;
> Nearest the Throne itself must be
> The footstool of humility."

This humbleness of mind is not incompatible with solid strength of character and a high self-respect. Unhappily it is allied in some minds with meanness of disposition, so that it is taken for granted that noble and chivalrous natures will recoil from it; but this arises from an entire misconception.

The man who truly humbles himself before God, exalts himself amongst his fellows, and acquires a personal dignity unknown to the vain and self-complacent; indeed, it is generally visible in his very mien. To "hold communion with the skies" is the surest way to command real respect on earth; nor is there any halo of glory so brightly radiant as that which encircles the head of a devout and consistent saint.

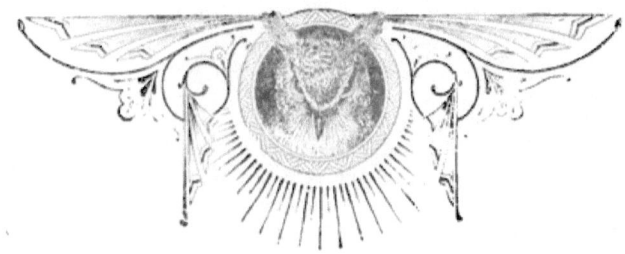

XI.

KEEPING THE HEART WITH DILIGENCE.

"KEEP thy heart with all diligence," says the wise man; literally, "above all keeping." Solomon has already exhorted us to take heed to our mouth, lips, eyes, feet; for each and all need to be carefully guarded. But, he virtually adds, give especial care to the custody of thy heart; and he supplies a very good reason, "For out of it are the issues of life." Even from a physical point of view this is perfectly true; but it is not less true in the moral and spiritual sense in which the writer meant it.

As I ponder this aphorism, the first thing that strikes me is that *some hearts are not worth the keeping*. The very best thing we can do is to get rid of them as soon as possible. The sooner we get new hearts the better. Scripture is most plain in telling us that no good can come out of these degenerate hearts that we have by nature. There is a vast amount of precious time lost, a great part indeed of many a man's lifetime thrown away, in vain efforts to get some good out of the natural heart, to amend the character and life, to do better for the future, to turn over a new leaf, without first of all getting a radical change within.

If every page of the book is soiled, to what purpose is it to "turn over a new leaf?" Ah! I have known men to spend the best years of their life in this hopeless business, only to give it up in despair; and then they came, just as they ought to have done at the beginning, to Him who says, "A new heart will I give you." There are not wanting among our public teachers those who are loud about cultivating the intellect, elevating the tastes, regulating the habits—all very good, but it is useless unless you begin at the heart. If the reservoir from which our houses are supplied with water contains some poisonous ingredients, what should we think of the sagacity of the counselor who advised laying down new pipes, or fitting up fresh cisterns, or introducing a newly-invented stopcock?

All would be fruitless till the fountain-head itself was made pure. So you may lay down excellent rules for your daily life. You may resolve to do this, and abstain from that, and to fashion your conduct according to some faultless standard—it is but a vain and profitless endeavor, until you have obtained a new heart.

Pursuing this metaphor on which Solomon's proverb appears to be based, it may be observed, secondly, that inasmuch as out of the heart are the issues of life, *it is important to keep the reservoir full.*

It is bad enough to have an empty head, but an empty heart is worse still. For, other things being equal, a man's force in the world is just in proportion to the fullness of his heart. We have known men who were seemingly without heart —icy, phlegmatic, cynical, unimpassioned beings, incapable of a really warm and generous impulse. Such men are mere ciphers in society—they accomplish no good. There may be a prim correctness about their behavior, but as regards any moral force in the world they are nobodies, they carry no momentum. Suppose the fires of a locomotive engine are out, or nearly out, you will not make it go at express speed by giving it a fresh coat of paint. But you may as well think to do so as expect by any outward culture to make one who is destitute of heart a real power in the world. Heart is power.

There may be no genius, there may be but slender intellectual acquirements; there may be very limited knowledge; yet, if there be a full and gracious heart, charged with zeal and fervor and enthusiasm, the man will make his impress on those around him. Better even the mistakes and blunders of an earnest and enthusiastic man, whose pulse beats strong, and whose soul is full to the brim and running over, than the cold correctness of one who never feels deeply about anything.

The third thing to note is, that if the heart is the reservoir out of which come the issues of life, *it is essential to keep it pure.* A full reservoir is not enough, the water must be clean. It is of no use having new pipes in our houses, and fresh mains under the streets, unless the source from which the supply comes is pure. Some time ago a good deal of just indignation was aroused among my neighbors on account of the character of the water supplied by the city water works, and a gentleman was known to remark that he could stock a fairly good aquarium with the animal life that found its way into his own cistern. A foul reservoir means spreading the seeds of pestilence and death. Precisely so. If the heart be not pure, you may be certain the thoughts will not be pure, nor the conversation, nor the life. It is impossible to overestimate the value of thorough transparency of character. Sometimes the remark is made regarding such and such a person, "I like that man, he is genuine and straightforward; you can see him through and through."

Fourthly, *the heart should be kept tranquil.* This is a source of comfort and strength. Not an easy thing in these days—we live in a fast, feverish age. With large numbers of commercial men the pulse beats too swiftly, the nerves are overstrained, the mind is held on the rack, and this state of things is far from being favorable to health, either of body or soul.

Be assured, without calmness of spirit the life will not be happy. The state of the heart has far more to do with one's comfort, success, and prosperity than most persons imagine. We are all but certain to meet with varied troubles. Some of us will get sadly knocked about in the world, will meet with many a reverse and disappointment; but a heart that is fixed on God can bear all these things with equanimity. You have often seen, possibly in your Bible, a map of Egypt and Palestine, with a curious zigzag line in red drawn across it, denoting the journey of the covenant people through the wilderness to the Promised Land. Truly did Moses say, "He led them about, He instructed them." Such is the pathway of nearly every Christian through this desert world; but what a blessed thing that the red track comes out at Canaan! Trusting in God, we can safely leave both present and future with Him.

There is a story of a Swiss martyr, who, on the day of his execution (he was burned at the stake) just before the fire was kindled, craved permission to say a word to the judge who had condemned him. In the presence of all the people, he addressed him thus: "Sir, I have but one last request to make, and it is that you will now approach, and place your hand first upon my heart and then upon your own, and tell this multitude which of the two beats more violently." It need not be said that the judge dared not fulfill the request, for he saw in the heroic martyr a calm tranquillity of soul to which he himself was a stranger. God help us to keep our hearts with all diligence, full and pure and transparent and tranquil, that from them, as from a clear mountain spring, there may issue influences of health and benediction to gladden our own lives and bless all around us.

XII.

A COMPLETE LIFE.

OF nearly every human undertaking it is a characteristic feature that, whatever energy of purpose may be thrown into its commencement, it remains at the last unfinished. Incompleteness is stamped on every mortal enterprise. The workman lays down his tools before his task is ended. Man puts his hand to many a job, the execution of which he is never to perfect.

Countless are the illustrations that at once offer themselves. There, in the studio of Michael Angelo, I see upon the canvas the inception of a splendid painting; but little more than the outline exists. Beside the easel lie oils and brushes as the artist left them; but already the fingers of the renowned genius are cold in death.

The chisel of Thorwaldsen is never to give the finishing touch to that fine group in marble which, at a glance, betrays the Danish sculptor's marvelous power.

Matthew Henry's "Commentary" has to be completed by another pen than that which wrote the bulk of those portly volumes.

On his study table, at Gad's Hill, lies the unfinished manuscript of the last novel that Charles Dickens began.

The grandest engineering achievement of our time, Brooklyn Bridge, was dedicated amid flying banners and universal congratulations; but the architect of that gigantic bridge which spans the East River never lived to see its completion. And so one might go on mentioning project after project which human enterprise started, but failed to carry through, and of whose sanguine originator it might be truly said, "This man began to build, but was not able to finish."

It is a still more sad and solemn fact that every man's life is, at the best, but a broken and imperfect thing. God gives to each of us a mission to accomplish, a task to fulfill; but, was there ever one but the faultless Redeemer who at life's close could dare to say, "I have finished the work which Thou gavest Me to do?"

The words may set us a-thinking; for the same testimony every man should aim at being able to bear. We learn, first, that *life is given us for work*.

Not so, thinks many a young man to-day. Life, he imagines, is given for pleasure, for frolic, for amusement. The world is a big playground provided for our diversion, and our best plan, as long as we remain in it, is to take the maximum of pleasure with the minimum of toil. Labor, says he, is the curse of the fall; therefore the more idle we are, the happier we shall be.

Never was there a greater mistake; but the notion explains the total failure in life of many a man who might have done fairly well. It would be more correct to say that the world is a vast workshop; and that every one is called upon to find his special department, and do his own share. The day is past for any one, man or woman, to command real respect whose time and talents are not turned to practical purpose.

Labor, the curse of the fall! Nothing of the kind. Before our first parent had conceived one sinful thought, his Creator had put him into a garden to keep it and to dress it. He was not placed there to lounge in idleness, or dream his hours away, reposing on flowery beds that needed no hand to trim them; industry was from the beginning an ordained law of his being. Mere occupation is not enough; the great bulk of our race are intended for work. A life of refined culture and literary ease has, no doubt, great attractions; but such a life is only for a select few. With the vast majority of men, and of women too, nearly every day must have its share of drudgery and toil. It is easier, as some one has truly said, to write a good biography than to spend a life that is worth recording. It is not, as a rule, men of genius, but men of action, that push their way to wealth and honor. Practical knowledge and plain common sense, together with vigorous energy of will, do more to command success than all the brilliant talents of dilettanti schemers who never put their own hands to the work.

The second suggestion is that *every one has his own specific work to do*.

It is not enough to be occupied; not enough to be busy; we must endeavor to find out the particular work which each of us has to do. Sydney Smith says, "Be what nature intended you for, and you will succeed; be anything else, and you will be ten thousand times worse than nothing." As truly as the key is made for the lock, and the pillar prepared for the socket, so has every one been sent into this world for a special design; and our first business is to find out the groove we are intended to fill.

Too often we hear of square men being occupied in filling round holes; not that round men are not to be found to fill them, for it is just as often the case that the latter class are vainly endeavoring to occupy the square holes. The skillful horticulturist well knows that certain plants are adapted for a clay soil, and that others are fitted for a sandy or gravel; and if he overlooks this fact, he only lays up for himself failure and disappointment.

Let every one then study his aptitudes, and decide what is the line of service for which his Creator made him; for, indeed, there is no irreverence in his appropriating the words of the Divine Master, and speaking of "the work which Thou gavest me to do."

You are not called to do another man's work, but one for which you have received a special endowment, and just as you buckle on earnestly to it will your qualification for the task increase.

There is yet a third thought that must not be missed: *the whole work of a Christian's life is to be viewed as truly a work for God*. It is an egregious mistake, but one into which many fall, to suppose that we are doing God's work only when we are engaged in some strictly religious service.

There are plenty of men who virtually write over their shop or office door, "Business is business," and over their church or chapel door, "Religion is religion," and who think these things should never be mingled; but that is a wrong notion altogether.

No doubt a godly man, however pressing his secular employment may be, will try to devote some portion of his time and energy to distinctly religious work; but even this is not his highest service, for the most effective of all ways by which we can honor God and commend Christianity to the world, is the consecration to Him of all our labor, and the feeling that in effectually discharging our common daily duties, we are truly fulfilling "the work He gave us to do."

The last thought that meets us here is the importance of *carrying through to the end* whatever undertaking is assigned to us. "I have finished the work;" I have not left it half done; I have not bungled nor shirked it, but completed its execution.

Better have a humble sphere, and thoroughly fulfill its duties, than occupy a great position whose responsibilities we only imperfectly discharge. The greatest benefactors of mankind are by no means the men who fill the most conspicuous spheres. How many a name might be mentioned that has no place on the roll of fame, but whose possessor lived a noble, self-denying and fruitful life!

> "Whate'er your *forte*, to that your zeal confine,
> Let all your talents there concentered shine;
> As shallow streams, collected, form a tide,
> So talents thrive to one grand point applied."

XIII.

THE BOW OF PROMISE.

WHEN traveling on the saddle, some time ago, with a party of congenial friends, along the coasts of Tyre and Sidon, and when near the site of the ancient town of Zarephath or Sarepta, my attention was suddenly directed to a remarkable natural phenomenon. None of the company had ever witnessed, nor even heard of, the like before. For at least two hours, from ten in the morning until noon—the weather being fine and bright, though slightly hazy—a perfect ring, brilliant with all the colors of the rainbow, and with a diameter of about thirty degrees, encircled the sun. Unlike an ordinary rainbow, it was not a mere segment of a circle, nor an arch with its two piers resting on the earth, but a complete circle overhead, with the sun for its centre, and all the prismatic colors clear and well defined. In order to have a full view and lasting impression of so unusual an appearance, we dismounted, and lying flat on our backs on the ground (and protecting our eyes as best we were able), we watched with intense interest for some time the singular phenomenon. What could be the cause of it? Was it that showers of fine rain were falling in the higher regions of the atmosphere above us, but were dissipated in vapor before they could reach the earth? Whatever the explanation might be, the meteor was as beautiful as it was rare. I afterward learnt from the Professor of Astronomy at the American College in Beirout, that he also, though not so distinctly, had observed it, and that, like ourselves, he had never before seen or heard of a circular rainbow so near the zenith, and with colors of such extraordinary brightness and beauty.

The singular appearance gradually faded away after mid-day, but left a vivid impression on our minds, especially in connection with the interesting spot where it was witnessed, a spot so closely identified in the mind of every Bible reader with the story of the widow woman whose wants the prophet Elijah miraculously supplied. To the devout Christian one important lesson of the rainbow is the same which Zarephath suggests; and to him, indeed, it possesses a peculiar interest beyond what it has to other men, both on account of what Moses tells us of its origin, and on account of what St. John in the Apocalypse tells us of its spiritual significance.

To some persons who are firm believers in the constancy of Nature's laws, there is a serious difficulty presented by the former passage. They cannot believe that it was not until Noah's time that that beautiful form was seen, that for at least two thousand years the earth had existed under its present conditions without a rainbow ever appearing in the sky.

But there is in reality no occasion for one to vex himself on the point, inasmuch as the original word rendered "I do set," may mean, I do constitute or appoint. So that the passage does not require us to conclude that the rainbow was now for the first time formed, that it was a new thing which human eyes had never looked on before. It is quite possible—and the words may mean no more—that the Creator now gave to it a significance it had not hitherto possessed, and made it a token or pledge of the faithfulness of His promise.

But even if we so read the passage as to understand that the beautiful arch to which God directed Noah's eye was the first of the kind which His hand had painted on the heavens, an explanation offers itself that is at least worthy of notice.

No doubt, under such atmospheric conditions as we are familiar with, the earth being visited with rain and sunshine, an occasional rainbow is a necessity of the case. But was this always precisely the order of things? If there was no rain, there would, of course, be no bow.

Now, we are not without some basis for the notion that prior to the Deluge the earth was moistened and refreshed after a different manner. There is, in point of fact, no mention of rain before the flood, except in this remarkable sentence: "For the Lord God had *not* caused it to rain upon the earth," with which is coupled the interesting statement, "But there went up a mist from the earth and watered the whole face of the ground." It is just possible, it is reasonably conceivable, that by the daily overspreading of a thick, vaporous mist over the land, depositing its watery contents upon every form of vegetation, the ground was quickened and fertilized; every day, therefore, having its period of coolness, when, so to speak, the brow of nature was refreshed. Can this be alluded to in the expression, "And they heard the voice of the Lord God walking in the garden in the cool of the day?"

No one, probably, will read the narrative in Genesis without concluding that the rainbow on which the patriarch gazed when the waters were assuaged, was not merely a pledge that no more would such a deluge overwhelm the earth, but also a guarantee of the perpetuity of the seasons, and was closely connected with the promise that "while the earth remained seed-time and harvest, and cold and heat, and summer and winter, and day and night, should not cease."

It is our privilege to look on every harvest as a fresh token of Divine faithfulness, and every fleeting rainbow should serve to quiet anxious thought, as it renews the pledge of the Almighty's bounty.

Indeed, to the eye of science, as well as to that of faith, the beautiful arch in the heavens is full of significance and promise. The primary or elementary colors are three in number—namely, blue, yellow, and red. The rainbow is, in reality, a triple arch, or three arches placed side by side, and partially overlapping, so that the colors blend into one another; and each of these arches is evidence of a certain power or influence resident in the beams of the sun. That glorious orb of day possesses three corresponding properties or influences. The first (for want of a better term) I must call the chemical influence, the second is light, and the third is heat. These three influences are linked and identified with the three colors I have named respectively. The blue is the chemical ray, the yellow the ray of light, and the red the ray of heat.

Now, the blue or chemical rays are those which, penetrating the soil more readily than the others, effect the germination of the seed, and the earliest growth of the infant plant. These are most abundant and powerful in the season of spring. The yellow or light rays, which are most abundant in early summer, are those which operate upon the plant chiefly when it has reached the surface of the soil, and they effect the formation of the stem or wood; whilst the red or heat rays, which exert their influence principally in the end of the summer and in autumn, cause the development of flower and fruit. I speak, of course, of a general and dominating law. The rainbow, therefore, intelligently observed and understood, is, in fact, a pictorial image of the analyzed powers of the sun; and so long as the solar rays, refracted by the raindrops, produce that beautiful meteor in the sky, so long we have evidence that the three great influences identified with spring, summer, and autumn—in other words, the powers of germination or seed-awakening, of lignification or stem-forming, and of fructification or fruit-producing—are still resident in the beams of the sun.

So that that bow in the cloud proclaims, as often as we behold it, the continuance of the three great energies of Nature, by which the soil is persuaded to yield its annual harvest.

Instead, then, of saying with the poet—

> " When science from Creation's face
> Enchantment's veil withdraws,
> What glorious visions yield their place
> To cold material laws!"

we should rejoice in the light which science throws upon nature's phenomena, and be stirred to yet higher notes of gratitude and praise.

> The sound, practical good sense of the counsels given by Dr. Davidson in the two following talks to young men renders them a fitting close to this volume.

COMPANIONSHIP WITH FOOLS.

EACH Book in the Bible has its own special characteristic; and it is well for us, when studying a particular passage, to keep in mind the main feature or end of the book in which it occurs, for thus we shall be more likely to arrive at its true meaning. Now, the distinguishing characteristic of this Book of Proverbs is, that it sets before us the highest wisdom, and religion as the highest form of prudence. This central thought gives a complexion to every sentence in the book. The godly man is viewed as pre-eminently the wise man; and the sinner as the simpleton and fool. There are, indeed, other parts of the Bible in which sin is spoken of as folly; but nowhere is this aspect of it so urged, and brought to the front, as it is here.

Sin is a *mistake* as well as a crime. In yielding to temptation, we not only offend God, but do ourselves damage. To do wrong is foolish, senseless, suicidal. Apart from every higher consideration, it is an act of gross stupidity. Sin never pays. Not once within these past six thousand years has a man acted wisely in doing a thing which was morally wrong.

You see, then, that the argument of King Solomon in this book is in great part utilitarian. I do not say that this is the highest form of argument; but yet it is not without its value. Placed as we are in this world, an appeal to our self-interest will always come to us with power. Self-love is a different thing from selfishness. The precepts alike of law and gospel, whilst they deprecate the latter, address themselves to the former. It is to our highest interest to be righteous; but "destruction shall be to the workers of iniquity."

That you will find or make companions is a matter taken for granted; but at the outset of life, it is well to weigh seriously this royal adage (as true to-day as when—a thousand years before Christ—it dropped from the pen of Solomon): "He that walketh with wise men shall be wise; but a companion of fools shall be destroyed." That is to say, a young man will very soon take the color of those with whom he associates. "Tell me with whom you go," says an old proverb, "and I will tell you what you are." Society you must have and will have. Man is a gregarious animal, and the sweetest pleasures, as well as the greatest dangers of life, are linked with this love of company, of which nearly all of us are conscious. So many thousands of young men have there been whose ruin is put down to bad companions, that I should be guilty of a great omission did I not take up this subject; and therefore, without further delay, I wish to speak a word of caution *as to the kind of associates you should be careful to avoid*. Satan has a big family, all of whom should be kept at arm's length; but there are two or three of them I would particularly mention, and warn you against, men who are "fools" in Solomon's sense of the word, and whose companionship can only be to your destruction.

Never make companionship with a buffoon. Do not choose for your associate the frivolous jester, the man who seems hardly capable of a grave or serious thought, but turns everything into an occasion for merriment. In dull times such a fellow is likely to be much run after. He keeps a company in good humor; his fund of ready wit is inexhaustible; his hits and jokes, and sallies are enough to banish care and keep any circle in a roar of laughter. Thus the lively wit is a general favorite; there is something in almost every sentence he utters, and even in the roguish twinkle of his eye, that seems to shed a sparkling light around, and make the burdens of life more easy to bear.

Well, I am not going to condemn witticism, and fun, and repartee. Not at all. As Solomon says, "there is a time to laugh," as well as "a time to weep." There is a time to be playful and jocular, as well as a time to be serious and solemn. I do not see any reason why a Christian's face should be longer than any other man's; but I see many a reason why it should be brighter and merrier.

Never in my life do I remember of more wit and humor, and buoyancy of animal spirits being crammed into one day than on a day which I once spent in the country in company with the late eminent Wesleyan minister, Dr. Punshon, who knew when to be grave and when to be gay, and whose dying words were, "Jesus is to me a living, bright reality." Not a bit of sympathy have I with the narrow-minded folk who think it a sin to laugh, and who have nothing but denunciation for those who are playful and humorous. I say God has created within us a faculty of mirthfulness, which He meant for use. When indulged in moderation, it is a wholesome thing, and helps to lighten the serious labors of life. If God has given you a little of this quicksilver, be thankful for it. Stone, and iron, and lead, though heavy and dull, are more useful articles; but every gift He bestows has its purpose.

But some men lay themselves out for habitual jesters, nor do they stop at anything—religion, worship, death, eternity—there is no subject so serious that they will not vent their wit upon it. Always punning, joking, quibbling; everything appears to have for them its comic or farcical side. And so they go on through life, as though they had no higher view of it than one prolonged amusement. "Note such men, and have no company with them, that they may be ashamed."

Have nothing to do with the cynic. He is a very ugly character, though somewhat hard to describe. He has a wondrous faculty of sneering; and is almost incapable of believing good of anybody. He can never see a sterling quality in any man, and is always ready with his insinuations and innuendoes. With him, all human actions but his own are either openly bad or secretly bad; and the more pure and virtuous they really are, the more hypocrisy does he detect in them. He is well-named "cynic," a word which comes from the Greek for dog; for like an ill-tempered cur, he snarls at every one. With him religion is cant, benevolence is just a cunning form of selfishness, and virtue is a sham. If you tell him such a man has contributed liberally to some charity, ten to one he will say it is a good advertisement. If you say of such another, he is a devoted member of the Church, he will add, it is to advance his business. Rotten at heart himself, he cannot conceive of such a thing as genuine principle; and roundly asserts that self-interest is the basis of every action.

A man like that is a pest and a curse to the community. He scatters poison wherever he goes. The young give him credit for wonderful far-sightedness and knowledge of human nature; and, therefore, rather court his society, as one who "knows what's what," and can pierce through all shams. Alas, we are all naturally ready enough to listen to anything that throws discredit on religion; and when a creature such as I have described gets among those who are not yet settled in their convictions, he may do as much mischief in a month as will take years to eradicate. Keep clear of the cynic as you would of a man steeped in smallpox; for his influence upon you will be "only evil, and that continually."

Give a wide berth to the skeptic. There is no fool so great as the man who says there is no God; and the companion of such a fool will be destroyed. I would most earnestly caution you against associating with any one who rejects the Bible, and denies the Christian religion, however amiable and virtuous may be his character.

It is getting quite the fashion with a certain class of young men to talk as though Christianity were now an exploded fable. They will tell you that some men have a religious instinct, just as most men have a taste for music, or for poetry, or for architecture, or for botany, or for some other art or science; and that there is no harm in gratifying that instinct by some form of devotion; but that all religions are alike good or bad: it is simply a question of taste or predilection; but the basis of all is superstition. They would put Jesus Christ on the same level with Plato, and Socrates, and Pythagoras, and Confucius, and Mohammed; and treat religion as a pure question of philosophy.

They forget that man has a moral nature and a conscience, as well as an intellect, and that these demand what only the Gospel can supply.

You will never reap any good from men of that stamp, but you will derive an enormous amount of injury. Doubt and unbelief, when once enkindled in the soul, are hard to eradicate. Far better strengthen your religious faith than imperil it. Never cultivate the friendship of one who would rob you of your trust in Christ. The internal evidence which the Bible possesses of its divine authority is of itself sufficient to silence the caviller, and command our reverent belief. All the attacks that have been made upon it—and no citadel on earth has been so stormed and assailed—leave it to-day impregnable as ever; its influence wider and mightier than it ever was before. Believe me, my brothers, you will only prepare for yourselves bitterness and regret, if you accept the companionship of men who have cast off the faith. Rather be it yours with the Psalmist to say, "I am a companion of them that fear Thee, and of them that keep Thy precepts."

Reject the company of the libertine. Most men have to fight a battle with the passions of their lower nature quite severe enough, without courting the society of those who will throw all their influence on the wrong side. One immoral and licentious youth may prove a curse to a score of as fine young fellows as ever came up to seek a living in a great city.

Such a man does not show his vileness all at once. On the contrary, there may be an air of polish and virtue about him, which completely deceives you on first acquaintance. The devil takes good care to scatter flowers over the pitfalls he has laid. You say, a more good-hearted fellow never lived. You get to like him. He is kind and generous, possesses lively spirits, sings a good song, can tell a capital story, is very free with his money, and, altogether, is "excellent company." So your acquaintance ripens, and—all the rest follows.

The man I am now entreating you to shun has no idea of hard work; with him pleasure is everything, and that pleasure of the grossest kind. As a matter of course, he drinks, for all his ideas of enjoyment are linked with a free use of alcohol. His nerves exhausted by sensual indulgence, he must needs resort to stimulants, and he is never satisfied unless others join with him in his potations. His haunts are the taverns and casinos and singing saloons. If he has money, most probably he gambles; or, at least, squanders it upon everything that is foolish and vicious. No mistake, he is a "fast man," for money, character, health, all quickly go; and, ten to one, he himself gallops into an early grave.

Of all the intimate associates of my young days, I had but one who turned out to be of this description. Born in affluence, with every advantage of culture and education, an only son, and possessed of pleasing manners as well as of a vigorous constitution, he seemed to have a happy career before him; but at sixteen years of age he began a career of vice, and before his twenty-first year was reached, might have been seen in the streets of ——, bloated and haggard, a very picture of wretchedness. Poor, miserable fellow! he never attained his majority, but died a profligate's death.

Most of you have heard or read of the learned Sir Matthew Hale. When quite a youth, he fell into the society of some vicious young men, who very nearly proved his ruin. Being invited to a great merrymaking, he met with an incident, which proved the turning-point in his career. During the carouse, one of the company drank so much wine, that at last he fell down as dead on the floor. All present were much alarmed, and did what they could to arouse him from his stupor; but Hale went into an adjoining room, and falling on his knees, besought God earnestly for his friend, and also that he himself might be forgiven, and then and there he made a solemn vow that he would henceforth shun such company, and " never drink another toast as long as he lived."

I dare say some of you think you are perfectly safe though you do associate with men whom you know to be living improper lives. You don't like to "cut" an old friend; you think you can still keep up the intimacy without falling into evil ways. Remember, these words are the words of divine wisdom, and are written here expressly for your warning, " The companion of fools shall be destroyed."

As in nature all bodies receive or give out heat, until there is an equilibrium of temperature, so there is a radiation of character upon character. Whether conscious of it or not, we are slowly and surely affected by the influence of those with whom we daily mingle. Any sign of want of sterling principle should be enough to make you draw back at once from another's society. If you detect too surely meanness, untruthfulness, or any form of incipient profanity, that should be quite sufficient to decide you to steer clear of such a person. Cowper's principle admits of wide application:

> "I would not enter on my list of friends,
> Tho' graced with polished manners and fine sense
> (Yet wanting sensibility), the man
> Who needlessly sets foot upon a worm."

Always select for your most intimate companions those for whom, in your inmost heart, you have a profound respect. Secure, if it be possible, the friendship of men in whom you see qualities that you admire, and would fain possess.

If you tell me *where you pick up your friends*, I shall have a good idea of their value. There are thousands of instances of an acquaintanceship that has sprung up casually on the street, or on the car, or at the tavern door, or in some place of questionable amusement; and too many of these prove woeful and disastrous. No lack of vampires—friends of the sucker order—who stick to you while they can get anything out of you, but not a moment longer. Leeches fasten on the living. but drop off from the dead. As Shakespeare says:

> " Every man will be thy friend
> Whilst thou hast wherewith to spend;
> But if store of crowns be scant,
> No man will supply thy want."

Lay this down as a sound principle; no Christian young man will find real satisfaction in the friendship of one who is not himself a Christian.

You cannot be too careful in your selection. Youthful years run very quickly away, and the companionships you then form will leave their impress on your whole life. Of course, in urging this cautiousness, I do not mean that I would have you to be saucy, or proud, or misanthropic. A warm-hearted man must have friends, he cannot be happy without them. It is only a mean, selfish nature that can be content to remain isolated and alone. Robinson Crusoe might glory on his lonely island in being " monarch of all he surveyed," but he was heartily glad when he got the company of the man Friday. Even the companionship of the dumb animals is better than none. Sir Walter Scott's dog, Maida, and Dr. Johnson's cat, Hodge, cannot be dissociated from their memory. The social, chatty hours spent with their chums by such men as Charles Lamb, and Sydney Smith, and Lord Macaulay, have an intense interest and attractiveness all their own. Many a pleasant day have I spent at Craigcrook, in Midlothian, where every room, and garden-seat, and tree seemed redolent with the fragrance of the delightful dialogues which Lord Jeffrey used to have there with his literary friends. Religion does not frown upon such enjoyment; rather does it develop and encourage it. There is no freemasonry to compare with the fellowship that unites those who love and serve a common Saviour.

Ah! brothers, the first friend I would have you all to seek and find is Jesus Christ Himself. To know the sweetness of His friendship you must first possess the joy of His salvation. Oh! what a happy, happy thing would it be if every one of you were a decided Christian. I would to God that I could persuade each of you to come over to the Lord's side. I know you mean to do so some day, but oh! delays are dangerous; and many, who have had the same intentions, have passed unprepared into the presence of their God. It is the most awful thing a man can do to reject the outstretched hand of the Divine Saviour. You say, God forbid that I should do that! But that is just what you are doing if you do not come right out of unbelief and worldliness, and with God's help be out and out a Christian. Decide at once between two worlds, one or other of which is to be your portion for ever. Is it possible, that, for the sake of hugging your sins a little longer, you will imperil your immortal soul? If there is but half a thought or wish in your heart just now to turn over a new leaf, and be a Christian, God Almighty fix that purpose, and make it permanent. How I should rejoice to know that some of you had been brought to the feet of the Saviour. Believe me, His is not a hard hand; His is not a cold heart. No frown upon His brow; no angry words upon His lips. Some of us can tell you, for we have proved Him, that "His is love beyond a brother's." "He will not quench the smoking flax, nor break the bruised reed." I advise every one of you to come to a decision. Choose ye whom ye will serve. Determine which of two eternities is to be yours. Select the road you are to travel, the goal you are to pursue, the company you are to take. "He that walketh with wise men shall be wise; but the companion of fools shall be destroyed."

THE CONCLUSION OF THE WHOLE MATTER.

AT the close of a volume, it is not an uncommon thing to have a brief epitome or *résumé* of the whole. In a few telling words you have the sum of the argument, the gist of all that has gone before, and are thus the better able to grasp it firmly in your memory. I like, in taking up a book, to find a "table of contents" at the beginning, or a good condensed summary at the end. It helps you. You cannot carry an octavo volume in your mind, but you can retain a few pithy, pungent sentences. You may not be able to remember a series of addresses, but you can grip the pointed "conclusions" at which the speaker arrives.

Though our subjects have been very varied, the scope, or drift, has been the same, and I have thought that I might try to show you what that scope is—what has been the drift of all our teaching—and the words of Ecclesiastes come ready to my hand, "Let us hear the conclusion of the whole matter: Fear God, and keep His commandments, for this is the whole duty of man."

To understand exactly the force of King Solomon's words, you must know what was the object he set before him when he wrote this book. He meant it as a record of the grand and unexampled experiments he made in search of man's highest good. He tells us in the second chapter that this was the great inquiry which he set himself to prosecute. "What was that good for the sons of men which they should do under the heaven all the days of their life?" How can man best fulfill the end of his being? How can he attain to the highest measure of happiness?

A noble inquiry indeed, and worthy of the wisest of men to pursue. Well, he had splendid materials for making it. Never man had such a chance as he. I suppose that since the world was made unto this day there has never been such wealth, such splendor, such magnificence, and, withal, so fertile a mind, able to extract from the resources of earth all the satisfaction and pleasure they could yield. The world seemed literally to exhaust itself upon that man. It emptied itself into his lap. It spread its treasures at his feet. It lavished on him all its luxuries and delights. It pressed the rarest wine to his lips. It set the richest gems in his crown. It warbled the sweetest music in his ear. He tells us in this book how he had everything material that fancy could prompt or heart could desire. Houses and gardens, and vineyards, and orchards, and pools for fish, and stately upholstery, and silver plate, and gold plate, till they actually trimmed the candles with snuffers of gold, and scooped out the ashes of the grate with shovels of gold.

I see before me, like a petrified dream, the regal palace, in all the snowy whiteness of its virgin marble. Around the towers there flutter birds of richest plumage and of rarest song. The gardens are gay with a floral beauty, to which every clime has been tributary; and I have read, that to this day, non-indigenous flowers are found by botanists near Jerusalem—flowers found nowhere else in Palestine—the lineal descendants of the very plants which Solomon collected from foreign lands. Listen to the strains of that wonderful orchestra. Inhale the perfumed spray of those glittering fountains. See the peacocks strutting under those spreading cedars. Mark those sculptured figures, almost breathing with life. Look at stair, and porch, and corridor, and gallery, adorned with all the embellishments of art. Curtains of Tyrian tapestry. Fragrance of cinnamon, and calamus, and frankincense. Glitter of jewelry, till the eye is dazzled and confused. And hark! the prancing of proud horses brought up to the palace gate, that the royal princes leap into the saddle for a grand parade; or to the thunder of chariots, whose fiery chargers, with throbbing nostril, and flaunting mane, and golden caparison, make the earth quake with their trampling hoofs.

To say all this, is only to begin an inventory of Solomon's resources. With an intelligence amounting to genius, and a wisdom that has never been equaled, he applied himself to the study of nature; and, five hundred years before Aristotle (whom some have called the "father of natural history") earned his laurels, Solomon had diligently explored the field. He was a large contributor to the literature of his day. His proverbs were three thousand, and his songs one thousand and five; whilst on botany, ornithology, and zoology, and chemistry, and I know not what else beside, he was *facile princeps*, the highest scholar of his age.

I think of Solomon as a walking encyclopædia. I think of his palace yonder, as library, museum, laboratory, herbarium, all in one. He was a thinker. He was a student. He was a philosopher. He was a man of extraordinary versatility. The accomplishments of twenty average men centred in him. He lived many lives in one. He tapped every conceivable resource of happiness.

And, all through, he kept this one life-aim before him, to find out wherein lay man's highest good, how he could best fill up his allotted term on earth. And

THE CONCLUSION OF THE WHOLE MATTER.

with what result? Lo, I see him thoughtfully standing in the vestibule of the palace; and, as he looks round upon all his vast domain, and recalls the experience of these past eventful years, he draws a long, deep sigh that whispers of " vanity and vexation of spirit," and then he says (and the weighty words have come echoing down the long corridor of ages). " This is the conclusion of the whole matter, Fear God and keep His commandments; for *this is the whole of man.*"

Did you notice that I left out a word just now? The word "duty," in the text, is printed in italics, indicating that it has been supplied by our translators, and does not exist in the original. Indeed, I think it mars the text; at least it makes it express but half its meaning. No doubt Solomon is pointing to duty, but this is not the main thought in his mind. He has been eagerly prosecuting the inquiry, how man can attain to his fullest and highest development, can reach his truest dignity, can fulfill the end of his being. The more he does so, the more shall he be in the line of his supreme happiness and duty. The Septuagint rendering brings this out exactly, " Fear God, and keep His commandments; for this is the whole man." Without religion, a man is not whole, not complete; there is a great gap in his being; let him have wealth, and rank, and honor, and fame, and knowledge, and art, and science, still he needs something else to make him a whole man, a " man " in the noblest sense of the word, a man as he was originally created in the image of his Maker; and that something else is here said to be the " fear of God, and the keeping of His commandments."

This expression stands for genuine personal religion, " the fear of God," denoting the inward principle; and " the keeping of His commandments" the outward practice.

Tell me, then, my brothers, is there a truth more important than this which I could urge on your consideration? or is there one which may be more truly said to hold within itself the condensed substance of all these monthly addresses? Why, sirs, if there is one wish for you that I have above another, it is that each of you may feel—aye, and may own—that you need true godliness to make you complete; that, without a living, earnest piety, though you may have every other endowment, there is still a sad, a terrible want about you—a want which nothing else can supply.

Do not prate, my dear brother, about your manliness, so long as you know not God; why, no matter what be your years, or your strength, or your gifts, or your resources, you are not yet a whole man till you have the grace of God in your heart. "God created man a living soul," not a dead soul: and so long as your soul is dead, you lack the supreme element of your dignity, and that which gives you your noble and peerless place in creation.

An old Arabian philosopher used to pray: " O God, be kind to the wicked. Thou hast been sufficiently kind to the good in making them good." And underneath that prayer there lies a great truth; for there is no endowment that any of you can possess that is half so precious as converting grace. I tell you, I do honestly feel, that if you take away from me my religion, you rob me of my manhood; you bring me down, by a quick descent, immeasurably nearer to the beasts of the field. To a vast degree, my self-respect, my dignity, my honor, have gone. You have quenched the light within my soul. I am now but a two-legged brute (with all the misfortune of knowing my wretchedness).

One of the Vice-Presidents of the United States (who was a sincere Christian of the old-fashioned sort, who had repented of his sins and put his trust in the Lord Jesus Christ), when addressing a body of young men, shortly before his sudden death, said, "I believe in a robust Christianity. If ever there was a time in our country, that time is now, when young men should read, reflect, think, and act according to the teachings of God's Holy Word, and give thought and effort to purify, lift up, and carry our country onward and forward, so that it shall be the leading Christian nation of the globe. You will be disappointed in many of your hopes and aspirations; but, gentlemen (he went on to say), when friends turn their backs upon you, when you lay your dear ones away, when disappointments come to you on the right hand and on the left, there is one resource for a true and brave heart; and that is an abiding faith in God, and a trust in the Lord Jesus Christ." Lord Bacon used to say that in the unforced tendencies of the young men of the age, you have the best materials for prophecy as to the social and political future of a nation. When Catiline attempted to overthrow the liberties of Rome, he began by corrupting the young men of the city; showing discernment enough to perceive that what constitutes the strength and safety of a community is the virtue and integrity of its rising youth.

Give us a generation of young men who "fear God and keep His commandments," and the highest prosperity of our country is secured. There is a power in a living Christianity, which even its enemies are unable to deny. Charteris, a notorious scoundrel of his time, once said to a man who was distinguished for his religious principles, "I would give a thousand pounds to have your good character." "Why?" inquired the other. "Because I could make ten thousand pounds by it," was the reply of the detestable rogue.

It was the testimony of the great Napoleon that in war the moral is to the physical as ten to one. When I resided in a wooded part of Scotland, I used to notice that the trees nearest the light at the edge of a dense forest had larger branches than those in the interior, and that the same tree would throw out a long branch toward the light, and a short one on the other side toward the dark recess of the forest. Just so, a man grows toward the light to which he turns. If you turn toward God, all your nobler powers and faculties will develop and strengthen, you will attain to a loftier manhood, your good principles will grow stronger, your character will acquire robustness and vigor; but if you turn toward mammon or the flesh, your nature will become dwarfed and stunted, and whatever manliness you have will eventually wither away. I would say this with more than wonted emphasis, because it is the thing that so many fools deny; who, running straight in the teeth of our text, talk as though religion imparts a softness and stupidness to its possessor, and takes what is manly out of him. Yes, most of us know something of the slang terms in which it is common with a certain class to throw ridicule upon decided and godly young men, as though they were namby-pamby "muffs" and simpletons; whereas it is on the side of the scoffers that there is cowardice, and all that is contemptible, and unmanly, and mean. This text of ours, which, though written a thousand years before the Incarnation, declares a truth as accurate to-day as when Solomon penned it, that nothing short of "the fear of God, and the keeping of His commandments," can make one a whole man.

Young men, equip yourselves as you like, physically, socially, intellectually; get on in business, and rise in the world to the full extent of your ambition; realize the highest culture and proficiency to which you can aspire—I say to you deliberately, in His name whose servant I am, that, unless your heart is dominated by "the fear of God," and your life ruled by the desire to "keep His commandments," there is still about you a radical, a deplorable, a fatal defect.

It is a defect, however, which, thank God, may at once be remedied; and I would most earnestly beseech as many of you as are not Christians to put it to yourselves, whether another of the most precious years of your life is to be allowed to close without your having settled the great matter, and joined yourselves to the followers of the Lord Jesus Christ. Oh, it is a grand thing, when one's feet are in early life turned in the ways of righteousness, and when you can say, as did the pious Obadiah to Elijah, "I, thy servant, fear the Lord from my youth."

The God who claims your reverent and trustful confidence (for this is really the meaning of the word "fear" in our text) is no such stern, implacable, and iron-armed tyrant as some of you have been wont to imagine; but a kind and merciful Father. The ignorant peasants of the Brocken mountains in Saxony sometimes see, at sunrise or sunset, a gigantic spectre on the mists of the opposite hills; and tremble before what they think to be a supernatural form; but it is only the shadow of their own bodies, thrown in colossal size on the masses of floating vapor by the rising or sinking sun. Such were the gods whom the heathen conceived of; such is the deity whom the natural heart always pictures—a grim and distorted representation of man himself; as Jehovah says, in the 50th Psalm, "Thou thoughtest that I was altogether such an one as thyself." The gospel brings to you a very different view of "Him with whom you have to do." It reveals to you a God who not only stretches out to you the hand of a father's love, but yearns over you with a mother's tenderness.

Did you ever hear what Napoleon Bonaparte said at St. Helena, when asked his opinion of the Christian religion? He replied, "Alexander, Cæsar, Charlemagne, and I myself have founded great empires; but upon what did these creations of our genius depend? Upon force. Jesus alone founded His empire upon love, and to this day millions would die for Him. This proves to me convincingly His Divinity."

My brothers, you will not misunderstand the words "Fear God" in our text. In one sense, I want you to get rid of the fear of Him. I want you to know Him so well, and trust Him so fully, that the thought of Him will never bring you terror or alarm. St. Paul expressly says, "God has not given to us the spirit of fear," that is, of dread and cowardice. And St. John says, that "perfect love casteth out fear." "The fear of God" in the Old Testament answers as nearly as possible to "faith in God" in the New; and the dual exhortation in our text is just a summons to the principle and practice of true religion, or to what the Apostles call "faith and works."

Let the thought of a personal and present God be the supreme factor in your daily life. Let not a morning dawn upon you, nor an evening close, without a visit to the cross of Christ, where faith shall ever find a Saviour, and penitence shall always find a Friend. Bind yourselves to a daily perusal of the Bible, and make it your companion and guide. From Sunday to Saturday let no day pass that shall not see you on your bended knees in prayer to God. Make it a fixed principle with you to keep the Sabbath holy. Join in fellowship with the saints, and attach yourselves openly to the Church of Christ. You who once were church-members in your country home, don't throw away your religion now, when it is more necessary to you than ever; don't keep your "lines" stowed away at the bottom of your trunk; don't withhold from us the note of introduction you received from a pastor or Christian friend; and don't be ashamed to have the Bible always lying on your table as a witness that you mean to live a Christian life.

Never allow an unclean or profligate man to cross your threshold. Whether you reside with a family, or live in a private lodging on the first, second, or third floor, determine that no bad book, or pamphlet, or newspaper, shall ever enter your room. Let your stock of books be select, and such as will benefit both heart and intellect.

Don't forget to write often to the dear ones at home. If you have a brother or a cousin far away, and exposed to special temptation, send him a letter of Christian counsel, and tell him from me not to forget the God of his fathers.

THE CONCLUSION OF THE WHOLE MATTER.

Oh, if any of you have up till now been running on the wrong line, I want you to switch at once: get upon the safe rails, and turn your face Zionward. Is it a hardship or an affliction, this godly life to which I beckon you? Nothing of the kind. As our text, rightly rendered, tells you, it comprises the whole happiness of man. I do not ask you to give up the pursuit of pleasure, but rather to seek it where alone it can be truly found. The old Grecian fable tells us that when Ulysses sailed past the island of the Sirens, those mysterious sea-nymphs, who had the power of charming by their songs all who were within hearing of their voice, he listened a moment to the sorcerer's music; and, to prevent himself and crew from being lured to the shore, he stopped their ears with wax, and had himself tied to the mast of the ship. Thus, as the story goes, they passed in safety the fatal strand. But, when Orpheus, in search of the Golden Fleece, went by the same coast, he being, you remember, a masterly musician, set up better music than that of the Sirens, and so enchanted his crew with his own sweet melodies, that, without the use of either thongs or wax, they all sailed safely past the sorcerer's isle.

I do not propose to fill your ears with wax, or to hold you back by thongs from the vain pleasures of the world; but, by sounding sweeter music in your ear, offering you richer joys than sense and sin can yield, I would disarm it of its spell.

Come over to the Lord, my brothers all; and you come from a frozen waste to perpetual summer; from a barren wild to the land of brightness and beauty, of flower and fruit, of sunshine and song.

The late David Burke said, toward the close of his days, that his life might be divided into a series of fits or manias: that he began it with a fit poetical, then a fit metaphysical, and a fit philosophical, and a fit rhetorical, and a fit political; each fit passing off in turn, and still leaving the heart empty and unsatisfied. This is just what, on a far grander scale, Solomon did: he pulled out in succession every stop of the world's great organ, struck every chord, sounded the full diapason of earthly delight; but lived to find that all such music soon palls upon the ear—lived to place on record, as the testimony of an experience never matched, and a wisdom never equaled, the weighty truth I leave with you, as "the conclusion of the whole matter," that in *the fear of God, and the keeping of His commandments* is comprised alike all the duty and all the happiness of man.

INDEX

A

Accuracy, illustrated, 138-144.
Adams, John, on Washington, 208.
Agassiz, devotion to science, 329.
Aim high, room at top, 216; case of low aim, 212.
Allen, Stephen, his rules of life, 26.
Amusement and recreation, 282-284.
Application, its character, 35-37; of Wilson, 58-60.
Aptitude followed, 177; of Smeaton, 178; of West, 178; of Sir John Franklin, 178.
Archimedes, his application, 35.
Arkwright, Richard, his cotton machinery destroyed, 53.
"As the man, so is his strength," 397-399.
Astor, John Jacob, origin and progress of, 32.

B

Barnes, Albert, his use of time, 168.
Bancroft, George, his recreation, 284; his patience, 87.
Beecher, Henry Ward, on books, 185; on money, 239.
Beginning in small way, 233-236; great things begin small, 39-41; of delays, 147-149.
Benevolence, give all you can, 248-251; of George W. Childs, 249; of Carey, 251.
Bible, on observation, 43; on singleness of purpose, 57; on perseverance, 63; on energy, 84; on industry, 92; on idleness, 97; on honesty, 201; and newspapers, 199; in business, 369-372.
Blakie, Professor, on character, 206.

INDEX.

Bloomfield, Robert, use of spare time, 168; how educated, 119; sought permanent values, 331.

Bow of promise, the, 416-418.

Boyhood of David Porter, 21; of Briggs and Lawrence, 22; of Gladstone, 28; of Grant, 212; of Franklin, 212; of Garfield, 214; of Peel, 216; of Whitfield, 217; of Canning, 217; of Dodge and Harper, 166; of Newton, 220; of Burritt, 222; of Washburn, 223; of Wilson, 58-60; of Drew, 76; of Carnot, 121; of Cameron, 88; of Reynolds, Jerome, and Henry M. Stanley, 312-314; of Pitt, 162; of N. P. Banks, 318; of Will Carleton, 146; of Roger Sherman, 319; of Moody, 152; of Farady, 260; of Jonas King, 363.

Bridgman, Laura, triumph over difficulties, 170.

Briggs, George N., son of a blacksmith, 22.

Bright, John, how used himself, 177; as a reader 182.

Brougham, Lord, on habit, 266; himself an illustration, 267.

Bruce, Robert, learning of a spider, 65.

Bryant, the poet, 103.

Budgett, Samuel, his punctuality, 82; on doing things well, 100; his industry, 92; his funeral, 92; on wasting time, 111; his honesty, 202; on economy, 246; religion in his warehouse, 362.

Bunyan, John, benefit of his trials, 109.

Burke, Edmund, rewrote a speech sixteen times, 103.

Burritt, Elihu, how he studied, 222; energy and progress, 223; what Everett said, 224; more push than Alexander or Cæsar, 224; a learned man 166; his letter to Everett, 154-156

Business, a school, 105-107; a great scheme, 53-55; education in, 255-257; religion in, 361-364; the Bible in, 369-372.

Buxton, on push, 222; his energy, 86.

C

Cæsar, Julius, use of spare time, 168.

Calhoun, Webster's reply to, 102.

Canning, the English statesman, poor but aspiring, 217; Lord Shelburne's prediction, 218.

Capital, the best, 173.

Carlyle, on self-reliance, 68; on readers, 184; on conversation, 306.

Carnegie, Andrew, his trials and triumphs, 195; his view of culture, 257.

Cecil on method, 110; advice to a young man, 382.

INDEX.   435

Character, good, 27; in chirography, 315; tested, 316; power of, 206-208; as capital, 208-210; of
　　Holland's people, 210; for companionship, 235; and accuracy, 143; and money, 241; and
　　self-respect, 130-133; and responsibility, 349-352.
Childs, George W., his great benevolence, 248, 249.
Christian duty, the compendium of, 406-409.
Chums, 388-390.
Claflin, Horace B., keeping promises, 290.
Clarke, Dr. Adam, his punctuality, 81.
Clay, Henry, how educated, 105.
Coffin, Charles Carleton, reading foundation of his success, 187.
Coleridge, lazy, 99; classification of readers, 188.
Colton, on reading, 183; on money, 242.
Columbus, his perseverance, 64; his faith, 358.
Common sense is tact, 218; discussed, 156-160; in using ideas, 322-324.
Companions, choice of, 237-239
Companionship with fools, 419-425.
Complete life, a, 413-415.
Conclusion of the whole matter, the, 426-432.
Contentment, adapting one's self to circumstances, 260-263.
Conversation, art of, 306-309.
Cook, Rev. Joseph, on reading, 189.
Cooper, Peter, beginning in a small way, 235.
Country parson, what he said, 214.
Courage, illustrated, 75-79; not self-possession, 233; and patriotism, 254.
Courtesy, what it is, 136-139.
Crabbe, on modesty, 124; on frank men, 164.
Criminal never did a day's work, 104.

D

Dearborn, General, his research as to success and failure, 31.
Debating, Canning's success, 218; discipline of, 316-318.
Decision, what, 71-75; and patriotism, 340.

INDEX.

Delays, how begin, 147 149.
Depew, Chauncey M., on college education, 257.
Diary, keeping one, 304-306.
Dickens, Charles, on genius, 122.
Difficulties, should not see them, 67; indecision invites, 75; what are they for, 168-172; how Curran overcame, 316.
Discrimination, 47-51.
Divine Plumb-Line, the, 400-402.
Dodge, William E., a store his school, 106; his industry, 93-95; his recreation, 284.
Doing things well, 99-101; Washburn's rule, 225; the United States judge, 67, 68; advantage of, 208-210; a striking case, 162; is to be accurate, 141-144; making perfect, 144-147
Douglas, Stephen A., his courtesy and success, 139.
Douglass, Frederick, colored orator, self-made, 119.
Drew, Samuel, his courage, 76.
Drink, the habit, 267-269; Gough on, 269.
Duty a watchword, 284-288.

E

Economy, keeping expense book promotes, 303; save all you can, 245-248; of nature, 248.
Edison, the electrician, on seizing opportunity, 271; and Ole Bull, 144; his faith in phonograph, 356; in electric light, 356; secrets of his mental growth, 149.
Education and health, Dr. Hooker on, 331; secret of, 149-154; not a foe to labor, 255-257; Dr. Arnold on, 255.
Eliot, George, and "Romolo," 103.
Emerson, Ralph Waldo, his thorough work, 103; on thinking, 194; on Napoleon, 255.
Emmons, Dr. N., his method, 109; lack of practical knowledge, 157.
Energy treated, 84-86.
Ericsson, John, his inventions show tact, 219.
Everett, Edward, comments on letter of Burritt, 154-156.
Expense Book, 301-304.
Eye service, what is it, 335-338.

INDEX.

F

Facts to be followed, not theories, 327-331.
Failure, how to avoid, 31-33; its lessons, 31; number who fail, 31; to be sought, 32; were Astor and Girard failures, 32.
Faith, place of, in true life, 356-359.
Ferguson, James, his father's clock and gentleman's watch, 49.
Filial tie, discussed, 295-298.
Flag, the American, 343; loyalty to, 343-345; poetic tribute to, 343; protects the poor, 347-349.
Fools, companionship with, 419-425.
Foster, John, and case of decision, 71; on reading, 187.
Franklin, Benjamin, greater than his business, 212; his proverbial sayings, 212; proverbs on work, 212; advice to young trader, 102; before kings, 95; not above business, 230; on leisure, 166; living cheap, 169; on wasting time, 111; his way to success, 161; great reader, 188; advice to girl on reading, 189; as debater in youth, 316; his faith, 358; on saving, 245.
Fraternal tie, discussed, 298-301.
Frederick the Great, his method of reading, 186.
Frost, Charles G., what an hour per day did for him, 167
Fuller on method, 110.

G

Garfield, James A., advice to young men, 211; on difficulties, 172; his filial love, 297; reading bad books, 191; what debate did for him, 317; Mrs. Garfield's girlhood, 258; his gratitude, 339.
Garibaldi, loyalty to country, 344.
Garrison, William Lloyd, his opportunity, in reform, 273; persecuted for an idea, 322.
Genius, what it is, 120-122.
Gibbon and memoirs, 103.
Girard, what Horace Mann said of him, 32; and the dude, 230.
Gladstone, William Ewart, statesman and orator, 28.
Goodhue, Jonathan, power of character, 208; and money, 244.

INDEX.

Grant, Ulysses, greater than business, 213; incidents of his life, 212, 213; his decision, 74.
Gratitude, a leading virtue, 338-340.
    his self-reliance, 69, 70; tender, 79; modesty of, 123; his common sense, 159; his magnanimity, 134; his individuality, 165.
Greater than business, 211-214.
Greeley, Horace, plea for persistence, 104; sought permanent values, 333.
Gurney Family, connection with Buxton, 74.
Gutenburg, inventor of printing, 320.

H

Habit, what, 265-267; drink habit, 267-269; tobacco habit, 269-271.
Hargraves, James, his spinning jenny, 53.
Harper, James, how began, 107; doing things well, 100.
Hasting to be rich, 394-396.
Hawthorne, his plea for punctuality, 82.
Haynes, his speech, 102.
Health, how secured, 261; sound body in sound mind, 277-279; how to make and keep a sound body, 279-282; alcohol inimical to, 267.
Heart, keeping the, with diligence, 410-412.
Heartiness, 379-381.
Henry, Patrick, his decision, 71; a thinker, 194.
Honesty, its value, 201-204; of A. Lincoln, 204-206; and keeping promises, 288-290; of Tudor, 132; of Three Brothers, 337.
Hood, Thomas, on reading, 183.
Hooker, Dr., on observation, 33.
Hopper, Isaac, in England, 211.
Howard, Gen. O. O., his filial love, 297.
Humboldt, his greatness and common sense, 160.
Hume, long application, 103.
Humphrey, President, courtesy of, 137.

I

Ideas in clay, 272; Paxton, working at, 272; worth of, 318-322; the ideal and real, 325-327.
Idleness discussed, 97-99; perils of, 353.
Ignorance of laws of health, 277-279; disgraceful to have fever, 278.
Impossible, adjective of fools, 214.
Individuality, what it is, 163-166.
Industry, illustrated 89-92; industry before kings, 93-95.
Infidelity, Franklin reading infidel book, 190; Lincoln reading one, 190; a foe to success, 364-367; infidel lawyer, 371.
Intemperance, how led to, 267-269.
Inventions of Ericsson, 219; of Newton, 220; of Hargraves, 53; of Arkwright, 53; suspension bridge, 56; of Watt, 56; of fly-shuttle, 53; how thought creates them, 53-56; of Gutenburg, 320; of Joseph Francis, 322-324; opposition to, 329; Edison's phonograph and electric light, 356; of Faraday, 260; Christianity uses, 361.

J

Jewett, Dr. Charles, his sharp observation, 43.
Johnson, Dr., on success, 31; on doing things well, 99; on genius, 120; on reading, 182; on man of one book, 192; on debt, 247.

K

Keeping a diary, 304-306; promises, 288-290.
Kitto, his method, 108; self-made, 119; recalling early life, 128.
Knowledge, successful men have most, 105; love of, with Locke, Franklin, and Murray, 37; and religion, 363.

L

Lafitte and the pin, 40.
Law of mental growth, 149-154.
Lawrence, Amos, career and views of riches, 22; punctuality of, 83; not above his business, 228; on leisure time, 166; his honesty, 202; on tobacco, 270; his benevolence, 230.
Lawyer, Lincoln as, 204-206; one ruined by success, 354; infidel, 371.
Lee, Gideon, a worker, 101; his method, 110.
Letter writing a fine art, 314-316.
Life, a complete, 413-415.
Lincoln, Abraham, his best teacher, 105; on Grant's perseverance, 63; his independence, 76; a statesman, 166; what honesty did for him, 204-206; his common sense, 158; his filial love, 296; his magnanimity, 135; reading infidel book, 190; influence of reading on him, 191; his gratitude, 338.
Little things, 39; minding, 39-41; want of a nail, 303; Lawrence on, 303; two cents, 141; Toosday, 142; inaccuracies of speech, 142.
Logan, General, his loyalty and courage, 77.
Longfellow, his views of success, 21.
Loyalty, the Roman sentinel, 285; loyalty, 343-345; reasons for, 347-349.
Luck, no such thing, 216; sorcery as real as luck, 37.
Luther, his decision and courage, 194; his words on character, 207; how made a thinker, 194.
Lyon, Mary, on wasting time, 110; sisterly love, 300; on duty, 285.

M

Magnanimity, what it is, 133-136.
Making things happen, 214-216; how Garfield did it, 214; how General Grant did it, 212, 213.
Mann, Horace, his application, 36; his poverty, 36; public service, 37; on dignity of labor, 92; on laws of health, 278.
Martyn, Henry, saved by one companion, 238.
Matthews, on genius, 122; on originality, 165; on money makers, 242.
Maxims, on doing things well, 99; of Franklin, 94, 166, 212; on observation, 43; on help, 68; of the Bible, 97; on little things, 41; on method, 107; on difficulty, 171; self-made, 118; on companions, 237.

INDEX. 441

Men, young, how many, 25; expense book for, 301–304; courteous, 136–139; honesty of a young man, 203; honesty necessary for, 203; how Providence uses, 361.
Method, its nature, 107–110.
Miller, Hugh, on observation, 43; how made, 166; knew how to use himself, 176.
Mills, Samuel, his self-reliance, 67.
Modesty, its value, 123–126.
Moltke, Count von, his modesty, 124.
Money, passion for, 32; what Lawrence said, 22; and character, 206; not a safe impulse, 239–242; making, 242–245; saving it, 245–248; given away, 248–251; perils of, 354.
Moody, Dwight L., secret of his mental growth, 152.
Morse, author of telegraphy, 320.

N

Napier, Sir Charles, on difficulties, 169.
Napoleon, not above business, 230; great worker, 255.
Nature on time, 83.
Newspapers, reading, 196–199.
Newton, Sir Isaac, his tact, 220; how educated, 221; his observation, 45; his application, 35; John Newton ruined, 238; Isaac's patience, 87; John on contentment, 262.
Notable eleven, a, 403–405.
Not above business, carrying coalhod, 72; Horace Mann on, 92; illustrated, 227–231.
Note-book, reading with, 188–190; including scrapbook, 196.

O

Observation, examples of, 29; what is it, 43–45; seen in location of Lowell, 54; and discrimination, 47; tale of the dervis, 47; degrees of, 50; its moral use, 50; promotes thinking, 194.
Occupation, low idea of it, 70; choice of, 177–180; natural bent, 175–179.
One or two fools I have met, 391–393.
Opportunities of our day, 25; seizing, 271–274; letting slip, 274–276.
Originality, consistent with study, 165; Sidney Smith on, 166.
Osborne, his definition of success, 21.

P

Palissy, Bernard, success of, 170.
Parton, James, talks with Maydole, 100; on little things, 234.
Pascal, Blaise, early observation, 48.
Passion, the master, 311-314.
Patience, art of waiting, 86-89.
Patriotism, what, 341-343; and loyalty, 343-345; illustrations of, 344, 345; reasons for, 347-349.
Pedro, Dom, accepting the situation, 261, 262.
Peel, Sir Robert, how trained, 216; what biographer says, 217; on filial love, 297.
Perils of success, 353-356.
Perseverance, illustrated, 63-66; of Jonas King, 363.
Peter the Great, not above business, 228.
Pilgrims, faith of, 358.
Pizarro, his courage, 78.
Pompey, his decision and courage, 72.
Porter, David, chimney-sweep, 21.
Possibilities for young in our land, 25; being prepared for, 258-260; the two daughters, 253.
Practice, and habit, 265; makes perfect, 144-147.
Principle, 225-227; Mrs. Wesley on, 225; case of a young man, 225; Biddle's clerk, 227; Victoria, 227; of Walter Scott, 90.
Printing, origin of the art, 320.
Prescott, his great perseverance, 66.
Promise, the bow of, 416-418.
Promises, keeping of, 288-290.
Prosperity and presumption, 382-384.
Punctuality, 81-84; Washington's practice, 81; Hawthorne on, 82; example of Budgett, 82; promptness of Lawrence, 83; nature on time, 83.
Push, energy, force, 222-224; what Buxton said of it, 222.

Q

Quiet meditation, 385-387.
Quotations, finding one's place, 29; discipline of business, 87; on push, 106; on striving to be best, 100; observation, 43; from Wilson, 60; on application, 35; on singleness of purpose,

36; on difficulties, 63; from Patrick Henry, 71; on energy, 84; on industry, 90; on letter-writing, 315; from Spurgeon, 97, 99; from Parton, 235; on method, 109; on money, 166; on wasting time, 111; on politeness, 138; on a rolling stone, 179; on self-made, 118; Holland and Lincoln, 205; on habit, 265; Gough, on drink, 269; on modesty, 124; on genius, 122; on reading, 183; on thinking, 193-196; on sticking to nature, 164; on health of school girls, 281; from Greeley, 333; Bacon, on money, 245; on keeping promises, 288.

R

Raleigh, Sir Walter, terrible worker, 104; and the potato, 234.
Raphael, the great painter, his self-respect, 132; his reimke to cardinals, 132.
Reading, of David Porter, 21; of Whitfield, 217; of Spooner, 105; of Wilson, 58-60; poor, 112; habit of, 265; place of, 181-184; what to read, 184-188; how to read, 188-190; what one book may do, 190-193; Garfield, reading bad books, 191; read few books, 192; without thinking, 193; how made Patrick Henry, 194; promotes thinking, 194; newspapers, 196-199; author of trashy, 274-275.
Recreation discussed, 282-284.
Religion, thought to be visionary, 325; relation to secular faith, 361-363; and money-making, 369-371; and personal responsibility of Miss Martin, 350; in secular affairs, 361-364; and infidelity, 364-367; Mountain Jim, 366.
Responsibility, personal, 349-352.
Rich, Isaac, his humble start, and rapid rise, 85.

S

Schiller, inquisitive boy, 106.
Scott, Walter, on industry, 90.
Self-control, relation to self-possession, 231-233; what, 115-118.
Self-help, how to do it, 175-184; wisdom of, 253-255.
Self-made, how, 118-120.
Self-possession, what it is, 231-233.
Self-reliance, of Porter, 21; of Briggs, 22; of Lawrence, 22; discussed, 67-70; with self-possession, 231.

INDEX.

Self-respect, is what, 130-133.
Seward, William H., his self-control, 115; on delays, 147.
Sheridan, Richard Brinsley, his decision, 72; Phil Sheridan's ride, 73.
Sherman, General, his magnanimity, 134; Roger, his boyhood, 319.
Shortening way to success, 161-163.
Sigourney, Mrs., on writing letters, 315; on conversation, 306.
Simplicity, illustrated, 127-129.
Singleness of purpose discussed, 57-61.
Smith, Adam, without tact, 219; Sidney on originality, 166.
Something for nothing, 290-293.
Spare moments, how Burritt used them, 166; of Drew, 76; what will do, 166-168; Dean Alfred on, 271.
Spooner, William B., made by business, 105; his good start, 175.
Stanley, Henry M., his master passion, 312; how went to Africa, 314.
Start, a good, 173-175; what Lawrence said of, 173; Farragut's, 173.
Starting right, illustrations, 21-23; chimney-sweep, 21; Allen, 26; Franklin, 212; Dodge and Harper, 106, 107.
Stephenson, George, had tact, 219; his locomotive, 330.
Stewart, Alexander T., said of Wanamaker, 29; demanded accuracy, 143.
Stowe, Harriet Beecher, on conversation at home, 308.
Success, 21-23; definitions, 21; degrees of, 22; how to succeed, 25; how great men won, 27; to be avoided, 31; secret of it, 29; what it is, 218; relation of work to, 144-147; Grigg's rise to, 241; its perils, 353-356.

T

Tact, what, 218-222; want of it, 156; seen in reducing ideas to practice, 322-324; boyhood of three brothers and tact, 337.
Talbot, Ex-Governor, his sense of personal responsibility, 351; a factory boy, 351.
Teachers, the farm, the shop, etc., 105; outside teachers, 55.
Theories, must stand on facts to be true, 327-331; of Agassiz on fish, 329.
Thompson, Rev. Dr., story of evil companions, 238.
Thoroughness, 379-418.

INDEX.

Thought, relation to labor, 53-56; art of thinking, 193-196; and seizing opportunity, 271-274; is real, 325-327; and mental growth, 149-154; promoted by diary, 304-306; helps to keep promises, 289.

Time, value of, 81; how squandered, 81; wasting, 110-114; how wasted, 112.

Tobacco, expense of cigars, 302; tobacco habit, 269-271.

Top, at the, 216; chance for, 258-260.

Truth, loyalty to, 287; Paul's loyalty to, 287; and keeping promises, 288-290; facing it, 364.

Turner, his secret of success, 102.

U

United States, their future, 25; their flag, 341-343.

V

Values, permanent, 331-334.

Vice, self-respect its foe, 130-133; how Newton ruined by, 238; and drink, 267-269; Aaron Burr's, 353.

Victoria, girlhood, and preparing for the throne, 227.

W

Wanamaker, John, what gave him success, 29, 30; what Stewart and General Grant said of him, 29; his magnanimity, 136.

Washburn, Ichabod, his career, 225, 226.

Washington, and the corporal, 229; power of his character, 208; his self-control, 117; modesty of his mother, 125; his filial love, 295; loyalty of, 345; faith of, 358.

Watt, James, and teakettle, 56.

Watts, Dr., his natural bent, 178.

Webster, Daniel, his plea for hard work, 102; and law student, 243; view of education, 105; Noah, his method, 110; anecdote on courtesy, 137; patience of Noah, 87; definition of magnanimity, 133; Daniel, on reading, 181; on delays, 148; on personal responsibility, 349.

Wellington, won Waterloo at Eton, 70; on duty, 286.

Wesley, Mrs., advice to son, 225; her husband's maxim on money, 242; only safe rule, 250.

Whitfield, George, bootblack, the best, 217.

Whittier, John G., what the newspapers did for him, 199; on opportunity, 274.

Will, the will and way, 214.

Wilson, Henry, his singleness of purpose, 57-60; what debating did for him, 317.

Women, young, how many, 25; self-possession of, 231; confusion of, 231; foresight of, 233; more idle, 98; need food and exercise like men, 279-282; must read newspapers, 198; know the real, 325-327; over ten hours a day, 256; example for, 258-260; one who missed, 259; adapting to circumstances, 260.

Work, condition of success, 101-104; desire for ease, 101; Gideon Lee's bargain with himself, 101; Franklin on, 102; Turner's and Webster's endorsement, 102; Bryant, Eliot, Emerson, Gibbon, Butler, Burke, Hume, Greeley, Raleigh, 103; work creates wealth, 104; I never did a day's work, 104; relation to thought, 53-56; work and culture united, 90-91; no place for idler, 98; division of, 108; of Palmerston and health, 279; and success, 141-147; ideas make work, 53-56; education not foe to, 255-257.

Y

Youth, how the punctual one thrives, 83; mistake work for genius, 102; limp, 214; importance of expense book, 301; their spare moments, 166; wasting time, 110; sticking to business, 179; what say to him, 120; honesty their wealth, 201-204; on companions, 237-239; need self-control, 118; getting something for nothing, 290; must have patience, 86-89; should love reading, 181; reading trash, 185; stick to nature, 165; not overworked in school, 281; must read newspapers, 196-199; what debate will do for, 316-318; expect opportunities, 272; not like school, 275; sowing wild oats, 276; be loyal, 343-345; should value ideas, 318-322; know that ideas are real, 325-327; stick to facts, 256; seek discipline, 330; example of Moody, 152; avoid vice, 153; want money, 239; Grigg an example, 241; save all you can, 245; keep promises, 288 290; avoid twaddle, 336; help themselves, 253-255; example for, 258; need contentment, 260-263; and infidelity, 364-367; Bible, 369-372.

www.ingramcontent.com/pod-product-compliance
Lightning Source LLC
Chambersburg PA
CBHW022144300426
44115CB00006B/333